Śrī Chaitanya's Life and Teachings

Explorations in Indic Traditions: Theological, Ethical, and Philosophical

Series Editor: Jeffery D. Long, Elizabethtown College

The region historically known as the Indian subcontinent (and more recently as South Asia) is rich with ancient and sophisticated traditions of intellectual and contemplative investigation. This includes both indigenous traditions (Hindu, Buddhist, Jain, and Sikh) and traditions that have found a home in this region (Islamic, Christian, Jewish, and Zoroastrian). This series is devoted to studies rooted in critical and constructive methodologies (such as ethics, philosophy, and theology) that show how these traditions can illuminate universal human questions: questions about the meaning of life, the nature of knowledge, good and evil, and the broader metaphysical context of human existence. A particular focus of this series is the relevance of these traditions to urgent issues that face humanity today—such as the ecological crisis, gender relations, poverty and social inequality, and religiously motivated violence—on the assumption that these traditions, far from being of merely historical interest, have the potential to enrich contemporary conversations and advance human understanding.

Conversations with Gurumaa: 21st Century Innovation in a Woman-Led Spiritual Community, by Angela Rudert

Śrī Chaitanya's Life and Teachings: The Golden Avatāra of Divine Love, by Steven J. Rosen

Śrī Chaitanya's Life and Teachings

The Golden Avatāra of Divine Love

Steven J. Rosen

LEXINGTON BOOKS
Lanham • Boulder • New York • London

Frontispiece courtesy of Drdha Vrata Gorrick www.divyakala.com.

Published by Lexington Books
An imprint of The Rowman & Littlefield Publishing Group, Inc.
4501 Forbes Boulevard, Suite 200, Lanham, Maryland 20706
www.rowman.com

Unit A, Whitacre Mews, 26-34 Stannary Street, London SE11 4AB

British Library Cataloguing in Publication Information Available
The hardback edition of this book was previously catalogued by the Library of Congress as follows:

Library of Congress Cataloging-in-Publication Data Available

ISBN 978-1-4985-5833-4 (cloth : alk. paper)
ISBN 978-1-4985-5835-8 (pbk. : alk. paper)
ISBN 978-1-4985-5834-1 (electronic)

∞™ The paper used in this publication meets the minimum requirements of American National Standard for Information Sciences—Permanence of Paper for Printed Library Materials, ANSI/NISO Z39.48-1992.

Printed in the United States of America

For Vrin and Prati

kānu vinā gīta nāī

"If there is no Krishna, there is no song."

sumekhala he parirambhan gauraṁ
māṁ veṣṭaya hi na kadācin muñca

"O charming belt that embraces Gaura!
Hug me tightly and never let me go."

Contents

Foreword xi
Jeffery D. Long

Acknowledgments xv

Introduction xvii

1 The Gauḍīya Tradition: From Veda to Rādhā 1

2 Śrī Krishna: Enter the Dark Lord 19

3 Śrī Gaura Tattva: From Black to Gold 39

4 The World of *Bhakti* 71

5 The Nectar of the Holy Name 87

6 Śikṣāṣṭakam: Eight Beautiful Prayers 105

7 Gauḍīya Vedānta: Inconceivable Unity in Diversity 123

8 Śrī Chaitanya and Other Traditions 135

9 Rāmānanda Rāya: The Viceroy of Devotion 159

10 Rāgānuga-bhakti: Śrī Chaitanya's Special Gift 173

Afterword: Mahāprabhu Comes West 193

Bibliography 209

Index 227

About the Author 231

Foreword

Jeffery D. Long

Series Editor

When I was first approached by Sarah Craig, the acquisitions editor for religion at Lexington Books, about the possibility of developing a series focused on Indian religious traditions, I saw it as a wonderful opportunity to develop a series with a constructive focus. The result has been the series of which I am delighted to say this volume is a member. *Explorations in Indic Traditions: Ethical, Philosophical, and Theological* arose from the very strong desire of a growing number of scholars of Indic traditions for venues in which to pursue constructive work of the kind we see many scholars pursuing under the rubric of Christianity: work which pursues questions of an ethical, philosophical, and theological nature *as such*, rather than simply describing the work that others have done in this regard from a more detached, historical perspective. Like many of our students, the work of a growing number of people who study Indic traditions is fueled by questions of this kind. We are not only interested, for example, in the fact that there are people who believe in reincarnation. We are ourselves interested in whether there really is such a thing as reincarnation and how one might argue for (or against) this idea. We are interested in ethical questions: questions of right and wrong. We are interested in questions about the ultimate meaning of existence. And many of us inhabit traditions that have a good many interesting things to say about these issues, and we would like the freedom to allow our work to be informed by these traditional conversations.

Many in the academy of religion of course have legitimate concerns about openly and unabashedly theological (and other kinds of constructive) standpoints operating as part of scholarly discourse, being far more comfortable keeping such standpoints at arms' length, as objects of study rather than as perspectives with which it might be desirable to engage substantively. It took a good deal of effort for the academic study of religion to free itself from the constraints of Christian theology: a project that is, arguably, even yet incomplete. The aim, though, is not for constructive thought to reassert a hegemonic space in the academy. Certainly, that is not the aim of those of us who are involved in this series. It is, rather, to open up a space in which constructive work can occur alongside, in dialogue, and even in collaboration, with what has come to be the more conventional social scientific approach of academic scholarship on religion—especially religions originating or widely practiced in India/South Asia.

In opening up such a space in an environment where scholars are often suspicious of constructive work, the burden of proof, fairly or not, is on those of us who advocate such work to show that it can be done in a rigorous fashion, which meets the academy's standards of logical argumentation and empirical evidence. We need to show, in short, that the perspectives of the practitioners of traditions are not merely confessional—not resulting merely in statements of belief—but are capable of producing substantive knowledge that contributes not only to a particular tradition, but to the wider academic discourse as well.

If one were looking for a representative of an Indic tradition whose work was capable of meeting this high standard—of embodying the values underlying this series—one of the first names which would come to mind would be Steven J. Rosen.

Steven has done outstanding work through the years, with books designed primarily with a popular audience in mind; as editor of the *Journal of Vaishnava Studies* (which has served as a venue for excellent work from some of the top scholars in the study of Vaishnava traditions); and with academically oriented books such as his *Essential Hinduism* and *Krishna's Other Song: A New Look at the Uddhava Gita* (both published by Praeger/Greenwood), which have been recognized and accepted by the academy and have long been used as textbooks for college courses in English-speaking countries. As an author of popular works, his writing has the virtue of being clear and accessible. Yet his knowledge of the traditions about which he writes is so great that he does not oversimplify the material he presents. His work has depth without obscurantism, clarity without superficiality.

As one might imagine, I was delighted to learn that Steven was interested in contributing a work to this series. And not just any work: it could well be argued that this volume is his magnum opus. While it is written with the clarity of his earlier work, there is scholarly depth here that makes this particular volume a substantial contribution to academic knowledge of the important, but under-studied figure of Śrī Chaitanya Mahāprabhu.

In this work, Steven contextualizes Śrī Chaitanya within the larger tradition of devotion to Krishna that was prominent in Chaitanya's time. The text includes a full rendition of Śrī Chaitanya's biography, as well as a list of key works in English for the interested reader who wishes to pursue the topic in greater depth. There is a full exposition of the central concept of *bhakti*, which is essential to any understanding of this tradition, and of how it relates to Śrī Chaitanya's life and work. There is an exposition on the importance of the name of Krishna in Gauḍīya Vaishnava doctrine and practice. Particularly exciting, from a scholarly perspective, is a fresh rendering of Śrī Chaitanya's eight verses, along with both a commentary and a history of the commentarial tradition on these verses. Of special philosophical interest, too, one finds here an excellent and clear section on Acintya Bhedābheda, the system of Vedānta that is associated with the Gauḍīya tradition. And there is more, including a chapter that analyzes Vaishnavism in light of other traditions, such as Islam and Buddhism; in-depth chapters on the profound dialogue between Śrī Chaitanya and Rāmānanda Rāya and on the intricate subject of Rāgānuga-bhakti—and even an Afterword thoroughly dealing with the coming of Śrī Chaitanya's teachings to the Western world. One would be hard-pressed to think of a more wide-ranging and comprehensive work on Śrī Chaitanya, his legacy, and its reception.

I am proud and delighted to offer this work as part of the series *Explorations in Indic Traditions*. It is a fine example of what this series hopes to achieve and the ways in which it hopes to advance the scholarly conversation.

Acknowledgments

First and foremost, I would like to thank my spiritual teachers, particularly His Divine Grace A. C. Bhaktivedānta Swami Prabhupāda, for without him I would know little if anything about Śrī Chaitanya. I also acknowledge a debt of gratitude to Śrīla B. R. Śrīdhara Dev Goswāmī Mahārāja and Śrīla Bhaktivedānta Nārāyaṇa Mahārāja, whose kindness, knowledge, and pure devotion have been a guiding light for me and for so many others. These three personalities have allowed Śrī Chaitanya's inimitable glow to pervade modernity.

I am also indebted to Jeffery Long, the series editor, who believed in this project from the beginning. His gracious Foreword is a key factor in setting the tone for this book, and I am deeply grateful for that. Sarah Craig should be thanked as well; her expert editorial assistance and pleasant demeanor succeeded in making the entire process doable. Drdha Gorrick, whose line-drawing beautifies the frontispiece, and Eduard Zentsik, artist extraordinaire, who rendered the cover painting of Mahāprabhu—both deserve my thanks.

Various scholars with whom I have developed friendships over the years, often through their participation in the *Journal of Vaishnava Studies*, have at least indirectly contributed to this work, before it was even conceived. Through related discussion and inspired exchange, they deepened my knowledge of Vaishnavism in general and Chaitanya Vaishnavism in particular: Ed Dimock, John Carman, Dennis Hudson, Alan Entwistle, Shrivatsa Goswami, Vasudha Narayanan, Jack Hawley, Frank Clooney, Joseph T. O'Connell, A. N. Chatterjee, June McDaniel, David Haberman, Donna Wulff, Thomas J. Hopkins, Dan Sheridan, Charles S. J. White, David Kinsley, Neal Delmonico, O. B. L. Kapoor, Phil Lutgendorf, Charles Brooks, Klaus Klostermaier, E. H. Rick Jarow, Fred Smith, Shyamdas, and others who should also be mentioned, though space grows short.

Additionally, I would like to specifically thank the following scholars and devotees, in no special order, for the fruits of their research and their direct assistance with this book in various ways. They were always available to help and to answer technical questions, particularly in terms of Sanskrit and Bengali texts, making this volume more rich and comprehensive than it otherwise would have been: Dhanurdhara Swami, Satsvarupa Dasa Goswami, Sacinandana Swami, H. D. Goswami (Howard Resnick), Giriraj Swami, B. V. Madhav Maharaj, Gerald Surya, Reverend David Carter (Hladini Shakti Dasa), Graham Schweig, Joshua Greene, Aleksandar Uskokov, Luis Gonzalez-Reimann, Vaiyasaki Dasa, Tukarama Dasa, Uttamasloka Dasa, Hari Parshad Das, Brijbasi Dasa, Dravida Dasa, David Buchta, Guy Beck, Abhi Ghosh, Lucian Wong, Baba Satyanarayana Dasa, Bhakti Vikasa Swami, Bhanu Swami, Rembert Lutjeharms, Larry Pugliese (Lakshmi-nrisimha Dasa), Kiyokazu Okita, Saul Porecki, Madhavananda Dasa, Ferdinando Sardella, Nityananda Dasa, Robert MacNaughton, Jan Brzezinski, Advaita Dasa, Kishora Dasa, Mans Broo, Urmila Devi Dasi, Eben M. Graves, Nagaraja Dasa, Rasik Mohan Dasa, Vasudeva Dasa, Ravi Gupta, and Vic DiCara, among others. Unless otherwise indicated, all English renderings of Sanskrit and Bengali texts in this book are my own, composed with the help of language specialists and in conjunction with existing translations (see bibliography).

Introduction

The Chaitanya Vaishnava tradition[1] is a balance of head and heart. As such, practitioners eschew mere sentiment or emotion in pursuance of their goals. Instead, they seek accomplishment through a scrupulous combination of scriptural study and a form of practice that leads to direct experience, ultimately resulting in blissful consciousness (*ānanda*).[2] Although there are exceptions in which the heart aspect is emphasized—as in, for example, the paradigmatic Vraja *gopīs*, the simple village girls who loved Krishna (God) as much as life itself, and who had absolutely no interest in academic pursuits—the overriding method is to combine scholarship and devotion.[3]

The *gopīs*' example of pure love is the undisputed goal of Chaitanya's Vaishnavism, whether or not it is accompanied by a deep, scholarly understanding of the tradition. Still, unless one naturally manifests such innate, spontaneous love, Vaishnava texts clearly recommend the cultivation of both knowledge and practice side by side, thus facilitating one's gradual advancement on the spiritual path. Indeed, despite its reputation as an "emotional" movement, even a cursory study reveals that Śrī Chaitanya's tradition greatly values intellectual understanding of its philosophy and teachings. Moreover, it safeguards the purity of its mission by requiring that teachers and practitioners, when they comment on the proof texts or otherwise represent the tradition, comply with universally accepted, intellectually sound standards. Invariably, we see that its greatest preceptors and exemplars throughout history have been lauded for their considerable intellectual prowess.

I recognized this from my earliest days as a devotee. Therefore, while I chose to access the tradition from the inside, I noted that rigorous scholarship—objectively exploring the practice, history, and literature of the tradition—could afford a certain context and holistic perception that is irreplaceable and which can be advantageous to the serious practitioner.

Along these lines, academia today recognizes that all informed perspectives have something to offer. But, more, whether one is a removed scholar or a committed acolyte, one necessarily approaches their chosen tradition from a point of origin, and this impacts their assessment of it. Every person begins at a certain place, with a certain background, engaging a certain motivation. The key, however, is to be honest about it and to proceed from that point. That's what I try to do. I am therefore mindful of both the advantages and disadvantages that accrue to me as a practitioner. And with that awareness in mind, I endeavor to sidestep the pitfalls of sentimentalism by applying scholarly standards to my assessment of the tradition in line with the rigorous criteria academe and the tradition itself require.

For me, scholarship has never been an end in itself. It has always been provisional. That is to say, it needs to lead somewhere, to achieve certain pragmatic ends. Like a man with fine taste in clothing, scholarship wears its best suit when it has somewhere to go. Knowledge for knowledge's sake certainly has value. But knowledge reaches its zenith when it is practically applied. Theoretical knowledge *tells* us the why of things, but practical knowledge—experiential knowledge—allows us to *inhabit* the why of things.

This is why I joined various Krishna *ashrams* in my youth—specifically in the Chaitanya tradition. I wanted to *know* that particular tradition, yes, but I also wanted to *live* it, for only by doing so, I knew, would I be able to ascertain its true value.

Consequently, I absorbed myself in the ancient literature of the tradition, even looking at the texts in their original languages. But beyond such basic studies, I found that by adhering to certain practices—such as quiet chanting, meditating, and the congregational singing of devotional songs—I gained entrance into the lineage in ways that scholarship, on its own, could never afford.

The sages of the tradition relate that experiencing Krishna is comparable to tasting honey. This analogy is not just a declaration of Krishna's sweetness. It has other components. For example, to fully appreciate honey, one must taste it. Intellectualizing about it, chemically analyzing it—or even writing a doctoral dissertation on it—will not allow one to experience its essence. To achieve that, one must open the jar of honey and actually taste the substance inside.

True, scholars, able to read the jar's label, acquaint themselves with the contents' minutiae, often more thoroughly than many practitioners. But this still does not constitute the actual tasting of honey. Analogically, certain aspects of a tradition unfold only through praxis. Clearly, that which is beyond the purview of the senses cannot be accessed by reading books. The full understanding of a tradition, again, is never solely intellectual. There is an emotional component as well.

The argument against this, of course, is that one must be objective, and emotional involvement can compromise objectivity. Thus, if one is going to research a tradition in a scholarly way, one must be somewhat removed.

Still, most will agree that balance is needed, as mentioned above. For example, Śrī Chaitanya's immediate followers, the Six Goswāmīs of Vrindāvan,[4] who were renowned for their scholarship, were also consummate practitioners. They perfectly evinced that aforementioned balance, fruitfully engaging both intellect and emotion in the service of higher understanding.

This has been my attempted approach to the Chaitanya tradition for the greater portion of my life. My study and practice has taken me into rarified association—including that of the modern tradition's greatest scholars and adherents. By their gracious association, I have learned, to a certain degree, what Chaitanya Vaishnavism has to offer, even as I still make my way toward its exalted goals, which remain very far away. What I am trying to say is this: Though I no doubt have numerous limitations, both as a scholar and as a practitioner, I have benefited immensely from the company of those more accomplished than I, and they have served to carry what I lack and preserve what I have. Indeed, they have enriched this book in ways that I could have never achieved without them.

As a result of that esteemed association, as well as my sustained study and practice, I hope this work offers new insights and, additionally, succeeds in presenting older insights in a new way. Because I have approached the tradition as a practitioner but no less as a scholar, I will attempt to make this a bridge book, of sorts, as valuable to Indologists and Religious Studies scholars as to practicing devotees. My invocation as this book commences, in fact, is that both scholar and practitioner, whether they are teachers or students, experienced or neophyte, will benefit equally from what I have to say, and that if any of this enhances their taste for Chaitanya Vaishnavism, or if they thereby learn something meaningful about it, the book will have served its purpose.

Śrī Chaitanya Mahāprabhu (1486–1533) holds a significant place in the study of "Hinduism."[5] Scholars such as Joseph T. O'Connell and Edward C. Dimock, Jr.,[6] had long ago brought him to the attention of the academic community, and the International Society for Krishna Consciousness (ISKCON)'s work from 1966 onward has done the same among spiritual seekers worldwide.[7] As a religious personality in the Indian subcontinent, Śrī Chaitanya's image has been installed as a worshipable deity in grand temples, and he has inspired writings, both scholarly and devotional, in the fields of theology, religion, and philosophy. He has been the subject of a commemorative postage stamp, a widely read and often reprinted comic book, and a museum dedicated to his memory, among other honors too numerous to mention.[8]

Oddly, then, there is something of a lacuna in terms of an overall biography for general audiences, a monograph that is up to date, incorporating both recent scholarly research and the perceptions of informed devotees. Several such works did indeed appear some thirty or forty years ago,[9] but that was before modern advances in scholarship and the contemporary findings of dedicated research specialists. Today, one finds volumes on isolated segments of Śrī Chaitanya's life and thought, or books that dance on the periphery of his biographical narrative, such as studies on sacred chant, *bhakti*, Gauḍīya philosophy, literature about his traditional biographies or in pursuance of his successors—and all of these are indispensable in the study of Mahāprabhu and in understanding who he was and what he represents—but an overview of his life and teaching, bringing to bear all we have learned thus far, at least in summary, is, again, notably lacking. This book attempts to fill that lacuna.

CHAPTER BREAKDOWN

Chapter One depicts the Vedic milieu from which Śrī Chaitanya emerges. "The Gauḍīya Tradition: From Veda to Rādhā" presents the background from which the Golden Avatāra (Chaitanya) arose, and shows how his "new dispensation" is connected to the predecessor tradition. Also pivotal to this first section is an analysis of why Gauḍīyas see Mahāprabhu as Krishna himself, and, more, as Krishna with the emotional disposition and inner spiritual identity of his feminine counterpart—he is revealed as the combined manifestation of both Rādhā and Krishna. After this, we offer an outline, first, of Vaishnavism in general, and then of Gauḍīya Vaishnavism in particular, highlighting its salient philosophical ideas and ritual practices, so that readers might be prepared for all that follows.

"Śrī Krishna: Enter the Dark Lord," the next chapter, presents a synoptical portrait of Krishna, depicting him not just philosophically, but also detailing his visual image, so strikingly etched into the heart of Śrī Chaitanya himself and, since the time of his advent, into the hearts of all Gauḍīya Vaishnavas as well. The chapter section focusing on the "Search for the Historical Krishna" does not attempt to prove or disprove the ontological existence of the lotus-eyed Lord; that determination is subjective and lies no doubt in the realm of faith and realization. Rather, this subsection of the chapter highlights historical scholarship on Krishna worship through the ages, showing that the many devotees who have revered him take part in a long and venerable tradition, predating even Christianity. We conclude this chapter by elaborating on a distinction crucial to understanding Chaitanya's mission, showing in "the Specific Krishna of Śrī Chaitanya's Era" that the Krishna who is the object of Chaitanya's adoration is incommensurate with other popular depictions of Krishna. For example, Mahāprabhu and his followers do not primarily focus on the Krishna of martial texts, such as the Mahābhārata, nor is it the sovereign and majestic Krishna of opulence and power, faithfully served in his kingdom of Dvārakā, who is the subject of Mahāprabhu's vision. Rather, Śrī Chaitanya is absorbed in the Krishna known as Vrajendra-nandana, the sweet and simple darling of Vraja, the lover of Śrī Rādhā, as found in the Purāṇas and in the later poets of the Vaishnava tradition. That is the cynosure of Mahāprabhu's life and thought. Thus, having looked at Gauḍīya Vaishnavism's Vedic background and its essential philosophy, along with Śrī Chaitanya's preferred understanding of Krishna, the reader is ready for a formal introduction to Mahāprabhu himself.

As the centerpiece for the entire volume, the Third Chapter is justifiably long. "Śrī Gaura Tattva: From Black to Gold" begins by posing the question, "Who is Śrī Chaitanya?" and then proceeds to serially interrogate the numerous responses that arise in answer to that initial query. Our journey takes us from the preliminary Gauḍīya understanding of Śrī Chaitanya's sainthood and his identification with the Puranic Vishnu to the culminating conception of his esoteric function as Rādhā and Krishna combined. This leads into an outline of important works on Śrī Chaitanya's life and teachings in the English language. Though not exhaustive, these works are clearly among the most significant and offer a substantial sampling of what has been written thus far. Most of these works tell us a story that will here be summarized yet again, using all of these texts and recent scholarly studies as a basis. The narrative of Śrī Chaitanya's life is then recapitulated as "The Early Period," "The Middle Period," and "The Final Period," approximating the sequence of events found in the Master's traditional biographies. This overview allows us to see him in all his glory, as a scholar, as an aesthete, and as God in the form of a devotee. Indeed, even among India's many divinities, Mahāprabhu is unique in terms of his Godhood—he shows a love for life, celebrating nature as he dances throughout the Indian countryside. In fact, he turns song and dance into *yoga*, bringing to mind the famous quote from Nietzsche: "I would only believe in a God who knows how to dance."[10]

With Śrī Chaitanya's life story now summarized, the reader is ready to delve into his teaching and practice. Chapter Four, "The World of *Bhakti*," introduces us to "devotional service" and elucidates its implications. *Bhakti* is a form of "spiritual action" that is at the heart of Śrī Chaitanya's method. We offer various definitions of the word *bhakti* itself, how it is used throughout the wisdom texts of India, and, most specifically, how it is employed by Mahāprabhu and his followers. The section ends with a brief history of the Bhakti Movement, a phenomenon that has been analyzed by modern scholars, and which culminates, in a sense, with Śrī Chaitanya's Vaishnavism, often seen as the fully developed, ultimate expression of the *bhakti* tradition.

One of the main practices of *bhakti* is mantra meditation, including the almost sub-vocal murmuring (*japa*) of Krishna's names while fingering a kind of rosary (in Sanskrit, a "*japa-mālā*" or "garland of sacred beads") and the heartfelt, animated call-and-response singing known as *kīrtana*. Thus, Chapter Five focuses on "The Nectar of the Holy Name." Beginning with a scriptural delineation of the practice according to the Purāṇas and other important Vaishnava texts, the chapter proceeds to then offer some philosophical explanation as to why such "nomenclature theology" would make sense. This is followed by an explanation of how such chanting was employed by Śrī Chaitanya's predecessors, by Śrī Chaitanya himself, and then by his immediate followers. After this, we specifically look at the Hare Krishna Mahā-mantra (Hare Krishna, Hare Krishna, Krishna Krishna Hare Hare/ Hare Rāma, Hare Rāma, Rāma Rāma, Hare Hare), a specific chant that is by far the most important and popular of the many sacred incantations used by Gauḍīya devotees worldwide. We offer references to the Mahā-mantra in sacred texts and then survey the catalogue of calamitous pitfalls that the tradition cautions practitioners to scrupulously avoid in the practice of the holy name.

The science of sound and how sound vibrations affect the consciousness is part of Śrī Chaitanya's central teaching. Thus, his "*Śikṣāṣṭakam*: Eight Beautiful Prayers," said to be the only original verses penned by the Master himself, is the subject of our Sixth Chapter. In addition to a thorough, albeit brief exposition on the blissful effects of chanting, the verses depict the sequence of developmental stages through which the soul passes on its journey to pure love of God. The text clearly articulates how at the beginning, in the neophyte stage, there is a lack of fully developed taste, which is gradually supplanted in due course by the dawning of a transformative humility accruing for the practitioner through his or her applied dedication. Thus a higher taste develops, and increasingly profound experiences ensue as the devotee enters ever more deeply into the intimate mysteries of the holy name. In fact, the verses reveal that the conscientious practitioner can through persistent practice eventually become witness to the ecstatic mood of Śrī Rādhā herself, both in the paradoxical joyfulness occasioned by the pain of separation, and in the consummate joy occasioned by the recurring experience of union after separation. The chapter ends with an outline of the text's history and commentarial tradition, showing how it permeates Gauḍīya sensibility.

If the *Śikṣāṣṭakam* can be compared to the "heart" of Gauḍīya Vaishnavism, then "Acintya-Bhedābheda"—the philosophical teaching that God and his energies are inconceivably and simultaneously one and different—is the Gauḍīya "head." Often referred to as the essence of Śrī Chaitanya's Vedāntic teaching, "Inconceivable Unity in Diversity" forms the substance of Chapter Seven. Here we explain the doctrine's meaning in terms of its scriptural basis and logic—despite the fact that it is only alluded to in scripture and transcends ordinary logic. While the concept can without doubt be found in early Indic texts, it was Jīva Goswāmī who coined the term as such, as we will see in this chapter. Primarily understood through three analogies—God and his energies are comparable to an ocean and a drop of water; a goldmine and a gold nugget; or the sun and its radiance—we explicate the tradition's full-bodied acceptance of this dense philosophical theory and why it continues to stand as the most complete of all Vedāntic postulates.

Chapter Eight focuses on "Śrī Chaitanya and Other Traditions." This is a complex subject, for Gauḍīya Vaishnavism sees itself not as yet another sectarian religion but as the essence of religious truth—as Sanātana Dharma, or the "eternal religion," or, as it is often styled, "the essential function of the soul." Still, historically, Śrī Chaitanya's Vaishnavism arose in a Bengal that was home to Muslims as well as Hindus, and this chapter addresses the tensions that beset the complex, sometimes shifting, and ultimately harmonious relationship that developed between the two. We also look at the Judeo-Christian tradition and its overlap with Śrī Chaitanya's doctrine and thought, even though, from a historical point of view, there is no record of the Master or his immediate followers interacting with actual practitioners of Occidental religion. After that, we examine how Śrī Chaitanya viewed both Buddhists and those of various impersonalistic schools of thought. Although he was fundamentally nonsectarian and universalist, he found the Voidist tradition of the Buddha (Śunyavāda) and the amorphous tradition of Śaṅkara (Māyāvāda) to be, in the final analysis, somewhat antagonistic to theistic devotion. Finally, we look at a series of Śrī Chaitanya's interactions with Vaishnavas of other denominations, outside the Gauḍīya tradition, and offer readers a helpful chart to see what aspects of the other *sampradāyas* (lineages) he considered most useful.

Next, in Chapter Nine, we explore Śrī Chaitanya's profound verbal exchange with Rāmānanda Rāya, a viceroy in South India who eventually became one of his most intimate followers. In the traditional biographies, the Master is known to have conversed with many stalwarts of his time, of which five were most prominent—Rūpa Goswāmī, Sanātana Goswāmī, Prakāśānanda Sarasvatī, Sārvabhauma Bhaṭṭācārya, and Rāmānanda Rāya.[11] The conversation with the Rāya is arguably the deepest and most complete of them all, espousing the full extent of divine love according to the truths of Gauḍīya *siddhānta*. Through Rāmānanda Rāya we learn of the intimate and esoteric relationships—five in number, either as a passive worshipper, a servant, a friend, a parent, or a lover—all living souls have with God in his eternal kingdom and the pinnacle of that loving exchange as exemplified by Śrīmatī Rādhikā, which the tradition views as A Love Supreme.

Finally, in Chapter Ten, "Rāgānuga-bhakti: Śrī Chaitanya's Special Gift" offers readers a glimpse into the methods and practices that allow practitioners to achieve the highest states of spontaneous love, beyond the strictures of scriptures and the formality of more structured adherence. Here, we look at esoteric texts and the insights of perfected devotees, who share their experiences and approaches for attaining the divine. They teach us how to find out who we truly are in relationship to Krishna, and how to cherish those with the most confidential relationships, the ones who bring both God and all living beings the most pleasure. By assisting these souls, say the Gauḍīya *ācāryas*, we can achieve the ultimate fruit of love of God.

In conclusion, our "Afterword" follows Mahāprabhu on his journey West. We begin by summarizing the initial expansion of his movement as he deputes his Six Goswāmīs and others to spread the teachings throughout India. We regard the trials and complexities his small group of committed followers faced, watching as certain of them succumb to deviations and splinter groups form, while others work diligently and succeed in delivering the Master's message without variance, as he intended. The movement grows exponentially, until all of India is modified by its existence. Ultimately, we see several pioneering luminaries board ships to bring Chaitanya's teachings to Western shores, albeit with only small success.

But we soon observe something remarkable, largely as a result of the Gauḍīya mission's persistence in its fledgling efforts. Namely, as these first bona fide representatives of Śrī Chaitanya continued to strive and to forge small but important inroads introducing Westerners to the breathtaking revelations of the "Krishna Consciousness" (Krishna Chaitanya) Movement, the table was set for the unprecedented accomplishments of the extraordinarily gifted preceptor and exemplar, A. C. Bhaktivedānta Swami Prabhupāda (1896–1977). Empowered with uncommon intelligence, erudition, determination, charm, and charisma, this one soul achieved what no one else could. We witness how in a few short years, with astonishing purity, courage, and expertise—*and against all odds*—this unexcelled world teacher founded an international society of considerable magnitude. The Swami saw his international society flourish, even in his own time, and it continues to flourish today, unabated, inundating the world with Mahāprabhu's distinctive message of Krishna-bhakti.

NOTES

1. Chaitanya Vaishnavism, also known as Gauḍīya Vaishnavism, or Bengali Vaishnavism, refers to the spiritual tradition that originates with Śrī Chaitanya, even if its roots are found in the earlier Vedic tradition. While Vaishnavism, or the worship of Vishnu (Nārāyaṇa, Krishna) can be traced to antiquity, this particular branch of the tradition arose in 16th-century Bengal.

2. For more on the interrelation of devotion and scholarship in the Vaishnava tradition, see Ravīndra Svarūpa Dāsa "The Scholarly Tradition in Caitanyite Vaishnavism: India and America," in *ISKCON Review* (Volume 1, No. 1, 1985), 15–23.

3. Certain esoteric texts reveal that even the *gopīs* embraced profound learning, their existence as "simple village girls" notwithstanding. For example, in Text 12 of the *Śrī Śrī Rādhā-kṛpā-katākṣa-stava-rāja* (part of the *Ūrdhvāmnāya-tantra*), Śrī Rādhā, the ultimate *gopī*, is glorified as the "queen of Vedic scholarship" (*tri-veda-bhāratīśvari*). Additionally, the *Śrī Rādhā-sahasra-nāma-stotra* (from the *Nārada Pañcaratra*) tells us in Text 20 that she is the "best of scholars" (*vid-uttamā*); in Text 153, that she is "a truly learned person" (*paṇḍitā paṇḍitā-guṇā*); and, in Text 162, that she is "the personification of knowledge" (*vidyā-svarūpiṇī*). And this superlative learning is not only attributed to Śrī Rādhā but to other *gopīs* as well. For example, in Rūpa Goswāmī's *Śrī-Śrī Rādhā-Krishna-gaṇoddeśa-dīpikā*, verses 181–183, we are told that Tuṅgavidyā, one of the primary *gopīs*, is well versed in India's 18 traditional branches of knowledge, including the *rasa-śāstra* and *nīti-śāstra*. In this regard, she is also described as the "*ācārya*" of the *gopīs*, indicating that she teaches these texts to the rest of them. Thus, in terms of ultimate truth (*tattva*), the *gopīs* are supremely knowledgeable, though their knowledge is subservient to their perfect love. But in terms of transcendental relationship (*rasa*), which is higher, they are simple village girls, and this is how their exchange with Krishna manifests and produces consummate pleasure. As an addendum, perhaps, Vaishnava commentators opine that particular Vraja *gopīs* were, in their previous lives, Vedic scholars who desired a loving relationship with Lord Rāma. Consequently, they were given the benediction of appearing during Rāma's subsequent incarnation as Lord Krishna to fulfill those desires. Thus, the culmination of their Vedic scholarship and their intense desire for Krishna allowed them to take birth as *gopīs* in Vrindāvan. This notion is found in the very first verses of the rather late "Krishna Upanishad" (said to be part of the *Atharva-veda*). See also His Divine Grace A. C. Bhaktivedānta Swami Prabhupāda, *Kṛṣṇa, the Supreme Personality of Godhead* (Los Angeles: Bhaktivedanta Book Trust, 1970), Volume 1, Chapter 31, "Songs by the Gopīs," 211.

4. The traditional dates of the Six Goswāmīs run as follows: Rūpa Goswāmī (1489–1564), Sanātana Goswāmī (1488–1558), Raghunātha Dāsa Goswāmī (1495–1571), Jīva Goswāmī (1513–1598), Raghunātha Bhaṭṭa Goswāmī (1505–1579), Gopāla Bhaṭṭa Goswāmī (1503–1578). See Bhaki Pradip Tirtha Swami, *Sri Chaitanya Mahaprabhu* (Calcutta: Gaudiya Mission, 1947), Appendix III, 98. These dates, Tirtha Swami tells us, come from Bhaktivinoda Ṭhākura (*Sajjana-toṣaṇī*, Vol. II, 1882), though in some instances they are admittedly problematic.

5. The terms "Hindu" and "Hinduism" are in fact misnomers, originating from Persian and Greek words for all peoples who lived near the Indus River. The terms were initially more a signifier of geographic and cultural considerations than religious affiliation. Gradually, these words became umbrella terms for the various religions of that region, such as Vaishnavism, Śaivism, Śāktism, and so on, despite the fact that these religions often differ with respect to their conceptions of divinity, scriptures used, and ritual practices. See John Stratton Hawley and Vasudha Narayanan, *The Life of Hinduism* (California: University of California Press, 2006), 10–11.

6. Joseph Thomas O'Connell (1940–2012) was among the first in the Western academy to bring attention to Chaitanya Vaishnavism. His Harvard Ph.D. thesis on the social implications of Gauḍīya Vaishnavism (1970) remains a classic work in the field

and his numerous articles on the tradition are considered seminal as well. Edward Cameron Dimock, Jr. (1929–2001), too, is a doyen of Gauḍīya studies in the West. His work on Vaishnavism and Vaishnava Sahajiyāism as portrayed in *The Place of the Hidden Moon* (The University of Chicago Press, 1966) and his major life's legacy, his translation, with Tony K. Stewart, of *Caitanya caritāmṛta of Kṛṣṇadāsa Kavirāja* (Harvard University Press, 2000), remain indispensable for scholars of the tradition.

7. ISKCON is an acronym for the International Society for Krishna Consciousness, founded in 1966 by His Divine Grace A. C. Bhaktivedanta Swami Prabhupada (1896–1977).

8. A commemorative "Chaitanya Mahaprabhu" postage stamp was issued by India's Department of Posts on March 13, 1986, celebrating "the 500th anniversary of his birthday." The comic book is called *Chaitanya Mahaprabhu*, Amar Chitra Katha, No. 90, editor, Anant Pai (Bombay: India Book House Education Trust, 1975). For a brief scholarly analysis, see Karline McLain, *India's Immortal Comic Books: Gods, Kings, and Other Heroes* (Bloomington, Indiana: Indiana University Press, 2009), 167–168. The museum was established on Śrī Chaitanya's 525th birth Anniversary by the Gaudiya Mission in Bagbazar, Kolkata, with the stated purpose of collecting, preserving and disseminating archival literature focusing on Mahāprabhu and his associates. Also significant perhaps are a few popular movies: *Shri Chaitanya Mahaprabhu* (1954) in Hindi, produced and directed by Vijay Bhatt, and the two-part Bengali epic, *Nader Nimai* ("Nimāi of Nadia," 1960), directed Bimal Roy, and *Nilachaley Mahaprabhu* ("Mahāprabhu of Purī," 1959), directed by Kartik Chattopadhyay.

9. See Chapter Three of this work, "Śrī Gaura Tattva: From Black to Gold," in which I outline the most important works in English to be released in the modern era.

10. See Friedrich Nietzsche, *Thus Spoke Zarathustra: A Book for All and None*, transl., Adrian Del Caro, ed., Adrian Del Caro and Robert B. Pippin (New York, N.Y.: Cambridge University Press, 2006), First Part, 29.

11. All five of these profound teachings are summarized in His Divine Grace A. C. Bhaktivedanta Swami Prabhupāda, *Teaching of Lord Chaitanya* (Boston: ISKCON Press, 1968). Reprinted as *Teachings of Lord Caitanya, the Golden Avatar* (Los Angeles, C.A.: Bhaktivedanta Book Trust, 1988).

Chapter 1

The Gauḍīya Tradition

From Veda to Rādhā

The sages of India tell us of a golden age,[1] millions of years ago, when people in general were pious and Vedic ritual (*yajña*) was the norm. These rituals were performed by highly evolved beings who, it is said, could see the divine in everyday phenomena: the stars, the sky, and the earth. Intricate Vedic ceremonies, brought to life by the hymns of the *Ṛg-veda* and its corollary texts, involved numerous complex sacrifices and the ingestion of a sacred if psychotropic beverage pressed from the soma plant.

Agni (fire) was deified and took center stage in these ancient rites, with flames rising high from deep within carefully constructed sacrificial pits. Visible to the priests and to other serious practitioners were the gods of the Vedic pantheon, who were pleased by these sacrifices. Indeed, the sacrifices themselves embodied the presence of none other than Vishnu (*yajño vai viṣṇuḥ*, as stated throughout Vedic texts), the supreme deity of the Vaishnava tradition.

THE NEW DISPENSATION

Indic scriptures forewarn that this was not to last. Lofty ages and their attendant practices, like everything else in the material world, deteriorate.[2] The physical law of entropy tells us that all matter breaks down, that energy tends to spread out until it reaches an even state, perpetually lessening in substance. The material world, in this sense, inevitably succumbs to planned obsolescence. In Indian theological terms, Satya turns to Kali.

There are four world cycles. These are comparable to the ages of the Greco-Roman tradition, in which virtue and goodness decline from one age to the next. With the cosmic succession of time cycles, people become more and more unfortunate, with decrease in strength, memory, intelligence, and discretion, along with a diminishing of their spirituality. There is a commensurate shortening of lifespan as well. While the classical ages of the West were named after precious metals, that is, Gold, Silver, Brass, and Iron, the nomenclature of the Vedic ages originated from the four throws of an ancient Indian dice game, in which rolls of four, three, two, and one were called Kṛta (Satya), Tretā, Dvāpara, and Kali, respectively.[3]

Despite the backward flow of these grand age cycles, or the inevitable disintegration and degradation outlined in the subcontinent's sacred literature, certain Indian texts refer to Kali-yuga, or the last of these ages, as Puṣya-yuga and Tiṣya-yuga. The terms *puṣya* and *tiṣya* indicate something "fortunate" or "auspicious." In fact, there is a portion of Kali that is sometimes even known as "Prema-yuga,"[4] or the age where divine love reigns supreme. So the question becomes this: Why use these words in relation to the age of Kali, especially when the scriptures are so clear that things in this Age just get worse and worse?

For those who embrace the Gauḍīya Vaishnava tradition, that is, followers of Śrī Chaitanya Mahāprabhu, the answer is found in the Purāṇas, sacred texts that serve as an accessible gateway to Vedic understanding. For example, an important, much-cited verse in the *Bhāgavata Purāṇa* (*Śrīmad Bhāgavatam*), lauded as the ripened fruit of the Vedic tree of knowledge,[5] tells us, "My dear King, even though Kali-yuga is an ocean of defects, there is still one good quality about this age: Simply by chanting the holy name of Krishna, one becomes free from material conditioning and is ultimately promoted to the supreme realm." (12.3.51) And further: "Whatever result was obtained in Satya-yuga by meditating on Vishnu, in Tretā-yuga by performing sacrifices, and in Dvāpara-yuga by serving the Lord's lotus feet—these can all be obtained in Kali-yuga simply by chanting the holy name of the Lord." (12.3.52)[6] The same truth is expressed in the *Vishnu Purāṇa* (6.2.17), the *Padma Purāṇa* (72.25), the *Bṛhan-nāradiya Purāṇa* (38.97), and elsewhere.

In fact, for Gauḍīya Vaishnavas, it is considered almost enviable to take birth in this age, for despite its many drawbacks, it has very particular spiritual advantages: "My dear King, the inhabitants of Satya-yuga and other ages eagerly desire to take birth in this Age of Kali, since in this age there will be many devotees of the Supreme Lord, Nārāyaṇa [Krishna]."[7] Even though Kali-yuga is overburdened by uncountable defects, we are told, there are consequential characteristics that more than make up for it: The means of God-realization is easier and, arguably, more effective than in other ages. And this is where Śrī Chaitanya comes in.

With firm scriptural support, as summarized above, Chaitanya and his followers assert that the Vedic *yajña* of old has been replaced by a new *yajña*. The contemporary Gauḍīya Vaishnava teacher Śacīnandana Swami elaborates: "Vedic *yajñas* are passé. The *yajña* for this age is Harināma Saṅkīrtana, the *yajña* of the holy name.[8]

"It is said that Mahāprabhu was once asked: 'If chanting the holy name is the *yajña* for the age, where is the sacrificial pit, which is used in all holy *yajñas*?'"

"Mahāprabhu's answer: 'Your ears are the sacrificial pit for this age.' A *nāma-yajña* is performed for the pleasure of Krishna, in which one and all become like Vedic priests. How does one become a priest of the holy name? Lord Chaitanya answers: 'Make your ears the sacrificial pit. The sacrificial spoon or ladle is your tongue. Use that tongue to pour the clarified butter (*ghee*) of the holy name into the ears—both yours and others—and then you will see how in your heart the fire of *bhakti* [devotion] will rise high and strong.' In other words, we should be like priests, who sit before the *yajña* pit and chant the *mantras* in order to invoke the presence of the Lord."[9]

THE "KRISHNA" WHO IS NOT KRISHNA

Śrī Chaitanya was understood as a divine incarnation (*avatāra*) of Krishna in his own lifetime. That his followers saw him in this way is a matter of public record.[10] In fact, various scriptural sources and numerous "proof texts" were marshaled by his earliest devotees and by the later tradition to show that he was the predicted incarnation of Kali-yuga.

Along these lines, there is a "Chaitanya Upanishad" associated with the *Atharva-veda*, and a host of other texts as well.[11] While these time-honored references are substantial and validating within the tradition itself, there are scholars who have questioned their authenticity.[12] Nonetheless, the evidence against their legitimacy is minimal, and so the tradition ratifies them as self-evidently sound and consistent with the report of Mahāprabhu's contemporaries.

Moreover, stalwarts in the Chaitanya lineage, such as Rūpa Goswāmī (1489–1564) and Jīva Goswāmī (c. 1513–1598), fully accept the bulk of these texts and explain them in terms of a larger philosophical corpus. In the end, Śrī Chaitanya's personal example and teachings—and that of his immediate followers—are overriding factors, above all else, for the truth of his value and incarnation comes from something more pragmatic than obscure proof texts: it is how his life and teachings impact the lives of those who follow them.

Still, the *Śrīmad Bhāgavatam* (11.5.32) offers an important predictive text for the tradition, if not because of its clarity then for its suggestive nuance:

kṛṣṇa-varṇaṁ tviṣākṛṣṇaṁ saṅgopāṅgāstra-pārṣadam
yajñaiḥ saṅkīrtana prāyair yajanti hi su-medhasaḥ

"In the age of Kali, intelligent people will engage in congregational chanting to worship the divinity who himself consistently sings the names of Krishna.

Although his complexion is not blackish [like Krishna's], he is nonetheless Krishna himself, always in the company of his associates, servants, weapons, and confidential companions."

The Sanskrit words *kṛṣṇa-varṇaṁ tviṣākṛṣṇaṁ* basically mean that he is blackish in color but, at the same time, he is not blackish as well. What could this possibly mean? Krishnadāsa Kavirāja Goswāmī examines these words in his 17th-century work, *Caitanya-caritāmṛta,* Ādi-līlā 3, verses 54–57: "The two syllables '*krish-na*' are always in His mouth; or, He constantly describes Krishna with great pleasure. These are two meanings of the word '*krishna-varṇa*.' Indeed, nothing else but Krishna issues from His mouth. If someone tries to describe Him as being of blackish complexion, the next adjective [*tviṣā akrishnam*] immediately restricts him. His complexion is certainly not blackish. Indeed, His not being blackish indicates that His complexion is yellow."[13] Clearly, for Kavirāja Goswāmī, the verse is talking about Śrī Chaitanya Mahāprabhu and no one else.[14]

As far as the original *Bhāgavatam* verse, context is important: Prior verses in the same chapter had already explained that Krishna incarnates in various colors in the different ages, Satya, Tretā, and Dvāpara, that is, white, red, and blackish,[15] respectively. And that he exhibits various characteristics and methods of worship according to his particular incarnation. It is only after discussing those three that the *Bhāgavatam* comes to the Kali-yuga *avatāra*, which is the subject of the verse in question.

Devotees of the Gauḍīya tradition read this text in various ways, depending on how a given commentator interprets the Sanskrit. Although the verse clearly indicates a divine person who does not appear in the darkish hue normally associated with Krishna, it simultaneously hints at Śrī Chaitanya's golden effulgence, as stated above, which in turn inspires his devotees with realization of his essence (*krishna-varṇaṁ*). Consequently, by seeing him, one is automatically seeing Krishna, not least because he is always chanting Krishna's name. It can also mean, say the commentators, that although he does not appear as Krishna directly but rather in the form of a devotee, he nonetheless reveals himself as the same dark-skinned Lord that the devotees know so well.

More, the verse tells us that each incarnation of Krishna can be identified by his special bodily features and ornaments (*aṅgas* and *upāṅgas*); his personal weapons (*astras*); and his associates (*pārṣadas*). All of this gives Gauḍīya Vaishnavas much on which to comment.

Chaitanya Mahāprabhu appears with all of these identifying features (*sāṅgopāṅgāstra-pārṣadam*): His main limbs (*aṅgas*), say Gauḍīya commentators, are Nityānanda and Advaitācārya, his two primary devotional companions; his ornaments (*upāṅgas*) are his other intimates, such as Gadādhara Paṇḍita and Śrīvāsa Ṭhākura; although he does not directly kill demons in this particular incarnation, he does "kill" the demonic mentality, if with the harmless "weapons" (*astras*) of his sheer beauty and his singing and dancing; and his intimate associates (*pārṣadas*), such as the Six Goswāmīs and others, are always at his side.

The word *saṅkīrtana* ("congregational chanting") in this verse is telling, too, for throughout history it has always been associated with Śrī Chaitanya more than with anyone else.

But for the objective scholar, this is all conjecture. The implicit reference to Śrī Chaitanya may be clear to Gauḍīya Vaishnavas, but it remains only an interpretation for those outside the tradition.

For this reason, Jīva Goswāmī, making prodigious use of his vast learning, adamantly confirms the esoteric reading of this verse and, in his *Tattva Sandarbha*, a central text of the Gauḍīya tradition, makes explicit that which had merely been implicit.

The very first verse of his *Sandarbha* replicates the key verse from the *Bhāgavatam* mentioned above. But then it is followed by an original verse penned by Jīva himself to clarify the identity of Śrī Chaitanya as the *Bhāgavatam*'s Kali-yuga *avatāra*. It fleshes out the mysterious or concealed Krishna alluded to in the *Bhāgavatam* verse, telling us clearly that the "not blackish" Krishna is in fact the golden one: Chaitanya Mahāprabhu. Gaura ("golden") and Gaurāṅga ("golden-limbed") are popular names of Śrī Chaitanya, and, in that context, Jīva wants to make it clear exactly who the *Bhāgavatam* is talking about. Here is Jīva Goswāmī's verse:

antaḥ kṛṣṇaṁ bahir gauraṁ, darśitāṅgādi-vaibhavam
kalau saṅkīrtanādyaiḥ sma, kṛṣṇa-caitanyam āśritāḥ

"[The Lord referred to here] is black on the inside [internally Krishna] and golden on the outside [externally Chaitanya], displaying all his riches, beginning with his bodily characteristics. In this Age of Kali, let us thus take shelter of Śrī Krishna Chaitanya by chanting together (*saṅkīrtana*) and adhering to other devotional practices."

As contemporary Gauḍīya theologian Tripurāri Swami eloquently words it: "Thus the color of his soul within is black (*antaḥ kṛṣṇaṁ*), yet he has accepted the disposition of his devotee to hide himself and is thus bearing an outward complexion that is golden (*bahir gauraṁ*)."[16] This is the Gauḍīya conception: that Śrī Chaitanya is the *channa* ("hidden") *avatāra*, or the Lord himself appearing in the guise of a devotee, as indicated by the words of the boy-saint Prahlāda Mahārāja: "In the age of Kali, you are disguised, never asserting yourself as the Supreme Lord, and therefore you are known as Triyuga, or the divinity who appears in three ages."[17] He hides, the tradition teaches, but is easily found by those who cultivate pure love of God.

Jīva is not alone in strongly asserting his interpretation of the original *Bhāgavatam* verse. Rūpa Goswāmī, Jīva's uncle and in many ways the central patriarch of the Gauḍīya tradition, had earlier composed a similar verse:

kalau yaṁ vidvaṁsaḥ sphuṭam abhiyajante dyuti-bharād
akṛṣṇāṅgaṁ kṛṣṇaṁ makha-vidhibhir utkīrtanamayaiḥ
upāsyaṁ ca prāhur yam akhila-caturthāśrama-juṣāṁ
sa devaś caitanyākṛtir atitarāṁ naḥ kṛpayatu

"By performing the sacrifice of congregational chanting, those who are learned in this age of Kali will worship Lord Krishna, who is now non-blackish because of a preponderance of bodily luster. He is the only worshipable deity for those who have attained the highest stage of *sannyāsa* (renunciation). May that Supreme Śrī Chaitanya show us his great causeless mercy."[18]

The reference to "bodily luster" is meant to connect Śrī Chaitanya with Krishna's divine consort Śrī Rādhā, the divine energy of the Lord (*hlādini-śakti*) and the very emblem of perfect devotion, for both Chaitanya and Rādhā glow with a hue of radiant gold—the illumination of a devotee absorbed in pure love of God.[19] Indeed, the Vaishnava poet-saint, Śrīla B. R. Śrīdhara Dev-Goswāmī Mahārāja (1895–1988), famously referred to Chaitanya as a "golden volcano of divine love," alluding to this divine connection. He writes,

> Diving deep into the reality of His own beauty and sweetness, Krishna stole the mood of Rādhāraṇī and, garbing Himself in Her brilliant luster, appeared as Śrī Chaitanya Mahāprabhu . . . . He was deeply absorbed in the mood of union and separation and shared His heart's inner feelings with His most confidential devotees. In the agony of separation from Krishna, volcanic eruptions of ecstasy flowed from His heart, and His teachings, known as *Śikṣāṣṭakam*, appeared from His lips like streams of golden lava. I fall at the feet of Śrī Chaitanya Mahāprabhu, the Golden Volcano of Divine Love.[20]

The association of Śrī Chaitanya's golden complexion with that of Śrī Rādhā and the *gopīs* (her assistant cowherd maidens) can be found in the earliest literature of the *sampradāya* (lineage). The opening verse of Kavi Karṇapūra's *Śrī Gaura-gaṇoddeśa-dīpikā*, for example, makes the connection clear: "Dark-complected Lord Krishna, whose form is eternal, full of knowledge, and bliss, formerly danced with the golden-complected *gopīs* in the land of Vrindāvan. By fully embracing them, he attained a golden complexion like theirs. In this golden form, he has now appeared in the town of Navadvīp [as Śrī Chaitanya]."[21]

The *Caitanya-caritāmṛta* (Ādi 1.5) attributes the overall concept (of Chaitanya Mahāprabhu being a manifestation of both Rādhā and Krishna) to one of the Master's earliest and most intimate associates, Svarūpa Dāmodara Goswāmī:

> The loving relationship of Śrī Rādhā and Krishna are transcendental manifestations of the Lord's internal, blissful potency. Although Rādhā and Krishna are ultimately one, they have eternally divided themselves [to relish loving interaction]. But in the form of Śrī Krishna Chaitanya, these two spiritual beings have reunited. I bow down to him, the Lord, who has manifested himself with the sentiment and complexion of Śrī Rādhā although he is Krishna himself.[22]

Later in the *Caitanya-caritāmṛta* (Madhya 8), in the section depicting the deep philosophical conversation between Śrī Chaitanya and Rāmānanda Rāya, detailed later in this book, we see this notion of Śrī Chaitanya as both Rādhā and Krishna in full development:

> Lord Śrī Kṛṣṇa is the reservoir of all pleasure, and Śrīmatī Rādhārāṇī is the personification of ecstatic love of Godhead. These two forms have combined as one in Śrī Caitanya Mahāprabhu. This being the case, Lord Śrī Caitanya Mahāprabhu revealed His real form to Rāmānanda Rāya.[23]

This view of Śrī Chaitanya has continued into the modern era. For example, Bhaktisiddhānta Sarasvatī Ṭhākura (1874–1937), the spiritual master of Śrīla A. C. Bhaktivedānta Swami Prabhupāda, sums up these ideas in a Bengali song:

> *mahāprabhu śrī caitanya, rādhā-krishna nahe anya rūpānuga janera jīvan*

"Śrī Chaitanya Mahāprabhu, who is nondifferent from Rādhā and Krishna, is the very life of those Vaishnavas who follow Rūpa Goswāmī." Along these lines, Śrīla B. R. Śrīdhara Mahārāja, quoted above, once said:

> The camp, the *sampradāya*, of Śrī Caitanya Mahāprabhu is known as the Rūpānuga-sampradāya. There our fate and our fortune is located. Now we have to conduct ourselves in such a way that naturally we can connect with that highest, purest spiritual conception from here. We must not allow ourselves to be satisfied with anything less than this highest ideal. That should be the highest goal of our life.[24]

Prabhupāda[25] explains it as follows:

> But the devotees know that Śrī Chaitanya Mahāprabhu is Krishna Himself: *mahāprabhu śrī caitanya, rādhā-krishna nahe anya.* "Śrī Chaitanya Mahāprabhu is none other than Rādhā and Krishna combined." In the beginning

> there was Krishna; then Krishna divided into two, Rādhā and Krishna. And then They again combined. That combination is Śrī Chaitanya Mahāprabhu.[26]

Thus, Śrī Chaitanya Mahāprabhu is seen by the tradition as a particularly esoteric incarnation of the supreme: Rādhā and Krishna lovingly fused into one form (*jugalāvatāra*). As John Stratton Hawley succinctly notes, "Early on he was regarded as divine by his followers—indeed, doubly divine: Rādhā and Krishna combined . . . ."[27] This, from the Gauḍīya perspective, makes Mahāprabhu the best of all possible manifestations of God. Most accurately, in fact, he is not a manifestation at all, but rather, as Krishna, he is the ultimate *manifestor*—that is, *avatārī*, the source of all *avatāras*—and as Śrī Rādhā, he is the divine energy of the Lord and an embodiment of the highest love.

The Gauḍīya tradition hopes to bequeath to its adherents the essence of the above esoterica, along with the bliss and peace that comes from the realization thereof. Some of their secrets and methods will be outlined in this book. In an upcoming chapter on Rāgānuga-bhakti, for instance, we will elaborate on just why Śrī Chaitanya descends to our world, elucidating Krishna's extremely confidential desire to taste Rādhārāṇī's incomparable love, and how Mahāprabhu wanted to give a glimpse of this superlative taste to anyone who would have it. But it starts in a stepwise fashion. Let us conclude this Introduction, then, with a brief definition of Vaishnavism as it is commonly understood, including a cursory outline of its central beliefs; we can then move forward to a few specifics about the importance of learning from within a legitimate lineage (*sampradāya*), as explained by authorities in the tradition, and bring this section to a close with some further notes on the specialty of Gauḍīya Vaishnavism itself, preparing the reader for all that follows.

GAUḌĪYA VAISHNAVISM

Vaishnavism is generally seen as one of the major traditions within Hinduism, along with Śaivism (worship of Shiva), Śāktism (worship of the goddess), and Smartism (the worship of all gods equally). That being said, Vaishnavism, in one form or another, constitutes the Hindu majority.[28] This is so because most Hindus venerate Vishnu or Krishna in one way or another, if not as Supreme God then as one of numerous manifestations of divinity.

Some basic teachings of Vaishnavism include the importance of *ahimsa* ("non-aggression"), taken to the point of vegetarianism;[29] chastity;[30] belief in an eternal soul and reincarnation;[31] and generally keeping pure in body and mind. Ultimately, the teaching prompts us to remember something deeply hidden in our soul—our lost relationship with God, or Krishna, which is rekindled through chanting his holy names and through a contemplative process of *smaraṇam* (remembrance through meditation).[32]

Bhaktivinoda Ṭhākura (1838–1914), one of the early theologians and reformers of modern Gauḍīya Vaishnavism, sums up the truths of his tradition in ten steps: (1) The *Vedas*, or literature in pursuance of the Vedic version, are a Vaishnava's principal scriptural evidence, which in turn expound the following nine principles; (2) Krishna is the Supreme Absolute Truth; (3) He possesses all energies; (4) He is the ocean of *rasa* (or the bliss that comes from transcendental interpersonal relationship); (5) The living entities are his separated parts and parcels; (6) These entities, due to their nature as marginal energy, may become conditioned by the material energy (*māyā*); (7) However, in the liberated condition, they are free of all mundane influence; (8) Everything in this material creation is inconceivably one and different from the Supreme Lord, Śrī Hari (i.e., *acintya-bhedābheda*, explained more fully in an upcoming chapter); (9) Pure devotional service is the highest duty for all living beings; (10) Pure love of Krishna is the living entity's ultimate goal of life.[33]

These truths may be expressed in various ways, according to the particular Vaishnava lineage with which one aligns. But in essence they hold true for all Vaishnavas, at least for those who subscribe to the all-important principle of accepting a guru in disciplic succession.

In the *Padma Purāṇa*, we find a verse that puts forward the absolute necessity of learning truth in a legitimate *sampradāya* (lineage): "If one does not affiliate with a bona fide disciplic succession, the *mantra* one chants will not bear the expected fruit: love of God. Therefore, in Kali Yuga, there will be four bona-fide *sampradāyas*."[34] These four may be enumerated as follows: Śrī Sampradāya, Brahmā Sampradāya, Rudra Sampradāya, and Kumāra (Haṁsā) Sampradāya, lineages systematized by Rāmānuja (circa 12th century), Madhva (circa 13th century), Vishnu Swami (dates unknown),[35] and Nimbārka (circa 11–12th century), respectively. Studying and practicing within these *sampradāyas* is said to be the proper way to reach perfection on the path.

Of course, there are several offshoot *sampradāyas* as well, such as the Vallabha Sampradāya, which is connected to the Rudra lineage, and, more pertinent in terms of our current project, the Gauḍīya Sampradāya, affiliated with the Brahmā-Mādhva line, and these are noteworthy exceptions.[36] Independent *sampradāyas*, such as the Rādhāvallabha Sampradāya and the Haridāsī Sampradāya have also become acceptable in the Vaishnava tradition, but such lineages are few and far between.

"Real" Vaishnavism, as described above, is viewed as Sanātana Dharma, or the eternal function of the soul, and not merely as yet another sectarian religion. It is seen as a sort of "science of spirituality" whose universal principles and practices will bear fruit for members of any religion and even for those who don't embrace any particular religious tradition.[37]

Accordingly, its conceptions of God are diverse, accommodating nearly every possible perspective of divine consciousness. Basically, it sees God in three overarching features—Brahman, Paramātmā, and Bhagavān. Brahman is God as an abstract force, in which he pervades everything. In this sense, it is a type of pantheism, that is, there is nothing that is not God, at least in terms of embodying his energy. Paramātmā is one step further, wherein he is seen as a localized entity, slightly more personal, entering into all that exists. This is comparable to panentheism. Finally, there is Bhagavān, or the Supreme Godhead. This is God as the ultimate person, who manifests as Krishna, Vishnu, or any of his many incarnations, and with whom one can enter into transcendental relationship. All three—Brahman, Paramātmā, and Bhagavān—are considered one divine truth, even if they are perceived variously, hierarchically, from less personal to more personal, according to one's realization.[38]

In terms of Bhagavān realization, which is considered the highest, it should be understood that this is a form of monotheism. Naturally, this can be confusing, since the "one Supreme Godhead" is viewed as having numerous forms and manifestations. Indeed, many have accused Vaishnavism of being polytheistic, just as most of India's other religions appear to be. In an attempt to offer some clarity, Graham M. Schweig coined the term "polymorphic monotheism," that is, a theology that recognizes many forms (*ananta-rūpa*) of the one, single, unitary divinity.[39]

In other words, from a superficial point of view, Vaishnavism appears to be a form of polytheism, in which numerous gods are worshipped and there is no Supreme Godhead. However, those who have studied the tradition with a discerning eye, and those who practice the religion under the direction of a spiritual master in disciplic succession, have a different story to tell. For them, Krishna is the same one Lord that is worshipped by members of all the great monotheistic traditions, and this is true whether he manifests as Vishnu or in any of his many other incarnations. Indeed, this holds true even if he appears as a golden-hued Brahmin in 16th-century Bengal.

Because Śrī Chaitanya's form of Vaishnavism began in Bengal, it is called "Gauḍīya"—the region of its origin was then known as Gauḍadeśa. This area extended throughout the southern side of the Himalayan Mountains and the northern part of the Vindhya Hills, which is called *Āryavarta*. The celebrated ancient capital of Gauḍadeśa, or Gauḍa, was situated in what is now the modern district of Maldah. The seat of the Sena dynasty, this capital was eventually transferred to the ninth or central island on the western side of the Ganges at Navadvīp, which is now known as Māyāpura (although at that time it was called Gauḍapura).[40] Chaitanya Mahāprabhu lived his early life in that area, and so Gauḍīya Vaishnavism took on the nomenclature to commemorate that event.

But because the term "Gauḍīya," in the sense expressed above, refers chiefly to a geographical location, some think it inappropriate as a name for the tradition itself. After all, the essence of Gauḍīya Vaishnavism, they say, implies far more than a mere place in time. Thus, they prefer to call the tradition "Chaitanya Vaishnavism" or "Chaitanyaite Vaishnavism" (even if some also refer to it as "Bengal Vaishnavism," clearly another throwback to its geographical origins). In fact, the religion is based, first and foremost, on the inspiration and teaching of Śrī Chaitanya, and that, or so the theory goes, should be reflected in its name.

All this being said, the tradition recognizes yet another etymology of the word Gauḍīya, well known to Vaishnava aesthetes: The primary noun, *guḍa* (anglicized as *gur*), literally refers to molasses, or sweetness, and is often associated with the adjective Gauḍa, the region, which, as mentioned, gives us the name, Gauḍīya Vaishnavism. Interestingly, in the long history of Vaishnava traditions, it is the Gauḍīyas who make it a special point of emphasizing sweetness.

This nectarean and indispensable ingredient, they say, comes from Śrī Rādhā, for it is her sweet devotion to Krishna that speaks to the essence of Gauḍīya Vaishnava thought.[41] Because of her singular and intense bhakti, or devotional mood, the Gauḍīya tradition focuses on mādhurya, or the sweet love of God, as opposed to aiśvarya, or God's majesty. Further, her *madhu-sneha*, or honey-like love, was not fully revealed before the time of Śrī Chaitanya, again, making her unique brand of burning devotion peculiar to the Gauḍīya tradition. From this perspective, then, the term "Gauḍīya" takes on new meaning and can without doubt serve as an appropriate title for Śrī Chaitanya's Vaishnava tradition.[42]

Śrīla B. R. Śrīdhara Mahārāja reveals just how far his teacher, Śrīla Bhaktisiddhānta Sarasvatī Thakura, took the notion of Gauḍīya Vaishnavas as actually being devotees of Rādhā: "So, Śrīla Prabhupāda [Bhaktisiddhānta] said, 'We are *śuddha-śāktas* [pure worshippers of the feminine]. We are *śāktas*, not Vaiṣṇavas, but not *vidhā-śāktas* [ordinary *śāktas*]. We are *śuddha-śāktas*. We are concerned with Kṛṣṇa because our mistress Rādhārāṇī has connection with Him. This is why we want Him, and not otherwise.' This is a clear statement."[43]

Sarasvatī Ṭhākura sums up: "A devotee of Vishnu is a Vaishnava, a devotee of Krishna is a Kārshna, and a devotee of Śrī Rādhā is a Gauḍīya."[44]

NOTES

1. See *Śrīmad-Bhāgavatam* 9.10.51; *Mahābhārata*, Shanti Parvan, 231.12–20; and *Vāyu Purāṇa* 57.29–32. See also Jean Antoine Dubois, *Description of the*

Character, Manners, and Customs of the People of India (London: Longman, Hurst, Rees, Orme, and Brown, 1817), 334–335. The most thorough modern analysis of the Indian world ages comes from Luis A. González-Reimann, *The Mahabharata and the Yugas: India's Great Epic Poem and the Hindu System of World Ages* (New York: Peter Lang Inc., 2002).

2. See *Śrīmad-Bhāgavatam* 12.2.1; Sir M. Monier-Williams, *Indian Wisdom* (London: W.H. Allen & Co., 1893), 333; and Nicholas Sutton, *Religious Doctrines in the Mahābhārata* (Delhi: Motilal Banarsidass, 2000) 259–60.

3. This is noted by Heinrich Robert Zimmer, *Myths and Symbols in Indian Art and Civilization* (Princeton, New Jersey, Princeton University Press, 1972), 13.

4. For more on the auspicious side of an otherwise degraded age, see Mans Broo, "Bhaktivedanta Swami and the Golden Age," in *Journal of Vaishnava Studies*, Volume 13, No. 2 (Spring 2005), 95–112. "Prema-yuga" is a term introduced by Kanupriya Goswami (1891–1975), the Bengali Vaishnava writer of the modern era.

5. *Śrīmad Bhāgavatam* 1.1.3.

6. *kaler doṣa-nidhe rājann/ asti hy eko mahān guṇaḥ// kīrtanād eva kṛṣṇasya/ mukta-saṅgaḥ paraṁ vrajet//* (51) *kṛte yad dhyāyato viṣṇuṁtretāyāṁ yajato makhaiḥdvāpare paricaryāṁkalau tad dhari-kīrtanāt* (52).

7. *kṛtādiṣu prajā rājan/ kalāv icchanti sambhavam// kalau khalu bhaviṣyanti/ nārāyaṇa-pārayaṇah//* (*Śrīmad Bhāgavatam* 11.5.38) The translation of these two verses are adapted from that of His Divine Grace A. C. Bhaktivedānta Swami Prabhupāda.

8. Śacīnandana Swami explains this in various ways. One online version: (http://www.iskcondesiretree.com/m/blogpost?id=2103886%3ABlogPost%3A241463). The metaphor originates in Locana Dāsa Ṭhākura's *Caitanya-maṅgala*, one of the standard biographies of Śrī Chaitanya from the 16th century. See Locana Dāsa Ṭhākura, *Śrī Caitanya-maṅgala*, Madhya-khaṇḍa, Chapter 9, Song 21, verses 81 and 82 (Calcutta: Bagh Bazaar Gaudiya Mission, 1991), 132. Summarized translation from Bengali: (81) The living entities ears are sacrificial openings. The tongue is a sacrificial ladle. The sound of Lord Krishna's glories is charming sacrificial *ghee*. (82) When the ladle of the tongue pours that ghee into the openings of the ears, the ghee enters the heart. In the heart the *ghee* adds fuel to the fire of ecstatic love. It makes that fire burn with great flames. The flames of that fire make the body tremble. They make the body hairs stand erect.

9. Ibid.

10. See Joseph T. O'Connell, "Historicity in the Biographies of Caitanya," *Journal of Vaishnava Studies*, Volume 1, No. 2 (Fall 1993), 102–32.

11. The *Chaitanya Upanishad* was first discovered in 1887 by Bhaktivinoda Ṭhākura, who wrote a commentary on it (http://www.salagram.net/caitanya-upanisad.html). The work is unique in being the only Upanishadic text that mentions the life and mission of Śrī Chaitanya, purporting to predict his appearance. For this reason, and because of its rather late discovery, its authenticity has been questioned in the academic community.A. C. Bhaktivedānta Swami Prabhupāda provides a number of other predictive proof texts in his commentary to the *Caitanya-caritāmṛta* (Ādi 2.22). A few prominent examples:

(a) *puṇya-kṣetre navadvīpe bhaviṣyāmi śacī-sutaḥ*: "I shall appear in the holy land of Navadvīpa as the son of Śacīdevī." (*Krishna-yāmala-tantra*)

(b) *kalau saṅkīrtanārambhe bhaviṣyāmi śacī-sutaḥ*: "In the Age of Kali when the *saṅkīrtana* movement is inaugurated, I shall descend as the son of Śacīdevī." (*Vāyu Purāṇa*)

(c) *atha vāhaṁ dharādhāme/ bhūtvā mad-bhakta-rūpa-dhṛk// māyāyāṁ ca bhaviṣyāmi/ kalau saṅkīrtanāgame//*: "Sometimes I personally appear on the surface of the world in the garb of a devotee. Specifically, I appear as the son of Śacī in Kali-yuga to start the *saṅkīrtana* movement." (*Brahma-yāmala-tantra*)

12. Most of the early predictive evidence for Mahāprabhu's divinity exists only in manuscript form and generally cannot be found in current editions of scripture. For example, I have searched for the *Vāyu Purāṇa* quote mentioned in the above endnote, but I have not been able to locate it. That being said, it is common in Indian scholarship to recognize various recensions of a given text and the loss of portions of scripture over time. Still, some of the Puranic and Tantric verses mentioning Śrī Chaitanya can be found in Teun Goudriaan and Sanjukta Gupta, *Hindu Tantric and Śākta Literature* (Germany: Otto Harrassowitz Verlag, 1981), 105–109. For an example of how some of these texts are questioned in terms of authenticity, see Jagadānanda Dāsa (Jan Brzezinski), "An Analysis of Three Suspicious Texts" (http://jagadanandadas.blogspot.com/search/label/Chaitanya%20Upanishad). As a side note, many in the tradition claim that Mahāprabhu's specific descent involved appearing as a "secret" *avatāra*, with his identity as the Lord being confidential. For this reason, they say, scriptural indications of his existence were purposely camouflaged in accordance with his desire.

13. This is Prabhupāda's translation. One may wonder why not being black indicates yellow or golden. *Krishna-varṇaṁ tviṣākrishnaṁ* can also mean, "although he is black, he is also the opposite of black," which in Puranic parlance indicates gold. For example, in Hindu astronomy, there are two kinds of fortnights, *krishna-pakṣya* and *gaura-pakṣya,* where it is understood that *gaura* (golden) is the opposite of *krishna* (black).

14. The *sandhi* compound, *tviṣākṛṣṇam* can be divided in two ways: *tviṣākṛṣṇam* or *tviṣāakṛṣṇam*. According to the pre-Chaitanyite commentator, Śrīdhara Swami (c. early 15th century), lauded by the Gauḍīya community as being among the most significant authorities on the *Śrīmad Bhāgavatam, tviṣākṛṣṇam* in this verse (11.5.32) is explained as follows: [The Lord's] luster (*tviṣā*) is *kṛṣṇam*: brilliant like that of sapphire (*indranīla-maṇi-vadujjvalam*), in contradistinction to the usual Gauḍīya interpretation of *tviṣā akṛṣṇam*, "a non-blackish luster." Thus, *tviṣākrishnaṁ* in this context can be interpreted as an allusion to Krishna instead of Chaitanya. [See *Śrīdhara Swami's Commentary on the Śrīmadbhāgavat Mahāpurāṇam,* ed., Pandit Rāmteja Pāndeya (Delhi: Chaukhambā Sanskrit Pratiṣthān Pub, 2011), Verse 11.5.32, 1,292.] Regarding the Lord's complexion in this verse, Śrīdhara also uses the words *rukṣatām vyāvarttayati*, which translates as "negates grossness." This is to indicate that his luster is not coarse but shiny, which can also suggest Krishna's splendid blackish hue. But, for later Gauḍīya commentators, it leaves an opening

that can also point to the effulgent Mahāprabhu. Additionally, Śrīdhara Swami sees the *Bhāgavatam*'s following two verses (33 and 34) as suggestive of Rāmacandra, even if Krishna is also evoked by these verses. [See also Srila Bhakti Ballabh Tirtha Maharaja, "Sri Ramacandra-avatara" (http://www.bvml.org/SBBTM/sra.html)] While Gauḍīyas acknowledge the veracity of this version without doubt, they simultaneously emphasize the inner reading of the Goswāmīs, wherein these verses are veiled references to Śrī Chaitanya.

15. There is also a tradition claiming that this *yuga* cycle is unique. According to Prabhupāda in his commentary to the *Caitanya-caritāmṛta*, Madhya 20.246: The four *yuga-avatāras* are (1) *śukla* (white) in Satya-yuga, (2) *rakta* (red) in Tretā-yuga, (3) *śyāma* (dark blue) in Dvāpara-yuga, and (4) generally *krishna* (black) but in special cases *pīta* (yellow) as Chaitanya Mahāprabhu in Kali-yuga . . . .

16. See Swami B. V. Tripurāri, *Jīva Goswāmī's Tattva-Sandarbha* (Philo, California: Harmonist Publishers, 2011), 16. The *Krama Sandarbha* further confirms that this verse refers to Śrī Chaitanya. Jīva quotes it in his auto-commentary to the first verse of the *Tattva Sandarbha* (See *Tattva* 1–2, *Sarva-saṁvādinī*).

17. *dharmaṁ mahā-puruṣa pāsi yugānuvṛttaṁchannaḥ kalau yad abhavas tri-yugo 'tha sa tvam* (*Bhāgavatam* 7.9.38).

18. See Rūpa Goswāmī, *Stava Mālā, Dvitiya Śrī Caitanyāṣṭakam*, Verse 1 (http://kksongs.org/songs/k/kalauyamvidvamsah.html).

19. Gauḍīya Vaishnavas tend to see Rādhā in two ways: (1) She is Krishna's female counterpart, that is, the female Godhead. That is, while he is the *predominating* aspect of deity, she is the *predominated* aspect of deity. But in reality they are one, comprising one supreme Godhead. In this connection, Bhaktisiddhānta Sarasvatī uses the obscure English term "moiety," which means "one of two equal parts." (https://www.merriam-webster.com/dictionary/moiety). His usage of this word in relation to Rādhā can be found throughout his writing and teaching, such as in his conversation with Dr. Stella Kramrisch in 1931 (http://srilabhaktisiddhantasarasvatithakuraprabhupada.com/legacy/conversations/talk-to-prof-dr-stella-kramrisch-m-a-ph-d-1931/). See also Bhaktisiddhānta Sarasvatī, "Sree Radhika," in *The Harmonist*, Volume XXX, No. 5 (November 1932). (2) Śrī Rādhā is the *hlādini-śakti* of the Lord, meaning that she is his internal pleasure potency, or his sublime energy in full form. "Śrī Rādhā is the full power, and Lord Krishna is the possessor of that power. The two are identical, as the scriptures say." See *Caitanya-caritāmṛta*, Ādi 4.96.

20. Swami B. R. Śrīdhara, *The Golden Volcano of Divine Love* (Nadiya, West Bengal: Sri Chaitanya Saraswat Math, 1996, reprint), 10.

21. Śrīla Kavi Karṇapūra's *Śrī Gaura-gaṇoddeśa-dīpikā*, trans., Kuśakratha Dāsa (Culver City, California: The Krsna Library, 1987), Text 1.

22. *rādhā kṛṣṇa-praṇaya-vikṛtir hlādinī śaktir asmād/ ekātmānāv api bhuvi purā deha-bhedaṁ gatau tau// caitanyākhyaṁ prakaṭam adhunā tad-dvayaṁ caikyam āptaṁ/ rādhā-bhāva-dyuti-suvalitaṁ naumi kṛṣṇa-svarūpam//* Also quoted in *Caitanya-caritāmṛta* 1.4.55, wherein Prabhupāda notes in his purport that this is taken from the diary of Svarūpa Dāmodara Goswāmī.

23. Madhya 8.282: *tabe hāsi' tāṅre prabhu dekhāila svarūpa'rasa-rāja' 'mahābhāva'—dui eka rūpa*. This is Prabhupāda's translation. The words indicating

Krishna and Rādhā in this verse are pregnant with meaning, elaborated upon throughout the tradition: Rasarāja-Mahābhāva, respectively. Briefly, Rasarāja indicates the king of all relationships, which can only be Krishna, and Rādhā is the embodiment of the highest love (she is known as Mahābhāva-svarūpiṇī). Thus, the title "Mahāprabhu" (i.e., "great master"), traditionally used for Śrī Chaitanya, is a sort of esoteric shorthand for these two words: "Mahā" indicates Mahābhāva and "Prabhu," indicates Krishna, the king of blissful interaction, Rasarāja. Although a number of great teachers in history have been called "Mahāprabhu," such as Vallabha, only Śrī Chaitanya can claim it in this esoteric sense.

24. Swami B. R. Śrīdhara, *Śrī Guru and His Grace* (Nabadvip: Sri Chaitanya Sāraswat Matha, 1999), 221.

25. Despite the fact that Gauḍīya masters such as Rūpa Goswāmī and Bhaktisiddhānta Sarasvatī, among others, are sometimes referred to as "Prabhupāda," when I use the name in this book it refers to His Divine Grace A. C. Bhaktivedānta Swami Prabhupāda, unless otherwise indicated.

26. A lecture by Prabhupāda, recorded in Māyāpur, India, on March 25, 1975, "Caitanya Mahāprabhu—Rādhā and Krishna Combined," published in *Back to Godhead*, Volume 33, No. 6 (November, 1999).

27. See John Stratton Hawley's American Academy of Religion review of Tony K. Stewart, *The Final Word: The Caitanya Caritāmṛta and the Grammar of Religious Tradition* (New York: Oxford University Press, 2010). The review can be found here: http://jaar.oxfordjournals.org/content/early/2010/11/30/jaarel.lfq097.

28. For evidence that Vaishnavism constitutes the numerically largest segment of the Hindu population, please refer to three consequential books: (1) Agehananda Bharati, *Hindu Views and Ways and the Hindu-Muslim Interface* (New Delhi: Munshiram Manoharlal, 1981); (2) Klaus Klostermaier, "The Response of Modern Vaishnavism" in Harold G. Coward, ed., *Modern Indian Responses to Religious Pluralism* (Albany: State University of New York Press, 1987), 129; and (3) Gerald Larson, *India's Agony Over Religion* (Albany: State University of New York Press, 1995), 20. The same fact was stated in the 1996 *Britannica Book of the Year*.

29. See Paul Michael Toomey, *Food from the Mouth of Krishna: Feasts and Festivities in a North Indian Pilgrimage Centre* (Delhi: Hindustan Publishing Corporation, 1994); also see Steven J. Rosen, *Holy Cow: The Hare Krishna Contribution to Vegetarianism and Animal Rights* (New York: Lantern Books, 2004).

30. See Steven J. Rosen, *The Four Principles of Freedom: The Morals and Ethics Behind Vegetarianism, Continence, Sobriety and Honesty* (New York: FOLK Books, 2002); see also "Why Celibacy?—A Hindu Perspective," by Swami Tyagananda: http://www.eng.vedanta.ru/library/vedanta_kesari/why_celibacy_a_hindu_perspective.php; and Yoga-sutra 2.38: When an awareness of the highest reality of chastity or celibacy (*brahmacharya*) is firmly established, then a great strength, capacity, or vitality (*vīrya*) is acquired (*brahmāchārya pratiṣthāyam vīrya labhaḥ*).

31. See (The Disciples of) A. C. Bhaktivedānta Prabhupāda, *Coming Back: The Science of Reincarnation* (Los Angeles: Bhaktivedanta Book Trust, Contemporary Vedic Library Series, 1982); also see Steven J. Rosen, *The Reincarnation Controversy: Uncovering the Truth in the World Religions* (Badger, California: Torchlight Publishing, 1997).

32. See Norvin Hein, "Caitanya's Ecstasies and the Theology of the Name," in *Hinduism: New Essays in the History of Religions* (Leiden: E.J. Brill, 1976), 22–23. For *smaraṇam*, see Dhyānachandra Goswāmī's *Śrī Gaura-govindārcana-smaraṇa-paddhati* (https://www.scribd.com/document/88069163/Gaura-Govindarcana-Smarana-Paddhatih-by-Dhyanacandra-Gosvami).

33. See Brijbasi Dasa (Kostyantyn Perun), "Daśa Mūla: The Ten Fundamental Truths" in *Journal of Vaishnava Studies*, Volume 23, No. 1, Fall 2014, 205–230.

34. *sampradāya-vihīnā ye mantrās te niṣphalā matāḥ*. Though this verse cannot be found in current editions of the *Padma Purāṇa*, it was cited (as a verse in that *Purāṇa*) in Kavi Karṇapūra's *Śrī Gaura-gaṇoddeśa-dīpikā* (21), which is an early Gauḍīya text. For this reason alone, it can be assumed that it was in earlier editions of the *Purāṇa*. The verse can also be found in the 18th-century *Bhakti-ratnākara*, Fifth Wave. A similar verse, almost identical, appears in the *Garga-saṁhitā,* which is a traditional *saṁhitā* in the Vaishnava tradition. (*Garga-saṁhitā*, Aśvamedha-khaṇḍa, 61.24–26) For more on this reference, see Viśvanātha Cakravartī's *Gaura-gaṇa-svarūpa-tattva-candrikā*, trans., Demian Martins (Vrindavan, U.P.: Jiva Institute, 2015), Introduction, xiii.

35. Tradition holds that there were three Vishnu Swamis, that is, Adi Vishnu Swami (circa 3rd century BCE, who introduced the traditional 108 categories of *sannyāsa*); Rāja Gopāla Vishnu Swami (8th or 9th century CE); and Andhra Vishnu Swami (14th century CE), thus accounting for the uncertainty in his dates.

36. For more on the four *sampradāyas* in a Gauḍīya context, see O. B. L. Kapoor, *The Philosophy and Religion of Śrī Caitanya* (Delhi: Munshiram Manoharlal, 1976), Chapter 3, entitled, "The Sampradāya of Śrī Caitanya," 36–52; see also William H. Deadwyler, "Saṁpradāya of Śrī Caitanya," in Steven J. Rosen, *Vaiṣṇavism: Contemporary Scholars Discuss the Gauḍīya Tradition* (New York: Folk Books, 1992). 127–140.

37. See His Divine Grace A. C. Bhaktivedānta Swami Prabhupāda, "The Religion Beyond All Religions" (http://www.krishna.com/religion-beyond-all-religions) and also his "Kṛṣṇa Consciousness: Hindu Cult or Divine Culture?" in *The Science of Self-Realization* (Culver City, California: The Bhaktivedanta Book Trust, 1977), 105–110; also see O. B. L. Kapoor, Ph.D., "*Bhakti*, the Perfect Science" *Back to Godhead*, Volume 1, No. 53, Spring 1973: http://www.backtogodhead.in/bhakti-the-perfect-science/.

38. The three-tiered levels of Godhead are best summarized in a much-quoted verse from the *Śrīmad-Bhāgavatam* (1.2.11): "The Absolute Truth is realized in three phases, though all of them are identical. These are expressed as Brahman, Paramātmā, and Bhagavān." (*vadanti tat tattva-vidas, tattvaṁ yaj jñānam advayam, brahmeti paramātmeti, bhagavān iti śabdyate*). See also Steven J. Rosen, *The Hidden Glory of India* (Sweden: Bhaktivedanta Book Trust, 2002), 42–45.

39. Graham M. Schweig, "Krishna, the Intimate Divinity," in Edwin F. Bryant and Maria L. Ekstrand, eds., *The Hare Krishna Movement: The Postcharismatic Fate of a Religious Transplant* (New York: Columbia University Press, 2004), 18. Ultimately, as Dr. Schweig points out, the tradition can be seen as a form of "polymorphic

bi-monotheism," since it acknowledges a dual-gendered divinity whose ultimate manifestation is Śrī Śrī Rādhā-Krishna. See *ibid.* 19.

40. See Bhaktivedānta Swami Prabhupāda's translation of the *Caitanya-caritāmṛta* (Ādi 1.19), purport.

41. For more on the theology of Rādhā, see John S. Hawley and Donna Wulff, eds., *The Divine Consort: Rādhā and the Goddesses of India* (Berkeley, California: Berkeley Religious Studies Series, 1982) and also their revised edition, *Devī: Goddesses of India* (Los Angeles: University of California Press, 1996). Also see *Journal of Vaishnava Studies*, Volume 8, No. 2 (Spring 2000) and Volume 10, No. 1 (Fall 2001). Both issues focused on Śrī Rādhā.

42. See Radhakanta Das's "From Fear to Love": http://backtobhakti.com/from-fear-to-love/.

43. See http://www.gaudiyadarshan.com/posts/the-quantity-and-quality-of-rasa/.

44. Quoted in Bhakti Vikāsa Swami, *Śrī Bhaktisiddhānta Vaibhava*, Volume 3 (Surat: Bhakti Vikas Trust, 2009), 34. It should be noted that Sarasvatī Ṭhākura makes this statement knowing full well that all Vaishnavas worship the three divinities in question. His statement is more in the line of emphasis and meant to be descriptive of the inner Gauḍīya mood. This preference for Śrī Rādhā gives insight into the heart of Gauḍīya Vaishnavism: Bhaktisiddhānta Sarasvatī spoke frequently about the Gauḍīya preference for Rādhikā. Once, when the Diwan of Bharatpur showed deep respect for Śrī Rādhā, Sarasvatī Ṭhākura declared: "Their angle of vision towards . . . Rādhārāṇī is different from ours. They recognize and revere Krishna. And because Rādhārāṇī is Krishna's favorite, they also have some reverence for Her . . . . But our vision is just the opposite. Our concern is with Rādhārāṇī. And only because She wants Krishna do we have any connection with Him." (http://scsmathinternational.com/library/LovingSearchForTheLostServant/LovingSearch-11-TheServiceOfSriRadha.php). Bhaktivinoda Ṭhākura goes further: "If your desire for the worship of Śrī Rādhā does not arise, then your so-called worship of Krishna is virtually dead." See *Rādhikāṣṭakam,* Song 8, Verse 1 (*rādhā-bhajane yadi mati nāhi bhelā kṛṣṇa-bhajana taba akāraṇa gelā*).

Chapter 2

Śrī Krishna

Enter the Dark Lord

Before attempting to understand Śrī Chaitanya, his life and precepts, one must first understand something about Lord Krishna. Insight into the supreme divinity of the Vaishnavas—whether viewed as Vishnu, Nārāyaṇa, Krishna, or any of his many incarnations—is prerequisite for delving into the golden *avatāra*. This is because the theological system surrounding Chaitanya and his tradition perceives Krishna as the Supreme Godhead, the basis, the underlying reality of all that is. Besides, Śrī Chaitanya loves him so much, and if you understand that which a person loves, you can understand much about the person.

The *Brahma-saṁhitā* (5.1), a traditional Indic wisdom text, defines Krishna's supreme position with clarity:

īśvaraḥ paramaḥ krishnaḥ
sac-cid-ānanda-vigrahaḥ
anādir ādir govindaḥ
sarva-kāraṇa-kāraṇam

"Krishna is the supreme being. He has a form that is composed of eternity, knowledge, and bliss. He appears as a cowherd boy (Govinda) who has no origin other than himself. He is the original cause of all causes."

This is no doubt a lofty attribution of divinity, but it is also repeatedly confirmed in numerous Indian scriptures, such as the *Bhagavad-gītā*. For example, the *Gītā* tells us that Krishna is the origin of every god in the Vedic pantheon[1] and, further, the source of all that exists.[2] Those who perform other kinds of worship, Krishna reveals in the *Gītā*'s pages, are ultimately worshiping only him, even if they don't quite know it, for he is the source and sustainer of all lesser deities.[3] He tells Arjuna, his interlocutor in the *Gītā*, that while various demigods may accept offerings from their worshipers, these demigods are really only his agents, accepting such offerings on his behalf. He is the ultimate enjoyer of all religious sacrifice.[4] In conclusion, at least in terms of our present context, Krishna tells Arjuna that he is the great Lord of all worlds[5] and the creator and sustainer of everything.[6]

In the course of their dialogue, Arjuna realizes Krishna's glory, too, affirming that his Master is indeed Lord of all: "He is the Supreme Brahman, the Supreme Abode, the Supreme Purifier, and the Supreme Divine Person," Arjuna says.[7] He further points out that Krishna is the God of all gods,[8] and the primeval person (echoing the words of the *Brahma-saṁhitā*).[9] Arjuna concludes that no one is equal to or greater than Krishna.[10]

Thus, Krishna, at least according to the *Gītā* and similar sacred texts, rises above the numerous gods or demigods (*devatās*) of the Vedic tradition. Śrī Chaitanya's Vaishnavism takes careful note of this.

Krishna's supremacy is also conveyed in the *Śrīmad Bhāgavatam*, considered the culmination of ancient India's Vedic revelation. The text literally begins and ends with Śrī Krishna, acknowledging him as Supreme. The very first verse tells us, "O my Lord, Śrī Krishna, son of Vasudeva, O all-pervading Personality of Godhead, I offer my respectful obeisances unto You. I meditate upon Lord Krishna because he is the Absolute Truth and the primeval cause of all causes of the creation, sustenance and destruction of the manifested universes."[11]

A key verse in that same first canto tells us that Krishna is the source of all divine manifestations. "All of these incarnations," the text tells us, after enumerating a number of divinities, "are either plenary portions or portions of plenary portions of the Lord, but Lord Śrī Krishna is the original Personality of Godhead."[12]

This is important for the Gauḍīya tradition, especially because other Vaishnava lineages tend to favor Vishnu or Nārāyaṇa. These other lineages present this more majestic aspect of the Supreme as the original "Personality of Godhead," as opposed to Krishna. But according to the *Bhāgavatam* and Śrī Chaitanya, Krishna is the source of Vishnu and not the other way around. Scholars of the Gauḍīya tradition put forward many scriptural and logical explanations to defend this perspective.[13]

Still, Vishnu and Krishna are also described as being various faces of the same one Supreme Being, and so the distinction between them is a technical point that need not concern us here. As the *Caitanya-caritāmṛta* (Madhya 9.153, 154) declares, "Lord Krishna and Lord Nārāyaṇa (Vishnu) are nondifferent . . . . It is an offense to see distinction between the various forms of the Lord (*kṛṣṇa-nārāyaṇa, yaiche eka-i svarūpa . . . īśvaratve bheda mānile haya aparādha*)." But the main point is that the *Bhāgavatam* glorifies Krishna/ Vishnu as supreme.

The very last verse of the *Bhāgavatam* (12.13.23), in fact, tells us that spiritual perfection is easily available to one who glorifies the holy name of Krishna (*kīrtana*). Such chanting leads to direct perception of divinity, say the Gauḍīyas, and so the question of just who occupies the place of supreme deity, Vishnu or Krishna, can easily be answered: just take to the chanting process and see for oneself. In any case, the *Bhāgavatam* leaves us with the essential practice of the age, connecting Krishna with the path promulgated by Śrī Chaitanya: Hari-kīrtana.[14]

IN SEARCH OF THE HISTORICAL KRISHNA

Although searching for Krishna in terms of historical data would have little meaning for the Chaitanya tradition, it might be fruitful to briefly explore the various archival and archeological evidences for his early existence in the world of three dimensions. There are, to be sure, Vedic (pre-Hindu) texts that mention Krishna[15] and a dynastic clan from which he is said to have emerged.[16]

Few scholars have looked into Krishna's historicity as thoroughly as Bimanbehari Majumdar (1900–1969), and his work, *Kṛṣṇa in History and Legend* lays bear the numerous reasons one might accept the dark-eyed Lord as an historical personality. In regard to the aforementioned dynastic clan, for example, Majumdar has this to say:

> Kṛṣṇa is a real historical personage. To call him a mythical or an allegorical figure is to ignore the evidence of the whole of the ancient Indian historical tradition. The genealogy of the famous royal dynasties was carefully preserved by distinct classes of persons called the Sūtas, Vyāsas, and the Paurāṇikas. As many as twelve out of the eighteen Purāṇas recount the names of ancestors of Kṛṣṇa. These Purāṇas were compiled in different regions of India and yet there is a remarkable agreement among them so far as the Yādava genealogy is concerned. Several variations in the names indicate that one list was not a slavish copy of the other.[17]

Still, it is difficult if not impossible to empirically prove the existence of anyone from prehistoric times. Nor is it necessarily desirable. In other words, the Krishna of the Chaitanya tradition is a Krishna of faith, revealed through realization if revealed at all. The founding fathers of the lineage ask adherents to perform Sādhana-bhakti, that is, devotional service in practice, and thereby gain personal experiential knowledge of Krishna and his truth. While practicing, one has recourse to the realization of one's forebears, or the great teachers in disciplic succession, who have seen Krishna, it is said, in their heart of hearts. One may also study the detail and logic afforded by scripture and the greater tradition, thus fortifying one's faith until realization ensues.

While the historicity of Krishna, much like that of Jesus,[18] is ultimately a question of faith, or, according to the believer, realization, many scholars—even those trained in the Western academy—seem to accept that there is some objective truth to his existence. This scholarly endorsement of said historicity comes after much study and deep exploration of the facts.

Historians like Horace H. Wilson, writing as far back as 1870, notes, "Rama and Krishna . . . appear to have been originally real and historical characters . . . ."[19] Similarly, Rudolf Otto wrote in the first part of the 20th century, "That Krishna himself was a historical figure is indeed quite indubitable."[20] Some years later, Dr. R. C. Majumdar tells us: "There is now a general consensus of opinion in favour of the historicity of Krishna."[21] Dr. Thomas J. Hopkins wrote in 1978: "From a strictly scholarly, historical standpoint, the Krishna who appears in the Bhagavad-*gītā* is the princely Krishna of the *Mahābhārata* . . . . Krishna, the historical prince and charioteer of Arjuna."[22] Perhaps more realistically, Diana Eck notes that even if Krishna lacks the usually historical documentation of a being who walked among us, he is nonetheless "a reality in the lives of people of faith."[23]

There *is* early evidence for the existence of Krishna worship, and that too lends itself to conceiving of him as a historical reality. For example, the Greek ethnographer and explorer Megasthenes, serving as an ambassador of King Chandragupta Maurya and hailing from the Seleucid dynasty in the 4th century BCE, wrote a book called *Indika*. Though the original text no longer survives, it has been quoted by ancient classical writers such as Arrian, Diodorus, and Strabo. From their quotes, we become privy to Megasthenes's description of the Sourasenoi, an Indian tribe who worshiped "Herakles"—or Hari-kul-isha, that is, "Hari, the supreme controller." We also read in those same texts about the two great cities of the Sourasenoi, known as Methora and Kleisobora, and a nearby river, the Jobares. Later commentators have noted that Methora is obviously Mathurā, where Krishna was born; Kleisobora is Krishna-pura, meaning "the city of Krishna"; and the Jobares is the Yamunā, the famous river in the Krishna narrative.[24]

Archeological evidence includes the Heliodorus column in Besnagar, northwest Madhya Pradesh, dated to around 100 BCE. The inscription on the pillar tells us that Heliodorus, a Greek ambassador of the Indo-Greek king Antialcidas, considered himself a "*bhagavata*," or a devotee of Bhagavān Śrī Krishna. His inscription is particularly noteworthy because it reveals that, even at this early date, a foreigner had actually been converted to Vaishnavism, and particularly to Krishna worship.

According to some, he was obviously not the first foreigner to adopt Krishnaite allegiances. As Thomas J. Hopkins mused, "Heliodorus was presumably not the earliest Greek who was converted to Vaishnava devotional practices although he might have been the one to erect a column that is still extant. Certainly there were numerous others including the king who sent him as an ambassador."[25] There are similar inscriptions, too, such as that of Ghosundi in Rajasthan and the Mora Well in Mathurā, establishing a considerable claim for Krishna worship in the pre-Christian era.

In recent decades, the most convincing archeological support for the historical Krishna comes from seabed discoveries found off the coast of modern Dwarka. To those who know the Krishna story as revealed in the scriptures, Dvārakā (Dwarka) served as Krishna's later kingdom in the state of Gujarat in northwestern India. This is where he settled as a prince after his early life as a cowherd in both Vrindāvan and Mathurā. It is considered one of the seven sacred cities of Hinduism.

The *Mahābhārata* (16.8.40–41) describes the flooding of Dvārakā with a few beautifully poetic verses, and then, in the *Harivaṁśa*, too, we find that Krishna's kingdom was "released into the ocean" (2.58.34). Indeed, it is said that, after his earthly existence, his regal dwelling was cataclysmically inundated by the Arabian Sea.

In the late 1970s into the 1980s, Indian archeologist, S. R. Rao, led a team of archaeologists and divers in Gujarat to see if there were remains of Krishna's ancient city. At first, they merely found simple pottery and other artifacts that were likely more than 3,000 years old, which was itself significant, but then they found other relics and monuments indicating the ruins of an ancient city.

Subsequent research conducted by famed archeologist Alok Tripathi, tells us that, "Ancient structural remains of some significance have been discovered at Dwarka, under water and on land, by the Underwater Archaeology Wing (UAW) of the Archaeological Survey of India (ASI)."[26] Rakesh Krishnan Simha, in an article called "The Historical Krishna," tells us, "Another important find by our divers was a seal that establishes the submerged township's connection with the Dwarka of the *Mahābhārata*. The seal corroborates the reference made in the ancient text, the *Harivaṁśa*, that every citizen of Dwarka carried such a seal for identification purposes. Krishna had ruled that none without the seal should enter his kingdom. A similar seal has been found onshore as well."[27]

While none of this, of course, is conclusive in terms of establishing a historical Krishna, it is certainly thought provoking and lends itself to deep contemplation on the nature of being. What, after all, makes someone an "historical" person? What determines if someone truly exists or not? Martin Kahler offers this insightful answer: "Is it not the person who originates and bequeaths a permanent influence? [or] . . . those dynamic individuals who intervene in the course of events?"[28] Kahler's response makes us think twice about what constitutes a historical person—it is, in the end, someone who has historical significance. Now, does the record show that Krishna was historically significant? Has he "intervened in the course of events" known as world history? That there are, and have been for centuries, millions of Hindus worldwide—this in itself attests to the legitimacy of an affirmative answer.[29]

The search for the historical Krishna is rich and compelling—but the image that emerges from it may well be unrecognizable to the devout practitioner. It doesn't look like the Krishna of the *Bhāgavatam* or the Krishna that appears of his own sweet will in the hearts of pure devotees. Both historiography and personal realization are important parts of human experience. Ideally, they complement each other. It serves us well to uncover facts—but not if we don't endeavor to truly understand them. Fact and interpretation must dance together in harmony, lest they be deemed unworthy, or worse, contrived. The historian may discover an objective truth, but to what end? If the beneficiaries of that truth derive no utility from its possession or an ennobling of character or behavior, then its value is questionable, at best. Conversely, if all the facts are not in place, but an acolyte embraces whatever little he or she understands to be true, and grows incrementally ennobled in character and behavior by that embrace, then that process can certainly be considered meritorious and laudable.[30]

TRUTH AND BEAUTY SUPREME

Who, then, is Krishna to Gauḍīya Vaishnavas? What is their vision of the Lord of all? Put simply, in addition to everything that has been outlined above, he is seen as beauty supreme. While he has opulent and awe-inspiring manifestations, such as Vishnu, or Nārāyaṇa, his supreme form, say the Gauḍīyas, would be rather unexpected, for it is disarming in its simplicity. Yet isn't the topmost beauty often the most natural, the most uncomplicated, the most sincere and direct?

Apropos of this, the preeminent form of God is the simple, village cowherd boy who lives in Vrindāvan. He is described as being *śyāma*, blackish, or dark-colored, like a fresh raincloud, or sometimes *nīla*, dark blue, like the petals of a blue lotus. Sometimes he is described as looking like the best of blue sapphires, a dark mound of blue musk, or like a newly unfurled leaf of a *tamāla* tree. His darkness evokes a sense of mystery, but, more, it points to his deep beauty.

He has blooming blue eyes like lotus petals[31] and is adept at playing on his magical flute, which not only shepherds and delights the cow, but, by its unparalleled melodiousness, also attracts all errant souls back to the inconceivable felicity of his company. His head is gorgeously crowned with a peacock feather; he wears glistening golden garments that offset his dark complexion; and the beauty of his face puts to shame the glorious splendor of the autumnal moon at the peak of its fullness. Vaishnava texts are replete with such descriptions of Krishna's unrivalled beauty. This is Krishna, whose name, unsurprisingly, is often translated as, "the all-attractive one."[32]

His life narrative, which appears in the tenth canto of the *Śrīmad Bhāgavatam*, functions both as a repository of wisdom teachings and a chronicle of his transcendental activities on earth, which, according to tradition, occurred some 5,000 years ago. But more, it functions as a resplendent ornament that enhances his appeal; it radiates and exponentially heightens the magnetism of his already incomparable beauty.[33]

But to fully understand these narratives, the tradition teaches, one must receive them from self-realized souls, pure devotees, for the seed of transcendence is carried by their potency, and Krishna will only allow himself to be accessed by their grace. Once introduced to Krishna and his realm through these sources—the sacred texts as conveyed by God's pure representatives—one gradually learns the inner truths of a divine kingdom that is both far away and as close as our own hearts. That is to say, Krishna is both transcendent and imminent.

His play (*līlā*), or "pastimes," as it is often translated (we will explain this word further in the next chapter), are separated into four periods: From his (apparent) birth to his fifth year is called *kaumāra*; from the beginning of his sixth year until his tenth is *paugaṇḍa*; from his 11th year until the end of his 15th is labeled *kaiśora*; and finally, everything after his sixteenth year is known as *yauvana*, or youth. Thus, Krishna, as the eternally youthful divinity of the Vaishnavas, does not visibly age beyond this final period in his "life," even when he is well over 100 years old on the battlefield of Kurukshetra (where the *Bhagavad-gītā* was spoken). These various ages that Krishna manifests—each eternal and never-ending, inconceivably—represent his specific desires to lovingly interact with his devotees in particular ways, according to their specific relationships with him. The overall narrative serves to lure his devotees back to him, and is detailed or blossoms in India's sacred texts.

In addition to the standard literature, there is a more advanced, essential reading of Krishna's activities as well, leading to the cultivation of pure devotion. This reading evolved as a secret meditation specifically promulgated by the Chaitanya tradition, encoded in texts that foster "remembrance" of one's eternal relationship with the alluring blue cowherd. These texts, it is said, facilitate an actual "entrance" into the spiritual world.

Rūpa Goswāmī, for example, wrote a short work called the *Smaraṇa Maṅgala* in which he details the "eight times of Krishna's day." This was a concept gleaned from early post-Vedic works, such as the *Padma Purāṇa* (Patala khaṇḍa, Ch. 14) and the *Sanat-kumāra Saṁhitā*, in which Krishna's typical day in celestial Vraja is broken down into distinct periods for meditative purposes. In this way, accomplished devotees on the path might learn to further focus on the Lord's intimate pastimes.[34] This eightfold meditation came to be called Aṣṭa-kālīya-nitya-līlā, or "the eternal eightfold daily pastimes," as we will explain in an upcoming chapter.

Śrī Rupa was not the only one to elaborate on the eight parts of Krishna's day. Kavi Karṇapūra, another early Vaishnava poet, outlined this same eightfold schema in his *Kṛṣṇāhnika Kaumudi*, and so did the early Gauḍīya mystic Dhyānachandra Goswāmī in his *Smaraṇa-paddhati*. Perhaps the most famous versions of Krishna's eight-part day come from Krishnadāsa Kavirāja Goswāmī, in his classic, *Govinda-līlāmṛta*, and Viśvanātha Chakravartī (circa, 1626–1708), in *Śrī Krishna Bhāvanāmṛta Mahāvākhya*.

Of course, this practice, meant for extremely advanced practitioners, is subservient to chanting the holy name, which the tradition puts forward as essential for spiritual attainment. Jīva Goswāmī thus writes, "If one's heart has become pure by surrender, *sādhu-saṅga* (the association of great souls), and hearing and singing the names, forms, attributes and pastimes of the Lord, one can then perform *smaraṇa*, or remembrance of the Lord." (*Bhakti-sandarbha*, Anuccheda 274). Jīva Goswāmī particularly recommends *kīrtana* (loud call and response chanting) over *smaraṇa*, so that when the heart becomes pure through such chanting, meditation will arise as a matter of course. (*Bhakti-sandarbha*, Anuccheda 276) In the very last line of Śrīla Bhaktisiddhānta Sarasvatī's song "Vaishnava Ke" (text 19), he thus leaves his readers with this: "The power of congregational chanting can automatically awaken remembrance of the Lord . . . ." (*kīrtana-prabhave, smaraṇa svabhave*). We will mention these references later as well, in a more specific context.

For our current purposes, however, the Aṣṭa-kālīya-līlā has considerable significance: The esoteric Krishna we find in this schema is clearly the Krishna of Chaitanya Vaishnavism. For example, Śrī Rādhā figures prominently in the eight times of Krishna's day. When we look at Chaitanya Mahāprabhu's love for Krishna, we find that Rādhā is central, both for Mahāprabhu's notion of divinity and as a prototype for the perfect devotee.

This preeminence of the divine Goddess arose in Bengal prior to the time of Śrī Chaitanya, who embraced it with full enthusiasm. According to Krishnadāsa Kavirāja Goswāmī in his *Caitanya-caritāmṛta*, Mahāprabhu deeply relished five devotional authors, all of whom laud Rādhā's special place in Vaishnava theology.[35] Their names should be known: Jayadeva, Caṇḍīdāsa, Vidyāpati, Bilvamaṅgala, and the Master's contemporary, Rāmānanda Rāya. By understanding the perspective of these poets, along with the *Bhāgavatam*, which is considered seminal for all Gauḍīya Vaishnavas, we will see how the Krishna conception favored by Śrī Chaitanya's teachings emerged historically.

THE KRISHNA OF ŚRĪ CHAITANYA'S ERA

It all begins with the *Bhāgavatam*. We learn of the *Bhāgavatam*'s special nature throughout its many pages (1.1.2–3): "Completely rejecting all religious activities which are materially motivated, this *Bhāgavata Purāṇa* propounds the highest truth, which is understandable by those devotees who are fully pure in heart. The highest truth is reality distinguished from illusion for the welfare of all. Such truth uproots the threefold miseries. This beautiful *Bhāgavatam*, compiled by the great sage Vyāsadeva [in his maturity], is sufficient in itself for God realization. What is the need of any other scripture? As soon as one attentively and submissively hears the message of *Bhāgavatam*, by this culture of knowledge the Supreme Lord is established within his heart. O expert and thoughtful men, relish *Śrīmad-Bhāgavatam*, the mature fruit of the desire tree of Vedic literatures. It emanated from the lips of Śrī Śukadeva Gosvāmī. Therefore this fruit has become even more tasteful, although its nectarean juice was already relishable for all, including liberated souls."

And further (1.7.7): "Simply by listening to this Vedic text, the feeling for loving devotional service to Lord Krishna, the Supreme Personality of Godhead, sprouts up at once to extinguish the fire of lamentation, illusion and fearfulness." The text concludes with similar praise (12.13.15): "*Śrīmad-Bhāgavatam* is declared to be the essence of all Vedānta philosophy. One who has felt satisfaction from its nectarean mellow will never be attracted to any other literature."[36]

Of the 14,000-plus verses found in the *Bhāgavatam*, the text's most lauded section involves Krishna and the *gopīs*: the five chapters of the Rāsa-līlā, or Krishna's round dance with the cowherd maidens of Vraja. Graham Schweig has written extensively on this subject[37] and points out that the Rāsa-līlā is the essence of all *līlās*, or the very heart of the *Bhāgavatam*.[38] That being the case, one can look to the Rāsa-līlā to see what the *Bhāgavatam* is really all about.

Interestingly, in that particular section, we find the most profound truths of Krishna devotion, including the complex subject of love in union (*sambhoga*) and love in separation (*vipralambha*, or *viraha*)—and we find both the presence and absence of Śrī Rādhā, who appears in the dance but is not specifically named.[39] We will return to Rādhā's mysterious presence in the *Bhāgavatam* in a few moments. First, we should devote a couple of paragraphs to the spiritual concepts of union and separation, both of which, again, are central to the Rāsa-līlā, and, as we shall see, to the entire Rādhā-Krishna relationship.

Anyone can understand the desire for union, since this is the coveted goal of all lovers, but where does separation fit in, at least in terms of being something positive? Rūpa Goswāmī tells us that "When the lover and the beloved meet, they are called *yukta* (connected). Previous to their meeting, they are called *ayukta* (not connected). Whether connected or not connected, the ecstatic emotion arising due to not being able to embrace and kiss each other as desired is called *vipralambha*. This *vipralambha* helps nourish emotions at the time of meeting."[40] Thus, rather than seen as an obstruction, love in separation is a much appreciated goal in the Vaishnava tradition, the flipside and enhancer of spiritual union.

To help understand the idea of love in separation and why it is so special, several quotes from the Vaishnava *ācāryas* might be helpful: In Rūpa Goswāmī's *Padyāvali* (240), for example, he has Rādhikā saying, "I prefer separation from Krishna to union, because in union I see Krishna only in one place, whereas in separation, I see him everywhere." Commenting on Rūpa's *Ujjvala-nīlamaṇi* (1.20), Jīva Goswāmī says that "the power of an elephant can only be seen when it is chained and using all its strength to break free; similarly, the power of Rādhā's love for Krishna can only be fully seen in her separation from him."

Śrīla A. C. Bhaktivedānta Swami Prabhupāda explains the underlying logic as follows: "The spontaneous attraction of Śrī Kṛṣṇa for His dearest parts and parcels generates an enthusiasm that obliges Śrī Kṛṣṇa and the *gopīs* to meet together. To celebrate this transcendental enthusiasm, there is need of a sentiment of separation between the lover and beloved. In the condition of material tribulation, no one wants the pangs of separation. But in the transcendental form, the very same separation, being absolute in its nature, strengthens the ties of love and enhances the desire of the lover and beloved to meet. The period of separation, evaluated transcendentally, is more relishable than the actual meeting, which lacks the feelings of increasing anticipation because the lover and beloved are both present."[41]

All of this brings us back to Rādhā and the Rāsa-līlā. In the chapters of the *Bhāgavatam* depicting the round dance, we find a reference to an unidentified *gopī* "who worships Krishna best." The verse in question (10.30.28) uses the phrase *anayārādhitaḥ*, meaning "by her the Lord is worshiped," and the tradition has gone to great pains to show that the unidentified *gopī* is in fact Rādhā,[42] a name derived from the root word *ārādhana* ("worship").[43]

In regard to love in separation, the Rāsa-līlā is important in the following way: Before the dance even begins, Krishna runs off when he sees that the *gopīs* become proud of being in his presence. He does so, ultimately, to set them right and to deepen their love. During this scene, he absconds with Rādhā, or, since she is not named, with that "one special *gopī*" who he loves so dearly. But then he escapes from her, too, allowing her to also taste the sweet pangs of separation—and to thus fall even more deeply in love with him.

This focus on Śrī Rādhā and the theology of union and separation goes well beyond the *Bhāgavatam*. As mentioned above by Kavirāja Goswāmī, these ideas can be found in the writings of the five authors favored by Mahāprabhu himself. We will briefly look at only two of them here, Jayadeva Goswāmī and Caṇḍīdāsa, just in terms of how they view Rādhā, or at least the part they play in her revelation, but that should be sufficient to make our point.

It is natural to begin with Jayadeva, who wrote the Sanskrit *Gīta-govinda* in the 12th century CE, since he was the earliest of the writers mentioned in the *Caitanya-caritāmṛta*. For academics, Jayadeva's work is viewed as the text that gives us our first look at Rādhā in full form.[44] Practitioners, on the other hand, would say that she is an eternal entity—Krishna's female counterpart and his *hlādini-śakti*, or blissful "pleasure potency." Devotees generally believe that Jayadeva merely *popularized* the Rādhā narrative, which could be located in esoteric texts all along.

In other words, most scholars give a relatively "late" date to the Purāṇas in general, including the specific Puranas that tell us details of the Rādhā story. But practitioners tend to see these texts as precursors to Jayadeva's work, opining that this literature existed long before his *Gīta-govinda* came into existence. There may be something to the practitioner perspective. As I have argued elsewhere,[45] scholarship on Puranic dating leaves us with more questions than answers. Ludo Rocher, one of the modern era's foremost Puranic scholars, writes: "I submit that it is not possible to set a specific date for any Purāṇa as a whole."[46] Friedhelm Hardy concurs: "On the whole, it is meaningless to speak of 'the date' of a Sanskrit Purāṇa, because many generations of bards, etc., have been involved in the accumulation of material which at some stage has been given a name."[47]

Interestingly, the *Brahma-vaivarta* and *Padma Purāṇas*, among others, afford us a portrait of Rādhā that is very much in line with Jayadeva's. The only question is this: did those Purāṇas influence Jayadeva (as is held by the orthodox tradition), or was it the other way around (as many modern scholars suggest)? We may never have objective evidence either way, since both scholars and devotees have their respective arguments. Whatever the case, Rādhā subsists and is an indispensable part of the tradition.

But let us move on to Caṇḍīdāsa, a Bengali poet of the 15th century, who wrote less than one hundred years before Mahāprabhu's time. Assessing Caṇḍīdāsa's work is sometimes complicated by the fact that several poets used his name: Ādi Caṇḍīdāsa, Kavi Caṇḍīdāsa, Dvija Caṇḍīdāsa, and Dina Caṇḍīdāsa. Nonetheless, after Jayadeva's *Gīta-govinda*, a debate arose in terms of Rādhā's marital status: the *svakīya* doctrine, which states that she is the wife of Krishna,[48] and *parakīya*, which opines that she is married to someone else but indulges in a relationship with Krishna anyway. The *parakīya* line of thought was articulated by poets like Caṇḍīdāsa and, further, by Gauḍīya stalwarts like Rūpa Goswāmī and Viśvanātha Chakravartī.[49]

This might seem surprising. Why would Vaishnavas, who are generally known as pillars of ethical and moral behavior, endorse a doctrine in which extramarital affairs are elevated to divine status? As one might suspect, all is not what it seems. In his purport to the *Caitanya-caritāmṛta* (Ādi 4.50), Prabhupāda explains *parakīya-rasa*: "The risks involved in such love of Godhead make this emotion superior to the relationship in which such risk is not involved. The validity of such risk, however, is possible only in the transcendental realm. *Svakīya* and *parakīya* conjugal love of Godhead have no existence in the material world, and *parakīya* is not exhibited anywhere in Vaikuṇṭha, but only in the portion of Goloka Vrindāvan known as Vraja [Gokula]."[50]

He explains further: "They're not married as husband and wife. Rādhārāṇī appears to be the wife of someone else, but She and Krishna were friends from childhood. Rādhārāṇī could never forget Krishna . . . . *Parakīya* means love—not by marriage, but by friendship. There, it is pure. There's no inebriety. 'Perverted' means the topmost thing has become the lowest. Here (in the material world), *parakīya*, loving another's wife or husband, is most abominable; it is adultery . . . . In order to make [Rādhā and Krishna's] pastimes more relishable, [however,] Rādhā is 'so-called' married to Abhimanyu. The intrigue of Them (Rādhā and Krishna) meeting in secret and planning and plotting against Jaṭilā [Abhimanyu's mother] and Kuṭilā [Abhimanyu's sister] always makes Their pastimes more relishable."[51]

In other words, *parakīya* is *only* a spiritual phenomenon. In the ideal world of Vrindāvan, Krishna is the center of attention, and all efforts are focused on his pleasure. While *parakīya* is completely inappropriate in the material world, it embodies the highest pleasure for Śrī Krishna in the spiritual realm as manifested in Gokula. It creates the excitement and thrill one might expect of *parakīya* in the material world, but without any negative side effects. No one gets hurt.

In the typical extramarital affair, the spouse will generally suffer as a result. But who is Rādhā's spouse? Prabhupāda mentions Abhimanyu.[52] The traditional literature tells us that Abhimanyu's marriage to Śrī Rādhā is a manifestation of illusion (*māyā*), a sham enacted for a greater purpose.[53] It is a magic show created for the Lord's pleasure, to increase the titillation of his secret relationship with Rādhā and thereby deepen their love. It is not real.

Abhimanyu is therefore often referred to as her "so-called" husband, as Prabhupāda does above. Further, as Jīva Goswāmī argues, all *gopīs*, including Rādhā, constitutionally "belong" to Krishna, since they are his energy manifesting as living beings for the sake of interpersonal relationship (*rasa*). In this sense, they enjoy a sort of *svakīya* relationship with him. Accordingly, the Goswāmīs, especially Śrī Jīva, sometimes think of them as his "wives."[54] Thus, what *parakīya* really represents is a spiritual conception and not a phenomenon of the material world. It's essence may be summarized as follows: love of God is meant to be total, absorbing, and without compromise or distraction, nor should it be limited by the strictures of conventional relationship.

This, in a nutshell, is the conception inherited and developed by Śrī Chaitanya and the Six Goswāmīs of Vrindāvan. Bhaktivinoda Ṭhākura thus writes that, "Although Caṇḍīdāsa, Vidyāpati, Bilvamaṅgala, and Jayadeva lived before Śrī Chaitanya Mahāprabhu was externally manifest within this world, Chaitanya Mahāprabhu's conception of *bhakti* [devotional love for Krishna] had arisen within their hearts and was expressed in their writings."[55]

In all of these teachers, we see the glowing personality of Śrī Rādhā, at first with just a glimmer and then with full force. Once Mahāprabhu appeared in Bengal, her divinity burst through in all its glory. It was his golden personality, say the teachers of the Gauḍīya tradition, that allowed her glistening nature to become fully visible for the fortunate few who had his association. By his grace, too, the Six Goswāmīs of Vrindāvan, led by Śrī Rūpa, expressed it for all who would seriously pursue spiritual life, in their writing and no less in their example—they fully explained the mood of Rādhā-dāsyam, loving service focused on Śrī Rādhā, specifically. What they conveyed is also known as Mañjarī-bhāva, wherein one aspires to assist the *gopīs* in their service to Rādhā and Krishna, with a special emphasis on Rādhā. As B. R. Śrīdhara Mahārāja once said,

> Rādhā-dāsyam has been said to be the highest attainment. Why? The quality and quantity of *rasa* that Rādhārāṇī can draw from Krishna can never be found anywhere else. So if you are situated just behind Rādhārāṇī, you'll be allowed to taste not only the quantity, but the highest quality of *rasa*. No other person can draw such high *rasa* from Krishna. The fullest, highest type of quality is drawn from Krishna: He gives Himself fully and wholly and deeply. So if you are in Śrī Rūpa's group, then you can have a taste of that sort of *rasa*.[56]

If Śrī Chaitanya brought Rādhā to the fore, it was she, too, who was to return the favor: She was the first to recognize him, albeit in a predictive dream. Viśvanātha Chakravartī, in his book *Śrī Stavāmṛta Laharī*, apprises us of this confidential incident, in a song called, "Svapna-vilāsāmṛtāṣṭakam." A summary of this song's contents can be rendered as follows:

> Once, Śrī Rādhā told Krishna of an astonishing dream she'd had. In this dream, she told him, there flowed a beautiful river reminiscent of the Yamunā, its banks beautified by dancers, *mṛdaṅga* players, and the most enchanting Brahmin boy with a golden hue.
>
> Fervently, the boy repeatedly called out, "O, Krishna," and sometimes, "O, Rādhā!" As he did, his striking beauty dilated prodigiously, ecstatic symptoms blossomed in his body and, before Śrī Rādhā's astonished eyes, he became the most beautiful, divinely intoxicated, all-attractive madman.

She continued: so contagious was his mood of spiritual enthusiasm that all his companions were elated, and they too spontaneously called out to Rādhā and Krishna and were transformed.

But, she was confused. Who was the mysterious beautiful person in her dream? Was it Krishna? Was it she? Or was it someone else, altogether? And why was she so utterly drawn to him?

Amused, Krishna responded to her inquiries cryptically: "When you saw me as Nārāyaṇa or in my numerous other forms, you were not confused. Why now?" Just then, Krishna playfully lifted the *kaustubha* jewel from his chest, and in the glimmer of that transcendent object, Śrī Rādhā saw her dream suddenly come to life.

She was stunned as the realization overtook her: this is no dream—it is reality.

Reflecting on the words of her beloved and the image revealed by the *kaustubha* jewel, she finally intuited the only possible identity of the Brahmin boy: He was Krishna himself. Otherwise, why was she so incredibly drawn to him? It had to be Krishna!

And, another, more astounding realization dawned as well, heightening her jubilation. Beautiful beyond compare, the golden youth was not only Krishna—he embodied her mood, complexion and essential nature as well. Thus, she beheld Śrī Chaitanya, and understood his esoteric identity.[57]

With that much as a backdrop, we can now explore Mahāprabhu's life and times.

NOTES

1. *aham ādir hi devānām* (10.2).
2. *ahaṁ sarvasya prabhavaḥ* (10.8).
3. *ye 'py anya-devatā-bhaktāḥ . . . yajanti mām avidhi-pūrvakam* (9.23).
4. *ahaṁ hi sarva-yajñānāṁ, bhoktā ca prabhur eva ca* (9.24).
5. *sarva-loka-maheśvaram* (5.29).
6. *sarvasya dhātāram* (8.9).
7. *paraṁ brahma paraṁ dhāma pavitraṁ paramaṁ bhavān puruṣaṁ śāśvataμ divyam . . .* (10.12).
8. *deva-deva* (10.14).
9. *ādi-deva* (10.12); *vam ādi-devaḥ* (11.38).
10. *na tvat-samo 'sty abhaydhikaḥ kuto 'nyaḥ* (11.43). I am grateful to Howard J. Resnick (H. D. Goswami) for bringing these verses, as expressed in endnotes 1–10, to my attention. See his article, "Kṛṣṇa in the *Bhagavad-gītā*: A Beginning Ontology from the Gauḍīya Perspective" in *Journal of Vaiṣṇava Studies,* Vol. 3, No. 2 (Spring 1995), 5–32.
11. *Śrīmad Bhāgavatam* 1.1.1, Prabhupāda's translation. (*janmādy asya yato 'nvayād itarataś cārtheṣv abhijñaḥ svarāṭ/ tene brahma hṛdā ya ādi-kavaye muhyanti*

yat sūraya// ḥtejo-vāri-mṛdāṁ yathā vinimayo yatra tri-sargo 'mṛṣā/ dhāmnā svena sadā nirasta-kuhakaṁ satyaṁ paraṁ dhīmahi//).

12. *Śrīmad Bhāgavatam* 1.3.28, Prabhupāda's translation. (*ete cāṁśa-kalāḥ puṁsaḥ kṛṣṇas tu bhagavān svayam*). There is a similar verse in the *Gīta-govinda* (1.15, 16): *daśākṛtikṛte krishnāya tubhyaṁ namaḥ* ("Obeisance to Krishna, from whom the ten incarnations emerge."). The implication here is that Krishna is the original form of God.

13. For a clear summarization of Gauḍīya arguments regarding Krishna's superiority over Vishnu, see Satyarāja Dāsa, "Who's First: Vishnu or Krishna?" in *Back to Godhead*, Volume 47, No. 3 (May/June, 2013).

14. *nāma-saṅkīrtanaṁ yasya/ sarva-pāpa praṇāśanam// praṇāmo duḥkha-śamanas/ taṁ namāmi hariṁ param//*

15. As but two examples of such texts, we can cite the *Ṛg-veda* 1.22.164 (*sukta* 31), which mentions a cowherd "who never falls," and the *Chandogya Upanishad* (3.17.6), revealing Vāsudeva Krishna as the son of Devakī. However, there is some contention regarding these texts' authenticity and interpretation, and that should also be noted.

16. The historical Krishna is aligned with a standard genealogy by way of his father, Vasudeva. The Vrishni-Yādava clan is mentioned in early Vedic texts, such as the *Taittirīya Saṁhitā* (2.9.3), the *Taittirīya Brāhmaṇa* (10.9.15), and the *Śatapatha Brāhmaṇa* (1.1.4).

17. See Bimanbehari Majumdar, *Kṛṣṇa in History and Legend* (Calcutta: University of Calcutta, 1969), 279. Because B. B. Majumdar was a scholar, with his above work noting inconsistencies and anomalies in the Krishna story, it is all the more significant that he views Krishna as an historical personality. He wrote a similar volume on Mahāprabhu: *Śrī Caitanya Cariter Upādān* (Calcutta: University of Calcutta, 1959).

18. Surprisingly, it is not an undisputed fact that Jesus walked the earth. Numerous scholars offer an "argument from silence," saying that there was virtually nothing written about him in his day from sources outside the Gospels. They note that the Jewish philosopher Philo of Alexandria, who wrote less than half a century after the alleged time of Jesus, did not so much as mention Jesus in his historical account of Pontius Pilate. Similarly, Josephus's *Antiquities of the Jews*, written sometime in 93–94 CE, includes two references to the biblical Jesus but may well be a product of Christian interpolation or forgery. See Michael Martin, *The Case Against Christianity* (Philadelphia, Pennsylvania: Temple University Press, 1993), 52.

19. Horace H. Wilson, *The Vishnu Purana* (Delhi: India: Nag Publishers, 1989), ii.

20. Rudolf Otto, *The Original Gita*, citied in Bimanbihari Majumdar, *Krishna in History and Legend* (Calcutta: University of Calcutta, 1969), 5.

21. R. C. Majumdar, *The History and Culture of the Indian people*, Volume 1 (Bombay: Bharatiya Vidya Bhavan, 1980). 303.

22. Thomas J. Hopkins in Steven J. Gelberg, ed., *Hare Krishna, Hare Krishna: Five Distinguished Scholars on the Krishna Movement in the West* (New York: Grove Press, 1983), 144.

23. Diana Eck, *Encountering God: A Spiritual Journey from Bozeman to Banaras* (New Delhi: Penguin Books, 1995), 90.

24. See R. P. Chanda, *Archeology and the Vaishnava Tradition* (Memoirs of the Archeological Survey of India, No. 5, 1920). See also Edwin F. Bryant, *Krishna, the Beautiful Legend of God* (London: Penguin Books, 2003), xvii–xviii, and Allan Dahlquist, *Megasthenes and Indian Religion* (Delhi: Motilal Banarasidass, 1962).

25. Steven J. Gelberg, ed. op. cit., 117. For more on the Heliodorus Column, see Suvira Jaiswal, *The Origin and Development of Vaiṣṇavism* (Delhi: Munshiram Manoharlal, 1967) and Benjamin Preciado-Solis, *The Kṛṣṇa Cycle in the Purāṇas* (New Delhi: Motilal Banarsidass, 1984).

26. See *The Hindu* (http://www.thehindu.com/todays-paper/Significant-finds-at-Dwaraka/article14724351.ece). See also S. R. Rao, *Lost City of Dvārakā* (New Delhi: Aditya Prakashan, 1999).

27. See http://www.esamskriti.com/essay-chapters/How-science-discovered-the-historical-Krishna-1.aspx.

28. Martin Kähler (1896), *The So-called Historical Jesus and the Historic, Biblical Christ*, trans., Carl E. Braaten (Philadelphia, PA: Fortress Press), 1964, reprint, 63.

29. This paragraph is adapted from an idea about Jesus derived from "The Historical Christ—Fact or Fiction?" by Kyle Butt, M.Div. (http://www.apologeticspress.org/APContent.aspx?category=10&article=187).

30. Is Krishna ultimately a myth? In the end, the practitioner perspective should be clear: "The pastimes of Sree Krishna and the milkmaids of Braja as explained in the *Srimad Bhagavata* are neither history nor allegory. They are not history because they are transcendental whereas our so-called history is only a record of our experiences of this world . . . . They are also not allegory for the reason that they happen to be the actual concrete Reality of which this world is the perverted reflection. As a matter of fact, it is this world and its happenings that are really allegorical and impossible of comprehension except relatively to the Real and symbolizing the reality." See Nisi Kanta Sanyal, *The Erotic Principle and Unalloyed Devotion* (Calcutta: Gaudiya Mission, n.d.), 25; reprinted in *The Harmonist*, Volume XXVI, No. 7 (December 1928).

31. One does not usually think of people from India as having blue eyes (exceptions do exist in Bihar and elsewhere), and this may be a further indication of Krishna's transcendence. That his eyes are blue is confirmed throughout sacred texts. See, for example, "*Śrī Rādhā-Kṛpā-Katākṣa-Stava-Rāja*," verse 7 (http://www.harekrsna.com/philosophy/radhakrsna/radharani/krpa-kataksa.htm). Further, Kavi Karṇapūra tells us in his *Ānanda Vrindāvan Campu* (Second Chapter) that "Krishna's two lotus eyes look like a pair of blue lotus buds." (http://www.salagram.net/jan-krsna-app.html); and Rūpa Goswāmī writes in his *Rādhā-Krishna-gaṇoddeśa-dīpikā* (2.6) that Krishna's "rolling eyes are as splendid as red and blue lotus flowers." (http://nitaaiveda.com/Compiled_and_Imp_Scriptures/Glories_of_Lord_Krishna/Krishna_the_Supreme_Absolute_Truth/Shri_Shri_Radha_Krishna_Gannodesha_Dipika.htm). This refers to blue eyes with red in the corners, as his eyes are described throughout Vaishnava literature.

32. Prabhupāda writes: "The name Krishna means 'all-attractive.' God attracts everyone; that is the definition of 'God.' We have seen many pictures of Krishna, and we see that He attracts the cows, calves, birds, beasts, trees, plants, and even the water in Vrindāvan. He is attractive to the cowherd boys, to the *gopīs*, to Nanda Mahārāja, to

the Pāṇḍavas, and to all human society. Therefore if any particular name can be given to God, that name is 'Krishna.'" See his *The Science of Self-Realization* (https://www.quora.com/Does-the-word-Krishna-refer-to-a-characteristic-trait-of-an-ideal-human-rather-then-referring-to-a-person-or-God). Although *krishna* generally means "blackish," an etymological reading for the above might run as follows: "The word '*krish*' is the attractive feature of the Lord's existence, and 'na' means spiritual pleasure. When the verb '*krish*' is added to the affix '*na*' it becomes Krishna, which indicates the Absolute Truth." [*Mahābhārata* (Udyoga-parva, 71.4), cited in *Chaitanya-caritāmṛta*, Madhya 9.30.]

33. Traditional versions of Krishna's full life story can be found in the *Śrīmad Bhāgavatam* (10–11); the *Brahma-vaivarta Purāṇa* (Śrī-Krishna-Janma-khaṇḍa 4); the *Padma Purāṇa* (Patala-khaṇḍa 69–99); the *Vishnu Purāṇa* (5); and of course the entire *Harivaṁśa*, which is appended to the *Mahābhārata*.

34. Eventually, Dhyānachandra Goswāmī, Viśvanātha Chakravartī Ṭhākura, and others applied the same principle to Śrī Chaitanya Mahāprabhu. Viśvanātha's text is particularly loved by Gauḍīyas: the *Mahāprabhor-aṣṭa-kālīya-līlā-smaraṇa-maṅgala-stotram*. In this text, Viśvanātha elaborates upon Mahāprabhu's "eightfold daily pastimes," thus giving experienced devotees facility for advanced meditation techniques in relation to this most confidential incarnation of Krishna. We will revisit this idea in our chapter on Rāgānuga-Bhakti. See Viśvanātha Chakravartī's *Śrī Gaurāṅga Līlāmṛta*, trans., Daśarath-suta Dāsa (Union City, Georgia: Nectar Books, n.d.).

35. See *Caitanya-caritāmṛta*, Madhya 2.77: "Night and day, in the company of Svarūpa Dāmodara and Rāmānanda Rāya, Mahāprabhu would sing or listen to the songs of Caṇḍīdāsa, Vidyāpati, the musical drama of Rāmānanda (*Jagannātha-vallabha*), *Krishna Karṇāmṛta*, and *Gīta-govinda*." (*caṇḍīdāsa, vidyāpati, rāyera nāṭaka-gīti, karṇāmṛta, śrī-gīta-govinda svarūpa-rāmānanda-sane, mahāprabhu rātri-dine, gāya, śune—parama ānanda*).

36. The preceding two paragraphs are Prabhupāda's translation.

37. Graham M. Schweig, *Dance of Divine Love: the Rāsa Līlā of Krishna from the Bhāgavata Purāṇa, India's Classic Sacred Love Story* (Princeton, New Jersey: Princeton University Press, 2005).

38. Quoting Krishnadāsa Kavirāja Goswāmī, Schweig notes that the Rāsa-līlā is the *līlā-sāra* ("the essence of all *līlās*"), and, quoting Viśvanātha Chakravartī, calls it *sarva-līlā-cūḍa-maṇi* ("the crown jewel of all *līlās*"). The former statement is found in the *Caitanya-caritāmṛta* (Madhya 21.44) and the latter one is found in Viśvanātha's commentary on the *Bhāgavatam* (10.29.1). See Graham M. Schweig, "Rāsalīlā Pañcādhyāya: The *Bhāgavata*'s Ultimate Vision of the Gopīs" in *Journal of Vaishnava Studies,* Volume 5, No. 4 (Fall 1997), 8.

39. Gauḍīya Vaishnava *ācārya* Śrīla Nārāyaṇa Mahārāja (1921–2010) offers an esoteric reading on why the speaker of the *Bhāgavatam*, Śukadeva Goswāmī, did not utter Śrī Rādhā's name directly: "A reason given as to why Śukadeva Goswāmī did not directly mention Śrīmatī Rādhārāṇī's name in the *Śrīmad Bhāgavatam* is because Mahārāja Parikṣit had only seven days to live, and uttering Rādhikā's name would have thrown Śukadeva into ecstatic trance for six months. In the *Brahma-vaivarta*

Purāṇa, it is mentioned . . . if Śukadeva Goswāmī uttered the name of Śrīmatī Rādhikā, he would at once remember Her pastimes. Due to his Rādhā-premā, he would have become *āviṣṭa-citta*, excited and fixed in remembering Her pastimes and activities in the service of Krishna. He would then have become internally fixed on Krishna and inert for six months. But Parikṣit Mahārāja had only seven days to live, and Śukadeva wanted him to have the benefit of the entire *Śrīmad Bhāgavatam*. . . . Why would Śukadeva Goswāmī go into an ecstatic trance at the mere mention of the name of Śrīmatī Rādhikā? In his commentary on his own *Bṛhad-bhāgavatāmṛta*, Sanātana Goswāmī writes, 'Śrīmatī Rādhikā was the worshipable goddess [*iṣṭadevatā*] of Śukadeva Goswāmī, so whenever he uttered Her name, he would become *āviṣṭa-citta*, internally spiritually excited and externally inert. So in the *Śrīmad Bhāgavatam* he has given the name of Rādhikā and other *gopīs* in a hidden way. Śukadeva Goswāmī has therefore not uttered Her name directly, but only indirectly.'" See *Sriya Suka and Radharani* (http://nimaipandit.ning.com/profiles/blogs/some-of-the-sweet-glories-of-sukadeva-goswami-the-sriya-suka-of).

40. *Ujjvala-nīlamaṇi* (Vipralambha-prakarā 3–4).

41. See his commentary on *Caitanya-caritāmṛta*, Ādi 4.31, purport.

42. Regarding Śrī Rādhā as the special *gopī* in the Rāsa-līlā, Mahāprabhu confirms this himself in his conversation with Rāmānanda Rāya. This exchange is retold in Kavirāja Goswāmī's 17th-century *Caitanya-caritāmṛta*, Madhya 8.99–101, so it is, technically speaking, a later reference, to be placed after the ones I will now mention. As far as being the unnamed *gopī* in the Rāsa-līlā, Sanātana Goswāmī affirms her identity in his *Bṛhad-vaiṣṇava-toṣaṇī* (commenting on 10.30.28), and it is repeated yet again by Śrī Jīva in his *Vaiṣṇava-toṣaṇī*, commenting on the same verse. Jīva also mentions this in his *Prīti Sandarbha*, referring not only to verse 28 but also to the one before it. This can be found in most online versions at Anuccheda 108 (http://nitaaiveda.com/All_Scriptures_By_Acharyas/Jiva_Goswami/Six_Sandarbhas/Priti-sandarbha_1.htm). However, in Bhanu Swami's version it is located at Anuccheda 106. Following his Goswāmī predecessors, Viśvanātha Chakravartī explains the word *anayārādhitaḥ* in the same way in his *Bhāgavatam* commentary, the *Sārārtha-darśini-ṭika*, when discussing 10.30.28.

43. Śrīla B. V. Nārāyaṇa Mahārāja gives a creative derivation of the name "Rādhā": The prefix "*rā*" indicates "*anurāga*" (deep loving attachment) and "*dha*" means "*dhavati*" (to run quickly and with great eagerness). She is always running toward Krishna with great love and is therefore called "Rādhā." See Nārāyaṇa Mahārāja, "The Glory of Śrī Rādhā, Part One," in *Śrī Rādhā: Our Supreme Shelter* (Vrindavan: Gaudiya Vedanta Publications, 2016), 77–78.

44. Of course, scholars accept that there are brief references to Rādhā prior to Jayadeva—her name appears in a *Ṛg-vedic* appendix (*Ṛk-pariśiṣṭa*), though here it is said to refer to a constellation as opposed to Rādhā herself; she is found in Hāla's 1st- to 7th-century *Sattasaī*; and in the writings of the 5th-century lexicographer, Amara Simha, to name a few. Such stray instances of "Rādhā" have been documented by Barbara Stoler Miller, *Love Song of the Dark Lord: Jayadeva's Gītagovinda* (New York: Columbia University Press, 1977), 27–35. But Rādhikā's more developed story, religious historians generally assert, arises with the *Gīta-govinda*.

45. See Introduction to the *Gīta-govinda* issue of the *Journal of Vaishnava Studies,* Volume 22, No. 1 (Fall, 2013), 3–4, and Steven J. Rosen, *Essential Hinduism* (Westport, CT.: Praeger, 2006), 140–141. Regarding the early existence of the Purāṇas, even those that include the Rādhā narrative, Barbara Stoler Miller argues that although the *Brahma-vaivarta Purāṇa* is usually dated to the 16th century, an older edition may have existed in as early as the 8th. If so, then perhaps it is this version that Jayadeva drew upon. See her *Love Song of the Dark Lord: Jayadeva's Gitagovinda*, ibid., 58.

46. Ludo Rocher, *The Purāṇas: A History of Indian Literature,* Volume 2, Fasc. 3. (Wiesbaden, Germany: Otto Harrassowitz, 1986), 103.

47. Friedhelm Hardy, *Viraha-bhakti—The Early History of Kṛṣṇa Devotion in South India* (Delhi, India: Oxford University Press, 1983), 486.

48. There is a "marriage" between Rādhā and Krishna enacted in Chapter Fifteen of the *Brahma-vaivarta Purāṇa.* It can also be found in the *Garga-saṁhitā* (1.16); the tenth act of the *Lalitā Mādhava*; and in the *Gopāla-champu* (Uttara 33.4), among other places. Philosophically, too, Jīva argues that as Krishna's divine energy, Rādhā is his "wife" in the truest sense, that is, they belong to each other. See Endnote 51.

49. For an extensive analysis of this subject, see Jan Brzezinski, "Does Krishna Marry the Gopīs in the End?" in *Journal of Vaishnava Studies*, Volume 5, No. 4 (Fall 1997), 49–110.

50. Prabhupāda's point here may be difficult to grasp. Some background information is needed. Gauḍīya tradition teaches that there are two divisions of Goloka Vrindāvan, or the highest region of the spiritual world. One is called Goloka, which is the unmanifest spiritual world proper, and then there is Gokula, which is considered the inner portion of Goloka and which manifests in "the material world," that is, the world visible to material eyes. So Prabhupāda is saying that in the spiritual Goloka, the marriage to Abhimanyu does not take place. In that supreme realm, Rādhā's relationship to Abhimanyu is only conceptual, to increase the love between Rādhā and Krishna. By officially "committing" to someone else, Rādhā increases Krishna's thrill with a sort of transcendental jealousy, because of which he wants to be with her even more. As his pastimes manifest in the material world (Gokula), such concepts take actual shape, and Krishna manifests Abhimanyu through his *māyā* potency, thus playing out the interpersonal exchange that is only suggested in the Goloka realm.

51. https://www.quora.com/Why-was-Radharani-married-to-Abhimanyu-if-she-loved-Lord-Krishna

52. Abhimanyu is often called Āyān in early Bengali literature, as in, for example, the work of Caṇḍīdāsa. It should be noted that Śrī Rādhā's marriage to Āyān is mentioned in the *Brahma-vaivarta Purāṇa* (2.51.34) and we find that the Āyān/ Abhimanyu character is prominent in Rūpa Goswāmī's plays as well, such as the *Vidagdha Mādhava*. [See Donna M. Wulff, *Drama as a Mode of Religious Realization: The Vidagdhamādhava of Rūpa Goswāmī* (Chico, California: Scholars Press, 1984).] Abhimanyu is also mentioned in Rūpa Goswāmī's *Rādhā-Krishna-Gaṇoddeśa-dīpikā* (text 174) and in his *Ujjvala-nīlamaṇi*, especially chapters 13 and 14 (http://www.bvml.org/SRG/SriUjjvalaNilamani.html); he is also in Jīva Goswāmī's *Mādhava-mahotsava* and in Viśvanātha Chakravartī's *Śrī Camatkara Candrikā*, among other places.

53. See *Ujjvala-nīlamaṇi*, 1.21, Viśvanātha Chakravartī Ṭhākura's commentary.

54. For an extensive discussion on Rādhā and the *gopīs* as Krishna's "wives," see Jan Brzezinski, "Does Krishna Marry the Gopīs in the End?" in *Journal of Vaishnava Studies*, op. cit., especially 69–78.

55. http://www.bvml.org/VS/sjg.html

56. See Śrīla B. R. Śrīdhara Mahārāja, "The Service of Śrī Rādhā" (http://www.bvml.org/SBRSM/tsosr.html).

57. This song comes to us through the 18th century pen of Viśvanātha Chakravartī. The original Sanskrit verses appear online: http://(http://kksongs.org/songs/p/priyesvapnedrsta.html). The rendering here is my own paraphrased translation.

Chapter 3

Śrī Gaura Tattva

From Black to Gold

Who is Śrī Chaitanya Mahāprabhu? At the risk of seeming evasive, the answer depends very much on whom you ask. Even in India, the average person doesn't really know who he is. One might, for example, question devout Hindus about his actual identity, but a clear understanding would still be wanting. For Vaishnavas of various denominations, he might be seen as one of history's many *avatāras* (literally, "descent"), or the divine in bodily form. For the historian of religion who knows something about Vaishnavism, he was a saint, a mystic from 16th-century Bengal who emphasized chanting as the most effective means of God-realization in the current epoch of world history. Joseph T. O'Connell, an expert on Bengali religion and culture, wrote of the traditional Gauḍīya Vaishnava perspective: "During Chaitanya's own lifetime it became axiomatic among his closer devotees that he was in some fashion Hari/Krishna (even Krishna with the feelings and complexion of Rādhā) descended in human form."[1]

Gauḍīya Vaishnavism explains that there are various levels in understanding Śrī Chaitanya.[2] For instance, in the Introduction to Edward C. Dimock Jr.'s massive edition of the *Caitanya-caritāmṛta*, Tony K. Stewart points out that there are several possible views of Chaitanya's divinity, which seem to evolve from the earliest biographies to the later ones.[3]

There are seven major hagiographical texts to which Stewart refers, most of which were written slightly after Mahāprabhu walked the earth and, for the final biography, almost a century later: (1) Murāri Gupta's first Sanskrit biography of Chaitanya; (2) Kavi Karṇapūra's initial work, *Śrī Caitanya-caritāmṛta Mahākāvya* and his (3) ten-act play, *Śrī Caitanya-candrodāya-nāṭakam*; (4) Vrindāvandāsa Ṭhākura's *Caitanya-bhāgavata*, the earliest Bengali biography of Śrī Chaitanya; (5) Locana Dāsa's *Śrī*

Caitanya-maṅgala; (6) Jayānanda's *Caitanya-maṅgala*; and the cap on the tradition, (7) Krishnadāsa Kavirāja Goswāmī's *Śrī Caitanya-caritāmṛta*.

In summary, Stewart notes that in the initial two biographies (written by Murāri Gupta and Vrindāvandāsa), Śrī Chaitanya is primarily viewed as an incarnation of Vishnu in the ancient Puranic sense. Accordingly, he is seen as appearing in this world to destroy evildoers, or at least the demoniac mentality, and to establish the *dharma* for the age. In Kavi Karṇapūra's first biography (he wrote an early one and also, later, a drama based on Mahāprabhu's life, as mentioned above), the view slightly shifts to include the Pañcha Tattva (Śrī Chaitanya in five features, discussed later in this chapter) and the specifics of *avatāra* theory. After that, Jayānanda's work, though considered questionable by the orthodox tradition, is more specific regarding Śrī Chaitanya as an incarnation of Krishna.

Then, in Kavi Karṇapūra's second biography, written many years after the first one, we become privy to the Lord's "feminine side"—Śrī Rādhā is specifically mentioned[4]—though the dual incarnation of Chaitanya as Śrī-Śrī Rādhā-Krishna does not yet fully emerge. Locana Dāsa, too, begins to tell us of the sweet *mādhurya* nature of Śrī Chaitanya in his rather late biography of Mahāprabhu. Finally, with Krishnadāsa Kavirāja Goswāmī's *Caitanya-caritāmṛta*, Stewart points out, we find the most developed conception of Chaitanya's divinity—Rādhā and Krishna combined, as understood by the tradition today. Stewart succinctly writes in his book *The Last Word*, "Images of Caitanya spanned well-known forms of Vaiṣṇava divinity from multi-armed, theriomorphic forms of celestial sovereignty, *aiśvarya*, to more gentle and beneficent forms, *mādhurya*."[5]

The varying conceptions of divinity attributed to Śrī Chaitanya should be carefully understood and distinguished, at least if one wants to understand how the tradition sees itself. While there is certainly merit to Stewart's thesis, it needs to be appreciated from within a certain context—for the practitioner, it is merely the *emphasis* that evolves, not the conception. The tradition avers that Mahāprabhu embodies all the various conceptions of divinity outlined in the sacred biographies, and that the authors were merely expressing them according to their personal *bhāva*, or inner emotion.

For example, as stated above, Vrindāvandāsa Ṭhākura, in his very early *Caitanya-bhāgavata*, sees Mahāprabhu as the Puranic Vishnu. But who is Vrindāvandāsa? According to the tradition, he is an incarnation of Vyāsa, the legendary compiler of the *Vedas* and the Purāṇas.[6] So it is natural that Vishnu or the more *aiśvarya* forms of Krishna would be his emphasis. Then, in the final biography, Krishnadāsa Kavirāja Goswāmī's *Caitanya-caritāmṛta*, we find the Rādhā-Krishna conception revealed in full, expressing what came to be understood as the summit of Mahāprabhu's divinity. But who was

Krishnadāsa Kavirāja? The later tradition identified him as being a *mañjarī* in his previous life, a maidservant who assists Śrī Rādhā herself.[7]

Thus, devotees opine that the various conceptions of Mahāprabhu's Godhood exist simultaneously, but are emphasized variously according to the devotee who expresses them. Stewart himself recognized that it is a question of emphasis (as opposed to evolution) in an interview conducted in 1992: "Well, it *is* one of emphasis, you are correct, because every biography captures both sides of that tension—the *aiśvarya* and the *mādhurya*."[8]

This is to say that, in the early biographies, we see intimations of the "Chaitanya as Rādhā" motif, at least to a certain degree, and in the later biographies, we see that he is still Vishnu or the Puranic Krishna. In fact, Kavirāja Goswāmī, the last of the biographers and the one who highlights the Rādhā-Krishna theme, attributes the idea of this dual divinity to Svarūpa Dāmodara,[9] who is one of Mahāprabhu's earliest associates. This would make the dual incarnation concept an early one and not merely the product of an evolving tradition.

As further proof that the "Chaitanya in the mood of Rādhā" motif exists in the earliest biographies as well as in the later ones, one need look no further than Vrindāvandāsa's *Caitanya-bhāgavata*. While this author's overriding conception is that of the opulent Godhood of the Lord, as Stewart notes, he reveals in certain sections of his work an understanding of the Lord's higher identity as the embodiment of divine energy (*śakti*) and the essence of *mādhurya*.

This can be seen, for example, in Madhya 18, where Mahāprabhu is depicted as dancing "in the guise of Lakṣmī" as part of a theatrical performance. The later tradition accepts this role-playing as indicative of a secret message regarding the Master's true identity. Interestingly, Vrindāvandāsa treats this episode more elaborately than other, similar exchanges, suggesting that, for the tradition, there is something special about it.

"At that time Viśvambhara [Śrī Chaitanya], the Lord of all, came on stage dressed as the supreme goddess," writes Vrindāvandāsa.[10] "The devotees wondered: 'Has Mahā-Lakṣmī or Pārvatī appeared in our presence? Has the treasure of Vrindāvan [Rādhārāṇī] personally come?'"[11] Further, "As the fair lion known as Chaitanya danced in the form of his original spiritual potency (*śakti*), the devotees happily watched. Their eyes were like bumblebees inescapably drawn to the lotus of his feet."[12]

This episode is considered so important that its author, Vrindāvandāsa, offers a blessing: "By hearing about the Lord's wonderful dance as a *gopī*, which is the treasure of the four *Vedas*, one attains devotional service to Krishna."[13] Then, Vrindāvandāsa, in summarizing the *līlā*, tells us: "Only one who is favored by Krishna can understand this confidential truth."[14] Thus, what was covert in the early Chaitanya tradition became overt for his later followers. In this sense, it can be admitted, as Tony Stewart suggests, that there was an evolution in the concept of Śrī Chaitanya's divinity.

EXPLORATIONS IN ENGLISH

Stewart, of course, is not alone among modern scholars in his focus on Śrī Chaitanya. Many deep thinkers have spilled ink over the golden Lord. Though there have been numerous Indian writers in the modern world who have explored his life and teachings, especially in regional languages, it would be beyond the scope of this work to list them here.[15] However, it would be worthwhile, I think, to at least document the earliest and perhaps most important books in English, for these show how Mahāprabhu made his way to modernity, developing a significant presence in current spiritual discourse.

We begin with Bhaktivinoda Ṭhākura. From all reports, his short English work on Mahāprabhu's life, *Shree Chaitanya Mahaprabhu: His Life and Precepts* (1896), is likely the first. In an upcoming chapter, we will discuss this more thoroughly. A year after Bhaktivinoda's work, several other studies come to light, notably Shishir Kumar Ghosh's *Lord Gaurāṅga, Or, Salvation for All* and a rare book by K. Chakravarti, *The Life of Chaitanya*, published by the Calcutta Yoga Samaj. Around this same time, too, a lengthy, serialized overview of Mahāprabhu's life appears in the *Journal of the Buddhist Text Society of India*, Vol. III–Vol. V (Calcutta: 1895–97), edited by one Sarat Chandra Das. In 1898, the author, Deena Nath Ganguli, self-published his series of articles as a book. Parts of this series might have even appeared in print prior to Bhaktivinoda's work.[16]

Many studies soon followed. Some of the more important titles deserving mention can be listed here: Jadunath Sarkar wrote *Chaitanya's Pilgrimage and Teachings, from his contemporary Bengali biography the Chaitanya-charit-amrita: Madhya-lila* (1913).[17] D. C. Sen, the famous historian of Bengali literature, then released two significant books in English, beginning with *Chaitanya and His Companions* (1917) and followed by *Chaitanya and His Age* (1924). Christian missionary M. T. Kennedy gave us *The Chaitanya Movement, A Study of Vaishnavism in Bengal* (1925) soon thereafter and this was followed by two other consequential English studies: Niskanta Sanyal's *Sree Krishna Chaitanya* (1933)[18] and Sambidānanda Dās's Ph.D. thesis from the University of London (1935), "The History and Literature of Gauḍīya Vaishnavas and Their Relation of Medieval Vaishnava Schools."[19]

Interestingly, these latter two books were pivotal in Śrī Chaitanya's teachings coming West. In the mid-1930s, when Bhaktisiddhānta Sarasvatī sent several disciples to Occidental shores, he equipped them with Sanyal's volume, confident that this work would adequately inform Western intellectuals of Śrī Chaitanya's life and thought.[20] One of the disciples sent West was Sambidānanda Dās, who completed his doctoral studies while abroad.

Sushil Kumar De wrote prodigiously on Mahāprabhu and his associates in the 1930s and 1940s, publishing his findings in the *Indian Historical Quarterly* and other Indological journals. The bulk of his work was published as a single volume in the mid-1940s under the title, *Early History of the Vaishnava Faith and Movement in Bengal*. Though not presented as a "life of Mahāprabhu" as such, it did include much biographical material, and this can be substantiated by a quick review of the table of contents. His work offers elaborate detail on the biographies, the life, the teachings, and the immediate successors (and their voluminous writing). This text has been reprinted a number of times and remains one of the most informative English volumes on Mahāprabhu and his era.

Another important book appeared in 1940: B. P. Tirtha Swami's *Sri Chaitanya Mahaprabhu*.[21] Significant in that it was a full-life study by a disciple of Bhaktivinoda, it was seen as an orthodox yet scholarly reading of Mahāprabhu's earthly sojourn written by an insider. Tirtha Swami was one of the few devotees that Bhaktisiddhānta Sarasvatī had sent to the West. He traveled on the same ship with Sambidānanda.[22] This important journey will again be mentioned in the Afterword.

There was a decade of relative quiet in the 1950s. But with the 1960s and the years that followed, Mahāprabhu scholarship—literature produced by academics and devotees—took on new life. A few evocative titles include but are not limited to, Aloka Lahiri, *Chaitanya Movement in Eastern India* (1960); A. C. Bhaktivedānta Swami Prabhupāda, *The Teachings of Lord Chaitanya* (1968); A. K. Majumdar, *Chaitanya: His Life and Doctrine* (1969); O. B. L. Kapoor, *The Philosophy and Religion of Sri Chaitanya* (1977); A. N. Chatterjee, *Śrīkṛṣṇa Chaitanya* (1983); Swami B. R. Śrīdhara, *The Golden Volcano of Divine Love* (1984); and, in many ways as a culminating force in the scholarly study of Mahāprabhu, mention should again be made of the Harvard University Press edition of Edward Dimock's *Caitanya-caritāmṛta* (1999), which was edited by Tony K. Stewart. Stewart's more recent volume is similarly significant: *The Final Word: The Caitanya Caritāmṛta and the Grammar of Religious Tradition* (2010), though it does not explicitly focus on Mahāprabhu's life.

A special note should underscore A. C. Bhaktivedānta Swami Prabhupāda's mammoth translation and commentary of the *Caitanya-caritāmṛta*. Originally published in 1975, the guru and his disciples worked day and night, tirelessly, achieving a miracle of book production in the course of only two months, though Prabhupāda, of course, had been working on his translation for years.[23] In the end, the Bhaktivedanta Book Trust released a deluxe 17-volume English edition, with color plates, based upon the traditional commentaries of Bhaktivinoda Ṭhākura (*Amṛta-pravāha-bhāṣya*) and Bhaktisiddhānta Sarasvatī (*Anubhāṣya*). The text was subsequently reprinted in an elegant 9-volume edition and is now available in numerous languages worldwide.[24]

THE MANIFEST LIFE OF ŚRĪ CHAITANYA

Let us now briefly review the details of Mahāprabhu's life. We will use as our primary resource the standard, traditional biographies provided by the tradition's early writers, both those in Sanskrit and those in Bengali. But equally important for our purposes, in a sense, are the summaries supplied by Bhaktivinoda and his successors. We will rely on them as well. Moreover, the lengthier academic studies listed above have also proved indispensable in this summarization process.

Before delving into Mahāprabhu's life narrative, however, we should mention that, according to his followers, he never exists in a vacuum. Like Śrī Krishna himself, he is always accompanied by his devotees, four of whom are especially prominent. Together, they are known as the *Pañcha Tattva*, or "Five Truths." This refers to Chaitanya himself, along with Nityānanda Prabhu, Śrī Advaita, Śrī Gadādhara, and Śrīvāsa Ṭhākura. Briefly, Krishnadāsa Kavirāja Goswāmī theologically analyzed these personalities as follows.

Mahāprabhu is Krishna with the mood and complexion of Śrī Rādhā; he is to be considered the supreme manifestation of all forms of Godhead (*īśa-tattva*). He is followed by Nityānanda Prabhu, who is Krishna's first expansion Balarāma, now also in devotee form (*bhakta-svarūpa*). Being Balarāma, he is considered the brother of Mahāprabhu, even as Balarāma is the brother of Krishna. Advaita Ācārya, the devotee form of Mahāvishnu (*bhakta-avatāra*), or the Lord of the universe, is also known as Sadāśiva, the origin of Shiva himself. The above three are Vishnu-tattva, or entities in the category of God.

Next, Gadādhara (*bhakta-śakti*) is a unique personality—while Mahāprabhu embodies the inner emotion of Rādhā in separation from Krishna, Gadādhara is also Rādhā but in the more conciliatory mood of Rukmiṇī, Krishna's chief consort in Dvārakā. Finally, there is Śrīvāsa (*śuddha-bhakta*), an incarnation of Nārada, representing all souls, particularly the devotees. These two—Gadādhara and Śrīvāsa—are in the category of Śakti-tattva, or the Lord's energy. The first is a manifestation of his *hlādini-śakti*, or internal energy, and the second is Jīva-tattva, or the marginal energy, that is, the minute living being.[25]

Thus, the Gauḍīya Vaishnavas pray:

jāya śrī-krishna-caitanya prabhu-nityānanda,
śrī-advaita gadādhara śrīvāsādi-gaura-bhakta-vṛnda

> "Let all victory go to Srī Krishna Chaitanya and his associates: Nityānanda Prabhu, Śrī Advaita, Śrī Gadādhara, and Śrīvāsa, along with all of Gaura's devotees."[26]

It would be prudent to consider one other philosophical point before looking into the specifics of Mahāprabhu's life. If the Chaitanya tradition accepts that he is God, and it clearly does, then what does his historical narrative really mean? How can we understand that he walked the earth or had an observable place in world history? What does it mean that he is born, or that he dies?[27] Clearly, these overt actions are a manifestation of something higher, of divine play (*līlā*), as it is called in Indian philosophical literature.[28] The phenomenal, external events of his life story provide the reader with an inner, confidential vision of a hidden, numinous reality, one that is meant to educate, and, more importantly, bring pleasure to both the Lord and his devotees. It is, according to the tradition, a glimpse into the transcendental realm, a sample of esoteric action, confidential and edifying, and nurturing for one's spiritual life. These are the implicitly understood reasons for God's *līlā*. With that in mind, say the guardians of the tradition, one may venture into Mahāprabhu's life story and, with faith, derive the expected benefits.

The Early Period

Mahāprabhu was born to Jagannāth Miśra and Śacīdevī, a pious Brahmin couple who settled near the Bhāgīrathī, a branch of the Ganges in Navadvīp (located in West Bengal, north of Kolkata). Today, the specific area of his birth is known as Māyāpur.

From Mahāprabhu's father's side, the family had originally come from Dakha Dakshin, a village in the Bangladeshi district of Sylhet, then known as Śrīhaṭṭa in East Bengal.[29] Several generations earlier, Mahāprabhu's paternal grandfather, Upendra Miśra, had settled there and raised seven sons: Kamsari, Paramānanda, Jagannāth, Sarbeśwar, Padmānabh, Janardan, and Trilokanāth.[30] It was Jagannāth, his third son, who had moved from Sylhet to Navadvīp (Nadia), a prominent center of learning at the time, and married Śacī. He specifically came to Nadia to study under Nīlāmbara Cakravartī, Śacī's father, who was a renowned astrologer of the time.

Śacī's ancestry is also traced to East Bengal. In fact, her family descendants still live in the village known as Magḍobā, in the district of Faridpur in Bangladesh. But Nīlāmbara, her father, had brought his family—consisting of two sons (Yogeśvara Pandit and Ratnagarbha) and two daughters (Śacī and Bhāgāvāthī)—to Navadvīp sometime before her marriage to Jagannāth.[31] When the wedding was proposed, Nīlāmbara welcomed his new student as the husband of his pious daughter.

In due course, Śacī gave birth to eight children, all daughters. Tragically, all died at birth. Misfortune would soon withdraw from the Miśra household, however, and as the fruit of Śacī's ninth pregnancy, a son appeared, whom the joy-filled parents named Viśvarūpa. Their family now prospered, and, after some years, in 1486 CE, another child appeared to them: On a beautiful full-moon night in the Hindu month of Phālguna (February/March), baby Mahāprabhu was born.[32]

Of course, the honorific "Mahāprabhu" was awarded Śacī's second son at a later time. In his infancy and youth, his names were simple descriptors of the circumstances of his birth, or signal characteristics of his person, that is, Śacīnandana ("son of Śacī"); Gaura ("the golden one"); Nimāi (for his being born under a *neem* tree). It was Nīlāmbara who conceived of his actual given name, Viśvambhara ("sustainer of the universe"). The appellation was inspired by the Paṇḍita's conviction, based on his reading of the child's birth chart and on the effulgence of his divine countenance, that this little Nimāi was a most extraordinary soul.

The *Caitanya-bhāgavata* (Ādi 3.16–21) indicates the enthusiasm with which Nīlāmbara recognized Nimāi's identity: "This infant is Lord Nārāyaṇa himself," he said, "and he will give the essence of all religion to the entire world. By his wonderful preaching, everyone will be liberated, freely receiving the treasure that Brahmā, Shiva, and Śukadeva yearn to attain. In fact, simply by seeing him, the entire world will become immersed in bliss, renounced, and merciful to all . . . . Even *yavanas* (foreigners), who are generally antagonistic to Lord Vishnu, will worship this boy's feet. Indeed, his glories will be sung in countless universes. Everyone, from intellectuals to children, will bow down before him."

The residents of Navadvīp dearly loved the beautiful baby. The ladies, in particular, affectionately designated him "Gaura Hari," thus celebrating both his beauteous golden hue and also his manifest divinity as confirmed for them by the pronouncements of the widely renowned and authoritative Nīlāmbara Chakravartī.

Krishnadāsa Kavirāja relates a remarkable dynamic that asserted itself whenever the child was visited by Śacī's friends and neighbors, and which served to exponentially heighten their affection for her son. With uncanny effect, the infant would begin to weep and wail so loudly and forcefully that all within earshot of his inexplicable distress feared for his well-being. And, except and until the assembled guests loudly and enthusiastically chanted the holy names, he was inconsolable. So, even though an unprecedentedly charming atmosphere arose whenever baby Viśvambhara was dandled and fussed over, that preternatural festival of mirth and smiles was manifest only on condition of enthusiastic chanting of God's names.

After a few years, it became clear that he would be a notoriously precocious little boy, but this only endeared him more to the people who surrounded him.

On one occasion, in a pastime with his mother Śacīdevī, the five-year-old Nimāi employed a veiled pedagogy accomplishing two ends. On the one hand, he deftly exposed the unsoundness of the Māyāvādī argument that "all is one," and on the other, he considerately and deliberately, albeit subtly, preserved the sweetness Śacī relished in her superior role as his parent. The story goes that Śacī once gave him some sweets to eat, but the child Nimāi, feigning an admixture of childish ignorance and playful impishness, ate dirt instead. Naturally she chastised him, but he defended his action by arguing that sweets and dirt were simply transformations of the same one energy, and thus identical. Why discriminate between the two, he suggested, when in fact they are one? Here he was indirectly calling attention to the fatuity of the "all is one" philosophy, and subtly inviting his mother to deliver a Vaishnava disquisition on its absurdity.

"Sweets or dirt—what's the difference?" Mother Śacī debated her little boy. "All matter exists in a special state and is adapted for special use," she told him. "Earth, while in the form of a jug, for example, can be used as a water-pot. But in the form of a brick, it can't be used to hold water. So, sweets," she concluded, "although also a form of matter, can be used as food, whereas earth cannot." Little Nimāi thanked her for this life lesson, which also served to convey the foolishness of "all is one" philosophy.

After his fifth year, Nimāi was admitted into a primary school where he applied himself to the study of basic Bengali and other elementary subjects. Soon thereafter, during this early period, there occurred an event that had profound impact on him and his parents: Nimāi's elder brother Viśvarūpa took the vows of *sannyāsa*, renouncing family life and departing from home. They never saw him again.[33] The family system was forever changed. Nimāi, for his part, became even more precocious as a result.

His parents, though, were devastated. They feared that Nimāi, if exposed to religious training in the school of Advaita Āchārya as his brother had been, might well follow in Viśvarūpa's footsteps and likewise be forever lost to them. Certain they could not bear the trauma of losing their beloved Nimāi, they delayed his education. Even so, by the time he was 14 he began school under the tutelage of Gaṅgādāsa Paṇḍita. It was at that time that everyone in the area recognized him as a child prodigy, a scholar, having mastered several languages, logic, rhetoric, hermeneutics, and philosophy.

With his mastery of Sanskrit and grammar, and his growing renown as a scholar, he soon opened a school of his own, though he was still only a teenager. And a fruitful time it was. During this period he met Lakṣmīpriyā, the young girl who would become his wife. Remarkably, though busy as a young husband and headmaster of a school, he authored his own commentary on *Kalāpa Vyākaraṇa,* a Sanskrit grammar. (Regrettably, that text is no longer extant.) His family life at this point is described as flourishing. Several years passed and his reputation grew. Indeed, at this time it was already manifest to all of Navadvīp that Nimāi was its preeminent scholar, and, still precocious, he exploited that fact. There was no one even remotely near to him in erudition, productivity, eloquence, charisma, and influence. And, again, Navadvīp was known specifically as the unparalleled intellectual capital of Bengal, if not of all of India.

On a journey to East Bengal to earn money for his academy, he decided to visit his ancestral village, where his grandfather and uncles still lived. Everyone along the coast enthusiastically greeted him, since his renown as an author, orator, and debater preceded him, and he extended his stay.

Particularly significant in East Bengal was his unexpected meeting with Tapan Miśra, father of Raghunātha Bhaṭṭa Goswāmī, who would later become one of Mahāprabhu's leading followers. Tapan Miśra was undergoing spiritual crisis, and although Nimāi, now known as Nimāi Paṇḍita, was, at this point, more an intellectual than a spiritual leader, he addressed Miśra's concerns: "Chanting the holy name of the Lord," Nimāi told him, "is the real object and goal of spiritual life." And with that, he gave him the Mahā-mantra: "Hare Krishna, Hare Krishna, Krishna Krishna, Hare Hare/ Hare Rāma, Hare Rāma, Rāma Rāma, Hare Hare."[34] This is the first time in Mahāprabhu's manifest *līlā* that he recites the full Mahā-mantra and shows proclivity for the process he will soon champion.

Though the biographers tell us that this was a promising and progressive period in Nimāi's life, fate would quickly take it all away—and, as often happens, replace it with something else.

While Nimāi was visiting East Bengal, his young wife died of snakebite. Some of the biographers say that it was "the poisonous snake of separation" that took her life, for she so missed her loving husband; others say it is to be taken literally. Whatever the case, at his mother's request, he quickly remarried. The new bride was Vishnupriyā, a dedicated young woman who would eventually become one of the most important female ascetics in the Gauḍīya Vaishnava community.[35]

Soon after, in 1508, when Nimāi was 22, tragedy struck yet again. His beloved father, Jagannāth Miśra suddenly passed away. As a result, Nimāi traveled to Gayā, Bihar, to perform the traditional rites of passage for him, known as the Śrāddha ceremony.[36] While there, he happened into a temple along the Falgu River, famous for its footprint of Vishnu carved into a basalt block. The image moved him deeply, so much so that he cried uncontrollably. Something stirred deep within.

But an even more significant event occurred in Gayā: he met Īśvara Purī, a renunciant of the Mādhva lineage.[37] It was from him that Nimāi took spiritual initiation into the ten-syllable Gopāla *mantra* (*gopījana-vallabhāya-svāhā*), which loosely translates, "Salutations to the beloved of the *gopīs* (i.e.,

Krishna)." He chanted it incessantly, repeatedly, and he could feel it change his life, engulf his being.

On his return to Navadvīp, he had a beatific vision of the beautiful lotus-eyed Krishna, playing on his flute. He considered this the culmination of the initiation process, and began chanting Krishna's name without stopping, like a man possessed.[38] He described his vision to his friends:

> I saw a young, beautiful boy, with a resplendent, dark complexion, blackish like the bark of a *tamal* tree. His dazzling curly hair was decorated with wild flowers, a fresh garland of *gunja* berries, and a colorful peacock feather. His jewelry and gems shined so brightly that it was difficult to see him properly. For this reason, it is impossible for me to adequately describe the beauty of his delicately ornamented flute, which he held tightly in his hand. His soft lotus feet were adorned with attractive ankle bells, and his strong, graceful arms easily surpassed the strength and beauty of large blue pillars. How will I describe the wonder of his golden silk *dhoti*, his dangling fish-shaped earrings, and his intoxicated-looking lotus-petal eyes? Smiling sweetly as he approached me, he gave me a gentle hug and then suddenly ran away.[39]

Nimāi Paṇḍita knew he would never be the same.

The Middle Period

The hagiographical texts tell us that for the next six years the transformed Nimāi, Chaitanya Mahāprabhu, was like a live wire, surcharging everyone he met with ecstatic love.

Upon his return from Gayā, the substratal shift in his consciousness caused as radical a shift in his vision of Navadvīp. He saw everyone he met as a devotee, with Krishna in their hearts. And it is related by Vaishnava commentators that the astonished residents of Navadvīp, because they noted so profound a change in him, began to speculate about his identity. Could it be that he was not only the embodiment of pure love of God, which was self-evident, but also, perhaps, the complete embodiment of Godhead?

No longer did he disport himself as a pompous academic, preoccupied as they commonly are with scholarly matters of rhetoric, pedantic debate, literary output, pedagogical innovation, and the like. Instead, he engaged exclusively in intensely animated advocacy of divine love for Krishna. Not only was it clear that he was in love with Krishna—the intensity of his love caused those who came in contact with him to manifest ecstatic symptoms themselves, much like his own.

Regarding his students, when he had initially returned from Gayā, they were shocked by his behavior, and eventually his school had to be closed down. His lectures were no longer about logic and grammar but about chanting the holy name. According to Vrindāvandāsa's *Chaitanya-bhāgavata*, Madhya 1, Śrī Chaitanya instructed those enrolled in his school as follows, "What you have heard and read for many days now make perfect by chanting the holy names of Lord Krishna." The students then asked him how they should chant. To this, he merely sang the various names of Krishna: *hare haraye namaḥ krishna yādavāya namaḥ, gopāla govinda rāma śrī-madhusūdana.* (Madhya 1, texts 405–407) The chanting became contagious, and his students followed suit.

"Hearing the *kīrtana*," Vrindāvandāsa tells us, "all who lived in neighboring Vaishnava homes ran toward the sound" (413). Seeing the Master's ecstatic trance upon chanting, the Vaishnavas felt great wonder (414). Madhya 2 tells us that the devotees gathered, one by one, at the Master's house (215). "Haribol!" Śrī Chaitanya roared, his voice reverberating in all directions. Then he fell to the ground, shaking. No one could hold him still (218). Seeing these wonders, the devotees happily sang the holy names with him. Nothing was able to contain their ecstasy. In this way, Śrī Chaitanya began the Saṅkīrtana movement. As witnesses to this—and as participants—the devotees in Navadvīp found that any suffering they may have previously experienced had become a thing of the past (220, 223).[40]

Advaita Ācārya's group of senior Vaishnavas embraced him warmly. They were certain that the visible transformation in his person that was electrifying Navadvīp was incontrovertible evidence that the divine had embraced him, and that he had fully embraced the divine. As a result, one by one, an inspired cohort of intimate associates, remarkable for their own divine attributes, began to join him: Nityānanda (Balarāma); Haridāsa (Brahmā, and the exemplar of the holy name); Gadādhara (Rādhā in the mood of Rukmiṇī); Śrīvāsa Paṇḍita (Nārada); and a host of others. Advaita Ācārya himself, again, was said to be Mahāvishnu/ Sadāshiva.

During this period, Mahāprabhu opened a nocturnal school of *kīrtana* (congregational chanting) in Śrīvāsa Paṇḍita's courtyard. There, for the refinement and development of his hand-picked companions, his biographers tell us, he exhibited very rare symptoms of the most advanced states of divine love, and the ecstasy arising from the ravishment of chanting God's holy names in the company of the faithful. With his now growing coterie of sincere followers, he gradually showed his divinity to a fortunate few, though he was insistent that his covered incarnation remains concealed.[41] His mission was to exist as a devotee, not as God, as already explained.

Śrī Chaitanya issued a mandate to Nityānanda and Haridāsa: "Go, dear ones, go through the streets of our town, door to door, and exhort one and all to sing the name of Hari with devotion."[42] The two enthusiastic preachers went out on Mahāprabhu's behalf and accomplished miracles. Vaishnava texts tell us that the most miraculous encounter of all occurred when the two preachers met Jagāi and Mādhāi. These two wayward brothers, although born in a most highly esteemed Brahminical family, were addicted to wine, women, and debauchery. They are described as guilty of iniquitous acts too reprehensible to recount in gentle company. It takes little imagination to picture the extreme incompatibility of the two parties upon their meeting, or to visualize the derisive and violent response of the two reprobate brothers when they were urged to take up meditation on God's holy names. When confronted with Nityānanda and Haridāsa, they ridiculed them, saying that they were fools to work on Śrī Chaitanya's behalf.

The two brothers further showed their lack of character by shouting obscenities at Nityānanda, chasing him and harassing him with their words. But the clash was aborted timely, and little harm was done, apart from verbal abuse. When Mahāprabhu learned that Nityānanda had attempted to preach to such fallen individuals, he applauded him.

The next day, however, Nityānanda tried again, but this time it would not end so easily. As soon as he approached the iniquitous brothers, Mādhāi dared to throw a piece of broken pot at him. Reaching its target, it slightly pierced Nityānanda's forehead, causing blood to flow. Nityānanda was not dissuaded, though, despite the inflicted wound. Instead, due to his intense compassion, and because he fully fathomed the depth of their perdition, he immediately forgave the two brothers and continued appealing to them to receive the mercy of the holy name.

Jagāi was impressed. He had seen many "holy people," both authentic and bogus. Nityānanda was clearly in a category of his own. As this realization planted itself in Jagāi's heart, he immediately beseeched Nityānanda to excuse his foolish brother, and Nityānanda's merciful glance revealed that the pardon was already in effect. Nonetheless, Mādhāi moved forward to cause Nityānanda more pain, but this time Jagāi stopped him, insisting that they both surrender to Nityānanda Prabhu.

Śrī Chaitanya suddenly appeared on the scene, maddened that someone had offended his dear Nityānanda. He raised his golden arm in the air, summoning his famous weapon—the weapon of Vishnu, the Sudarśana disc—preparing to kill the two offenders. However, Nityānanda stepped in, insisting that the Lord show mercy. He reminded him of his mission to liberate the most sinful, that his was a mission of love, of peace; and that the only killing would be that of the demoniac mentality, not a literal taking of life. Nearly everyone in this age, said Nityānanda, is comparable to Jāgai and Mādhāi. Should Mahāprabhu kill them all?

Hearing the words of his dear devotee, Mahāprabhu accepted Jagāi and Mādhāi as his own, but only on the condition that they reform their behavior. According to *Caitanya-bhāgavata* (Madhya 13. 298–302), they agreed to do as he says and, in reciprocation, he immediately took away all of their sins. As a result, before everyone's eyes, the Master's body became a deep blackish hue. All present naturally began comparing him to Lord Krishna. But he assured them, "This blackness comes from the sins of these two, Jagāi and Mādhāi." He then told the assembled devotees to perform *kīrtana*, so that the sins accumulated in his body would be transferred to blasphemers of the Lord. After this, the once wayward brothers became devoted followers of Śrī Chaitanya's Saṅkīrtana movement.[43]

Another significant episode in Mahāprabhu's middle period concerns his interaction with Islam,[44] particularly a political leader in Navadvīp: Chand Kazi, who served as the city magistrate under Hussein Shah (reigned 1493–1519), the independent sultan of Bengal. Some say that the Kazi's full name was Maulānā Sirājuddin; others say it was Habibar Rahmān. His descendants still live in the vicinity of Māyāpur, and pilgrims regularly come from various quarters to see his nearby tomb, formally known as "Chand Kazi's Samādhi."[45]

Śrī Chaitanya preached his doctrine of divine love throughout the Kazi's area of authority and was becoming more and more visible because of his large chanting parties. While the Muslim population remained tolerant, at least to some degree, it was the caste-conscious Hindus who complained and created difficulty for Mahāprabhu's mission, their conventional understanding of Hinduism virtually forcing them to deprecate his new religion of love.

Thus, the Kazi, reacting to the complaints of his constituency, journeyed to Śrīvāsa Paṇḍita's house and witnessed the *kīrtana* for himself. At that time, he issued fair warning, saying that the congregational chanting should stop at once, especially in public, and that if the devotees ignored his reprimand, he would have their instruments confiscated and perhaps even forcefully convert them to Islam. It is said that he also broke one of their *mṛdangas* (drums) at that time, to show the seriousness of his warning. He had hoped that this would put an end to their "religious fanaticism." But that was not to be.

The disruptive incident was brought to Mahāprabhu's attention. In response, the Master spoke out against the Muslims of Bengal, issuing threats. Although he was clearly infuriated by the Kazi's attempt to disturb his mission, in the end his methods were peaceful. He adhered to the principle of nonviolent resistance. In pursuance of this, he sent out word to the townspeople that they should take to the streets that evening, singing the holy names with torches in hand, which, in actuality, brought great fear to the Kazi and his constables. Many thousands gathered on Śrī Chaitanya's behalf, chanting and determined to help. They divided into fourteen groups, each one growing as they marched to the Kazi's home.[46]

Upon their arrival, Mahāprabhu and a few of his main followers confronted the Muslim leader, though he was visibly frightened, and a long conversation ensued. In the end, the Master communicated the essence of his Vaishnava tradition, drawing on both the Vedic scriptures and the Koran, since the Kazi was a Muslim. The Kazi, touched by his words and person, began to cry, admitting that he was wrong to stand in his way. More, he felt the need to embrace Śrī Chaitanya's doctrine and felt pangs of ecstatic love merely by being in his presence. The Kazi then joined the chanting parties waiting right outside, and everyone rejoiced.[47]

Interestingly, the Kazi had already, before their meeting, made up his mind to support the Saṅkīrtana movement. Apparently, as he told Mahāprabhu during their discussion, he had had a dream right after the breaking of the drum: "As I slept that night," said the Kazi, "I saw a greatly ferocious creature, roaring very loudly—his body was like a human being's but his face was like that of a lion. In my dream, the lion jumped on my chest, laughing and showing his sharp teeth. Placing his nails on my chest, he said in a scary voice, 'I shall immediately break open your chest as you broke apart the *mṛdanga* drum!'" The lion was, according to tradition, the half-man/ half-lion *avatāra* known as Nṛsiṁhadeva. After telling Mahāprabhu this story, the Kazi showed Mahāprabhu his chest, which bore the actual marks of the lion's nails. Because of this, he had already asked his men to cease and desist, giving full endorsement to the Saṅkīrtana movement. Meeting Mahāprabhu served to further nourish and enhance his newfound devotional sentiments.[48]

The Final Period

I will treat this period very briefly, since the upcoming chapters will further elucidate several of the incidents described here.

In the beginning of 1510, when Mahāprabhu was 24—after only a short period of distributing his unique brand of divine love in Navadvīp and neighboring villages—he traveled to nearby Katwa, where Keśava Bharatī, an important renunciant of the time, initiated him into the renounced order of life (*sannyāsa*).

Getting to Katwa was not easy. The terrain was difficult and his intimate followers didn't want him to go. Their love, in this instance, caused them deep consternation: they couldn't bear the thought of him adopting the difficult path of a mendicant, for it would be a hard, austere life. The traditional biographies thus describe them as being like the *gopīs* of Vrindāvan, who cried piteously when Krishna chose to leave Vrindāvan and go to Mathurā. Keśava Bhāratī, the *sannyāsa* guru, is compared to Akrūra, who was responsible for taking Krishna out of his cherished forest dwelling.[49]

It is recounted that even Madhu, the barber who was to cut Mahāprabhu's raven locks at the *sannyāsa* ceremony, wept with full remorse. Devoted onlookers, such as Nityānanda, Ācāryaratna, and Mukunda Datta—others were there as well—watched the ceremony with dread, praying that their beloved Gaurāṅga would somehow come back to them. Still, they knew this was something he had to do: His intention was to show by example that single-minded determination and focus were indispensable in attracting the Lord, and that a life of asceticism, unencumbered by worldly responsibilities, could be advantageous in this regard.[50]

Also, the religious institutions of the time expressed deep regard for *sannyāsīs*, and if he were to sway them to his religion of love, he knew, he needed to look like them, to speak their language, and to move in their circles, all of which he would do in the years to come. Indeed, although he would preach *bhakti*, devotional love, as the essence of all Vedic religion in no uncertain terms, he would often couch it in their terminology, drawing on the *Vedānta-sūtra* and other intellectual traditions of the day. His earlier training in life had prepared him for this.

Whatever the feelings of his closest followers and friends, the *sannyāsa* ceremony finally occurred. Keśava Bhāratī sat before the young Mahāprabhu, acknowledging that although he, Bhāratī, was acting as guru, he was in fact the disciple: Who could be the guru of God? He wanted this truth reflected in the name he awarded to Mahāprabhu: "I will not give him the *Bhāratī* name, which he would normally receive, coming in my line. Instead, I will give him a name befitting his special spiritual stature."[51] Thus, it was during this ceremony, that Mahāprabhu received the name by which he would be known forevermore. "You have aroused everyone's 'spiritual consciousness' (Chaitanya) and inspired the entire world to chant Lord Krishna's holy name," Bhāratī told him. "Thus, you will henceforward be called 'Krishna Chaitanya'" (a name that basically means, "Krishna Consciousness").[52]

After taking *sannyāsa*, Mahāprabhu wanted to visit Vrindāvan, the land of Krishna. For three days and nights he wandered in a trance-like state in the Birbhum-Bardhaman area (on the west bank of the Bhāgīrathī) with his associates, who couldn't accept that he would no longer be with them in Navadvīp. Though he loved them deeply, his mind and heart were focused elsewhere, searching for Krishna, his beloved, always anticipating a vision of his dark-eyed Lord.

Because of Śrī Chaitanya's God-intoxicated state, Nityānanda Prabhu was able to trick him into going to Śāntipura instead of Vrindāvan—he convinced him that the Gaṅgā, which flows through Navadvīp, in West Bengal, was actually Vrindāvan's Yamunā River. Due to his being so overwhelmingly absorbed in thoughts of Krishna's holy land, Mahāprabhu couldn't really tell the difference, and so he was once again reunited with his Navadvīp followers, including his mother. The disconsolate Śacī took the opportunity to ask him if he would establish nearby Jagannāth Purī as his central headquarters. In this way she would regularly hear of his activities. He eventually did this to accommodate her request. But his journey to Vrindāvan was never far from his mind.

By March 1510, Mahāprabhu arrived in Purī, Odisha, not only to fulfill his mother's desire but to see the deity of Lord Jagannāth, who is Krishna himself in a distinct, uncommon, and very particular form.[53] Approaching the temple in a state of ecstasy, he indeed saw Jagannāth and immediately fainted as a result of ecstatic love. It was under these circumstances that he first met Sārvabhauma Bhaṭṭāchārya, a renowned monistic philosopher of the period who had established the school of Nava-Nyāya in Navadvīp before relocating to Purī. The celebrated philosopher was living in the land of Lord Jagannāth under the patronage of Pratāparudra, king of Odisha.

Sārvabhauma knew that there was something special about this young *sannyāsī* from the very beginning, but seeing him lying there on the floor of the Jagannāth temple, apparently lifeless, was something new. He had never experienced such a thing. Bringing Mahāprabhu to his home, he tested him in various ways to make sure that his ecstatic trance was authentic. Satisfied that it was, he tried to revive him by standard means. Nothing seemed effective. But when the Master's followers arrived, they knew exactly what would work: loud chanting of Krishna's holy name. This in fact revived him, and Sārvabhauma was in awe.

The Vedāntic teacher and Mahāprabhu then proceeded to have a lengthy discussion on the subtle implications of the Upanishads and Vedānta. Sārvabhauma had never heard such explanations before, which refuted Śaṅkara and the common impersonal understanding of the Supreme. He did his best to counter Śrī Chaitanya's *bhakti* conclusion, but his endeavors were fruitless. He was surpassed by Mahāprabhu's in-depth knowledge of the scriptures, his logic, and his spiritual presence. Sārvabhauma admitted defeat, his consciousness was revolutionized, and he became a dedicated follower of Śrī Chaitanya.[54] Conversion of such a celebrity brought numerous new acolytes, who enthusiastically served the Saṅkīrtana mission, causing it to spread throughout India.

Soon after this incident with Sārvabhauma, Mahāprabhu traveled south, where he met Rāmānanda Rāya, governor of Rājmundrī (near Madras), on the banks of the Godāvarī River. This too was an historic meeting of considerable importance, for here, with his intimate associate (Śrī Rāmānanda was an incarnation of the *gopīka* known as Viśākhā),[55] Mahāprabhu engaged in profound dialogue, revealing the innermost dimensions of Gauḍīya Vaishnava thought. Moreover, it was at this meeting that Mahāprabhu brought forth his identity as a dual manifestation of Rādhā and Krishna. For these reasons, I have devoted a chapter to their exchange later in this book.

That same summer—roughly from August to November of 1510—Śrī Chaitanya spent time at the famous temple at Raṅga-kshetra (also called

Śrīraṅgam). There he met the three pious brothers, Vyeṅkata Bhaṭṭa, Tirumalla Bhaṭṭa, and the famous Prabodhānanda Sarasvatī, and explained to them the intricacies of Gauḍīya Vaishnavism. At that time, he also spent time with Vyeṅkata's little boy, Gopāla Bhaṭṭa, who, in later years, became one of the Master's most important theologians: Gopāla Bhaṭṭa Goswāmī, one of the famous Six Goswāmīs of Vrindāvan.

After this, Mahāprabhu visited the major temples of the Deccan, revealing the glories of the holy name. He met individuals in their homes and led chanting parties in the streets. Then, after continuing his travels throughout South India—spanning a total of two years—he returned to Jagannāth Purī. It was the summer of 1511 or 1512 and he was twenty-five years of age. At this time, he attended the Ratha-yātrā festival, and millions came to see him. By now, he was well known throughout the subcontinent. People came from all over to meet with him, to learn from him, and to surrender to his mission.

In 1514, once again he ventured out from Purī. By the fall of that year, when roughly 28 years old, he again felt the need to see Śrī Krishna's land of Vrindāvan. On the way, too, he hoped to meet the two brothers Dabīra Khāsa and Sākara Mallika,[56] important and learned officials in the Islamic government of North India—they would later become Rūpa and Sanātana Goswāmīs, in many ways the most important patriarchs of the Gauḍīya tradition. Prior to meeting him, they had written him lengthy letters, expressing dissatisfaction with the state and political life in general. They wanted to participate in his Saṅkīrtana movement but felt their entanglement in mundane affairs too overwhelming, stopping them from pursuing spiritual life with the commitment it warranted.

Thus, on his way to Vrindāvan, Mahāprabhu stopped in Rāmakeli, in Bengal, where the two brothers were stationed. He met them, instilled even deeper inspiration in their hearts, and accepted them as his disciples. At that time, he also gave them their life mission of writing scholarly literature on the Krishna tradition, both in poetry and prose, and reclaiming the lost holy places of Vrindāvan, which they did in earnest. Importantly, their nephew Jīva Goswāmī, only a little boy at the time, is said to have seen the Master at this point, too, or at least was inspired by him,[57] setting the course of his life to come—he would later emerge as the preeminent philosopher of the Gauḍīya tradition, without equal.

Once again, however, Śrī Chaitanya did not consummate his trip to Vrindāvan.

By that summer he was back in Purī, having decided for various practical reasons to postpone his trip to the holy land. His love for Krishna conquered his pragmatic side every time, however, and after a few months, he found himself once again on the path to Vrindāvan. This was in 1515, when he was twenty-nine, and somehow, though overcome with bliss, he actually arrived.

It was his third attempt and, for him, it was well worth the wait. Merely approaching the outskirts of Vrindāvan proper, he shivered and the hairs of his body stood on end; he experienced all the various symptoms of devotional ecstasy. As he entered the actual area where Rādhā and Krishna had engaged in their loving pastimes some 4,500 years earlier, he felt their presence everywhere, and could not contain his unending joy.

As fall turned to winter in 1516, he left Vrindāvan via Allahabad, which was then called Prayag. There he spent months with Rūpa Goswāmī, instructing him in the details of man's relationship with God, information that Rūpa would later organize into the many books he would produce for the Gauḍīya tradition. He then sent Rūpa to Vrindāvan (to unearth long lost holy places and to build temples) and left for Benares on the road back to Purī. At Benares, he instructed Sanātana Goswāmī in the philosophy of *avatāras* and other Vaishnava minutiae. After explaining these things at length, he asked him to go to Vrindāvan (to work with Rūpa). While in Benares, too, Mahāprabhu converted one of India's most famous monists, Prakāśānanda Sarasvatī, who, like Sārvabhauma before him, brought thousands of followers to Mahāprabhu's feet through his own surrender.

In that same year, by age 30, Mahāprabhu settled in Purī, never to leave again. Everything he needed to do outside of that sacred area was already accomplished. So in the association of his most intimate followers, like Rāmānanda Rāya and Svarūpa Dāmodara Goswāmī, he allowed himself to be fully captivated by Rādhā-bhāva, the ecstasy of Rādhārāṇī's love for Krishna. For 18 years, while in this state of enhanced spiritual ecstasy, he engaged in loving pastimes with the devotees in Odisha, pastimes that are especially detailed by Kavirāja Goswāmī in his *Caitanya-caritāmṛta.*

The last twelve years were particularly intense. Special attention is given to the profound ecstatic symptoms he exhibited during this period. He was in a state of *divyonmāda*, divine madness, Kavirāja Goswāmī tells us, and it often resulted in strange consequences. For example, his bodily limbs would periodically recede and then expand out again, like a turtle, as he wept uncontrollably with love for Krishna. When his body would contort in this way, the only thing that would set him right was the chanting of Krishna's names. These ecstatic symptoms are called *sāttvika-bhāvas*—involuntary bodily transformations, of which eight are most prominent: paralysis, crying, perspiration, change of color, fainting, horripilation, trembling, and stuttering. According to Gauḍīya spirituality, such symptoms only appear in the later stages of love of God, known as *mahābhāva*—an exalted level of devotion, rarely achieved.

In his very last days, he lived in the garden-house of Kāśī Miśra, completely gripped by rapturous spiritual emotions. At this point he would often succumb to a level of ecstatic bewilderment called Prema-vilāsa-vivarta, wherein the spiritual world and the material world become indistinguishable, causing one to see all material phenomena as nondifferent from the elements of Krishna's *līlā*.

For example, Mahāprabhu saw a sand dune and confused it with Govardhana Hill, unable to resist running up to it and embracing it with full force. When he saw the Ganges, he was convinced it was the Yamunā. And because the Yamunā, for him, was inextricably related to the divine couple, he nearly ended his life by jumping into her waters while in a barely conscious state of spiritual ecstasy. Though the spiritual world is far away, it is as close as our skin. Mahāprabhu thus spent the final six years of his life in euphoric transcendence, after which, say the biographers, he simply departed for the spiritual realm, at age 48. The year was 1533.

The devotees could not bear his leaving, and some of them passed away shortly thereafter. Others were able to stay on for many years, in service to his movement. The biographies mention King Pratāparudra's reaction to Mahāprabhu's demise, and his story relates the mood quite well, as an example of how his devotees reacted. It is said that he was so grief-stricken that he left Purī, bequeathing his kingdom to his son. According to *Bhakti-ratnākara* (3.217–221), "When the king heard that Śrī Chaitanya had departed, he fell to the ground and lamented uncontrollably. Hitting his head again and again, he finally fell unconscious, and only the company of Rāmānanda Rāya kept him alive. The king was unable to bear the absence of Śrī Chaitanya, and so he left Purī, staying elsewhere, incognito, for the rest of his days."[58]

A few words should be said about Mahāprabhu's miraculous death story. The major biographies, from Vrindāvandāsa's *Chaitanya-bhāgavata* to Kavirāja Goswāmī's *Caitanya-caritamrta*, are generally silent regarding the details. They tell us that he "disappeared" (*antardhāna*), and sometimes they mention the year of its occurrence, but they are reluctant to explore it more deeply. This is no doubt because of the emotional trauma they would endure by contemplating their Master's demise.

There are those, however, who venture toward disclosure, allowing us some insight into Mahāprabhu's departure. Among the biographers, the first to discuss this uncomfortable subject is Locana Dāsa Ṭhākura in his *Caitanya-maṅgala* (Śeṣa-khaṇḍa 15.15–38). He tells us that Mahāprabhu merged into the deity of Lord Jagannāth, perhaps while the deity was residing at the Guṇḍicā Maṇḍira.[59] Śrīla A. C. Bhaktivedānta Swami Prabhupāda seems to concur with this point of view,[60] as do numerous Odia writers from ancient times to present.

An alternate theory is that the Master merged into the deity of Ṭoṭā-gopīnātha, which at the time was being cared for by Mahāprabhu's intimate, Gadādhara Paṇḍita. This version is mentioned in the *Bhakti-ratnākara* (8.354–359) and is endorsed by Bhaktivinoda Ṭhākura.[61] To this day, a golden streak can be seen on the deity's thigh. Local priests assure all visitors that this streak can be traced to Mahāprabhu's disappearance. Bhaktisiddhānta Sarasvatī has mentioned the Ṭoṭā-gopīnātha version as well.[62] Interestingly, this is considered the earlier theory, having first been articulated by Vāsudeva Ghosh, a poet who was Mahāprabhu's contemporary.[63] We may never know what actually happened, but, like the various miracles that make up his life, it should not be of central interest. It is his life itself and the inspiration and the teachings that it implies—this is what Mahāprabhu is all about.

Miracles, in fact, were not in short order in his life's narrative. On this score, some would put him on a par with Jesus. A few examples should suffice to make our point: Once, when Śrī Chaitanya's *kīrtana* associates expressed their desire for mangoes (even though the fruit was then out of season), he took a mango seed and buried it in Śrīvāsa's courtyard. Immediately, the seed sprouted, miraculously appearing as a full-grown mango tree right before their eyes. It supplied enough ripened fruits to accommodate each of them, and it continued to do so for the rest of their lives.[64]

On another occasion, Mahāprabhu journeyed to Purī through the dense jungles of the Jhārikhaṇḍa Forest, even though he knew well that numerous wild beasts made it their home. The biographers inform us, however, that the spiritual potency of his chanting transformed the otherwise perilous forest into something resembling the fabled "peaceable kingdom." All resident creatures responded to his presence by joyfully dancing together—tigers with deer, wild boar with pheasants—creating an image of biblical proportions. Hearing Śrī Chaitanya chant the names of Krishna, it is said, they all howled in their respective tongues.[65]

Another signal instance of Śrī Chaitanya's miraculous performances—inarguably on a par with those ascribed to the Nazarene, or the Hebraic prophet Elijah, or the celebrated Islamic Master Al-Khidr—was his curing of Vasudeva's leprosy[66] simply by his loving embrace. But more, the canon even records the miraculous resurrection of Śrīvāsa Ṭhākura's dead son,[67] which was witnessed by many of Chaitanya's intimate followers, and recorded by his biographer Vrindāvandāsa in the *Caitanya-bhāgavata*. Most such miracles were not witnessed by the masses, but only by his inner circle of friends and associates. It is easy, therefore, to relegate them to the realm of hagiography or even interpolation. But they are unequivocally accepted by the tradition, as believing Christians accept Jesus's miracles.

Some of Mahāprabhu's supernatural actions, however, are said to be public events, seen by the multitudes: Perhaps the most famous of these occurred in Purī, during the Ratha-yātrā festival. Once, at this massive celebration, in which three huge, wheeled chariots carrying the deities Jagannāth (Krishna), Baladeva (his brother), and Subhadrā (his sister) are pulled by hundreds of enthusiastic devotees, with hundreds of thousands more as witnesses, the cart suddenly stopped. No number of able-bodied men, however strong and however many, could budge the strangely immobile chariot. Again and again, all the assembled devotees tried with their combined strength not only to pull it with its attached massive ropes, but also to push it forward from behind. Their endeavor, in the end, proved unsuccessful. The gigantic elephants of Purī's royal house were brought in, but they, too, failed to move the cart. Everyone present was bewildered by this inexplicable course of events, not knowing what to do. Just then, Mahāprabhu arrived and placed his head up against the back of the immovable cart. Applying minimal pressure, the enormous vehicle finally moved forward, to everyone's astonishment. Thousands of devotees shouted "Haribol!" in appreciation of Śrī Chaitanya's miracle.[68]

Another such event occurred at Ratha-yātrā: His many followers saw him dancing in the midst of seven *kīrtana* groups at once! The chanters in each group, not realizing that the Master had expanded himself by his spiritual potency, thought he had favored them, appearing only in their party. Later, they realized that he chanted in all seven simultaneously.[69]

Whether public or private, miracles are not the point, as stated above. To highlight this perspective, Bhaktivinoda Ṭhākura writes as follows:

> We leave it to our readers to decide how to deal with Mahaprabhu. The Vaishnavas have accepted Him as the great Lord, Shri Krishna Himself . . . . Those who are not prepared to accept this perspective may think of Lord Chaitanya as a noble and holy teacher. That is all we want our readers to believe . . . . We make no objection if the reader does not believe His miracles, as miracles alone never demonstrate Godhead. Demons like Ravana and others have also worked miracles and these do not prove that they were gods. It is unlimited love and its overwhelming influence that would be seen in God Himself.[70]

Bhaktivinoda's words should be deeply considered. Still, in practice, Gauḍīya Vaishnavas do view Mahāprabhu as more than just a saint. They teach that he is God himself, and, not only that, he is God in his highest feature—a particularly esoteric form of Rādhā and Krishna combined, as already discussed. Exactly how Gauḍīyas see him is nicely summarized in the following apocryphal story. Let us conclude an already long chapter with the insights it conveys.

> One day, Krishna sat beside Rādhikā in the forest of Vrindāvan. Taking one of her hands in his, he pleaded, "Please give me something special today . . . ." Inwardly, Śrī Rādhā's heart melted at his request, but outwardly, she concealed her secret mind with a studied silence. Speaking no words, but by the tilt of her head, her sidelong glance, and the sign language of her lotus hand, she invited Krishna to tell her what he wanted. And Śrī Krishna eagerly obliged her silent invitation with an outburst: "Please, give me your love!"

Rādhikā smiled and responded playfully: "Aho, but Krishna, this love of mine would be too heavy for you to bear."

Just then, the best of Śrī Rādhā's devoted girlfriends, the saucy Lalitā, chimed in, "Rādhā's love *would be* too heavy for you, Krishna. You should know just how intense it is—when you are not near, her anxiety knows no limit. And though we try our best, no remedy can be found to assuage her distress. We anoint her body, blazing from the fire of separation, with cooling sandalwood paste, but the sandalwood flies from her golden limbs like dried leaves of paper. We bid her lie on a shaded bed we prepared, strewn with dampened lotus petals, but the fragrant petals are incinerated by the fever of her longing. So, it is true, none but the queen of Vraja could bear that weight. It would be too heavy for you."

Hearing these words, Krishna grabbed hold of Rādhārāṇī's other hand, and with tears coursing from his lotus eyes, implored once more: "But I cannot live without tasting the nectar of this love!"

Astonished by joy, Śrī Rādhā's broadly smiled, and as if orchestrated by her heartbeat, all of Vraja fell silent, eavesdropping to hear her jubilant declaration, "All right, beloved, I will give you this love you crave. But there's something more. You will need the sanctuary of my golden complexion to shield your beautiful blackish body, because the intensity of my love will cause you to stumble and fall. And without the protection of my golden effulgence, you would be bruised. This golden hue will indemnify you instantly; no harm will ever overtake your soft body, which is more dear to me than life itself."

So Krishna was concealed by the molten gold of Śrī Rādhā's dazzling complexion, which causes him to adopt her mood and inner disposition. His limbs began to tremble and dance in jubilation, and he began to cry out, as Rādhā does: "O Krishna, where are you? Where are you? O ascendant moon risen from the dynasty of Nanda Mahārāja and Yaśodā? O beloved of my life breath, Where are you?" As soon as Krishna possessed—and was possessed by—this love, his amorous cries transformed the landscape: the stones within earshot melted in ecstasy; the trees began to dance; and the ardor of the love he felt caused him to crash down like a tree torn from the earth by a gale, and cast to the ground. And then it was that Śrī Rādhā's beautiful golden effulgence protected him, just as she had promised . . . . This is the notion of Gaurāṅga Mahāprabhu found in the line of Rūpa and Raghunāth . . . .[71]

Let us now look at Mahāprabhu's religion of love. Indian tradition sometimes refers to it more generically as *bhakti*, devotion, and it developed over the centuries as a systematic science, but never as it did in the hands of Śrī Chaitanya and his followers.

NOTES

1. Joseph T. O'Connell, "Historicity in the Biographies of Chaitanya," in *Journal of Vaishnava Studies*, Volume 1, No. 2 (Fall 1993), 110.

2. See Tony K. Stewart, "On Changing the Perception of Chaitanya's Divinity," in Joseph T. O'Connell, *Bengal Vaisnavism, Orientalism, Society, and the Arts* (Michigan state University, 1985), 38. Also see Tony K. Stewart's unpublished Ph.D. thesis, "The Biographical Images of Kṛṣṇa-Caitanya: A Study in the Perception of Divinity" (University of Chicago, 1985).

3. *The 'Caitanya Caritāmṛta' of Kṛṣṇadāsa Kavirāja*, translated with commentary by Edward C. Dimock, Jr. and edited by Tony K. Stewart, with an introduction by the translator and the editor (Harvard Oriental Series, No. 56, Cambridge, MA: Harvard University Press, 1999), 82–106. See also Tony K. Stewart, *The Final Word: The Caitanya Caritāmṛta and the Grammar of Religious Tradition* (New York: Oxford University Press, 2010), Chapter Three, "Early Formal Theories of Manifest Divinity," 99–138.

4. Kavi Karṇapūra's drama, Act 3, Texts 23 and 24, and especially 136, among others. See Gerald T. Carney, "Entering the Dynamics of Vaishnava Devotion: The Inset Play in Act III of Kavikarṇapūra's *Caitanyacandrodaya*," in *Journal of Vaishnava Studies*, Volume 5, No. 1 (Winter, 1996)

5. *The Final Word: The Caitanya Caritāmṛta and the Grammar of Religious Tradition*, *op. cit.* (http://oxfordindex.oup.com/view/10.1093/acprof:oso/9780195392722.003.0003).

6. See Kavi Karṇapūra's *Gaura-gaṇoddeśa-dīpikā* (109): *veda-vyāso ya evāsīd dāso vṛndāvano'dhunā* . . . .

7. Krishnadāsa Kavirāja Goswāmī's identity as Kaustūrī Mañjarī is mentioned in Dhyānachandra Goswāmī's *Śrī Gaura-govindārcana-smaraṇa-paddhati* (text 341): "Next, the particulars of Śrī Kaustūrī Mañjarī are described . . . . In Kali-yuga, in Gaurāṅga-līlā, she is known as Śrī Krishnadāsa Kavirāja Goswāmī." This is also mentioned in David Haberman, *Acting as a Way of Salvation: A Study of Rāgānuga Bhakti Sadhana* (New York: Oxford University Press, 1988), 110–111.

8. See Tony K. Stewart, "The Biographies of Śrī Chaitanya and the Literature of the Gauḍīya Vaishnavas," in Steven J. Rosen, *Vaiṣṇavism: Contemporary Scholars Discuss the Gauḍīya Tradition* (New York: FOLK Books, 1992; reprint, Delhi: Motilal Banarsidass, 1994), 116–117.

9. The key verses here are found in *Caitanya-caritāmṛta,* Ādi 1.5, 6, and Ādi 4, where Kavirāja Goswāmī attributes this most confidential knowledge as coming from Svarūpa Dāmodara. Prabhupāda notes in his commentary to Ādi 4.55, which repeats the exact verse found in 1.5, that this concept originates in Svarūpa Dāmodara's diary. This view is also supported by Bhaktivinoda Ṭhākura in *Jaiva Dharma* 14, *Nitya-dharma, Sambandha, Abhidheya* and *Prayojana*, Part Two, Śakti-vicāra, "A Description of the Potencies of Śrī Krishna."

10. *Caitanya-bhāgavata,* 2.18.120 (*henai samaye sarva-prabhu viśvambhara, praveśa karilā ādyā-śakti-veṣa-dhara*).

11. *Caitanya-bhāgavata,* 2.18.127 (*kibā mahālakṣmī, kibā āilā pārvatī? kibā vṛndāvanera sampatti mūrtimatī?*). For the *rasika* associates of Śrī Chaitanya, the reference to the "treasure of Vrindāvan" in this context was clear—it refers to Rādhā.

12. *Caitanya-bhāgavata,* 2.18.154.

13. *Caitanya-bhāgavata,* 2.18.216 (*adbhuta gopikā-nṛtya cāri-veda-dhanakṛṣṇa-bhakti haya ihā karile śravaṇa*).

14. It is a secret pastime: *Caitanya-bhāgavata,* 2.18.220. (*kṛṣṇa-anugraha yāre, se e marma jāne*). It should be noted that a similar dramatic performance can be found in Act III of Kavi Karṇapūra's play, *Śrī Caitanya-candrodāya-nāṭakam*, and there too one finds the same hidden truth: Mahāprabhu plays the role of Rādhā, revealing his true identity. Gerald T. Carney, whose Ph.D. thesis focused on Kavi Karṇapūra's play, sums up, "In theological terms, the inset-play becomes a sort of scrim through which the Lord's play in all reality is perceived through the eyes of those who have cultivated devotional sentiment, the *rasikas*. The play is ultimately that of Chaitanya himself, Kṛṣṇa assuming the feelings of Rādhā, just as Chaitanya takes the role of Rādhā in the play . . . . Chaitanya's assuming the role of Rādhā in the inset play reflects the reality of his devotional feelings and the deepest meaning of his appearance." See Gerald T. Carney, "Entering the Dynamics of Vaishnava Devotion: The Inset Play in Act III of Kavikarṇapūra's *Caitanyacandrodaya*," op. cit., 61.

15. I would like to mention just a few that are particularly important: Haridāsa Dāsa, *Śrī-śrī-gauḍīya-vaiṣṇava-jīvana*, 2 vols., in Bengali (Nabadwip: Haribola Kuṭīra, 1951); Bimānbihāri Majumdār, in Bengali, *Śrī-caitanya-caritera-upādāna* (Calcutta: Calcutta University Press, 1959); Bhakti Siddhānta Sarasvati Gosvami, ed., *Śrī Caitanya-bhāgavata of Vrndāvana Dāsa Thākura,* Third Edition (Calcutta: Bāgbāzār Gaudiya Matha, 1961); Haridāsa Dāsa, *Śrī-śrī-gauḍīya-vaiṣṇava-ahidhāna*, 4 vols., in Bengali (Navadwip: Haribol Kuṭīra, 1976); and Nareśacandra Jānā, in Bengali, *Vṛndāvanera-chaya-gosvāmī* (Calcutta: Calcutta University Press, 1970).

16. The series appearing in the Buddhist journal concludes with a brief acknowledgment of Bhaktivinoda's efforts, indicating that the author was aware of his work and, consequently, Bhaktivinoda's book must have come first. Still, other short works in English may have preceded Bhaktivinoda's, but, to my knowledge, these were just brief analyses of Mahāprabhu's philosophy and not biographies as such. One example is "Chaitanya and the Vaishnava Poets of Bengal" from 1873 (http://www.sacred-texts.com/journals/ia/cvpb.htm).

17. This book was renamed in its second edition: *Chaitanya's Life and Teachings; from his contemporary Bengali biography the Chaitanya-charit-amrita* (Calcutta, 1922).

18. This was originally envisioned as a three-volume set, but, unfortunately, during the author's lifetime (and for many decades thereafter), only the first volume was released. The second volume, however, was recently published: *Sree Krishna Chaitanya*, Volume II (Kolkata: Gaudiya Mission, 2004). We do not know if the third volume was ever written.

19. For many years, this massive study remained unpublished, at least in its complete form, and was merely circulated as a photocopied manuscript. A severely abbreviated version did appear in various published editions. See, for example Sambidānanda Dās, *Sri Chaitanya Mahaprabhu* (Madras: Sree Gaudiya Math, 1986, originally published in 1958). The full Ph.D. thesis was finally released as *The History & Literature of the Gaudiya Vaishnavas and their relation to other Medieval Vaishnava Schools: Complete Work of Dr. Sambidānanda Dās* (Chennai: Sree Gaudiya Math, 2007).

20. See Ravīndra Svarūpa Dāsa, *Śrīla Prabhupāda: The Founder-Ācārya of ISKCON* (India: ISKCON GBC Press, 2014), 36–37.

21. The later reprint would be a beautiful hardbound edition: Bhakti Pradip Tirtha, *Sri Chaitanya Mahaprabhu* (Calcutta: Gaudiya Mission, 1947).

22. See Ferdinando Sardella, *Modern Hindu Personalism: The History, Life, and Thought of Bhaktisiddhānta Sarasvatī* (New York: Oxford University Press, 2012), 146.

23. The book consists of 62 chapters ("*paricchedas*") divided into three parts ("*līlās*"). In total, the text includes 11,555 verses, out of which the author, Śrīla Krishnadāsa Kavirāja Goswāmī, composed 10,525 Bengali verses ("*payāras*") and 97 original Sanskrit *ślokas*; the remaining 933 Sanskrit verses were quoted from other traditional sources. This information comes from Brijabasi Dasa, "The 400th Anniversary of Sri Caitanya-caritamrta" (http://www.dandavats.com/?p=17215).

24. What Dimock and Stewart's edition is for scholars, Prabhupāda's is for practitioners: A. C. Bhaktivedānta Swami Prabhupāda, *Śrī-Śrī Caitanya-caritāmṛta*, Nine Volumes (Los Angeles: Bhaktivedanta Book Trust, 1996, reprint of original 1975 edition).

25. "Lord Chaitanya in Five Features," *Caitanya-caritāmṛta*, Ādi 7. See also Steven J. Rosen, *Śrī Pañca Tattva: The Five Features of God*, (New York: Folk Books, 1994).

26. All Gauḍīya Vaishnavas sing this traditional prayer daily. The translation is my own.

27. Indeed, the tradition doesn't use the Sanskrit and Bengali words for "birth" and "death" in relation to God or his incarnations. Instead, they say *āvirbhāv* ("appearance") and *tirobhāv* ("disappearance"), or similar words along those lines. The traditional analogy is clarifying: The sun rises in the east, but it does not originate there. We can say it "appears" from the east and then becomes visible for us, wherever we may be. Similarly, the sun sets in the west; it "disappears" at that time, but it does not go out of existence. The sun is always the same but merely appears before us or escapes our vision, depending on our perspective.

28. The rich Sanskrit word "*līlā*" means, "play," "sport," "spontaneity," or "drama"—and also, more colloquially, "divine pastime." It refers to the effortless, free, or playful activity of God, in which he enjoys his associates and they enjoy him.

29. There is a theory, originating, perhaps, in Jayānanda's *Caitanya-maṅgala*, that Mahāprabhu's ancestors had originally migrated from Odisha and lived in Sylhet for sometime before relocating to Navadvīp, but there is little evidence to support this.

30. *Caitanya-caritāmṛta,* Ādi 13.58.

31. Śacī's clan information is neatly conveyed in Sambidānanda Dās, *Sri Chaitanya Mahaprabhu*, op. cit., 2.

32. Scholars of the tradition say the exact day was Friday, February 18, 1486. See Bhakti Pradip Tirtha, *Sri Chaitanya Mahaprabhu*, *op. cit.*, 14.

33. It is said that Mahāprabhu's later tour of South India was instigated by his desire to find his brother. Tradition has it that Viśvarūpa, after taking *sannyāsa*, was given the name "Śaṅkarāraṇya Purī" and traveled to Pāṇḍarapura in Maharashtra, where he "passed away" by entering the body of Nityānanda Prabhu.

34. See *Caitanya-bhāgavata,* Ādi 14.143–47.

35. All manifestations of Vishnu have three energies, known as Śrī, Bhū and Nīlā (or Līlā). Lakṣmī, Mahāprabhu's first wife, is a manifestation of *śrī-śakti*, serving his

majestic Gaura-Nārāyaṇa form; Vishnupriyā, his second wife, is his *bhū-śakti*, the earth goddess; and Navadvīp, the land of his *līlā*, is his *līlā-śakti*. For more, see Śrīla Bhakti Ballabha Tīrtha Goswāmī Mahārāja, "Śrīmatī Vishnupriyā Devi (http://www.bvml.org/SBBTM/svd.htm).

36. The senior male child performs a death ritual for the departed parent. This is called a Śrāddha ceremony, which enables the deceased person's soul to journey to the land of the forefathers (*pitri*).

37. According to Viśvanātha Chakravartī's *Gaura-gaṇa-svarūpa-tattva-candrikā* (Verse 26, 27), Īśvara-purī was Gargamuni in his previous incarnation.

38. *Caitanya-bhāgavata,* Madhya 2.179–185.

39. *Caitanya-bhāgavata,* Madhya 2. See Śacīnandana Swami, "Kanai Natashala: Where Śrī Chaitanya's Ecstasy Awakened" in *Back to Godhead* (September/October 2006). Edited for clarity. (http://btg.krishna.com/kanai-natashala-where-sri-chaitanyas-ecstasy-awakened).

40. The origins of the Saṅkīrtana Movement can be found in the pages of the *Chaitanya-bhāgavata*, Madhya-khaṇḍa, chapters one and two, both entitled, "Śrī Saṅkīrtanārambha-varṇana ("Description of the Saṅkīrtana Movement's Beginning"). In Navadvīp, just after the Master returned from Gayā, many Vaishnavas gathered in devotees' homes to chant with Śrī Chaitanya (particularly in Śuklāmbara's, Śrīvāsa's, and Śacīdevī's, all of whom were especially dear to him). This is where the great sound of Mahāprabhu's *kīrtana* resounded for the first time, as well as among his students, as mentioned in this section. See Vrindāvandāsa Ṭhākura's *Śrī Caitanya-bhāgavata* (Complete in One Volume), trans., Kuśakratha Dāsa (Alachua, Florida: The Kṛṣṇa Institute, 1994).

41. Interestingly, despite his "disguised" incarnation, Mahāprabhu revealed his divinity on several occasions. Significantly, there is an episode called Mahābhāva-prakāśa, where, for twenty-one hours, he showed his many divine forms to all his intimate devotees in Śrīvāsa Ṭhākura's courtyard. This is detailed in Vrindāvandāsa's *Caitanya-bhāgavata,* Madhya 9 and 10. Some other examples may be cited as follows: He showed Śrīvāsa his form as Vishnu (*Caitanya-bhāgavata*, Madhya 2.256–258); Murāri Gupta saw both his Varāha Avatāra (*Caitanya-bhāgavata,* Madhya 2.3) and Rāma Avatāra (*Caitanya-bhāgavata*, Madhya 2.10); Advaita Ācārya, Śrīdhara, and Śacī saw his form as Krishna (*Caitanya-bhāgavata*, Madhya 2.6, 2.9, and 2.8, respectively); Nityānanda, Sārvabhauma, and Pratāparudra viewed his six-armed form (*Caitanya-bhāgavata*, Madhya 2.5, *Caitanya-caritāmṛta,* Ādi 17.13, and Murāri's *Kaḍacā* 3.16.13, respectively); Advaita saw his universal form (*Caitanya-bhāgavata*, Madhya 24.32–55); and Rāmānanda Rāya saw his combined manifestation as Śrī-Śrī Rādhā and Krishna (*Caitanya-caritāmṛta,* Madhya 8.282–284).

42. See Bhaktivinoda Ṭhākura, *Sri Chaitanya: His Life and Precepts* (http://www.purebhakti.com/mission/bhakti-is-love-mainmenu-75/799-life-of-sri-chaitanya-mahaprabhu.html).

43. While this incident seems uncharacteristic of Mahāprabhu, who tended to show mercy rather than rage, it is said that he was attempting to bestow his love through Nityānanda on this particular occasion, so that his followers would fathom the depth of, and fully appreciate, the unprecedented compassion of his spiritual brother, which demonstrably exceeded his own. On a separate note, in commenting

on this pastime, the tradition relates that Jagāi and Mādhāi are incarnations of the same gatekeepers, Jaya and Vijaya, who were cursed to take three births as demons, that is, Hiraṇyākṣa and Hiraṇyakaśipu, Rāvaṇa and Kumbhakarṇa, and Śiśupāla and Dantavakra. See *Śrimad Bhāgavatam* 7.1.33–47 and 7.10.35–38. The tradition's textual source for claiming that Jagāi and Mādhāi were a fourth incarnation of Jaya and Vijaya can be traced to the *Gaura-gaṇoddeśa-dīpikā* (115): "Jaya and Vijaya, the two doorkeepers of Vaikuṇṭhaloka, voluntarily appeared in Śrī Chaitanya's pastimes as the two devotees Śrī Jagannāth and Śrī Mādhava." These latter names were awarded to Jagāi and Mādhāi after they converted to Vaishnavism.

44. Muslim presence in Bengal dates back three centuries prior to Mahāprabhu, when Muhammad Bhakhtyār and his troops defeated the Sena dynasty. This led to various sultanate regimes, which became a sustained dimension of North India's political and religious landscape. By the mid-14th century, the Ilyas Shāhī dynasty began to reign in Bengal and continued until just before Mahāprabhu's era, when Abyssinians, initially migrating from Africa as slaves, took power. It is with the end of Abyssinian rule, in 1493, that Husain Shāh brought the area under his influence.

45. *Caitanya-caritāmṛta*, Ādi 17.124, Prabhupāda's edition, purport.

46. Many consider this an early instance of "nonviolent civil disobedience," predating both Mahatma Gandhi and Martin Luther King, Jr. As Prabhupāda notes: "He was the first man in the history of India who started this civil disobedience movement. It is not Gandhi who is the originator of civil disobedience; it was Chaitanya Mahāprabhu." See A. C. Bhaktivedānta Swami Prabhupāda, morning walk conversation, Montreal, August 26, 1968 (http://vaniquotes.org/wiki/He_was_the_first_man_in_the_history_of_India_who_started_this_civil_disobedience_movement._It_is_not_Gandhi_who_is_the_originator_of_civil_disobedience;_it_was_Caitanya_Mahaprabhu._He_said_that_%22Defy_the_order_of_the_Kazi). That being said, the *Chaitanya-bhāgavata* (Madhya 23) version of this story is somewhat abbreviated. Gone is the mood of reconciliation and the prolonged discussion between Mahāprabhu and the Kazi, which lends itself to a mood of passive resistance. Kavirāja Goswāmī offers more detail, enabling readers to see the episode as, in its ultimate conclusion, an instance of nonviolent civil disobedience.

47. Bhaktivinoda Ṭhākura offers an esoteric dimension to the story in *Śrī Navadvīpa Dhāma Māhātmya*, Parikramā-khaṇḍa, Chapter 6: "When Nityānanda Prabhu and Jīva Goswāmī entered Chand Kazi's village, Nityānanda said, 'O Jīva, hear My words. The Chand Kazi's village is nondifferent from Mathurā. After performing *kīrtana*, Gaurāṅga gave love of God to the Kazi and liberated him. Mathurā's King Kaṁsa of Krishna-līlā became Chand Kazi in Gaura-līlā. For that reason Gaurāṅga addressed the Kazi as his maternal uncle, and out of fear the Kazi took shelter of Gaurāṅga's lotus feet. Under orders from Hussain Shah, who was the king of the Bengal Empire and Jarāsandha in Krishna-līlā, the Kazi caused disturbance during *kīrtana* performance by breaking the *mṛdangas*. The Lord, appearing in the form of Nṛsiṁha, put fear in the Kazi's heart. Like Kaṁsa, the Kazi cowered in fear. Śrī Caitanya, however, gave him *prema* and thus made the Kazi a great devotee . . . ." (http://www.krishnapath.org/Library/Goswami-books/Bhaktivinoda-Thakura/Bhaktivinoda_Thakura_Sri_Navadvipa-Dhama-Mahatmya.pdf).

48. *Caitanya-caritāmṛta* Ādi 17.178–191.

49. According to Verse 52 of Kavi Karṇapūra's *Gaura-gaṇoddeśa-dīpikā*, Keśava Bhāratī was Sāndīpani Muni (Krishna's teacher) in his previous life. However, Verse 117 of this same text tells us that, according to others, Keśava Bhāratī was Akrūra, which is particularly noteworthy in this context. Such parallels are brought out in particular *kīrtana* songs, showing a distinct connection between Krishna-līlā and Gaura-līlā. There is a form of *kīrtana*, in fact, called Gaurachandrikā, in which an activity of Śrī Chaitanya is glorified (*līlā-kīrtana*), to set the proper mood, and then a corresponding activity from Krishna-līlā is sung in support of it. See Edward C. Dimock, Jr. "The Place of Gauracandrikā in Bengali Vaiṣṇava Lyrics," in *Journal of the American Oriental Society*, Volume 78, No. 3 (1958), 153–169. Also see Edward C. Dimock, Jr., and Denise Levertov, *In Praise of Krishna: Songs from the Bengali* (University of Chicago Press, 1967), xi–xii.

50. *Chaitanya-bhāgavata,* Antya 3.67.

51. *Chaitanya-bhāgavata,* Madhya 28.169–172.

52. See Bhumipati Dasa, trans., Śrīla Vrindāvan Dāsa Ṭhākura, *Śrī Chaitanya-bhāgavata*, Madhya-khaṇḍa, Chapter 28, verses 175–176 (New Delhi: Vrajraj Press, 2002), 563–564.

53. See "The Truth About Lord Jagannāth: A Personal Meditation" in *The Agni and the Ecstasy: Collected Essays of Steven J. Rosen* (London: Arktos, 2012), 163–165.

54. For an in-depth but readable article about the meeting of Śrī Chaitanya and Sārvabhauma Bhaṭṭāchārya, see Jayādvaita Dāsa Brahmacārī, "The Logician and Lord Caitanya" in *Back to Godhead*, Volume 1, No. 48, 1972 (http://www.backtogodhead.in/the-logician-and-lord-caitanya-by-jayadvaita-dasa-brahmacari/).

55. There are diverse opinions about Rāmānanda Rāya's spiritual identity. According to the *Gaura-gaṇoddeśa-dīpikā* (124), " . . . Rāmānanda Rāya is the incarnation of Lalitā-gopī, Arjuniya-gopī, and Pāṇḍava Arjuna." But according to Dhyānachandra Goswāmī's *Śrī Gaura-Govindārcana-Smaraṇa-Paddhati*, Text 214, Rāmānanda Rāya is Viśākhā. Thus, the tradition offers a certain latitude when it comes to Rāmānanda's previous incarnation. That being said, the mass of Gauḍīya stalwarts tends to accept Dhyānachandra's version. In the late 17th century, for example, Viśvanātha Chakravartī writes in his *Gaura-gaṇa-svarūpa-tattva-candrikā* (text 79): "The illustrious *gopī* named Arjunika (or Arjuniya), a plenary portion of Viśākhā, has now become Rāmānanda Rāya, the dear friend of Chaitanya." Bhaktivinoda Ṭhākura clearly expresses this preference, too, in his commentary on *Caitanya-caritāmṛta* (Madhya 8.23), and Prabhupāda, while elsewhere giving credence to the Lalitā option, also comments on Madhya 8.23 in the same way, writing, "Śrīla Rāmānanda Rāya was an incarnation of the *gopī* Viśākhā. Since Śrī Chaitanya Mahāprabhu was Lord Kṛṣṇa Himself, there was naturally an awakening of love between Viśākhā and Kṛṣṇa."

56. Dabīra Khāsa ("private secretary") and Sākara Mallika ("high minister") were titles given to Rūpa and Sanātana by the Muslim authorities of Bengal. But these were not their original names. Some scholars say that their birth-names were Amara and Santoṣa. The veracity of this claim, however, is questionable, and even something of a mystery, since no one seems certain about where or how these names first arose. According to Nareśacandra Jānā, in his authoritative Bengali work, *Vṛndāvanera*

chaya gosvāmī (Calcutta: Calcutta University Press, 1970), 22, "some people say their names were Amara and Santoṣa, but these names cannot be found in any of the tradition's early sources." See also D. C. Sen, *The Vaisnava Literature of Mediæval Bengal* (Calcutta: University of Calcutta, 1917), 28–29; and Prabhudayāl Mital, *Braj ke Dharma-Sampradāyo kā Itihās* (Delhi: National Publishing House, 1968), 311.

57. Interestingly, whether or not Jīva actually saw Mahāprabhu at Rāmakeli could be determined by the year of his birth, which, if it were later rather than sooner (there are various opinions about when he was born), would probably disallow his having had that pivotal experience. In other words, most scholars say he was born too late for that to occur. The traditional text usually cited for Jīva's seeing Mahāprabhu in person is *Bhakti-ratnākara* 1.638, which is anything but clear. This is further confused by a subsequent verse in that same chapter (1.713), as noted by Jan Brzezinski, which says that Jīva Goswāmī saw Mahāprabhu in a dream. Of course, seeing him in a dream does not preclude the possibility of seeing him in person, and so Brzezinski's thesis in not necessarily accurate. See Jan Brzezinski, "Jīva Goswāmī: Biography and Bibliography," in the *Journal of Vaishnava Studies*, Volume 15, No. 2 (Spring, 2007), 54.

58. See Jan Brzezinski's three-part article on King Pratāparudra (http://jagadanandadas.blogspot.com/search/label/Prataparudra).

59. See Radhacharan Das (Ravi Bains), "The Disappearance Lila of Shri Chaitanya Mahaprabhu" (https://www.scribd.com/document/190193533/The-Disappearance-of-Shri-Chaitanya-Mahaprabhu-Paper). A similar incident is mentioned in the *Advaita Prakāśa* 21.63–66.

60. Śrīla A. C. Bhaktivedānta Swami Prabhupāda, recorded conversation with disciple Hayagrīva Dāsa, "Outline of Lord Chaitanya Play," San Francisco, April 5 & 6, 1967. (https://old.prabhupadavani.org/main/Conversations/128.html).

61. Bhaktivinoda Ṭhākura, *Sri Chaitanya Mahaprabhu: His Life and Precepts*, 24 (http://www.sevaashram.org/media-resources/written-word/math-publications/Srila-Bhaktivinoda-Thakur/Life-and-Precepts.pdf).

62. Bhaktisiddhānta Sarasvatī, *Rai Ramananda* (Madras: Shree Gaudiya Math, 1932; reprint, 1975), 28. Sarasvatī Ṭhākura seems to indicate that the Ṭoṭā-gopīnātha and Jagannāth versions can both be true. Indeed, when dealing with transcendental truths, such as the "birth" or "death" of God, would normal restrictions or limitations necessarily apply? As the tradition suggests: Just as Mahāprabhu entered seven *kīrtana* parties at the same time, so, too, can he, inconceivably, enter into several deities at once.

63. Tony K. Stewart confirms the Vasu Ghosh poem as an early source of this theory. See Stewart's thorough analysis of Mahāprabhu's departure: "When Biographical Narratives Disagree: The Death of Kṛṣṇa Caitanya." *Numen* 38, No. 2 (1991), 231–60. In addition to the two major theories, which are both accepted by the orthodox, there is a third: Mahāprabhu died of septic fever as a result of a foot injury. This latter version is only found in Jayānanda's *Caitanya-maṅgala* (Uttara-khaṇḍa 119–155), which is not accepted by the tradition and is likewise considered suspect from a scholarly perspective. The skepticism with which both scholars and devotees, in general, view Jayānanda's biography is summarized in the words of Walther Eidlitz: "This work, provided it is not a downright forgery, was unknown until the mid-18th century and it

is neither read nor recited by the followers of Caitanya . . . . The work contains dozens of historical errors and many untrustworthy events which are in contradiction to all other biographies." See Walther Eidlitz, *Krsna-Caitanya, The Hidden Treasure of India: His Life and His Teachings* (Kid Samuelsson 2014, based on the German original, *Krsna-Caitanya: Sein Leben und Seine Lehre*, Stockholm: Almqvist & Wiksell, 1968), 576.

64. *Caitanya-caritāmṛta,* Ādi 17.79–87.

65. *Caitanya-caritāmṛta,* Madhya 17.1.

66. *Caitanya-caritāmṛta*, Madhya 7.137–8.

67. *Caitanya-caritāmṛta,* Ādi 17.227–229, and *Caitanya-bhāgavata*, Madhya 25, the latter of which gives a more thorough account). Bhaktivinoda Ṭhākura developed the story further in *Śoka Śātana*, trans., Daśaratha-sūta Dāsa (Georgia: Nectar Books, n.d.).

68. *Caitanya-caritāmṛta,* Madhya 13.189–190.

69. *Caitanya-caritāmṛta,* Madhya 13.52: "Śrī Caitanya then exhibited another mystic power by performing *saṅkīrtana* simultaneously in all seven groups." (*āra eka śakti prabhu karila prakāśa, eka-kāle sāta ṭhāñi karila vilāsa*) Also see Ravīndra Svarūpa Dāsa, "Lord Caitanya at Ratha-yātrā" in *Back to Godhead*, Volume 19, No. 8 (1984), 27–32. (http://www.krishna.com/lord-chaitanya-ratha-yatra)

70. Bhaktivinode Ṭhākura, *Shri Chaitanya Mahaprabhu: His Life and Precepts* (Madras: Sree Gaudiya Math, 1896; reprint, 1984), 60–61.

71. The story appears in Narahari Chakravartī's 18th-century *Narottama-vilāsa*, in a rare Bengali appendix called the *Naraharir viśeṣa parichaya*, written by Ānanda-Nārāyana Maitra (one of Chakravartī's disciples). This version is adapted from Śacīnandana Swami's commentary on Verse Two of Raghunātha Dāsa Goswāmī's *Śrī Manaḥ-śikṣā: Splendid Instructions to the Mind*, Volume 2 (Hillsborough, NC: Padma, Inc., 2016), 289–290. This is my paraphrased rendering of his version.

Chapter 4

The World of *Bhakti*

The essence of Śrī Chaitanya's philosophy is embodied in one simple word: *bhakti*. Though it is often translated as "devotion," or "devotional service," and is primarily associated with Indic traditions, the followers of Mahāprabhu see it as more far-reaching than that: Addressed in various ways in the world religions, in various languages, it refers to the heart's nonsectarian adventure, begun when the soul's longing impels the search for a lasting love relationship with God. At that time, one embraces the methods for attaining him and the state in which one revels in him. This is all *bhakti*. Throughout history, it has been revealed by prophets according to the capacity of their respective audience, and in the ancient Vaishnava tradition it has been articulated as a complex science, with as much nuance and detail as the mind can accommodate.

OF ROOTS AND RELATIONSHIPS

If we look at Monier Williams' *Sanskrit-English Dictionary*, we find that *bhakti* and its various linguistic permutations—especially its verbal root √*bhaj*—have numerous meanings, including, primarily, "distribution," "partition," and "separation." It also refers to "division," "a portion," or "a share."[1] Williams considers these to be primary definitions because his method is chronological. That is to say, he begins by defining words in terms of literature that is considered the oldest, like the *Ṛg-veda*, perforce informing his readers as to how the words were used in that context.

Accordingly, in the earliest portions of the *Vedas*, *bhaj* was primarily understood as "sharing," "dividing," and "distribution," or even "participating in," while the noun *bhakta*, also derived from *bhaj*, meant "devotee," as it does today.[2] Finally, Monier Williams affirms that *bhakti* more generally means "attachment," "devotion," "fondness for," "devotion to," "trust," "homage," "worship," "piety," "faith," or "love (as a religious principle or means of salvation)."[3]

From a Vaishnava perspective, the earlier definitions for *bhaj* are intriguing. Consider, for example, the primary meanings of "separation" or "division." While *yoga*—to call upon another popular Indic concept—refers to "union," *bhakti* refers to a diametrically opposed phenomenon: "division." And yet the words are often used together, as in the compound Bhakti-yoga. Why is that? What is the harmonizing concept that allows division and union to be spoken of in the same breath?

Consider this: For there to be devotion or love, *there must be separation*. This is why the root *bhaj* has come to mean "worship": If there is division, there are at least "two," and when there are two, worship is possible. A unitary entity does not worship itself (except in extreme cases of narcissism). To quote a famous devotee, "I don't want to *become* sugar, I want to *taste* sugar." Sugar, of course, cannot taste itself.[4]

According to the followers of Śrī Chaitanya, then, "oneness" causes relationship to evaporate. We may wax poetic, romantically talking about the oneness of lovers, for example, but, in the end, for lovers to love, they must be two, not one. The reference to a so-called "oneness" in this usage is merely a feeling of complete harmony, of oneness in purpose, oneness in sensibility. Love, by extension, then, is a connection that dissolves all differences. But it is not ontological oneness. Rather, it is "twoness" that facilitates love. This was how Śrī Chaitanya appreciated and understood *bhakti*.

Thus, while the words *bhakti* and *yoga* might mean entirely opposite things,[5] they are aiming for the same goal: closeness or intimacy with God. And not just ordinary closeness, but a closeness so total and all-encompassing that one might call it a kind of oneness.

Indeed, the "origin" of the eternal phenomenon known as *bhakti* can be seen in the initial "separation" of Rādhā and Krishna—the supreme unitary Truth manifesting in two eternal forms, female and male Godhead, respectively. As stated in the *Caitanya-caritāmṛta* (Ādi 4.56): *rādhā-kṛṣṇa eka ātmā, dui deha dhari', anyonye vilase rasa āsvādana kari'*. ("Rādhā and Krishna are nondifferent, but they have taken on two bodies. Thus, they enjoy each other's essence, tasting the exchanges of love.") That is to say, the one absolute truth *divides* to enjoy relationship (*rasa*), which is the essence of *yoga*.

Further, in Gauḍīya Vaishnava theology, the idea of Vipralambha-bhāva or Viraha-bhakti, which is "love in separation," resonates with *bhakti* as defined in the earliest of Vedic texts: If one is separated from God, one might long for him, thereby enhancing one's love. For this reason,

Viraha-bhakti is considered the zenith of loving exchange with Krishna. It is Viraha-bhakti, in fact, that nourishes Sambhoga, or "union with God," a concept more in harmony with *yoga* as commonly defined. Both phases are considered perfect, but in separation there is an intense yearning that is naturally absent in union, making one's love more intense and, in the end, more fully developed.

DEVOTIONAL "SERVICE"

The traditional Vaishnava etymology of *bhakti* is revealing. If we look to the ancient *Garuḍa Purāṇa* (Pūrva-khaṇḍa 231.3) we find the verbal root *bhaj* explained as follows:

bhaj ity eṣa vai dhātuḥ
sevāyāṁ parikīrtitaḥ
tasmāt sevā budhaiḥ proktā
bhaktiḥ sādhana-bhūyasī

"The root *bhaj* is used to convey 'service.' Therefore, the wise explain *bhakti* as engagement in the service of the Lord, and as a yet better practice."

Sixteenth-century Vaishnava theologian Jīva Goswāmī quotes this verse in his *Bhakti Sandarbha* (Anuccheda 215) in an attempt to show what *bhakti* "really means." Śrī Jīva's 18th-century successor, Baladeva Vidyābhūṣaṇa, quotes this same verse in commenting on *Bhagavad-gītā* 6.47. Today, Western Sanskrit scholars also tend to acknowledge that *bhakti* means "service" as opposed to some abstract form of love. In the words of Karen Pechilis:

> *Bhakti* is "doing" something that is in honor of the divine—service, ritual worship, cleaning the temple, pilgrimage, reciting the divine name, singing hymns of praise. I would look for two criteria especially: The activity is generated by the devotee's love for the divine, and it is done by the devotee her or himself. Thus, as I've stated before, I think "participation" better captures the dynamic, with "devotional participation" as an accessible gloss.[6]

This translation—"devotional participation"—correlates with the teaching of Chaitanya Vaishnavism as expressed by Śrīla A. C. Bhaktivedānta Swami Prabhupāda. He consistently translated *bhakti* as "devotional *service*"—with an emphasis on active service. For Prabhupāda, *bhakti* was not a "lip service" kind of love. Rather, it meant action. As he would often say when explaining the ramifications of the word, "If you love me, then you do something for me. *Bhakti* is not just a matter of feelings."[7]

Here are some examples from his writing and lectures:

> The word *bhajate* is significant here. *Bhajate* has its root in the verb *bhaj*, which is used when there is need of service. The English word "worship" cannot be used in the same sense as *bhaj*. Worship means to adore, or to show respect and honor to the worthy one. But service with love and faith is especially meant for the Supreme Personality of Godhead. (*Bhagavad-gītā As It Is*, 6.47, Purport)
>
> *Bhakti* means application of love. *Bhaja sevayā*. When you love, you serve somebody. That is called *bhakti*. (Lecture on *Śrīmad Bhāgavatam*, 1.2.6, Hyderabad, November 26, 1972)[8]
>
> *Bhakti* means service, *bhaja-sevāyām*. The *bhaj-dhātu*, it is used for the purpose of rendering service, *bhaja*. And *bhaja*, there is Sanskrit grammar, *kti-pratyaya*, to make it noun. This is verb. So there are *pratyayas, kti pratyaya, ti pratyaya, many pratyayas*. So *bhaj-dhātu kti*, equal to *bhakti*. So *bhakti* means to satisfy Krishna. (Lecture on *Bhagavad-gītā*, 2.6, London, August 6, 1973)[9]

Thus, Prabhupāda was insistent on translating *bhakti* as "devotional service." One of his earliest disciples, Satsvarūpa Dāsa Goswāmī, in fact, notes this in his Introduction to the *Nārada Bhakti Sūtra*, and contemplates its implications:

> I was surprised, on receiving the translation for the first aphorism, to see how Śrīla Prabhupāda translated the word *bhakti*. The edition he was using translated *bhakti* as "devotion" or "Divine Love." But Śrīla Prabhupāda translated *bhakti* as "devotional service." Even by this one phrase he indicated that *bhakti* was active and personal. He would not tolerate any hint that *bhakti* was a state of impersonal "Love."[10]

Prabhupāda's articulation of *bhakti* as devotional service has support not only from the *Garuḍa Purāṇa*, Jīva Goswāmī, Baladeva Vidyābhūṣaṇa, and modern Sanskritists, as mentioned above, but also in terms of inherent word meaning: In the Sanskrit lexicon, there is a traditional text known as the *Dhātupāṭhaḥ* ("recitation of word origins"). It includes some 2,200 primary verbal roots from which all Sanskrit words derive. Interestingly, the *Dhātupāṭhaḥ* tells us that the meaning of the root *bhaj* is *sevā*, plain and simple, defined as "going or resorting to," "visiting," "service," "attendance on" . . . "to be in the service of," "worship," and "homage." In other words, it refers to active service.[11]

So, for the Gauḍīya tradition, *bhakti* means to participate in some form of devotional activity. In fact, the word is formed by adding the primary suffix "*ti*" to the root *bhaj*, which makes it an "action noun." A similar phenomenon exists in English. All English words ending in "-tion" are Latin action nouns, as in, for example, the words "motion," "portion," "participation," and "devotion." These are all nouns implying action, as opposed to passive cognitive states, and, interestingly, the "-tion" part of the word is cognate with the Sanskrit "*-ti*." In other words, implied in the word *bhakti* is the need to engage in active service, thus confirming the grammatical rigor, scholarly precision, and perspicuity of Prabhupāda's translation. This, as we can see, is true even in terms of standard grammar.

BHAKTI IN PRACTICE

Sixteenth-century Vaishnava master Rūpa Goswāmī, in many ways Śrī Chaitanya's most important follower, has compartmentalized *bhakti* into three categories: *sādhana*, *bhāva*, and *premā*, with exhaustive details on how to navigate one's way through each stage.

Sādhana-bhakti is *bhakti* in practice—at this stage, one might or might not have the emotional disposition of a devotee. Still, the aspiring practitioner intellectually understands the importance of *bhakti*, or at least the need to follow the rules and regulations facilitating spiritual advancement. He or she desires to act in a proper way, in accordance with scripture, perhaps because of an appreciation of pure devotion, or the desire to obtain a pure devotee's qualities.

Such practice, when executed with determination and persistence, can lead to Bhāva-bhakti, wherein spiritual emotions start to well in one's heart. At this stage, true love dawns, howbeit unfledged, and one begins to gain experiential knowledge of a higher order. A fortunate few will then graduate to Prema-bhakti—a rare state of enhanced God-consciousness, as exhibited by Mahāprabhu and his followers—and spiritual perfection is achieved.

The texts of the Goswāmīs offer elaborate instructions for such advancement, explaining how to gradually evolve from one level to the next and what to look for on one's spiritual journey, that is, how to gauge one's spiritual advancement. These classifications and categories were conceived by Rūpa Goswāmī in an attempt to delineate a methodical means for achieving heightened spiritual perfection, as seen in the person of Chaitanya Mahāprabhu.

It should be briefly noted here: There are two different forms of Sādhana-bhakti, one that is prompted by rules and regulations (Vaidhī-bhakti), as cited above, and the other a more passionate desire to follow in the footsteps of Krishna's eternal and spontaneous associates (Rāgānuga-bhakti), complete with an inner meditation specifically meant for this kind of practice.[12] The distinction between these two forms of *sādhana* will be explored more fully in an upcoming chapter.

For now, we offer the reader two verses from Rūpa Goswāmī's *Bhakti-rasāmṛta-sindhu,* and these will serve to define the essence of devotional life, whether one is a Vaidhī-sādhaka or a Rāgānuga-sādhaka. The first is Śrī Rūpa's own composition and the second is quoted from the *Nārada Pāñcaratra*:

ānyābhilāṣitā śunyaṁ jñāna-karmādy anāvṛtam
anukūlyena kṛṣṇānu-śīlanaṁ bhaktir-uttamam

"When the highest form of devotional service develops, one will be devoid of all material desires, knowledge obtained by monistic philosophy, and fruitive action. The devotee must constantly serve Krishna favorably, according to Krishna's desire" (1.1.11).

In other words, the topmost form of *bhakti*, for which all practitioners aspire, must be free from all impurities, even *karma* (fruitive action) and *jñāna* (knowledge that is superfluous to Krishna devotion). In short, pure *bhakti* is devoid of any attempt to attain material fulfillment, especially through the cultivation of mundane assets and material knowledge. Moreover, it is *favorable* cultivation of service to Krishna, that is, attempting to give Krishna what he wants with both a happy spirit and accommodating mood.

Śrīla A. C. Bhaktivedānta Swami Prabhupāda comments on this verse as follows:

> . . . Śrīla Rūpa Gosvāmī clearly states that if anyone wants to execute unalloyed devotional service, he must be freed from all kinds of material contamination. He must be freed from the association of persons who are addicted to fruitive activities and mental speculation. When, freed from such unwanted association and from the contamination of material desires, one favorably cultivates knowledge of Kṛṣṇa, that is called pure devotional service. *Ānukūlyasya saṅkalpaḥ prātikūlyasya varjanam* (*Hari-bhakti-vilāsa* 11.676). One should think of Kṛṣṇa and act for Kṛṣṇa favorably, not unfavorably. Kaṁsa was an enemy of Kṛṣṇa's. From the very beginning of Kṛṣṇa's birth, Kaṁsa planned in so many ways to kill Him . . . . Thus while working, while eating and while sleeping, he was always Kṛṣṇa conscious . . . but that Kṛṣṇa consciousness was not favorable, and therefore in spite of his always thinking of Kṛṣṇa twenty-four hours a day, he was considered a demon, and Kṛṣṇa at last killed him. Of course anyone who is killed by Kṛṣṇa attains salvation immediately, but that is not the aim of the pure devotee. The pure devotee does not even want salvation. He does not want to be transferred even to the highest planet, Goloka Vṛndāvana. His only objective is to serve Kṛṣṇa wherever he may be.[13]

The next verse from *Bhakti-rasāmṛta-sindhu*:

sarvopādhi-vinirmuktaṁ tat-paratvena nirmalam
hṛṣīkeṇa hṛṣīkeśa-sevanaṁ bhaktirucyate

"*Bhakti* necessitates using our senses in the service of the Lord, the master of the senses. When one renders such service, there are two corollary effects:

One is freed from all material designations, and one's senses are completely purified" (1.1.2).

In essence, these verses tell us that one who engages in pure *bhakti* is not distracted by anything else. While this is not expected of the novice, it is something to aspire for. In other words, the devotee gradually develops a desire to please Krishna (*anukūlyena*) in a consistent way (*ānu-śīlanaṁ*) and by so doing becomes situated in his or her constitutional position as an eternal servant of Krishna (*jīvera 'svarūpa' haya-krishnera 'nitya-dāsa'*).[14] As this occurs, albeit gradually, one finds that one's senses are becoming purified (*hṛṣīkeṇa*) and one no longer identifies with external designations, such as those arising from the material body (*sarvopādhi-vinirmuktaṁ*).

The spiritual master thus brings his disciples to ever higher levels of consciousness by engaging them in one (or several) of the nine types of devotional service as mentioned in the *Śrīmad Bhāgavatam* (7.5.23–24): "The process of devotion to Vishnu involves hearing, chanting and remembering him; it also involves serving his feet, worshiping, offering prayers, always considering oneself his eternal servant and friend and dedicating everything unto him. These nine dimensions of devotional service should be performed . . . ."

Jīva Goswāmī states in his *Krama-sandarbha-ṭīkā* on *Śrīmad Bhāgavatam* 7.5.23–24 that out of the nine processes of devotional service, *kīrtana*, or the loud chanting of the holy name, is most important. He encourages devotees to engage in the other processes, according to their nature, but by all means, he says, *kīrtana* should be embraced by all.

One last note in this regard: While the process of *bhakti* is initially meant to free one of all false designations (*sarvopādhi-vinirmuktaṁ*), it is also meant, in the advanced stages, to reveal one's eternal relationship with Krishna. In other words, it at first takes you away from whom you are *not*, and eventually allows you remembrance of whom you *are*. As Mahāprabhu says:

nāhaṁ vipro na ca nara-patir nāpi vaiśyo na śūdro
nāhaṁ varṇī na ca gṛha-patir no vanastho yatir vā
kintu prodyan-nikhila-paramānanda-pūrnāmṛtābdher
gopī-bhartuḥ pada-kamalayor dāsa-dāsānudāsaḥ

"I do not identify myself as a Brahmin, Kṣatriya, Vaiśya, or Śūdra. Nor am I a Brahmacārī, a Gṛhastha, a Vānaprastha or a Sannyāsī. I identify myself only as the servant of the servant of the servant of the lotus feet of Śrī Krishna, the maintainer of the *gopīs*. He is like an ocean of nectar and the cause of universal bliss" (Rūpa Goswāmī's *Padyāvali* 74).

In other words, *bhakti*, properly performed, will lead one away from illusory, temporary identification, and establish one in the Self, whereby one very gradually begins to recognize who one is in the spiritual world. While the above verse focuses on *gopī-bhāva*, Śrī Chaitanya's preferred emotion, it should be noted that there are five possible relationships with which one might interact with Krishna. These are, briefly, *śānta* (neutral, peaceful, and passive), *dāsya* (helpful, devoted, and service-oriented), *sakhya* (friendly, caring, and a sense of camaraderie), *vātsalya* (protective, nurturing, and parental), and *mādhurya* (intimate, romantic, and erotic)[15]:

tat-tad-bhā' vādi-mādhurye
śrute dhīr yad apekṣate
nātra śāstraṁ na yuktiṁ ca
tal lobhotpatti-lakṣaṇam

"When an advanced, realized devotee hears about the activities of the devotees in Vrindāvan—with their loving relationships of *śānta, dāsya, sakhya, vātsalya* and *mādhurya*—he becomes inclined in that way, and his intelligence becomes attracted. Indeed, he begins to passionately desire that particular type of devotion. When such a desire is awakened, one's intelligence no longer depends on the instruction of *śāstra*, revealed scripture, logic or argument." (*Bhakti-rasāmṛta-sindhu,* 1.2.292, quoted in *Caitanya-caritāmṛta*, Madhya 22.155.)[16] This subject will be discussed more thoroughly in Chapters Eight and Nine, which focus on Mahāprabhu's esoteric conversation with Rāmānanda Rāya and Rāgānuga-bhakti, respectively.

TRADITIONAL DEFINITIONS

The above will suffice as a general definition of *bhakti* as explained by Mahāprabhu and his successors. There are other, related, definitions, however, that may be helpful, and these should be acknowledged as well.

Chapter Two of the *Nārada Bhakti Sūtra* (NBS), for example, is called "Defining Bhakti" and it includes the insights of various sages—our analysis of *bhakti* would be incomplete without recourse to their comments: Vyāsadeva, the compiler of the Vedic literature, for example, says that *bhakti* is "adoring attachment for worshiping God in various ways" (NBS 2.16). Gargamuni, another great Vedic sage, augments this definition by adding that "*bhakti* engenders a certain fondness for narrations about the Lord, by the Lord, and so on" (NBS 2.17). Śāṇḍilya, famous for writing texts on devotion and mysticism, offers, somewhat cryptically, "*bhakti* results when one removes all obstructions to taking pleasure in the Supreme Self" (NBS 2.18).

While all of these definitions have merit, Nārada himself, like Rūpa Goswāmī, points to exclusive *bhakti* as best summarizing what the word actually means. He tells us that, "the highest form of devotional service consists of offering one's every act to the Supreme Lord and feeling extreme distress in forgetting him" (NBS 2.19). Ultimately, he says, "the cowherd women of Vraja (the *gopīs*) are emblems of the purest form of *bhakti*, for they gave Krishna everything, heart and soul, asking for nothing in return" (NBS 2.21). This is the essence of Chaitanyite *bhakti*.

It might also be pointed out that, according to the *Bhakti-rasāmṛta-sindhu* (1.1.18), there are six characteristics of *bhakti*: (1) it bestows all auspiciousness; (2) it renders liberation insignificant; (3) it destroys all misery; (4) it is rarely achieved; (5) it brings intense blissfulness; and (6) it is capable of attracting Krishna—and in fact it is the only thing that attracts him.

In terms of this sixth point, one can only marvel at the power of *bhakti*. But this is the magic of pure devotion. Krishna says it himself in the *Bhagavad-gītā* (18.55), "One can fully know me only by unmotivated devotional service" (*bhaktyā mām abhijānāti*). And he confirms it again in the *Bhāgavatam* (11.14.21): "Only by single-minded devotional service am I attainable" (*bhaktyāham ekayā grāhyaḥ*). The *Māthara-sruti* makes it clear: "Devotion attracts him, devotion reveals him; the Lord is influenced by devotion. Nothing is more powerful than devotion (*bhakti*)."[17]

There is one final point about the word itself, at least in terms of its essential definition. We initially said that *bhakti* means, among other things, "to share." Indeed, scholars from Harvard University's "Pluralism Project" have noted this derivation and have emphasized its value in terms of cooperation among the world's religions.[18]

That being said, it is significant that Gauḍīya Vaishnavism includes a major tenet known as "the Saṅkīrtana principle." What this means, in essence, is that part of the process is *sharing* Krishna-bhakti with others. Sometimes it is done by going out and chanting in public places; it can also be accomplished through public lecturing, or in the distribution of books or sacred foodstuffs (*prasādam*), and so on. The main point is that one who has *bhakti* naturally wants to give it to others. It is a matter of sharing something precious, which is a natural impulse in caring souls. Like love or kindness, *bhakti* increases in the souls of those who share it. It is enhanced by apportionment, not diminished. And, remarkably, all of this is embedded in the word itself.

THE BHAKTI MOVEMENT

Apropos of this sharing principle, *bhakti* has historically emerged as a "movement" with outreach that extended, initially, throughout the Indian subcontinent, and, eventually, the world. Though it has certainly not manifested as a unified, singular conglomerate of devotees as such, but rather as a disparate coterie of somewhat related traditions, loosely based on the same methods and principles, they all share a will to spread out and offer their fruits to others.[19] John Stratton Hawley's recent book, *A Storm of Songs*,[20] explains this movement well, even as he muses on how it is both a movement and not a movement, how each segment or regional incarnation of the *bhakti* phenomenon so clearly relates to one another while at the same time originates under different circumstances and thus expresses itself differently. In a recent interview, he notes:

> . . . this is one of the great mysteries: for instance, how did the *padas* of Jayadev relate to the contemporary *patikams* of the Tamil country? Tagore wondered about this. As we zero in on close connections between Marathi *abhangs*, Gujarati *padas*, Hindi *pads*, and Telugu *padams*, the mystery becomes more palpable: how did these close echoes between different language streams get formed in historical time? Yet there it is: it did happen—the handful of verses in each *pada*, the presence of rhyme and metre, the vocal register, and very importantly the name of the poet as a "seal" at the end. The fact that different languages could in this way talk the same language is a wonder. And the fact that different individuals with different regional and social associations could be named there adds *masala* to this single metrical, musical form.[21]

The Bhakti movement, as such, might be traced, in its early stages, to the 7th through 12th centuries, with the Śaivite Nāyanmārs, yes, but more importantly for our purposes, the Ālvārs, the twelve Vaishnava poet-saints from Tamil country who were "drenched" or "immersed" (*ālvār*) in devotion to Krishna in his many forms.[22] Based on Puranic literature, such as the *Bhāgavatam*, and assorted tantric texts, in particular, the Vaishnava *ācāryas* began to emerge and preach their respective doctrines according to personal realization and inspiration, allowing for the systemization of distinct *sampradāyas*. This gave way to an especially rich period of creativity, in terms of *bhakti*'s outward expression—painting, poetry, and the arts—ranging, in its most intense form, from perhaps the 14th to 16th centuries. We have already noted the all-important songs of Jayadeva, Caṇḍīdāsa, and Vidyāpati, but there were many others. Bards and mystics, such as Rāmānanda, Sūrdāsa, Tulsīdāsa, and Tyāgarāja made similar contributions, developing Vaishnava themes in their own distinct ways, the above mainly through devotional lyric.

It was at this point, too, that the "movement," if we can call it that, began to show just how diverse it can be, particularly by articulating two different streams in the *bhakti* tradition: *saguṇa* ("God with attributes") and *nirguṇa* ("God without attributes").[23] The latter construction became particularly popular in Maharashtra, Rajasthan, and the Punjab, with poets like Jñāneśvara, Nāmdeva, Eknātha, and Tukārāma.[24] Their poetry, beautiful though it was, espoused a doctrine in which God is formless—a divine being who is wholly impersonal, an abstraction that can be felt but not seen. This, of course, ran counter to the Vaishnavism of the four traditional lineages, whose practitioners often found it confusing, that is, a bit too close to Śaṅkara's Advaita Vedānta.

This "*nirguṇī*" tradition has often confounded scholars, too, because it offers, as David Lorenzen notes, "heart-felt devotion to a God without attributes, without even any definable personality."[25] Scholars thus naturally wonder how such a thing is even possible. Wendy Doniger concludes that it isn't, and that *nirguṇa-bhakti* is basically a misnomer, an invention by the later tradition: "*Nirguṇa-bhakti* is . . . an Irish bull (or, as the Hindus say, *vandhyāputra* '[as meaningless as] the son of a barren woman).' . . . [It] is a concoction that monistic Hindu philosophers imposed upon a *saguṇa-bhakti* tradition that managed, somehow, to absorb it."[26]

The Gauḍīya tradition would concur. In the *Caitanya-caritāmṛta*, Madhya 17.129, therefore, Mahāprabhu is quoted as saying, "Māyāvādīs or impersonalists are offenders to Lord Krishna." (*māyāvādī kṛṣṇe aparādhī*) And, further, in Madhya 6.169, "If one follows the commentaries of Māyāvādī philosophers, all real understanding is doomed." (*māyāvādi-bhāṣya śunile haya sarva-nāśa*). Due to his unabashed love for Krishna, Mahāprabhu could not tolerate anyone denying the Lord's form, or relegating him to mere abstraction.

This is not to suggest that practitioners of the *nirguṇa* path did not have a role to play and were not appreciated on a certain level, even in Mahāprabhu's form of *bhakti*. After all, his Acintya-bhedābheda doctrine would accommodate both impersonal and personal schools of thought. (See our upcoming chapter on this subject.) He accepted God as both Brahman (impersonal) and as Bhagavān (the Supreme Person), and even appreciated the Lord's all-pervasive feature (Paramātmā) as well. But even here there are hierarchical considerations. Bhagavān is more inclusive, more complete, embracing and accommodating the other two.

In other words, there are forms of *bhakti* that are considered "weak," and forms that are considered "strong." The more impersonal aspects offer less in the way of *bhakti*'s greatest assets, diminishing the accomplishment of her practitioners, whereas the more personal dimension can easily catapult one to the summit of *bhakti* experience. This is because the essence of *bhakti* is love, and love, again, is an exchange between *people*. One cannot love an abstraction or an impersonal force. But you *can* love a person.

Krishna says this directly in the *Bhagavad-gītā* (Chapter 12, verses 1–7): Arjuna asks him about his preference regarding his devotees, or about whose understanding he considers more perfect: those who engage in devotional service, directed toward him as a person, or those who worship the impersonal Brahman, the unmanifested. Krishna answers that it is the former, the one whose mind is fixed on his personal form, that is greater, although those who worship the unmanifested, which lies beyond the senses—they, too, will achieve him, even if their journey will be more arduous.

This notion of *bhakti* as being either weak or strong, less effective or more effective, is alluded to in the *Bhāgavata-māhātmya* (1.48–50), six short chapters that traditionally form a part of the *Padma Purāṇa*.[27]

Composed in the form of a dialogue between Nārada and Bhakti personified, the *Māhātmya* tells us about a journey, "*bhakti*'s journey," with various geographical regions that either nurture her or find her virtually incapacitated. She begins in Draviḍa, in the south, and matures in Karnataka. From there, she journeys to Maharashtra and Gujarat, but something interesting happens during this leg of her journey. She is weakened and becomes almost unrecognizable due to illness. Her two "sons," knowledge and renunciation, weaken her further, for they are often not genuine, and, besides, they miss the essential point of *bhakti*. But the ending is a happy one: She arrives in Vrindāvan and is rejuvenated. She is lovely once again, reinstated in her original blissful form.

The weakened state, where she loses her charm, seems to occur during the Maharashtrian/Gujarat sojourn, and this conforms to our thesis of *saguṇa*- versus *nirguṇa-bhakti*. Indeed, it is here, in the Maharashtra region, that *nirguṇa-bhakti* rose to the fore, emphasizing the formless and impersonal aspect of divinity.

Interesting, too, is that she reaches her height in Vrindāvan, bringing us back to the Chaitanya tradition, which might be considered the zenith of personalist philosophy. Shrivatsa Goswami makes careful note of the Chaitanyaite ending to this story,

> So this gives, beautifully, the historical development of the medieval *bhakti* tradition. The *bhakti* movement took birth in South India with the Dravidian saints, the Ālvārs, and so on. Then, a little later, Rāmānuja, the first systematic philosopher of *bhakti*, appeared in the Tamil country . . . . After Rāmānuja, the next great devotional thinker was Mādhva, who was born in Karnataka at the end of the twelfth century. After that, the movement got a big boost from different saints who appeared throughout India, including Maharashtra, during the fourteenth, fifteenth, and sixteenth centuries. These centuries were very crucial for the growth of the *bhakti* movement. But the *bhakti* movement did not attain its highest development, as the passage implies, until it reached Vrindāvan. [*Bhakti* reached Vrindāvan], of course, in the form of Chaitanya Mahāprabhu because it was Chaitanya who, along with his followers the Six Goswāmis, was the founder of Vrindāvan in the early part of the sixteenth century. So the whole history of the *bhakti* movement is summarized here quite beautifully.[28]

Śrī Chaitanya Mahāprabhu represents the culmination of the *bhakti* movement, with his "Saṅkīrtana Movement" the highpoint of the tradition. Apropos of this, congregational chanting (*saṅkīrtana*), inevitably associated with Mahāprabhu himself, is considered the heart of the entire *bhakti* enterprise.

As the *Caitanya-caritāmṛta*, Antya 4.70–71 tells us, "In the realm of *bhakti*, the ninefold path is best.[29] This is because it has the uncanny ability to give one both Krishna and love for Krishna. And among all nine options, chanting the holy name (*nāma-saṅkīrtana*) is supreme, for if one chants without offense, one easily attains the treasure of divine love."[30] Let us now look more closely at the highly esteemed chanting process of the Gauḍīya Vaishnavas.

NOTES

1. Sir M. Monier Williams, *A Sanskrit-English Dictionary* (Delhi: Motilal Banarsidass Publishers, India, 1993 reprint), 743. It should be noted that, traditionally, *bhakti* is etymologically related to two root-words: Most commonly, as stated, it is traced to "*bhaj*," which is defined above. But it is also sometimes traced to "*bhañj*," which refers to "breaking apart" or "splitting." This definition, of course, is included in the meaning of *bhaj* as well. See Monier Williams, *A Sanskrit-English Dictionary, Etymologically and Philologically Arranged, With Special Reference to Greek, Latin, Gothic, German, Anglo-Saxon, and Other Cognate Indo-European Languages* (Oxford: The Clarendon Press, 1862), 695–696. Some say that *bhañj* is just a nasalized extension of *bhaj*.

2. Ibid.

3. Ibid. Interestingly, we find in the *Śvetāśvatara Upanishad* (6.23) one of the earliest uses of the word *bhakti*, and here it has been translated as "love of God." Quoted in W. N. Brown, *Man in the Universe: Some Continuities in Indian Thought* (Berkeley: University of California Press, 1970), 38–39.

4. Ironically, this quote is often attributed to Ramprasad Sen (1718–1775), a Śākta poet who, according to most Vaishnavas, is associated with monistic philosophy (http://www.poemhunter.com/i/ebooks/pdf/ramprasad_sen_2012_8.pdf).

5. The word *yoga*, from the Sanskrit word *yuj,* means to yoke or bind and is often interpreted as "union" or "oneness," first as oneness with one's own body and mind, then with nature, and finally with God.

6. Personal correspondence with Karen Pechilis, Chair of Department and Professor of Asian and Comparative Religions, Drew University (May 5, 2014). She also eloquently says, "The word *bhakti* should not be understood as uncritical emotion, but as committed engagement." See *The Embodiment of Bhakti* (New York: Oxford University Press, 2014), 19–21.

7. As is often the case, Prabhupāda may here be following the cue of his spiritual master, Bhaktisiddhānta Sarasvatī, who in at least one specific instance wrote of *bhakti* as "devotion, service." See Ferdinando Sardella, *Modern Hindu Personalism: The History, Life, and Thought of Bhaktisiddhānta Sarasvatī* (Oxford University Press, 2013), 205–206: "In his introduction to Bhaktivinoda's book *Sree Caitanya Mahaprabhu: His Life and Precepts*, completed on July 15th, 1924 . . . . [Bhaktisiddhānta Sarasvatī] translates the word *bhakti* not merely as 'devotion,' but as 'devotional service,' conveying the idea of practical engagement rather than contemplation."

8. Lecture available online: http://vaniquotes.org/wiki/Love_of_Godhead_means

9. Lecture available online: http://vaniquotes.org/wiki/This_bhakti_word_is_applicable_only_in_relationship_with_God,_or_Krsna

10. Of course, there were exceptions where Prabhupāda translated *bhakti* as merely "devotion," especially when context demanded it. One prominent example is the title of his book, *The Nectar of Devotion*, which is a translation of the Sanskrit phrase, *Bhakti-rasāmṛta-sindhu*. He could have translated it "The Nectar of Devotional Service," but he didn't. There are other instances, too, but overall he preferred the more accurate "devotional service."

11. *Dhātupāṭhaḥ*, ed., J. L. Shastri (Delhi: Motilal Banarsidass, reprint 1996), Column 1, 22. I am grateful to Gaura Keshava Dasa (Greg Jay) for this reference.

12. Rāgānuga-sādhana begins when one develops *lobha* or *laulyam* (spiritual yearning or even "greed"). As a result of this *lobha*, one learns to meditate on one's eternal spiritual form (*siddha-rūpa*), but such *smaraṇa* (remembrance) is difficult to practice. Thus, one must accept the guidance of a spiritual preceptor who is expert in this discipline. (See *Bhakti-rasāmṛta-sindhu*, 1.2.295) Along these lines, there are higher echelon aspects to the science of *bhakti*, such as Rasa Tattva, wherein one learns about the five types of relationships one may have with God in the spiritual world, as already discussed.

13. See A. C. Bhaktivedānta Swami Prabhupāda, *Bhagavad-gītā As It Is* (Los Angeles: Bhaktivedanta Book Trust, 1972), 11.55, purport.

14. *Caitanya-caritāmṛta,* Madhya 108–109 (*jīvera 'svarūpa' haya-kṛṣṇera 'nitya-dāsa'kṛṣṇera 'taṭasthā-śakti' 'bhedābheda-prakāśa'sūryāṁśa-kiraṇa, yaiche agni-jvālā-cayasvābhāvika kṛṣṇera tina-prakāra 'śakti' haya*).

15. Interestingly, while all of these relationships are considered equal, that is, Krishna relishes each and every one of them (even if *śānta* is not counted among the higher relationships), there is simultaneously a hierarchy here: As one analyzes the *rasas* from *śānta* to *mādhurya*, one sees a progression in complexity in which the qualities of the prior one are found in the latter one, which is always more inclusive. In the end, *mādhurya* accommodates the qualities of all the rest. In the words of Tony Stewart: "While *dāsya* may include elements of *śānta*, *sakhya* will embrace both, and *vātsalya* all four. Only *śṛṅgāra* [*mādhurya*] can range through the full permutation of forms, for lovers variously experience the feelings of friendship, of being a parent or a child, of being a servant, and even being overawed by the mate." See Tony K. Stewart, *The Final Word*, op. cit., 211. For more, see *Caitanya-caritāmṛta*, Madhya 8.86: "As the qualities increase, so the taste also increases in each and every relationship. Therefore the qualities found in *śānta-rasa, dāsya-rasa*, *sakhya-rasa* and *vātsalya-rasa* are all manifested in conjugal love (*mādhurya-rasa*)."

16. This verse describes the dawning of *rāgānugā-bhakti*. It is Prabhupāda's translation.

17. The *Māthara-sruti* is quoted in Swami B. P. Puri Maharaja, *Art of Sādhana: A Guide to Daily Devotion* (San Francisco, California: Mandala Publishing Group, 1994), 14.

18. "The word *bhakti*, from a root meaning 'to share,' conveys the sense of 'sharing' inherent in the love of God." (See http://www.pluralism.org/religion/hinduism/introduction/bhakti, Accessed on May 10, 2014)

19. Intellectual historian Krishna Sharma problematizes the entire notion of the Bhakti Movement, particularly its origins, contending that it was largely formulated or conceived by Western Indologists and their Christian orientation. See Krishna Sharma, *Bhakti and the Bhakti Movement: A New Perspective* (New Delhi: Munshiram Manoharlal, 1987), 32–36.

20. John Stratton Hawley, *A Storm of Songs: India and the Idea of the Bhakti Movement* (Cambridge: Harvard University Press, 2015).

21. See Anuradhan Raman's interview with John Stratton Hawley in *The Hindu* (January 10, 2016), "*Bhakti* challenges communal religion" (http://www.thehindu.com/opinion/'Bhakti-challenges-communal-religion'/article13990462.ece).

22. Friedhelm Hardy, *Viraha-Bhakti: The Early History of Kṛṣṇa Devotion in South India* (Delhi: Oxford University Press, 1983). See also *Journal of Vaishnava Studies* Volume 22, No. 2 (Spring 2014), special issue on the Ālvārs.

23. It can be argued, as Jack Hawley does, that there was once a time and mindset in which the strict polarization of *nirguṇa* and *saguṇa* was considered unimportant or even nonexistent. "Yet it is worth asking just how true-to-life this dichotomy is, how long has it actually been felt?" muses Hawley. See John Stratton Hawley, *Three Bhakti Voices: Mirabai, Surdas, and Kabir in Their Times and Ours* (New Delhi: Oxford University Press, 2005), 71. In this connection, it should be noted that the term *nirguṇa* can also mean, "God without 'material' qualities," as opposed to "God without any attributes at all." The former would be acceptable to most Vaishnavas, for God's characteristics are necessarily spiritual, whereas the latter would be considered inaccurate and even offensive.

24. See Winand M. Calewaert, "The Name in Nirgun Bhakti," in the *Journal of Vaishnava Studies*, Volume 2, No. 2 (Spring 1994), 163–174.

25. David Lorenzen, *Praises to a Formless God: Nirguṇī Texts from North India* (New York: State University of New York Press, 1996), 2.

26. Wendy Doniger, *On Hinduism* (New York: Oxford University Press, 2014), 152.

27. See John Stratton Hawley, *A Storm of Songs*, op. cit., 59–98. See also Interview with Shrivatsa Goswami in Steven J. Gelberg, ed., *Hare Krishna, Hare Krishna: Five Distinguished Scholars on the Krishna Movement in the West* (New York: Grove Press, 1983), 211–212.

28. Shrivatsa Goswami, ibid., 212. Shrivatsa also analyzes the word *videśam* in the *Bhāgavata-māhātmya*. He interprets it as meaning "not this country," indicating that *bhakti* would travel abroad, that she would, in fact, move "outside the subcontinent" due to the efforts of Swami Prabhupāda, who brought her to western shores. This is the reading that Shrivatsa offers in his commentary (244–245).

29. Again, though mentioned above, the nine process are "hearing, chanting and remembering him; serving his feet, worshiping, offering prayers, always considering oneself his eternal servant and friend and dedicating everything unto him."

30. *bhajanera madhye śreṣṭha nava-vidhā bhaktikṛṣṇa-prema, kṛṣṇa dite dhare mahā-śakti tāra madhye sarva-śreṣṭha nāma-saṅkīrtana niraparādhe nāma laile pāya prema-dhana.*

Chapter 5

The Nectar of the Holy Name

Kīrtana means glorification of Lord Krishna. It refers to loud recitation of the holy name, whether alone or in a group, but is most commonly used for call-and-response chanting. It is a central practice for all Vaishnavas, especially those in the Gauḍīya tradition. *Saṅkīrtana*, which is sometimes used interchangeably with *kīrtana*, has an expanded meaning: The prefix *saṅ* means "complete" or "in association." So *saṅkīrtana* refers to "complete glorification" or "chanting with others." It is mainly used to connote "many persons coming together to chant and dance for Krishna's pleasure."

The notion of *kīrtana* goes back to the *Vedas*, where priests are described as "telling, narrating, and describing" (*anukīrtana*, *anukṛti*) the glories of the divine. According to Monier Williams, the Sanskrit root *kīrt* means, "to mention, tell, name, call, recite, repeat, relate, declare, communicate, commemorate, celebrate, praise, or glorify."[1] This derivation was expanded in Puranic literature, where it is used as devotional "singing" or "call-and-response chanting," as it is defined today.

There are various kinds of *kīrtana*—*nāma-kīrtana* (chanting Krishna's names), *guṇa-kīrtana* (chanting about his qualities), *rūpa-kīrtana* (chanting about his form), *līlā-kīrtana* (chanting about his activities) and *parikara-kīrtana* (glorifying his associates)—and the Vaishnava community embraces them all.

Unsurprisingly, from region to region the flavors evolve, transform, and transmogrify, the nomenclatures change, and notable nuances appear. All of these permutations are attributable to the varieties of regional and cultural influence. Still, whether it is called Abhang (among devotees of Krishna in Maharashtra), Samaj Gayan (for those in the Nimbārka, Haridāsī, or Rādhāvallabha Sampradāyas), Haveli Sangeet (in the Puṣṭi-mārga of Vallabhāchārya), or what have you, it is still the same basic principle of glorifying the supreme through musical vocalizing, and its practice goes back to the earliest moments of spiritual longing.[2]

In pre-Chaitanya Bengal, *kīrtana* was generally referred to as Pālā-kīrtana, or Padāvalī-kīrtana, which is extended narrative poetry parlayed in strikingly embellished language. This developed into a powerful spiritual technique by Mahāprabhu's time, with specific styles and approaches peculiar to the Gauḍīya tradition. Still, Śrī Chaitanya himself gave special emphasis to Nāma-kīrtana, or the chanting of the holy names, in a simple and straightforward manner, for reasons that will be discussed below.

Soon after Mahāprabhu's manifest pastimes, however, Narottama Dāsa Ṭhākura (1534–1625?) and others developed *kīrtana* further, reinvigorating the older Padāvalī-kīrtana tradition.[3] Narottama himself was a consummate musician, and as a poet his literary contribution is of bardic stature. Indeed, he was to become one of the most renowned devotional singers of his time. His approach to Padāvalī-kīrtana included highly ornamented music replete with rhythmic (*tāla*) and melodic (*rāga*) complexity, as well as episodic dance movements depicting a farrago of intense emotions (*nāṭyam*), often displaying impeccable interpretive and improvisational artistry.

He would begin his *kīrtana* with Gaurachandrikā lyrics, or chanting in glorification of Mahāprabhu. This was a new development in the realm of Padāvalī-kīrtana. Only after introducing the chanting session with a song about Mahāprabhu would the singer allow it to morph into Rādhā-Krishna *kīrtana*, using lyrics that show parallels between the golden Lord and the blackish one.

Narottama's *kīrtana* starts slowly and meditatively, provoking thought about the words being uttered, but then builds momentum until those participating find themselves in an excited state of heightened bliss. His method came to be known as Garāṇhāṭi, after a subdivision of Kheturī, his hometown in Bangladesh. Garāṇhāṭi *kīrtana* is said to be "the Bengali equivalent of classical Dhrupad,"[4] which is high praise in Indian musicological circles.

During Narottama's lifetime and soon thereafter, other forms of *kīrtana*, with styles distinctly their own, also arose, including Śrīnivāsa's Manoharśāhi and three others: Reṇeti, Mandārini, and Jhārakhandi. While there are experts who still know the intricacies of these medieval techniques, they are few and far between. Overall, the classical forms are fading from memory. Thankfully, however, *kīrtana* is ultimately an affair of the heart, and no loss of technique can diminish its spiritual potency.

SCRIPTURAL SUPPORT

Among all forms of *kīrtana*, *nāma-saṅkīrtana* is considered best. Śrīla Sanātana Goswāmī, one of the earliest saints of the Gauḍīya Vaishnava tradition, confirms this in his seminal work, the *Bṛhad-bhāgavatāmṛta* (2.3.158):

> *kṛṣṇasya nānā-vidha-kīrtaneṣu*
> *tan-nāma-saṅkīrtanam eva mukhyam*
> *tat-prema-sampat-janane svayaṁ drāk*
> *śaktaṁ tataḥ śreṣṭha-tamaṁ mataṁ tat*

"*Nāma-saṅkīrtana* is considered primary among the various types of Krishna-*kīrtana*. This is because it has the power to quickly invoke the highest love for him."

Sanātana Goswāmī bases his glorification of *kīrtana* on the all-important *Śrīmad Bhāgavatam,* which also underlines the importance of faith in the name and chanting it profusely (*nāma-śravaṇa, nāma-saṅkīrtana*).

Soon after the *Bhāgavatam* opens, we are confronted with a basic existential question: "What is the duty of a man who is about the die?" After a number of verses meant to establish and augment the text's essential narrative, the initial answer to this question is found in 2.1.5, which hints at the importance of *nāma-saṅkīrtana*: "Hear this, descendant of King Bhārata: The Lord vanquishes all miseries for those souls who hear about, glorify (*kīrtitavyaḥ*), and remember him."[5]

Several verses later, it is stated more directly (2.1.11): "O King, those who consistently chant the holy name of Hari (*nāmānukīrtanam*) will know freedom from doubt and fear and ultimately achieve success. This is true even for those who are desirous of material enjoyment, those who are free from material desires, and even for those who are already self-satisfied, like the *yogīs*."[6]

Significantly, the *Bhāgavatam*'s very last verse (12.13.23) also supports chanting the name: "[Śukadeva says:] I offer my deepest respects unto the Supreme Lord, Hari, for the congregational chanting of his holy name (*nāma-saṅkīrtanaṁ*) destroys all sinful reactions, and upon offering obeisance unto him, one becomes relieved of all material misery."[7] Thus, the *Bhāgavatam*'s first teaching and its last are both about *nāma-saṅkīrtana*, highlighting its central importance not only for the Vaishnava tradition in general but for Śrī Chaitanya's Vaishnavism in particular.

The *Caitanya-caritāmṛta* (Ādi 7.93) also confirms that *nāma-saṅkīrtana* is at the heart of the *Bhāgavatam*'s many teachings. Spoken by Śrī Chaitanya himself, the text reads as follows: "My spiritual master taught me a verse from the *Śrīmad-Bhāgavatam*," says Mahāprabhu. "It is the essence of all the *Bhāgavatam*'s instructions. Therefore, he recited this verse again and again."[8]

So, which of the many *Bhāgavatam* verses is Śrī Chaitanya referring to? The *Caitanya-caritāmṛta* is clear. It is 11.2.40: "By eagerly chanting the holy name of the Lord (*nāma-kīrtyā*), one develops attachment for him. Soon, the heart melts with ecstatic love, and the chanter laughs loudly or cries or shouts. Sometimes he sings and dances like a madman, indifferent to public opinion."[9] Thus, the importance of *nāma-saṅkīrtana* is firmly established in the Gauḍīya tradition.

Moreover, it is said that nothing can compromise the efficacy of the holy name, even if the chanter has glaring disqualifications. For example, the *Bhāgavatam* (6.16.44) informs us that if a *caṇḍāla* (outcaste, untouchable) hears the name but once, he or she can be freed from the cycle of birth and death.

Along similar lines, the *Bhāgavatam* relates the story of Ajāmila, an errant, elderly Brahmin who calls out the name of his son Nārāyaṇa while on his deathbed. And because his son's name is also a name for God, Ajāmila achieves liberation. Thus, by even indirectly calling upon the divine name, one achieves the goal of spiritual life.[10] (Still, it should be noted that the Ajāmila text (6.2.49) promotes calling out the name with faith and love, *śraddhayā*, even if, in this case, it was love for his son.)

Commentator Viśvanātha Chakravartī says that, in point of fact, the very day Ajāmila named his son Nārāyaṇa, all his sins were already excused, so formidable is the strength of the name.[11] Later, as mentioned, he was liberated, or saved from hell, because of his inadvertent chanting, even though such chanting is only a shadow of divine sound (*nāmābhāsa*). After this, the narrative goes on to relate that a chastened Ajāmila, having seen the error of his ways, went on pilgrimage to Haridwar, where he engaged in *sādhana*, perfected his chanting, and gradually attained pure love of God.[12] None of this would have been possible without the grace and mercy of the name, despite the fact that, in this instance, it was initially chanted in a compromised way.

What the story is really meant to show is that if one can achieve great heights with even a semblance of the holy name, what might be possible if one chants purely? This is called Kaimutya-nyāya, or the logic of "how much more so." For example, one might say, "If this small fire is hot enough to melt iron, how much more quickly and efficiently would a large fire melt it?"[13] In the present context, the reader is left with the idea that, "If Ajāmila—who was not a seasoned, pure-hearted chanter but only calling out for his son—could achieve a liberated state by his imperfect intonation of the name, how much might I achieve if I actually applied myself?" In this way, the tradition hopes to encourage its earnest practitioners.

The tradition tells us that whether one chants imperfectly or while in a state of pure love—chanting is without doubt the recommended process for Kali-yuga, and all souls are encouraged to take part in it.

Mahāprabhu's premier spokesmen, such as Sanātana and Rūpa Goswāmīs, praise the chanting of the name as the best of all possible endeavors. For example, Sanātana, in his *Bṛhad-bhāgavatāmṛta* (1.9), writes: "All glories, all glories to the all-blissful form of Krishna's name, which causes his devotees to give up all conventional religious duties, meditation, and worship. When one utters it even once, it grants supreme liberation. This is the highest nectar. It is my very life and my only treasure."[14]

Similarly, Rūpa Goswāmī writes in his *Nāmāṣṭaka* (verse 2): "All glories, all glories unto the holy name, who is the abode of blissful nectar, the supreme truth incarnate in a perfect combinations of letters. In order to shower blessings on your own devotees, you have appeared as your names, thus showing the greatest compassion on everyone."[15]

It is in Śrī Rūpa's work, too, that we find perhaps the most famous Gauḍīya Vaishnava verse on the holy name, one that clearly shows how deeply esteemed and revered it is in the tradition:

> *tuṇḍe tāṇḍavinī ratiṁ vitanute tuṇḍāvalī-labdhaye*
> *karṇa-kroḍa-kaḍambinī ghaṭayate karṇārbudebhyaḥ spṛhām*
> *cetaḥ-prāṅgaṇa-saṅginī vijayate sarvendriyāṇāṁ kṛtiṁ*
> *no jāne janitā kiyadbhir amṛtaiḥ kṛṣṇeti varṇa-dvayī*

"I cannot calculate how much sweet nectar one can find in the two syllables 'Krish-na.' When this name is chanted, it appears to dance in one's mouth. As a result, we naturally desire numerous mouths. Similarly, when the name enters our ears, we desire many millions of ears. And when it dances in the courtyard of the heart, it conquers the movements of the mind, making all the senses inert."[16] Quotes such as these are plenteous and could be the subject of many volumes.[17]

Gauḍīya Vaishnavas teach that, ideally, one should hear the holy name from one who is self-realized, who has pure love for Krishna—that is when its potency really comes through. As Prabhupāda wrote soon after arriving in America: "When the *mantra* is chanted by a pure devotee of the Lord in love, it has the greatest efficacy on hearers, and as such this chanting should be heard from the lips of a pure devotee of the Lord, so that immediate effects can be achieved."[18] This notion intersects well with the above point about technique being secondary: If one receives the holy name from a pure devotee, and chants it as he or she directs, the sound has opportunity to enter one's heart, with all other considerations—musical style, social status, age, race, gender, and mental disposition—becoming less important.

The basic teaching is this: When one hears directly from a pure soul—or even from one who has heard from a pure soul—one imbibes the seed of *bhakti*, which will eventually sprout. This will start a chain reaction, of sorts, purifying anyone who comes into contact with it. This is why the Chaitanya tradition promotes *nāgara-saṅkīrtana*, or street chanting—all listeners, they say, will become purified by hearing the name and, if they then take up the chanting themselves, will also become carriers of divine sound.

THE THEOLOGY OF THE HOLY NAME

The basic theology of the name is straightforward: Being absolute, the Lord and his name are nondifferent. Gauḍīya Vaishnavas trace this teaching to the *Padma Purāṇa*:

nāma cintāmaṇiḥ kṛṣṇaś
caitanya-rasa-vigrahaḥ
pūrṇaḥ śuddho nitya-mukto
'bhinnatvān nāma-nāminoḥ

"The name of Krishna is spiritual substance, identical to Krishna himself. It is spiritually absolute, an embodied form of transcendental consciousness (*chaitanya*) and relationship (*rasa*). It is fully pure, eternal, complete, and never material under any circumstances—it is the essence of Krishna's own potency. Ultimately, there is no difference between Krishna and his name."[19]

That is to say, here, in the relative world, a person and his name are two different things. If we call out a person's name, he or she is not thereby summoned, or at least they are not personally present merely by the calling of their name. In the spiritual, absolute world, therefore, the opposite must be true. This seminal idea has been articulated by devotees throughout the history of the tradition, from Mahāprabhu's time to the present. For example, Hamsadutta Dasa, a contemporary Gauḍīya Vaishnava, illustrates this point with a graphic example: "A thirsty man's cry—'Water! Water! Water!'—will never satisfy his thirst, because the name water and the substance water are completely different. In the absolute world, however, there are no such differences. There, an object and its name, or a person and his name, are one. Therefore, simply by vibrating the holy name of God, one associates with God directly."[20] Premier Gauḍīya philosopher Jīva Goswāmī supports this idea throughout his considerable literary oeuvre.

In addition, Śrī Jīva identifies and substantiates a number of other theological conclusions about the holy name. In his *Bhakti Sandarbha* (248), for example, he says that such chanting relieves one of all sinful reactions (*pāpa-viśodhana*), but that even this is not the ultimate result of the chanting process. Rather, chanting Krishna's name, he writes, gives direct experience of God's attributes (264) and, more, it awakens intense passion (*anurāga*) for him, causing one to dance, cry, scream, and laugh like a madman (263). Jīva further tells us that singing the names out loud (*anugīyate*) is much more effective than quiet recitation, as in chanting *japa*, a practice also embraced by Gauḍīya devotees, and that people who engage in such loud chanting (*kīrtana*) are humanity's greatest benefactors (269). This latter point, again, speaks to the phenomenon of *nāgara-saṅkīrtana*, or street chanting, for, as the teaching goes, if even a non-believer merely hears the transcendental sound, he or she becomes purified and their spiritual life moves forward.

It would thus be worthwhile to briefly expound on the notion of "loud chanting." It was Haridāsa Ṭhākura, the great 16th-century "master of the holy name" (Nāmāchārya)—a title given to him by Mahāprabhu himself[21]—who initially taught that loud chanting is in fact 100 times more powerful than chanting to oneself, what to speak of silent meditation.[22]

Haridāsa further says that this emphasis on loud chanting is the real import of all sacred literature, and he augments this information with a logical observation: "If one silently chants the names of Krishna, then he liberates only himself; but if one chants loudly, then he liberates others as well."[23] Haridāsa concludes with an analogy couched in a rhetorical question, "Which is better—to feed yourself, or to feed yourself and simultaneously feed a thousand others?"[24]

Sanātana Goswāmī highlighted the glory of loud chanting as well, indicating some of its practical benefits: "For we [the inhabitants of the spiritual world] consider loud call-and-response chanting [*kīrtana*] to be the absolute best form of *bhakti*, much more effective than mere 'remembering' [*smaraṇam*], which appears only in one's own troubled heart. This is so because chanting engages not only the faculty of speech, which it uses directly, but also the mind and the sense of hearing. And chanting helps not only the person practicing it but others as well."[25]

"If the faculty of speech," Sanātana continues, "is brought under consistent control through *kīrtana*, then the mind becomes stable and can properly engage in transcendental remembrance of the Lord. Remembrance thus develops as the fruit of chanting, and not the other way around."[26]

Another important verse about chanting loudly comes from Rūpa Goswāmī's *Stava-mālā* (*Chaitanyāṣṭaka,* 6): "Śrī Chaitanya chants the Hare Krishna Mahā-mantra in a loud voice (*uccaih*), making the holy name dance on his tongue as he counts the number of recitations with his effulgent hand. His eyes are large, and his arms are long and graceful, reaching down to his knees. When will I be granted his audience again?"[27] Rūpa Goswāmī here mentions the Hare Krishna Mahā-mantra specifically, and, indeed, that should be the subject of our next section.

THE HARE KRISHNA MAHĀ-MANTRA

Although Śrī Chaitanya and the entire Gauḍīya line have embraced a number of mantras and names of God—as in, for example, the chanting of *hari haraye namaḥ krishna yādavāya namaḥ*, and so on—it is the Mahā-mantra that has always been their focus and raison d'être.[28] The mantra runs as follows: Hare

Krishna, Hare Krishna, Krishna Krishna, Hare Hare/ Hare Rāma, Hare Rāma, Rāma Rāma, Hare Hare.

From the Gauḍīya perspective, it is first and foremost an urgent or forceful call to Śrī Rādhā for engagement in divine service: "O Rādhe! Please engage me in Krishna's service!"[29] By chanting "Hare," one beseeches Mother Harā (another name for Rādhā) for her undivided attention. "Hare" is thus the vocative form of the word. Basically, according to Prabhupāda, the entire mantra can be translated like this: "O Lord, O Energy of the Lord, please engage me in Your service."[30] This is so because she, Rādhā, is the embodiment of such service. Indeed, according to Gauḍīyas, she is God in the form of active devotion (*bhakti*).

Regarding the distinct Gauḍīya reading of the *mantra*—with Rādhā as its main focus—this is perhaps best summed up by Prabhupāda's guru, Bhaktisiddhānta Sarasvatī. He clarifies that the *mantra* is embraced by each person according to his or her own preponderant internal proclivity—for those inclined toward awe and reverence, they will read it in one way, but for those given to the sweetness of *mādhurya*, they will read it in quite another:

> . . . when the words "Hare Rāma" are pronounced in a mood of reverential service to God, they indicate Śrī Rāma, the son of Dasarātha in Ayodhyā. However, devotees who worship in the mood of conjugal service understand Krishna, the son of Nanda in Vrindavan, as the lover of the cowherd girls (*gopī-rāmana*), and thus Rāma. When the word "Rāma" indicates service to Krishna, the lover of Rādhā (Rādhā-rāmaṇa), the term of address or "Harā" (Hare is the vocative form) indicates Rādhā, understood as the metaphysical or internal energy (*parā-śakti*) of God. In accordance with this understanding, the names Hare, Krishna, and Rāma refer to Rādhā and Krishna alone.[31]

Aside from understanding "Hare" as Rādhā and Rāma as Krishna, the Gauḍīyas promulgate various novel understandings consistent with the deepest aspects of their philosophy. For example, an esoteric reading of the *mantra* runs as follows: "Hare Krishna, Hare Krishna"—the first four words of the *mantra*—refer to Rādhā and Krishna in union, celebrating their love in each other's company (*sambhoga-bhāva*). But then, the next two words, "Krishna Krishna," indicate their separation from each other (*vipralambha-bhāva*). In other words, while separated, Rādhārāṇī is calling, "Krishna! Krishna! Where is my Krishna? Oh, please tell me, where are you?" In the next two words, Krishna reciprocates her love, feeling the same disturbing emotions: "Hare! Hare! Where is my sweet Rādhā?"

In the first half of the *mantra*, then, one finds the emotions of both union and yearning, but then, in the second half of the mantra, these same feelings intensify. Here, Krishna is called Rāma because he is the source of all pleasure (*rāma*): "Hare Rāma, Hare Rāma" means that Krishna is feeling extreme delight in the company of his beloved. That is to say, the divine lovers, Rādhā and Krishna, are reunited, enjoying the ecstasy of intimate association.

But then, "Rāma Rāma." Once again, they are separated, and Rādhā is crying: "Where is my blissful partner? Where is Krishna?" So intense is her longing that she calls him twice: "Rāma! Rāma!" Not to be outdone, he shares her grief: "Hare! Hare! Where is my beloved, Rādhārāṇī? Where is she?" So in both halves of the *mantra* there are, conjoined, both the unprecedented ecstasy of their union, and the acute devastation precipitated by their separation. And as one advances in the chanting process, it is taught, one can appreciate these emotions more and more.[32]

It should be emphasized that the Mahā-mantra encodes the entirety of the tradition. The accomplished practitioner, merely by vibrating these divine syllables, can access the secrets of Rādhā and Krishna and the deepest aspects of their transcendental relationship. In this sense, the *mantra* can be viewed as a sonic reenactment of the Rāsa-maṇḍala, or the circular dance of the Lord and his most intimate devotees. In the words of Graham Schweig:

> This *mantra* consists of a series of alternating names of God in the vocative case, both calling out for and praising the presence of the divine. When the *mantra* is recited repeatedly in meditation or song, it worshipfully enthrones the Soul of the soul within the heart of the devotee, forming a sonic *maṇḍala* . . . . The *mantra* begins and ends with feminine names, enclosing the masculine names, just as the *gopīs* engulf Krishna when they encircle him during the commencement of the Rāsa dance. When practitioners recite the *mantra* over and over, the divine names form a circular pattern imitative of the exchange between the feminine and masculine partners in the Rāsa dance.[33]

Mahā-mantra in Sacred Texts

Originally, the *mantra* itself is mainly found in Puranic texts, *Vaiṣṇava-āgamas,* and *Sātvata-tantras.*[34] However, it is traceable to one *śruti* text as well—*the Kali-santaraṇa Upanishad*, part of the Krishna-yajur-veda—even if, according to some, that text is sometimes considered a later addition to the Upanishadic corpus.[35] Whether early or late, however, the Upanishad in question is considered authentic by scholars within the tradition, and it offers practitioners the complete *mantra* with full Vedic authority:

> *hare kṛṣṇa hare kṛṣṇa kṛṣṇa kṛṣṇa hare hare*
> *hare rāma hare rāma rāma rāma hare hare*
> *iti ṣoḍaśakaṁ nāmnāṁ kali-kalmaṣa-nāśanam*
> *nātaḥ parataropāyaḥ sarva-vedeṣu dṛśyate*

"These sixteen names counteract the evil effects of the Kali-yuga. After searching through the gamut of Vedic texts, one cannot find a method so sublime as the chanting of these names."[36]

The *Ananta-saṁhitā,* another ancient text, echoes the words of the *Kali-santaraṇa* Upanishad, making clear that it is talking about the same Mahā-mantra by enumerating the entire mantra and mentioning the exact number of words and syllables it contains:

> Hare Krishna, Hare Krishna, Krishna Krishna, Hare Hare/ Hare Rāma, Hare Rāma, Rāma Rāma, Hare Hare. This sixteen-name, thirty-two syllable mantra is the Mahā-mantra in the age of Kali, and it is by this mantra that all living beings can attain salvation. One should never abandon this mantra, adopting other religious processes practiced by less qualified souls. Nor should one chant contrived combinations of Krishna's names that contradict the pure conclusions of the scriptures or are filled with illegitimate emotions. Regarding this entirely spiritual Mahā-mantra, which frees one from material existence, the original teacher, Lord Brahmā, has said, "The Kali-santaraṇa Upanishad has declared this mantra to be the best means of deliverance in the age of Kali." Because they heard all this from Brahmā, his sons and disciples, beginning with Nārada, all accepted the Hare Krishna Mahā-mantra and, having meditated on it, attained perfection.[37]

We see a similar occurrence in the *Sanat-kumāra-samhitā*:

> "The words "Hare Krishna" are to be repeated twice, then "Krishna" and "Hare" are repeated separately twice. Similarly, "Hare Rāma," "Rāma," and "Hare" are also to be repeated in the same way. The mantra will thus be chanted as follows—Hare Krishna, Hare Krishna, Krishna Krishna, Hare Hare/ Hare Rāma, Hare Rāma, Rāma Rāma, Hare Hare.[38]

There are many Puranic texts confirming the *mantra* as well. For example, in the *Brahmāṇḍa Purāṇa* (6.59–60), we find: "By engaging in *nāma-saṅkīrtana* (congregational chanting), specifically with the Hare Krishna Mahā-mantra, one situates oneself in complete spiritual reality."[39] And here's another from the *Padma Purāṇa* (Svarga-khaṇḍa 50.6): "If one worships Śrī Hari, the Lord of all lords, by chanting the Mahā-mantra, all sinful reactions are automatically removed."[40] There are numerous scriptural quotes along these same lines, and even more if one considers the many verses composed by Gauḍīya sages throughout the centuries.

A Brief Note on Offenses to the Holy Name

The *Padma Purāṇa* (Brahma-khaṇḍa 25.15–18, 22–23) offers a cautionary list of pitfalls to avoid in chanting the holy name. These are called *nāma-apārādha* (offenses against the name).[41] In the Gauḍīya tradition, the list can initially be found in the *Hari-bhakti-vilāsa*, Eleventh Vilāsa, texts 521–524.[42] The notion was then carried into Jīva Goswāmī's work, both in his commentary on Rūpa Goswāmī's *Bhakti-rasāmṛta-sindhu* (1.2.120) and in his *Bhakti Sandarbha* (Anuccheda 265).[43] Viśvanātha Chakravartī also highlights the importance of this list by citing it in his *Bhakti-rasāmṛta-sindhu-bindu* (Pūrva-vibhāga, First Wave, text 7).[44]

Within the tradition these offenses are taken very seriously, and though variously enumerated and delineated in specific texts, Gauḍīya commentary always emphasizes scrupulously avoiding their commission. Without any further ado, then, the basic list appears as follows:

1. To blaspheme or criticize the devotees of the Lord.
2. To consider the names of Shiva or other *devas* to be equal to Vishnu's.
3. To disobey the order of the guru or to consider him an ordinary person.
4. To disrespect scriptural authority.
5. To interpret the meaning of the name.
6. To consider the name's glories imaginary.
7. To carelessly commit sin with the idea that the name will relieve one of reaction.
8. To express the glories of the name to the unfaithful.
9. To consider the chanting of the name as mere pious activity.
10. To not have complete faith in the name after being given due instruction.

It is also considered a major offense to be inattentive while chanting.

Though these offenses can be taken at face value, meaningful elaboration can be found in the writings of Bhaktivinoda Ṭhākura, particularly his *Jaiva Dharma*, Chapter 24, and *Hari-nāma-cintāmaṇi*, Chapter 4, the latter of which devotes thirteen chapters to the subject. Prabhupāda also explains them in detail throughout his writings.[45]

It is significant that in *Jaiva Dharma*, Bhaktivinoda underlines the fact that one should chant with devotees, not with those who are faithless or who offend the holy name (*nāma-aparādhī*), thus giving credence to the above quote from Prabhupāda saying that one should hear the name from the lips of a pure devotee. "It is not proper," notes Bhaktivinoda, "for Vaishnavas to participate in congregational chanting in which *nāma-aparādhīs* are prominent or the lead singer himself is a *nāma-aparādhī*. However, there is no fault in chanting with pure Vaishnavas or even average devotees who are *nāma-ābhāsīs* (not pure and thus only invoking a shadow of the name). On the contrary," he concludes, "such chanting is desirable and will invoke great bliss."[46]

Significant, too, is that the word *aparādha* is composed of two syllables: *apa* which means "against," "without," or "to take away"; and *rādhā* which means "success," "to please," "to worship," or "flow of affection." Thus, according to Śrīla B. P. Purī Mahārāja (1898–1999), a Gauḍīya Vaishnava leader of considerable renown, the etymological development of the word *aparādha* is *rādhāt arthāt ārādhanat-apagataḥ*, which means, "to be distanced from worship." Naturally, given the placement of the word "*rādhā*" in this context, Purī Mahārāja relates *aparādha* to the worship of Krishna's consort: ". . . in a higher sense [*nāma-aparādha*] means to be removed from the service of Śrī Rādhā. All divine service to Krishna is being conducted under her direction. To offend her servitors [or the holy name] is to make one unfit for her divine service. The whole aim of Krishna consciousness is Rādhā-dāsyam, the divine service of Śrī Rādhā, and offenses . . . make one unfit for such service."[47] Thus, the word *aparādha* means "against or without Rādhā." For the Gauḍīya Vaishnava, then, *nāma-aparādha* refers to inferior chanting, or that unfortunate realm where Krishna (*nāma*) exists without (*apa*) Rādhā (*rādhā*).

CONCLUDING REFLECTIONS

"Indeed, among all spiritual practices," writes Bhaktisiddhānta Sarasvatī, "*saṅkīrtana* is the best and foremost means of attaining the grace of the Supreme Lord Śrī Krishna. Other types of *sādhana*, or devotional practices, are worthy of being called such only if they favorably assist the performance of *saṅkīrtana*; otherwise they should be known as obstructions to actual *sādhana*. Whether one is a child or an old or young man, male or female, learned or illiterate, rich or poor, beautiful or ugly, pious or sinful—regardless of the condition of life someone may be in—there is no spiritual practice for him other than Śrī Krishna *nāma-saṅkīrtana*."[48]

Apropos of this, Bhaktisiddhānta acknowledged that the principle of *saṅkīrtana* could be extended to other activities—virtually anything that spreads the holy name to one and all. He highly lauded book printing and distribution, in particular, and he even referred to the printing press as the *bṛhat-mṛdaṅga*, or "great drum." In a brief article on his life and teachings—one among many—this notion of extending *saṅkīrtana* through the larger drum is explained: "[Bhaktisiddhānta Sarasvatī] thought of the printing press as a *bṛhat-mṛdaṅga*, a big *mṛdaṅga*. The *mṛdaṅga* drum played during *kīrtana* could be heard for a block or two, whereas with the *bṛhat-mṛdaṅga*, the printing press, the message of Lord Chaitanya could be spread all over the world."[49]

But of what value are books that merely sit on a printing press or gather mold and mildew in a warehouse? With this in mind, Bhaktisiddhānta Sarasvatī not only glorified the spreading of the holy name and the literature that espouses its importance, but also side by side the devotees who go out into the world and share these spiritual commodities with others. He called them *jīvanta-cetana-mṛdaṅga*, or "living drums of consciousness," for while books extend the range of Hari-nāma beyond an ordinary *kīrtana*, these very books and the name itself would never reach the mass of people without the brave and enthusiastic souls who go out and distribute them.[50]

Upon embracing such service, say the Gauḍīya Vaishnava *ācāryas*, one eventually attains the highest destination. Initially, the holy name purifies one's consciousness and facilitates devotional service, as explained above. But when one reaches perfection in chanting, one becomes a self-realized lover of God. As Bhaktivinoda Ṭhākura poetically tells us in his masterwork, *Śaraṇāgati*:

> *pūrṇa vikaśita hañā, vraje more yāya lañā,*
> *dekhāya more svarūpa-vilāsa*
> *more siddha-deha diyā, kṛṣṇa-pāśe rākhe giyā,*
> *e dehera kare sarva-nāśa*

"Upon fully blossoming, the name takes me to Vraja and shows me his divine pastimes. He gives me an eternal body, keeps me by Krishna's side, and completely vanquishes this material body, granting me supreme perfection."[51]

NOTES

1. M. Monier-William, *Sanskrit-English Dictionary*, 2nd edition (Oxford University Press, 1899).

2. For a thorough history of *kīrtana*'s evolution in the overall Indic tradition, particularly in Vaishnavism, see Guy L. Beck, "Kīrtan and Bhajan," in *Brill's Encyclopedia of Hinduism*, ed., Knut A. Jacobsen, (Leiden: Brill Academic Publishers, 2010), Volume 2, 585–598.

3. See Guy L. Beck, "An Introduction to the Poetry of Narottam Dās," in *Journal of Vaishnava Studies*, Volume 4, No. 4 (Fall 1996), 17–52.

4. See Ramakanta Chakrabarty, "Vaishnava *kīrtana* in Bengal," in *Journal of Vaishnava Studies*, Volume 4, No. 2 (Spring 1996), 190. See also Endnote 43 in Chapter 2.

5. *tasmād bhārata sarvātmā/ bhagavān īśvaro hariḥ// śrotavyaḥ kīrtitavyaś ca/ smartavyaś cecchatābhayam//.*

6. *etan nirvidyamānānām/ icchatām akuto-bhayam// yogināṁ nṛpa nirṇītaṁ/ harer nāmānukīrtanam//.*

7. *nāma-saṅkīrtanaṁ yasya/ sarva-pāpa praṇāśanam// praṇāmo duḥkha-śamanas/ taṁ namāmi hariṁ param//.*

8. *eta bali' eka śloka śikhāila more, bhāgavatera sāra ei—bale vāre vāre.*

10.*evaṁ-vrataḥ sva-priya-nāma-kīrtyā/ jātānurāgo druta-citta uccaiḥ// hasaty atho roditi rauti gāyaty/ unmāda-van nṛtyati loka-bāhyaḥ//.*

10. The Ajāmila story, found in *Śrīmad Bhāgavatam*, Canto Six, Chapter 2, informs us that at the time of death, Ajāmila helplessly and very loudly called out the holy name of the Lord, Nārāyaṇa. In this case, he was actually beseeching his young son, to whom he had given the same name. Still, this chanting freed him from the reactions to all his sin, which was considerable. This same effect, the *Bhāgavatam* tells us, is awaiting those who chant the holy name in any way, even if they chant indirectly (to indicate something else), jokingly, for musical entertainment, or even neglectfully. See especially chapter 6, text 14.

11. See Śrīla Nārāyaṇa Mahārāja, "Criticize, and Lose the Holy Name" (http://bvml.org/SBNM/calthn.html).

12. See *Śrīmad Bhāgavatam* 6.2.39–40. This latter part of the story, where Ajāmila travels to Haridwar and reaches perfection is nicely retold in Bhaktivedānta Nārāyaṇa Gosvāmā Mahārāja, *Guru-devatātmā: Accepting Śrī Guru as One's Life and Soul* (New Delhi: Gauḍīya Vedānta Publications, 2012), 19, and Satsvarūpa Dāsa Goswāmī, *The Wild Garden: Collected Writings from 1990–1993* (Port Royal, PA: GN Press, Inc., 1994), 238.

13. Manindranath Guha, *Nectar of the Holy Name,* trans., Neal Delmonico (Kirksville, MO: Blazing Sapphire Press, 2005), 83.

14. *jayati jayati nāmānanda-rūpaṁ murārer/ viramita-nija-dharma-dhyāna-pūjādi-yatnam// kathamapi sakṛd-āttaṁ muktidaṁ prāṇīnāṁ yat/ paramam amṛtam ekaṁ jīvanaṁ bhūṣaṇaṁ me//.*

15. *jaya nāma-dheya muni-vṛnda-geya he/ jana-rañjanāya paramākṣarākṛte// tvam anādarād api manāg udīritaṁ/ nikhilogra-tāpa-pa-ṭalīṁ vilumpasi//.*

16. This verse is originally found in Rūpa Goswāmī's *Vidagdha-mādhava* (1.15) and is quoted in *Caitanya-caritāmṛta* (Antya 1.99).

17. There have been numerous books attempting to document the many scriptural quotes on the holy name and elaborate on their essential teaching. Some important volumes that have helped in this study would include, Rāghava Chaitanya Dāsa, *The Divine Name* (Bombay: self-published, 1954); Śacīnandana Swami, *The Nectarean Ocean of the Holy Name* (Germany: Gayatri Publishers, 1999); Manindranath Guha, *Nectar of the Holy Name,* trans., Neal Delmonico, op. cit.; and Satyanārāyaṇa Dāsa, *Nāma Tattva* (Vrindavan: Jiva Institute, 2001). There are many more, including an important article: Norvin Hein, "Chaitanya's Ecstasies and the Theology of the Name," in Bardwell. L. Smith, Ed., *Hinduism: New Essays in the History of Religions* (Leiden, Netherlands: E. J. Brill, 1976), 16–32.

18. Prabhupāda's essay on chanting was reprinted in the book *Chant and Be Happy* (http://www.harekrishna.com/col/books/YM/cbh/introduction.html).

19. Quoted in *Caitanya-caritāmṛta*, Madhya 17.133.

20. See Hansadutta Dasa, "Why Chant Hare Krishna?" (https://theharekrishnamovement.org/2011/04/).

21. For more on this important Muslim convert to the Chaitanya tradition, see Rupa-vilāsa Dāsa, *Nāmācārya: The Life of Haridāsa Ṭhākura* (Badger, California: Torchlight Publishing, 2010).

22. See *Chaitanya-bhāgavata, Ādi* 16.273–283.

23. Ibid., 16.281 (*japile shri-krishna-nāma apane se tare ucca-saṅkīrtane para upakara kare*).

24. Ibid., 16.289.

25. See Sanātana Goswāmī, *Bṛhat-bhāgavatāmṛta* 2.3.148.

26. Ibid., 2.3.149. In these two verses, Sanātana is indirectly addressing those members of the tradition who prematurely embrace Rāgānugā-sādhana, with its esoteric practice of *līlā-smaraṇa*. He is trying to show how chanting the holy name is superior to this practice and essential to its perfection.

27. *hare kṛṣṇety-uccaiḥ sphurita-rasano nāma-gaṇanā-kṛta-granthi-śreṇī-subhaga-kaṭi-sūtrojjvala-karaḥ viśālākṣo dīrghārgala-yugala-khelāñcita-bhujaḥ sa caitanyaḥ kiṁ me punar api dṛśor yāsyati padam.*

28. As a side note, due to Śrī Chaitanya's identification with Krishna, devotees of the Gauḍīya tradition revere Chaitanya's many names as being on a par with those of Krishna himself. In Bhaktivinoda Ṭhākura's *Jaiva Dharma*, for example, we read, "Worshiping Gaura by chanting Gaura-nāma mantra awards the same benefit as worshiping Kṛṣṇa by chanting His holy names in Kṛṣṇa-nāma-mantra. Worshiping Gaura through the Kṛṣṇa mantra is the same as worshiping Kṛṣṇa by the Gaura mantra. Those who believe that there is a difference between Gaura and Kṛṣṇa are extremely foolish; they are simply servants of Kali." See *Jaiva Dharma, Our Eternal Nature*, trans. by Śrī Śrīmad Bhaktivedānta Nārāyaṇa Gosvāmī (Vrindavan: Gaudiya Vedanta Publications, 2001), Chapter 14, 349. Śrīla Prabhupāda elaborates on this point as well in his commentary on the *Caitanya-caritāmṛta*, Antya 2.31: "Śrīla Bhaktivinoda Ṭhākura explains the Gaura-gopāla mantra in his *Amṛta-pravāha-bhāṣya*. Worshipers of Śrī Gaurasundara accept the four syllables *gau-ra-aṅ-ga* as the Gaura mantra, but pure worshipers of Rādhā and Kṛṣṇa accept the four syllables *rā-dhā kṛṣ-ṇa* as the Gaura-gopāla mantra. However, Vaiṣṇavas consider Śrī Caitanya Mahāprabhu nondifferent from Rādhā-Kṛṣṇa (*śrī-kṛṣṇa-caitanya rādhā-kṛṣṇa nahe anya*). Therefore one who chants the mantra Gaurāṅga and one who chants the names of Rādhā and Kṛṣṇa are on the same level." See His Divine Grace A. C. Bhaktivedānta Swami Prabhupāda, trans. and commentary, Krishnadāsa Kavirāja Goswāmī's *Śrī Caitanya-caritāmṛta*, 9-volume set (Los Angeles, California, 1996, reprint), Antya 2.31, purport. The name "Nimānanda," to cite yet another, more confidential example, is considered extremely important, as we learn from *Bhakti-ratnākara* 5.2164–2167: "Of all Mahāprabhu's names, the main one is 'Nimāi Paṇḍita,' which Nityānanda Prabhu liked the best. Seeing the followers (*sampradāya*) of Mahāprabhu in Nadia, now everyone calls them the 'Nimāi Sampradāya,' and because Nimāi gave so much joy (*ānanda*) to the world, his name 'Nimānanda' is so well known." (*prabhura nāma madhye mukhya nimāi paṇḍita/ nityānanda prabhura e nāme ati prīta// prabhura vaiṣṇava gaṇe dekhi nadiyāya/ nimai sampradā bali adyāpiha gāya//nimāi pradāna kaila jagate ānanda/ ei hetu abani vikhyāta nimānanda*).

29. "Hare" can also refer to Krishna, or "Harati," indicating that he unties the knot of material existence." See *Chaitanya Upanishad*, Mantra 12 (*The Glories of Śrī Chaitanya Mahāprabhu*, trans., Kuśakratha Dāsa, New York: Bala Books, 1984). Thus, the "Hare" in the Mahā-mantra can be seen as either Rādhā or Krishna. The Rādhā understanding, however, is more representative of Gauḍīya *siddhānta*, and has a history that goes back to the beginning of the tradition. It can be found in commentaries on the Mahā-mantra by both Gopāla Guru Goswāmī and Jīva Goswāmī, among others. See Śrīmad Bhaktivedānta Nārāyaṇa Mahārāja, trans., *Śrī Hari-Nāma*

Mahā-mantra (Mathura, U.P.: Gauḍīya Vedānta Publications, 2001, 2nd Edition), 27–30. Interpreting Hare as Rādhā can also be found in Narahari Chakravartī's *Bhakti-ratnākara* 5.2,214 to 2,218, but this is obviously a later text.

30. This interpretation can be found throughout Prabhupāda's prodigious literary contribution. (http://www.krishna.com/info/hare-krishna-mantra).

31. Quoted in Ferdinando Sardella, *Modern Hindu Personalism* (Oxford University Press, 2013), 81, footnote 82. This originates in one of Bhaktisiddhānta Sarasvatī's letters, dated October 10, 1928 (*Prabhupādera Patravali*, Volume 1, 57).

32. Though I have been unable to trace an early source for this explanation of the Mahā-mantra as representing both union and separation, it can be found in modern Gauḍīya literature. Two examples: Śrī Bhaktivedānta Nārāyaṇa Mahārāja's commentary on Bhaktivinoda Ṭhākura's *Śrī Bhajana Rahasya* (Vrindavan: Gaudiya Vedanta Publications, 2003), Prathama-yama-sādhana, 1.6, 16–19; and Mahanidhi Swami, *The Art of Chanting Hare Krishna* (Self-published, ISKCON Vrindavan, 2002), 160–161.

33. See Graham M. Schweig, *Dance of Divine Love: the Rāsa Līlā of Krishna from the Bhāgavata Purāṇa, India's Classic Sacred Love Story* (Princeton, N.J.: Princeton University Press, 2005), 179. Comparing the Mahā-mantra to the Rāsa-līlā is high praise. Viśvanātha Chakravartī refers to the Rāsa-līlā as "the crown jewel of all *līlās*" (*sarva-līlā-cūḍa-maṇi*). See Viśvanātha's commentary on the *Bhāgavatam* 10.29.1.

34. Much of this section is based on Kostyantyn Perun (Brijbasi das), "Hare Kṛṣṇa Mahā-Mantra From the Caitanya-Vaiṣṇava Perspective" in *Journal of Vaishnava Studies*, Volume 24, No. 2 (Spring 2016), 179–222.

35. Doubts about the *Kali-santaraṇa Upanishad* are given only minimal consideration, however, because the text is indeed listed as number 103 in the *Muktikā Upanishad*. This is a list of the standard, long-accepted 108 Upanishads, making it part of the original, established Vedic corpus. That being said, there is another Vedic text known as the *Chaitanya Upanishad* (*Caitanyopaniṣad*), which is also sometimes put forward as an instance of the Mahā-mantra in ancient scripture. But this one is not listed among the original 108 and so we will not address it here. I did, however, mention it briefly in the Introduction.

36. In certain manuscripts of the *Kali-santaraṇa Upanishad*, the Mahā-mantra appears with the "Hare Rāma" part first. This is a complex subject and has been thoroughly addressed in Brijbasi das, op. cit., 185–187, and also in Bhaktisiddhānta Sarasvatī, the *Gauḍīya*, Volume 11, No. 7 (October 22, 1932), 101. See also Śrīmad Bhaktivedānta Nārāyaṇa Mahārāja, trans., *Sri Hari-Nāma Mahā-mantra*, op. cit., 3–15.

37. Quoted in Brijbasi das, op. cit., 186–187.

38. Ibid. *Sanat-kumāra-saṁhita*, as quoted by Dhyānachandra Goswāmī in his *Gaura-Govindārcana-smaraṇa-paddhati*, verses 132–133.

39. http://www.krishna.com/some-scriptural-references-hare-krishna-maha-mantra.

40. Ibid.

41. According to Vaishnava scholar Hari Pārṣad Dāsa in personal correspondence (1.16.17): "[The ten offenses] can still be found in the *Padma Purāṇa*. However, they

are listed as offenses to Lord Shiva's name. We Vaishnavas have taken them as it is and applied them to the names of Lord Vishnu, because Lord Shiva is a *guṇa-avatāra* of Lord Vishnu . . . The list of *aparādhas* ends with the phrase, *shivanāmāparādhaḥ*. Traditional translators thus take it as offenses to Shiva's names, but the *Hari-bhakti-vilāsa* interprets *shivanāmāparādhaḥ* in a Vishnu-centric way." Indeed, the name Shiva (which means "auspicious") is known in Vaishnava circles as one of Krishna's holy names.

42. See Sanātana Goswāmī's *Hari-Bhakti-Vilāsa*, Volume 3, trans., Bhumipati Dāsa (Vrindavan: Rasbiharilal & Sons, 2006), 140–142.

43. See Jīva Goswāmī, *Śrī Bhakti Sandarbha*, Volume 3, trans., Satyanārāyaṇa Dāsa and Bruce Martin (Vrindavan: Jiva Institute, 2006), Anuccheda 265, 883–891.

44. See Viśvanātha Chakravartī Ṭhākura, Śrī *Bhakti-rasāmṛta-sindhu-bindu*, trans., Śrīmad Bhaktivedānta Nārāyaṇa Mahārāja (Mathura: Gaudiya Vedanta Publications, 1996), 116–117.

45. For example, see his commentary on *Śrīmad Bhāgavatam* 2.1.11. There is also a thorough explanation in *The Teaching of Lord Chaitanya*, Chapter 1, "Teaching to Rūpa Goswāmī" (Culver City, C.A.: Bhaktivedanta Book Trust, 1974, reprint), 29–30.

46. See Bhaktivinoda Ṭhākura, *Jaiva Dharma*, trans., Śrīmad Bhaktivedānta Nārāyaṇa Mahārāja (Mathura, U.P.: Gaudiya Vedanta Publications, 2001), Chapter 24, 573–574.

47. Bhakti Pramode Purī Goswāmī Mahārāja, *The Heart of Krishna*, Introduction (San Francisco: Mandala Media, 1995), 1.

48. Bhaktisiddhānta Sarasvatī, "Śrī Nāma-saṅkīrtana" in *The Gauḍīya*, Volume 23, No. 10. Translated in *Rays of the Harmonist*, No. 19 (2009), 22–23.

49. See "Śrīla Bhaktisiddhānta Sarasvatī Ṭhākura" (http://harmonist.us/2016/12/srila-bhaktisiddhanta-sarasvati-thakura/).

50. See Śrīla Bhakti Prajñāna Keśava Goswāmī Mahārāja, "Svadhāme Atīndriya Prabhu," translated in *Rays of the Harmonist*, No. 20 (2009), 38.

51. Bhaktivinoda Ṭhākura, "Śrī Nāma-Māhātmya," Verse 7, in *Śaraṇāgati*, (http://www.gaudiyadarshan.com/wp-content/uploads/2013/03/Sharanagati.pdf).

Chapter 6

Śikṣāṣṭakam

Eight Beautiful Prayers

If chanting the holy name is at the center of Mahāprabhu's profound philosophical system, his eight beautiful prayers, known simply as *Śikṣāṣṭakam* (*śikṣā*, teaching; *āṣṭakam*, eight verses), tell us what chanting is really all about.

Indicative of the fact that it is consummate Sanskrit poetry, Śrī Chaitanya's *Śikṣāṣṭakam* undertakes and achieves an extraordinary feat. With remarkable economy, in language perfectly evincing the highest standards of aesthetic Vedānta, it bestows four key teachings indispensable for achieving perfection on the path of *bhakti*: (1) It presents a virtual compendium of instructions for progress in devotion; (2) It delineates seven distinct effects of chanting, merely in its first verse; (3) It portrays the devotional mood spontaneously achieved by an ardent chanter; and (4) finally, it unveils the highest spiritual realm, the region to which chanting transports its resolute practitioners, the domain of pure, unequalled love of God.

In this chapter, I begin by offering a fresh, original rendering of these eight Sanskrit verses,[1] enlarging my perspective to identify and focus on their overall (quintessential) meaning rather than remain stranded on the restricted banks of literal accuracy (transcription). After each rendering, I include a brief, running commentary, just touching on the essence of each verse, and then, after all eight are addressed, I briefly explain their historical revelation and the insights of traditional commentators.

THE EIGHT VERSES

(1)
ceto-darpaṇa-mārjanaṁ bhava-mahā-dāvāgni-nirvāpaṇaṁ
śreyaḥ-kairava-candrikā-vitaraṇaṁ vidyā-vadhū-jīvanam

ānandāmbudhi-vardhanaṁ prati-padaṁ pūrṇāmṛtāsvādanaṁ
sarvātma-snapanaṁ paraṁ vijayate śrī-kṛṣṇa-saṇkīrtanam

"Let the highest victory go to Śrī-krishna-saṅkīrtana, the congregational chanting of the holy name, for it cleanses the mirror of the mind/heart; extinguishes the blazing fire of worldly life; sheds moonlight upon the white lotus of good fortune; is comparable to the wife of learning; invigorates the ocean of bliss; allows one to taste full ambrosia at every step; and refreshes one's entire being."

This first verse of the *Śikṣāṣṭakam* is modeled, at least in part, on the *Ṛg-veda* (1.146.1),[2] showing that, for Gauḍīyas, its authority should be considered on a par with the *Vedas* themselves—high praise in Indian culture.

In the ancient Vedic tradition, the "blazing sacrificial fire" is associated with the fire-god Agni, also known as Saptajihva, "having seven tongues."[3] In the Vaishnava context, the "seven-tongued flame" refers to the seven characteristics of Śrī-krishna-saṅkīrtana, as described by Bhaktivinoda Ṭhākura in his *Sanmodana-bhāṣya* commentary. Bhaktisiddhānta Sarasvatī elaborates:

> The Vedic scriptures describe fire as having seven tongues, each of a different color according to its intensity . . . . In the same way, Śrī Gaurasundara has sung the glories of the fire of *saṅkīrtana*, which also has seven tongues. They are *ceto-darpaṇa-mārjana* and so forth. Unless the fire of *saṅkīrtana* is kindled and blazes, one's material existence will not be destroyed at the root, and salvation's highest goal, *premā*, will never be achieved.[4]

Thus, in Mahāprabhu's first verse, he highlights the exclusive and special nature of chanting the holy name, and the effects one might expect if one chants it properly. First, he reminds us, the mind and heart are thoroughly cleansed (*ceto-darpaṇa-mārjanaṁ*). The great forest fire (*mahā-dāvāgni*) of material life is completely extinguished (*nirvāpaṇaṁ*). Then he poetically invokes the spotless and all encompassing "white lotus" of loving service to God (*kairava*),[5] aroused and nourished by the holy name, which is the expansive moonshine of good fortune and auspiciousness (*candrikā-vitaraṇaṁ*).

Next, he says that all knowledge comes to those who sincerely chant the name (*vidyā-vadhū-jīvanam*)—these fortunate souls, he tells us, are inevitably drenched in bliss (*ānandāmbudhi-vardhanaṁ*), which creates a soothing sensation deep in the heart. Thus, those who embrace the name, Śrī Chaitanya says, enjoy the full nectar of life at every step (*prati-padaṁ pūrṇāmṛtāsvād anaṁ*) and their whole existence becomes bathed in supreme transcendence (*sarvātma-snapanaṁ paraṁ*).

An esoteric addendum: Although generally overlooked, the word "*śrī*" in *vijayate śrī-krishna-saṇkīrtanam* is especially significant. The devotees are advised not only to glorify Krishna's name—but that of Śrī (Rādhā), too. "*Śrī*" traditionally represents the energy of the Lord, and in the context of praising Krishna it is necessarily indicative of his pleasure potency, Rādhikā.[6]

(2)
nāmnām akāri bahudhā nija-sarva-śaktis
tatrārpitā niyamitaḥ smaraṇe na kālaḥ
etādṛśī tava kṛpā bhagavan mamāpi
durdaivam īdṛśam ihājani nānurāgaḥ

"O Almighty Lord! By your mercy, you have bestowed upon the world a multiplicity of names by which you can be remembered, and you have endowed each of them with your full potency. More, you have made no restrictions in terms of chanting them, whether it be according to time, place or circumstance. Alas. Despite your leniency, I have no taste for chanting them."

Mahāprabhu here shows the ideal mood of a fledgling devotee. He begins by expressing appreciation for Krishna, who makes himself available and accessible by supplying humankind a plethora of divine names to choose from. This variety is offered so that anyone, according to taste and inclination, can relish chanting. Mahāprabhu further notes that, when it comes to Krishna, there is no difference between the name (*nāma*) and the named one (*nāmī*), or as Vaishnavas tend to say: *abhinatvaṁ nāma-nāmīnaḥ.*[7] This is suggested by the words *nija-sarva-śaktis*, that is, that the name includes all of his potencies—he, his *śakti*, and everything in direct relation to him are embodied in the name.

In this first line, we see another allusion to Vedic texts. When Mahāprabhu says *nāmnām akāri bahudhā nija-sarva-śaktis*, he is referring to the Lord's multiplicity of names. This harkens to the *Ṛg-veda* (1.164.46), where we are told that although Truth is one, it is called by numerous appellations. In fact, the exact same word, *bahudhā* ("many," "variety"), is used, albeit in a slightly different context. Thus, both in the *Veda* and in this second of the eight *Śikṣāṣṭakam* verses, we are told that God has many names, or that truth is expressed variously.

There is yet more Vedic resonance. Mahāprabhu tells us that the holy names are not beleaguered by everyday restrictions. This is in direct contrast to Vedic *mantras*, which can only be chanted by Brahmins, at a certain time of day, under very specific circumstances. Conversely, the holy names can be chanted by anyone, anywhere, without consideration of social status, time of day, or mental disposition. It is simply a matter of vibrating the *mantra*. Indeed, Rūpa Goswāmī makes clear in his *Bhakti-rasāmṛta-sindhu* (1.2.60–71) that the blessings of *bhakti* are open to all. The exact word he uses is *sarvādhikāritā*, that is, "everyone is eligible."

Finally, Mahāprabhu, assuming the guise of a neophyte chanter, expresses his "misfortune": The aspiring devotee should recognize that his taste for chanting is never what it should be, for no matter how much he wants to chant, it is a mere shadow of what he *should* want—so glorious is the holy name. In other words, if one understood the name's true glory, Mahāprabhu suggests, one would want to chant more and more, certainly more than one currently chants, both in terms of quality and quantity.[8] This mood of humility will be further developed in the next verse.

(3)
tṛṇād api sunīcena
taror api sahiṣṇunā
amāninā mānadena
kīrtanīyaḥ sadā hariḥ

"He who is humbler than a blade of grass, more forbearing than a tree, giving due honor to others without requiring it for himself—such a person is ever worthy of chanting the holy name and can do so without limit."

A tree is blown mercilessly by the wind; endures the elements; allows all to eat of its fruit; is abused by animals and children; and withstands being pruned or even cut down. Yet, would that it could, it never complains. We are advised to be similarly flexible and strong, forbearing, and supremely tolerant. Such tolerance comes from seeing oneself in perspective, as a tiny soul in a very large universe.

It is through a genuine sense of humility, says Śrī Chaitanya, that one becomes eligible for chanting the holy name. The humble devotee knows that Krishna is all that is, and that he is meant to be his humble servant. Moreover, the devotee recognizes that, because all living beings exist as parts of Krishna, he is meant to serve them as well. Thus, the *Caitanya-caritāmṛta* (Madhya 22.78–80) lists twenty-six qualities that are incumbent upon serious practitioners. *Amāninā*, meaning "humble," or "free from false prestige," is one of them—and among the most important. Indeed, the *Caitanya-caritāmṛta* (Antya 20.26) tells us: "If one chants the holy name of Lord Krishna in this mindset, he will certainly awaken his dormant love for Krishna."

According to Vaishnava teaching, most people are unfortunately intoxicated by the need for prestige. They lose track of all that is good and true whenever made to feel that they are better than others. The ego thus bewilders us with a sort of magic-show, making us forget reality and replacing it with an inflated conception of the self. The word *prestige*, in fact, comes from the French, meaning "illusion, glamour," and it is cognate with the Latin *praestigium,* "illusion, or conjuring tricks." Prestige thus tends to make us lose our grip on substantive truth. "Magic moments in life," writes Satsvarūpa Dāsa

Goswāmī, "[like when] the actor receives applause, when the writer receives a prize of recognition, when a person meets and conquers his ideal love-mate—all are 'juggler's tricks.'"[9] This type of illusion, or *māyā,* is destroyed at the root when one cultivates *amāninā.*

Vaishnava sages warn practitioners to scrupulously avoid *pratiṣṭhā,* the desire for respect and adoration, which can be seen as an antonym of *amāninā.* Bhaktisiddhānta Sarasvatī compared *pratiṣṭhā* to a tigress (*bhāginī*), for just as the tigress is known to eat her prey whole, so too does the offense of *pratiṣṭhā* "swallow" the practitioner's entire mood of devotional surrender.[10] Thus, the desire for respect and adoration can potentially end a person's spiritual life.

(4)
na dhanaṁ na janaṁ na sundarīṁ
kavitāṁ vā jagad-īśa kāmaye
mama janmani janmanīśvare
bhavatād bhaktir ahaitukī tvayi

"My dear Lord: I do not long for riches, friends, relatives or followers, nor do I desire beautiful women—I only ask that my heart clings to you with selfless devotion, lifetime after lifetime, in whatever birth I take."

Mahāprabhu lauds selfless devotion and exclusive attachment to the Lord. While Gauḍīya Vaishnavism outlines a path for the gradual elevation of one's consciousness, the ultimate fruit of love of God is only attained through pure devotion, unobstructed by any distraction or deviation. As the *Bhāgavatam* (1.2.6) asserts, "The supreme duty for all humankind is devotional service (*bhakti*). Such service must be unmotivated (*ahaitukī*) and uninterrupted (*apratihatā*) to completely satisfy the self."

Mahāprabhu is thus herein expressing the realization that this single-minded devotion is required if one is to reach the perfectional state of Krishna Consciousness. More, he teaches that one who achieves such a state will hanker for nothing, not even *mokṣa* (liberation from the repetition of birth and death), the coveted goal generally sought after in the Hindu tradition. Rather, a first-class devotee relishes the thought of serving the Lord lifetime after lifetime, without any concern about the kind of body he or she takes or the assets accrued.

(5)
ayi nanda-tanuja kiṅkaraṁ
patitaṁ māṁ viṣame bhavāmbudhau
kṛpayā tava pāda-paṅkaja-
sthita-dhūlī-sadṛśaṁ vicintaya

"O son of Nanda! I am your humble servant, and I have fallen into this ocean of ignorance, i.e., the material world. Kindly show me your mercy and lift me up, placing me as a particle of dust at your lotus-like feet."

The devotee sees himself as an eternal servant of Krishna, temporarily caught in an inhospitable material world. The process of *bhakti*, specifically chanting, is meant to lift the devotee up to his original, constitutional position, whereby he is reminded that his real life is with Krishna in the spiritual world. But cognizant of his fundamental inability to extricate himself from the thralldom of material entanglement, the humble devotee wholeheartedly implores Krishna's mercy, realizing its necessity for lifting him up to the platform of eternal loving service.

Great souls in Vaishnava history have expressed this desire in various ways. Lord Brahmā, for example, beseeches the Lord, "I am most humbly praying to you for birth within Vrindāvan forest, so that I may be favored by the dust of your devotees' feet. Even if I am given the chance to grow just as humble grass in this land, that will be a glorious enough birth for me. I beg to be allowed to take birth even just outside the immediate area of Vrindāvan, so that when the devotees go out they will walk over me."[11]

The great devotee Uddhava, to cite another example, humbly prays, "Please let me be fortunate enough to be one of the bushes, creepers or herbs in Vrindāvan, because the *gopīs* trample them and thus bless them with the dust of their feet."[12] Mahāprabhu similarly teaches us to approach God with humility—*dhūlī-sadṛśaṁ*, "like a particle of dust."

The word *kiṅkaraṁ* in this verse is significant. Derived from the two words *kim* ("what") and *karomi* ("I do"), it means, "What can I do for you?" or "How can I serve you?" But in this context, these are not casual questions—it refers to the mood of being willing to do anything, absolutely anything, for one's beloved. This mood of unending and totally dedicated service becomes pivotal in the later tradition, and is associated with word *pālya-dāsī*, which indicates the inner nature of a maidservant, simple, protected, and loved. These two words are used to depict the *mañjarīs*, the intimates of Śrī Rādhā, whose high level of service will be described in an upcoming chapter.

(6)
nayanaṁ galad-aśru-dhārayā
vadanaṁ gadgada-ruddhayā girā
pulakair nicitaṁ vapuḥ kadā
tava nāma-grahaṇe bhaviṣyati

"When, I wonder, will my eyes know streams of tears, my voice falter, and my hairs stand on end as I chant your name?"

As the dawning of true love approaches, certain ecstatic symptoms appear on one's body—the eight types of physical transformations known as *sāttvika-bhāvas*. Although in this verse Mahāprabhu prays for only three of them, these three are meant to be representative of the rest. His begging for these symptoms is, however, pedagogical, a teaching device, as we see in Verse Two, when he had bemoaned the fact that he has no taste for chanting. Here, by his anxious inquiry regarding the ecstatic symptoms, his followers learn how to pray and thereby unselfconsciously imbibe *bhāva* (higher spiritual emotions). The implication is that devotees should anticipate and long for these intense feelings of love, along with the bodily symptoms that accompany them.

And in Mahāprabhu's manifest pastimes, for the instruction of all souls, these visible bodily characteristics come to unforgettably vivid life. As mentioned in the *Caitanya-caritāmṛta* (Antya 14.92–96): "The flesh at each of His pores erupted like pimples, and His hair, standing on end, appeared like *kadamba* flowers. Blood and perspiration flowed incessantly from every pore of His body, and He could not speak a word but simply produced a gurgling sound within His throat. The Lord's eyes filled up and overflowed with unlimited tears, like the Ganges and Yamunā meeting in the sea. Biographers relate that his bodily color faded entirely to the stark whiteness of an unblemished conch shell, and his trembling flesh quivered across his frame like windswept waves racing across an agitated sea. Quaking thus, he fell to the ground."[13]

Observing these symptoms in Mahāprabhu, the Goswāmīs of Vrindāvan documented exactly how they can be replicated in ordinary souls, from rudimentary practice, where the ecstatic symptoms are appreciated in theory, to advanced states of consciousness, wherein one experiences them directly. Rūpa Goswāmī in particular wrote about these symptoms in great detail.[14]

(7)
yugāyitaṁ nimeṣeṇa
cakṣuṣā prāvṛṣāyitam
śūnyāyitaṁ jagat sarvaṁ
govinda-viraheṇa me

"Being separated from Govinda [Krishna] makes a moment seem like an eon. As a result, my eyes shed more tears than clouds in the rainy season, and the entire world seems hopelessly void without him."

Mahāprabhu begins the seventh stanza by addressing Krishna as Govinda, "one who pleases the senses." The irony should be clear: Separation from Krishna (*viraheṇa*), which he specifically addresses in this verse, assaults the senses rather than pleases them, and so he petitions Krishna by using the name that is relevant here.

Though I have translated *yuga* as "eon," it can also mean "millennium" and, according to the tradition, "twelve years."[15] The point here is that in the unbearable grief of separation from Govinda (*govinda-viraha*), each moment feels like an unmanageably long period of time. The "twelve years" reading, however, is particularly meaningful in a Gauḍīya context, for it harkens to Mahāprabhu's final twelve years in Purī. It was then and there that he felt deep separation from Krishna, which is suggested in this verse.

Separation from Krishna becomes intolerable for one steeped in love of God. Such a person goes transcendentally mad (*divyonmāda*), with involuntary symptoms overtaking his body. He experiences *prāvṛṣāyitam*, "tears flowing like torrents of rain," and his eyes become *varṣāra megha-prāya*, "like clouds in the rainy season." In such a state, it seems like a day never ends (*divasa nā yāya*) and all hope is lost.[16] Nevertheless, this seemingly dismal state of affairs is in fact the prelude that yields *sambhoga*, the ecstasy of union, engendering a pleasure unknown in this world.

(8)
āśliṣya vā pāda-ratāṁ pinaṣṭu mām
adarśanān marma-hatām-hatāṁ karotu vā
yathā tathā vā vidadhātu lampaṭo
mat-prāṇa-nāthas tu sa eva nāparaḥ

"Whether Śrī Krishna, my beloved, offers me his sweet embrace, or simply tramples me underfoot—or even if he tortures me by staying away altogether—he is always and forever my Lord, unconditionally, even though he is a debauchee (*lampaṭaḥ*) illicitly spending time with others."

In this final verse, Mahāprabhu is totally gripped by the mood of Śrī Rādhā. Love has taken over. He is willing to make any concession to win Krishna's heart, without stipulation. Krishna must be his, at all costs. And he will do *anything* to be with him, to serve him, to love him.

Śrī Rādhā's emotional disposition is particularly evident in the final line, for only she would dare to call him a debauchee. This comes from her possessive nature. She speaks out because she alone must be his.

Chandrāvalī, Rādhā's chief competitor for Krishna's love, is compliant, and her love is therefore called *ghṛta-sneha*, or love that "melts like clarified butter." It is characterized by the feeling of "I am yours," meaning that she totally gives herself to Krishna. Śrī Rādhā, on the other hand, embodies a love called *madhu-sneha*, which is an emotion that is "sweet like honey." The character of this love is more intense, high-spirited, if you will, with the feeling of "you are *mine*." It is more confident and more possessive. From the Gauḍīya perspective, it is the highest form of love.[17]

HISTORY AND COMMENTARIAL TRADITION

Although Mahāprabhu emphasized the importance of chanting the holy name, he did not compile volumes of literature to explicate his doctrine, a fact that is explicitly stated by Kavi Karṇapūra in his *Śrī-Caitanya-candrodaya-nāṭakam* (1.13–14). Mahāprabhu did, however, bequeath the loving task of writing to his followers—the Six Goswāmīs and others. Producing numerous Sanskrit volumes, they extensively articulated his inner emotion and thought through well-developed philosophy, drama, and poetry, the likes of which, it can be argued, the world had never seen before, and has not seen since.

Mahāprabhu himself wrote only the *Śikṣāṣṭakam*, the famous eight prayers outlined above, as confirmed by noted scholars of the tradition, such as S. K. De: "The only work that can be ascribed to him with certainty consists of the eight verses which are attributed to him in Rūpa Gosvāmin's *Padyāvali* . . . ."[18] Edward C. Dimock makes the same claim in his edition of the *Caitanya-caritāmṛta*: "[T]he *Śikṣāṣṭakam* is traditionally said to be the only piece of writing left by Caitanya himself . . . ."[19] Sanskrit scholar David Buchta is specific: "While a handful of works have been attributed to Caitanya, the only work he can confidently be said to have penned is the *Śikṣaṣṭaka*, a *stotra* consisting of eight somewhat disconnected verses glorifying *bhakti* and the recitation of Kṛṣṇa's names."[20]

Gauḍīya practitioners support this notion as well. Three examples should suffice. Bhaktivinoda writes: "In order to understand the teachings of Lord Chaitanya, we must refer to the *Śrī Caitanya-caritāmṛta*. Lord Chaitanya Himself did not leave any written works, except the eight verses of the *Śikṣāṣṭaka* . . . ."[21] Contemporary Gauḍīya leader, Bhakti Charu Swami declared in a lecture, "So we will discuss about *Śikṣāṣṭakam* [which] has eight verses. Śrī Chaitanya Mahāprabhu gave the most sublime and most elevated spiritual wisdom but in written form He gave only these eight verses."[22] And Jan Brzezinski (Jagadānanda Dāsa) sums up, "No short account of Krishna Chaitanya's life fails to note something like, 'Chaitanya only left eight verses by which we can know his belief system.'"[23]

It is thus broadly accepted that Śrī Chaitanya "wrote" only eight verses. One might legitimately wonder, however, what "writing" in this context actually means. Does it refer to tangibly jotting down verses for oneself, in longhand, or perhaps merely composing them, singing them out loud, while others did the actual writing? There is an oral tradition, in fact, asserting that Mahāprabhu's secretary, Svarūpa Dāmodara Goswāmī, did the physical writing of these verses, while the Master merely enunciated them during ecstatic trance.[24] Along similar lines, Vyāsadeva, the legendary compiler of the Vedic literature, is said to have *written* the *Mahābhārata*, when upon closer examination the tradition reports more precisely that he recited the inspired text, while Shiva's son Gaṇeśa committed the spoken words to the page, fulfilling the role of a scribe.

Whatever the specifics, there are today no early manuscripts of Mahāprabhu's *Śikṣāṣṭakam*. There is, however, a "handwritten *Bhagavad-gītā*" said to have been rendered by the Master himself; it can still be viewed at the Gauridasa Pandita Mandira in Ambika Kalna, Bengal—the sacred text is even mentioned in the 18th-century *Bhakti Ratnākara* (7.338–341), legitimating it for the believing tradition. Goswāmī literature from that period, too, is available for viewing at the Vrindavan Research Institute, the Bhaktivedanta Research Centre in Kolkata, and elsewhere as well.

Śikṣāṣṭakam's Origin and Unique Nature

We first find the *Śikṣāṣṭakam* verses as individual lines in Rūpa Goswāmī's *Padyāvali* (*ślokas* 22, 31, 32, 71, 94, 95, 328, and 341), not in the *Caitanya-caritāmṛta*, the text that made them famous. Interestingly, they are found scattered throughout the *Padyāvali*, without any indication that they are an *āṣṭakam* (a single poem of eight lines).

It was Krishnadāsa Kavirāja Goswāmī, in his *Caitanya-caritāmṛta*, it seems, who positioned them as eight consecutive prayers, separated only by Bengali stanzas of elaboration. Indeed, he was the one to initially refer to them as "*Śikṣāṣṭakam*" (as in Antya 20.65, 138, and 139), combining them as a group. And by placing the verses toward the end of his masterwork, he grants them even greater status as a kind of summary and essence of Mahāprabhu's entire life and teachings.

It is likely that Mahāprabhu composed the verses early in his career, even if he recited them toward the end in a state of ecstasy. This is indicated by Kavirāja Goswāmī himself, for as he elaborates on them in Antya 20, verses 63–65, he writes: "Thus, overwhelmed by ecstatic love, Śrī Chaitanya spoke like a madman, sporadically reciting suitable verses. The Lord had formerly composed these eight to teach people in general. Now, he personally tasted their meaning: these verses are called the *Śikṣāṣṭaka* . . . ."

The fact that these are "his" stanzas distinguishes them from the many other utterances attributed to him—and there *are* others. For example, there is a famous *śloka*, also originating in Rūpa Goswāmī's *Padyāvali*, quoted in the *Caitanya-caritāmṛta*: "I am not a Brahmin, Kṣatriya, Vaiśya or Śūdra. Nor am I a Brahmacārī, Gṛhastha, Vānaprastha or Sannyāsī. What am I? I am the eternal servant of the servant of the servant of the *gopīs*, who are servants of Lord Krishna."[25] In Bhaktisiddhānta Sarasvatī's commentary on this verse, he writes that this particular *śloka* was "uttered" or "spoken" by Śrī Chaitanya (*śrī-krishna-caitanyokta-ślokaḥ*), and basically says the same for Madhya 2.45, *Chaitanya-bhāgavata*, Antya 6.124, and several others.

Indeed, in Antya 20, verse 62, Kavirāja Goswāmī himself asserts that the entire Bengali song used to illuminate the *Śikṣāṣṭakam*'s eighth verse was also recited by Mahāprabhu (*pade kailā arthera nirbandha*), if not composed by him. The *Śivāṣṭaka*—eight prayers glorifying Lord Shiva—is also sometimes attributed to the Master. This poem can be found in Śrī Chaitanya's very first biography (*Śrī-Caitanya-carita-mahākāvya*), written by Murāri Gupta, a personal associate and firsthand witness to the Master's pastimes.

These Shiva prayers are recited during Mahāprabhu's South Indian tour: Upon entering a Shiva temple, he spontaneously praises the matted-haired *deva* with these specific stanzas. That being said, scholars have noted that the verses themselves too closely resemble a similar *āṣṭakam* written by Ādi Śaṅkara many centuries earlier, and so must be seen as a Vaishnava variation on a Shaivite theme, which was certainly not "composed" by Śrī Chaitanya. The same is true of the famous *Jagannāthāṣṭaka*.[26] In the end, while Śrī Chaitanya recited numerous lyrics and verses, noted down by the sages of the Gauḍīya tradition, none of these are considered his original "compositions." That is a distinction reserved solely for the *Śikṣāṣṭakam*.

Few Commentaries

Despite its importance for the tradition, we find little commentary on the *Śikṣāṣṭakam* until the 19th century.[27] It was Bhaktivinoda Ṭhākura, the great Gauḍīya Vaishnava reformer, who wrote the first comprehensive Sanskrit elucidation, known as the *Sammodana-bhāṣya* (1886), and, soon after that, he revisited the verses in his Bengali poem, *Gītāvalī* (1893). Finally, he explained the inner meaning of the *Śikṣāṣṭakam* more fully in his highly mystical work, *Bhajana-rahasya* (1902), a supplement to his earlier *Harināma Chintamaṇi* (1900).

It is in the *Bhajana-rahasya*, especially, that we gain full entrance into the secrets of Mahāprabhu's eight verses. Here Bhaktivinoda shows how they correspond to Gauḍīya Vaishnavism's traditional nine steps leading to perfection in worship, gradually taking novitiates from deep faith (*śraddhā*) to love of God (*premā*).[28] In this same work, he also analyzes the *Śikṣāṣṭakam* in terms of Gauḍīya esoterica, including Krishna's eight times of the day in the spiritual world (Aṣṭa-kālīya-līlā), where he elucidates the intimate love of Rādhā and Krishna. Finally, Bhaktivinoda shows how Śrī Caitanya's eight prayers correspond to the various elements of the *mahā-mantra*—a quatrain of four lines (*pāda*), each comprised of eight syllables. He systematically takes readers from the first pair of names ("Hare Krishna"), wherein one learns to overcome ignorance and embrace the holy name with faith, to the final pair ("Hare Hare"), which takes its chanter to the height of spiritual perfection (*gopī-bhāva*).[29]

Thus, using the *Śikṣāṣṭakam*, Bhaktivinoda offers the Vaishnava world a step-by-step procedure for attaining the Supreme, employing the philosophical categories of relationship with Krishna (*sambandha*), the methods of acting according to that relationship (*abhidheya*), and the truths of what is ultimately to be attained (*prayojana*).

Bhaktivinoda's son, Bhaktisiddhānta Saraswatī, composed a "sub-commentary" on his father's initial Sanskrit work on the eight verses, and as he concludes his analysis, he briefly summarizes the meaning of each stanza:

> In a general sense, the first *śloka* teaches the process of congregational chanting; the second, how one can realize his ineptitude to take up this chanting; the third, the procedure of chanting the holy name; the fourth, how to rid oneself of deception and detrimental mundane desires; the fifth, the soul's original spiritual identity; the sixth, how one experiences his good fortune of coming closer to the Lord; the seventh, the mood of separation after one obtains the required spiritual elevation; the eighth, how to obtain the highest perfection in the matter of finding one's absolute necessity or goal . . . . The first five *ślokas* describe *sādhana-bhakti* [devotional service in practice], and the next two *bhāva-bhakti* [the dawning of true love]. The sixth to the eighth *ślokas*, and especially the seventh to the eighth, deal with *prema-bhakti* [fully developed love of Godhead].[30]

Gauḍīya Vaishnavas continue commenting on the *Śikṣāṣṭakam* even today, utilizing all of the insights and terminology of the tradition and that of modernity as well. Śrīla A. C. Bhaktivedānta Swami Prabhupāda, for example, not only translates the verses in his *Teachings of Lord Chaitanya* and in his monumental edition of the *Caitanya-caritāmṛta,* but goes further to explain them for his modern readers in contemporary language, so that they can understand the text and see its relevance in their day to day life. Other modern editions of the *Śikṣāṣṭakam* have made similar contributions. Three prominent examples are those of Swami B. V. Tripurāri;[31] Śrī Ananta Dāsa Bābājī Mahārāja;[32] and Bhakti Tīrtha Swami.[33]

CONCLUDING REFLECTIONS

"The reason Śrī Caitanya wrote nothing besides these eight verses," Bengali author Manindranath Guha tells us, "is because he had no need to: they above all, and in a nutshell, perfectly summarize his entire teaching, identified as *nāma-prema*—the holy name and love of Krishna."[34]

It might be asked why a practitioner should subject himself to the pain of separation as depicted in Śrī Chaitanya's *Śikṣāṣṭakam.* After all, spiritual life is meant to be blissful, fulfilling in a way that material life could never be. This is true enough, and Gauḍīya Vaishnavas answer convincingly: To cogently dispel the confusion understandably raised by this undeniably counterintuitive notion, Vaishnavas elaborate two distinct points. First, the apparent "pain" of separation is only external. And second, by opening oneself up to it, one experiences an internal taste of nectar more relishable than any other, and unavailable by any other means. This has been beautifully articulated by Swami B. V. Tripurāri:

> What then is the value of Mahāprabhu's pain of separation? While on the outside the effects of *premā* appear like poison, on the inside they are filled with *ānanda.* Although the ocean of Gaura's love caused him suffering in its low tide of separation, his love in separation on the shores of Jagannātha Purī made the ocean of love for Krishna accessible to all. As he entered that ocean in low tide, so shall we—following his example through love in separation—and in so doing taste, as he did, the high tide of union discussed in the final stanza of *Śikṣāṣṭakam.*[35]

The tradition teaches that Mahāprabhu's verses should be recited daily. They are described as being like precious seeds that grow into the great tree of *bhakti*, even if that tree is not at first visible. Encoded in these stanzas, we are told, one can access all the mysteries of Gauḍīya Vaishnavism, if one but learns to hear them properly, entering into their understanding. B. T. Swami entices readers further:

> As we deeply access all the amazing literature, stories and understandings available, we can begin to realize the powerful treasure contained within these eight verses. We should recognize this valuable key that can open sacred doors to the spiritual world. As we recite these *ślokas* daily, we should constantly endeavor to enter more deeply into their meaning and mystery. This *Śikṣāṣṭaka* states the conclusion of Krishna Consciousness and offers the culmination of all the *Vedas*; therefore, it is the necklace that all Vaishnavas should wear. A necklace worn around the neck practically touches the heart. These verses are essential for us and should always be kept close to our hearts.[36]

NOTES

1. The *Śikṣāṣṭakam* appears in the *Caitanya-caritāmṛta* 3.20, verses 12, 16, 21, 29, 32, 36, 39, and 47. My English rendering is based on the Sanskrit original in conjunction with the existing translations found in Śrīla A. C. Bhaktivedānta Swami Prabhupāda, *The Teachings of Lord Chaitanya* (New York, N.Y.: ISKCON Press, 1968), pp. XXXVII–XXXIX; Bhakti Pradip Tirtha, *Sri Chaitanya Mahaprabhu* (Calcutta: Gaudiya Mission, 1947), Appendix II, pp. 43–45; and Tripurāri Swami, *Śikṣāṣṭakam of Śrī Caitanya* (San Rafael, C.A.: Mandala Publishing, 2005), pp. 4–5, 26–27, 44–45, 62–63, 80–81, 92–92, 106–107, 120–121.

2. See RV 1.146.1: *trimūrdhānaṁ sapta-raśmiṁ gṛṇīṣe 'nūnam agniṁ pitror upasthe* (Translation by Ralph T. H. Griffith, [1896]: "I laud the seven-rayed, the

triple-headed, Agni all-perfect in his Parents' bosom, sunk in the lap of all that moves and moves not, him who hath filled all luminous realms of heaven.") Also see *Muṇḍaka Upanishad* (1.2.4), along with Śaṅkara's commentary.

3. In its poetic elegance, the verse allows both the hardship of material existence and the bliss of *saṅkīrtana* to partake of the "blazing fire" metaphor, if each in their own way.

4. See Bhaktsiddhānta Sarasvatī Ṭhākura, "*Vijayate śrī-kṛṣṇa-saṅkīrtanam*" in *Śrī Gauḍīya Patrikā*, Volume 24, No. 3. Translated in *Rays of the Harmonist*, No. 16 (2006), 17–20.

5. Edwin F. Bryant explains the metaphor of the white flower evoked in this verse: "The imagery here is that as the *kairava* is a night-blooming lotus that is nourished by the moon, while other conventional day-blooming lotuses are asleep, so those who chant the names of Kṛṣṇa are awakened to love of God while most living entities are asleep under the influence of *avidyā*." See Edwin F. Bryant, *Bhakti Yoga: Tales and Teachings from the Bhāgavata Purāṇa* (New York: North Point Press, 2017), p. 642. As a side note, some commentators refer to the *kairava* as a lily (Nymphaea) as opposed to a lotus (Nelumbo). There is some basis for this. The lotus is in fact an Asian water lily and so, for many years, there was some confusion about the relationship between the two. According to Gauḍīya Vaishnava scholar Ravīndra Svarūpa Dāsa, "The *kairava*, according to the Monier-Williams dictionary, is 'the white lotus-flower (blossoming at night).' In fact, the dictionary gives, as an appellation of the moon, the compound word *kairava-bandhu*, 'friend of the [*kairava*] lotus-flower.' In order to blossom, the *kairava* depends upon the kindness of the moon. . . . [That being said] the *kairava*, strictly speaking, is not a lotus (genus Nelumbo), but a lily, belonging to the Nymphaea genus. However, its specific scientific name is Nymphaea lotus, a nomenclature that probably both reflects confusion and adds to it as well. The *kairava*'s common names in English include: Egyptian Lotus, Egyptian Water-Lily, Tiger Lotus, Tropical Night-Blooming Water Lily, Waterlily, White Egyptian Lotus, White Lotus, White Water-Lily." For more, see Ravīndra Svarūpa Dāsa, "Flowers of Devotion": https://iskconnews.org/flowers-of-devotion,1365/.

6. See Śrī Śrīmad Bhakti Vijñāna Bhāratī Gosvāmī Mahārāja, *Viśuddha Caitanyavāṇī: An Anthology of Hari-kathā* (Vrindavan: Gaudiya Vedanta Publications, 2016), 179.

7. Elaborated in Bhaktsiddhānta Sarasvatī Ṭhākura, "When Will I Realize that The Holy Name is Directly Kṛṣṇa?" in *Rays of the Harmonist*, Volume 6, No. 3 (2013). See online (http://www.purebhakti.com/resources/harmonist-monthly/90-year-6/1372-when-will-i-realize-that-the-holy-name-is-directly-krsna).

8. The lack of taste for the holy name is said to come from the fourfold impediments: (1) ignorance of eternal principles; (2) frailties of heart; (3) evil propensities; and (4) offenses. See Bhakti Pradip Tirtha, *Sri Chaitanya Mahaprabhu, op. cit.*, Appendix II, 43. This is based on Bhaktivinoda Ṭhākura's *Bhajana-rahasya*.

9. See Satsvarūpa Dāsa Goswāmī, *Vaiṣṇava Behavior: The Twenty-Six Qualities of a Devotee* (Port Royal, P.A.: The Gita-nagari Press, 1983), 181.

10. Quoted in Śrī Śrīmad Bhakti Vijñāna Bhāratī Gosvāmī Mahārāja, *Volcanic Energy: Lessons From the Life of Śrī Śrīmad Bhakti Dayita Mādhava Gosvāmī Mahārāja* (Vrindavan: Viśuddha Caitanya-vāṇī Publications, 2016), 107.

11. This is Prabhupāda's translation of the tenth canto. See his summary in *Kṛṣṇa, The Supreme Personality of Godhead*, Chapter 14, "Prayers Offered by Lord Brahmā to Lord Kṛṣṇa" (http://krsnabook.com/ch14.html)

12. See *Śrīmad Bhāgavatam* 10.47.61.

13. Prabhupāda's translation.

14. See Rūpa Goswāmī's *Bhakti-rasāmṛta-sindhu*, Chapter 27 and 28.

15. Swami B. R. Śrīdhara, *The Golden Volcano of Divine Love*, op. cit., 138. Interestingly, both Apte and Monier Williams offer "twelve" as an option in translating *yuga*, albeit an obscure one. Vaman Sivaram Apte, *The Student's Sanskrit-English Dictionary*, Second Edition (Delhi: Motilal Banarsidass, 1970), 458: "An expression for the number 'four,' rarely for 'twelve' . . . ." Monier Williams specifically associates *yuga* with the number twelve in the realm of astrology (http://www.sanskrit-lexicon.uni-koeln.de/mwquery/), though it may also refer to twelve in regard to the number of syllables in a Sanskrit meter, as in the *jagatī* meter (which consists of 4 verses of 12 syllables each).

16. See *Caitanya-caritāmṛta*, Antya 20.40: "In my great aggravation, a day never ends, for every moment seems like an entire *yuga*. Shedding innumerable tears, my eyes are like the clouds of the rainy season." (*udvege divasa nā yāya, 'kṣaṇa' haila 'yuga'-sama, varṣāra megha-prāya aśru variṣe nayana*).

17. The *ghṛta-sneha/ madhu-sneha* dichotomy appears in seed form in Rūpa Goswāmī's *Ujjvala-nīlamaṇi* (Sthāyi-bhāva-prakaranam 79–83, 84–85). Bhaktivinoda Ṭhākura outlines it for the tradition in *Jaiva Dharma*, Chapter 36, and for a scholarly assessment see Donna M. Wulff, "Rūpa's Rādhā: Passionate, Worshipful, Strong-willed, Divine" in *Journal of Vaishnava Studies*, Volume 8, No. 2 (Spring 2000), 86–87.

18. S. K. De, "Doubtful Works Ascribed to Chaitanya." *Indian Historical Quarterly* (1934), 310–317.

19. See *The 'Caitanya Caritāmṛta' of Kṛṣṇadāsa Kavirāja*, translated with commentary by Edward C. Dimock, Jr., edited by Tony K. Stewart, *op. cit.* This statement about the *Śikṣāṣṭakam* appears as a footnote for Antya 20, verse 3, 993.

20. See David Buchta, "Pedagogical Poetry: Didactics and Devotion in Rūpa Goswāmin's *Stavamālā*," Ph.D. Thesis, University of Pennsylvania, 2014, 10.

21. See Bhaktivinoda Ṭhākura, *Śrī Caitanya-śikṣāmṛta* (1.2).

22. His Holiness Bhakti Charu Swami, "ŚIKṢĀṢṬAKAM LECTURE 1—Belgium, Radhadesh, August 2, 2011" (http://www.bhakticharuswami.com/2011/08/1297109/).

23. Brzezinski continues, "But the authorship of even these verses has been cast into some doubt by scholars on the basis of statements by Karṇapūra and others, who declare unequivocally that Chaitanya wrote nothing at all. Over time, a number of a number of works have been attributed to Chaitanya, but few of these claims are credible. Even the most consistently attributed text, the *Rādhā-prema-rasāyana-stotram*, has not been accepted as Chaitanya's own writing by the tradition. In any case, a perusal of the works in question, where they are available, shows little of interest that would strike the hearts of the devotees as the work of the Supreme Lord himself . . . . On the other hand, the verses known to us as the *Śikṣāṣṭakam* ("eight verses of teaching") have had a resilience that has not only endured, but continues to grow, with several new commentaries, primarily in Bengali, being published

in recent decades." See Jan Brzezinski, "Śrī Chaitanya's *Śikṣāṣṭakam*," *Journal of Vaishnava Studies*, Volume 12, No. 1 (Fall 2003), 87–111.

24. Śrīnātha Ṭhākura, *The Teaching of Chaitanya Mahaprabhu* (Delhi: Three Ways Publishing, 1975), 31.

25. See *Padyāvali* 74; quoted in the *Caitanya-caritāmṛta*, Madhya-līlā, 13.80 (*nāham vipro na cha nara-patir nāpi vaiśyo na śūdro nāham varṇī na cha gṛha-patir no vanastho yatir vā kintu prodyan-nikhila-paramānanda-pūrnāmṛtābdher gopī-bhartuḥ pada-kamalayor dāsa-dāsānudāsaḥ*).

26. There are others as well. Some of these poems are alluded to in Haridāsa Dāsa's *Gauḍīya Vaishnava Abhidhāna*, a voluminous encyclopedia focusing on the Chaitanya-Vaishnava tradition. In the entry, "Krishna Chaitanya" (Volume 2, 1,183), the author notes that, "The commentator Viṭṭhaleśvara considers '*Śrī Krishna-premāmṛta-stotra*' as having manifested from the moonlike mouth of Śrī Krishna Chaitanya. There are other small *āṣṭakams* and other works that are ascribed to Mahāprabhu, too, but their authenticity is not free from doubt." Haridāsa Dāsa then proceeds to say that although it is unlikely that Mahāprabhu wrote any work other than the *Śikṣāṣṭakam*, he infused his *śakti* into Rūpa, Sanātana and the other Goswāmīs to write on his behalf. This is the general conclusion of the tradition as a whole.

27. Although the *Śikṣāṣṭakam* is rarely mentioned in the period between Krishnadāsa Kavirāja Goswāmī and Bhaktivinoda Ṭhākura, there are a few exceptions, the most notable perhaps being the *Karṇānanda* of Yadunandanadāsa (mid-17th century). In this work, there is a section wherein Rāmacandra Kavirāja espouses the basics of Gauḍīya theology. He cites many verses to substantiate his view, and when he comes to the topic of *saṅkīrtana* he begins with the first verse of the *Śikṣāṣṭakam* and then includes the others. Although the verses are cited as being from the *Padyāvali*, they are presented in the same order as in Kavirāja Goswāmī's *Caitanya-caritāmṛta*. See Yadunandanadāsa, *Karṇānanda*, in Bengali, edited by Rāmanārāyaṇa Vidyāratna (Murshidabad: Haribhaktipradāyinī Sabhā, 1891), 66–69.

28. The nine stages of perfection: (1) *śraddhā* (faith); (2) *sādhu-saṅga* (association of saintly people); (3) *bhajana-kriya* (performance of worship); (4) *anartha-nivṛttiḥ* (decreasing unwanted attachments); (5) *niṣṭhā* (steadiness); (6) *ruci* (taste); (7) *āsakti* (attachment); (8) *bhāva* (love); and (9) *prema* (purest love). This schema is originally found in Rūpa Goswāmī's *Bhakti-rasāmṛta-sindhu* (1.4.15–16) and developed by Viśvanātha Chakravartī in his *Mādhurya-kadambini*. In Bhaktivinoda's analysis, the first verse of the *Śikṣāṣṭakam* corresponds to *śraddhā*, the second to *sādhu-saṅge bhajana-kriya anartha-nivṛttiḥ*, the third to *niṣṭhā*, the fourth to *ruci*, the fifth to *āsakti*, the sixth to *bhāva*, and the seventh and eighth to *premā* (both in union and separation, respectively).

29. For more on the correlation between the eight verses and the *mahā-mantra*, see "Confidential Secrets of Bhajana: An Overview of Srila Bhaktivinoda Thakura's Bhajana-Rahasya" (Lectures given during Kartika in Vrindavan; October–November, 1996, by Tridandi Svami Sri Srimad Bhaktivedanta Narayana Maharaja), 12–15. See http://cincinnatitemple.com/downloads/confidentialsecretsofbhajana.pdf.

30. Toward the end of Bhaktisiddhānta's commentary on the *Sammodana-bhāṣya*, we find this succinct paragraph (http://www.krishnapath.org/Library/Goswami-books/Bhaktivinoda-Thakura/Bhaktivinoda_Thakura_Sri_Sanmodana_Bhasyam.pdf).

31. Swami B. V. Tripurāri, *Śikṣāṣṭaka of Śrī Caitanya* (San Rafael, C.A.: Mandala Publishing, 2005).

32. *Śrī-Śrī Śikṣāṣṭakam of Śrī Caitanya Mahāprabhu with the Commentary of Śrī Ananta Dāsa Bābājī Mahārāja,* translated by Advaita Dāsa (Radha-kunda: self-published, 1989).

33. B. T. Swami, *Reflections on Sacred Teachings—Volume One: Sri Siksastaka* (Capitol Hill, Washington, D.C.: Hari-Nama Press, 2002).

34. Quoted in Jan K. Brzezinski, "Śrī Chaitanya's *Śikṣāṣṭakam*," in *Journal of Vaishnava Studies*, Volume 12, No. 1 (Fall 2003), 88.

35. Swami B. V. Tripurāri, *Śikṣāṣṭaka of Śrī Caitanya,* op. cit., 116.

36. B. T. Swami, op. cit., 226.

Chapter 7

Gauḍīya Vedānta

Inconceivable Unity in Diversity

Throughout history, philosophers have endeavored to understand the many contrasting and conflicting aspects of the world around us.[1] They seek to penetrate the nestled layers of polydimensional reality in an attempt to comprehend the inner foundational essence that evades our grasp. Some would articulate this reality and the attempt to reconcile it as a natural progression through thesis, antithesis, and synthesis. The Hegelian dialectic, for example, teaches that concepts naturally include their opposites and even find reconciliation in a higher notion that contains both concept and contradiction.[2]

According to Hegel, an idea can only reach its full potential when its opposite ("negation") is accepted without compromise. Both positive and negative, he says, initially coexists with tension.[3] But as a sort of "negation of negation" develops in due course, a higher perception eventually ensues that will include both sides of the equation. In Hegel's view, then, two contradictory notions can support each other and even bring out their highest dimensions.

Hegel's thinking harkens to the philosophical ideal called *dialetheism*, the belief that a statement and its opposite can somehow both be true. This goes beyond *paraconsistent* (meaning "inconsistency-tolerant") logic, which merely seeks to accommodate contradiction, not confirm it. Indeed, dialetheism takes us from the usual "either-or" sensibility to a realm where "both-and" makes more sense. Such ideas point in the direction of Śrī Chaitanya's Acintya-bhedābheda Vedānta.

ŚRĪ CHAITANYA'S VEDĀNTIC TEACHING

Acintya-bhedābheda refers to the sphinxlike relationship between the Lord (*śaktiman*) and his energies (*śakti*), which exists in a perpetual state of simultaneous oneness and difference. This is supported by an age-old Vedāntic aphorism: "There is no difference between potency and the possessor of potency" (*śakti śaktimator abhedaḥ*).[4] Yet the possessor of potency is unquestionably prior, the source, and also distinguished as an independent entity. The potency, on the other hand, is not distinguished in the same way, but rather manifests as both the cosmos and as spiritual beings who are dependent on their source as his separated and individualistic parts (*vibhinnāmśa*).[5] They are both distinct (*bheda*) and non-distinct (*abheda*) from the Lord, inconceivably (*acintya*), and hence the term *actinya-bhedābheda*.

In other words, the Lord's *śakti* is an inseparable part of his self-existent nature. It is, in a sense, who he is, for a person and his energy are nondifferent (see clarifying analogies below). Nonetheless, because God is by nature absolute, his energy is imbued with personality and distinction, manifesting separately—apart from him—for his pleasure. Thus, what reality sets before us is God and all things directly related to God, on the one hand, and, simultaneously, it gives us those things that are *not* God, that emanate from him but only partially exhibit his spiritual nature, on the other. Both "God" and "not God," Vaishnava texts tell us, are in some sense one, if also obviously different.

The notion of Acintya-bhedābheda, then, seeks to harmonize these contradictory elements of reality. As Gauḍīya Vaishnava theologian O. B. L. Kapoor (1909–2001) writes,

> The concepts of identity and difference are both inadequate to describe the nature of being. Exclusive emphasis on the one leads to a virtual denial of the world as illusion, while exclusive emphasis upon the other bifurcates reality into two and creates an unbridgeable gulf between God and the world. Both concepts . . . seem to be equally necessary. Identity is a necessary demand of reason, and difference is an undeniable fact of experience. An ideal synthesis of identity and difference must be the cherished goal of philosophy. But the synthesis, though necessary, is not possible or conceivable. This is the final test of human logic. It fails. But the logic of the infinite succeeds where our human logic fails. In the perfect being there is no conflict between necessity and possibility. Here, what is necessary actually is. The clue to the solution of the problem, according to the school of Śrī Chaitanya, therefore, lies in the inconceivable power (*acintya-śakti*) of God, by which the concepts of identity and difference are transcended and reconciled in a higher synthesis.[6]

THE IMPORTANCE OF ANALOGY

Although Acintya-bhedābheda is fundamentally paradoxical and thus inexplicable, one can get a glimmer of its truth through analogy. This is precisely the technique the Goswāmīs of Vrindāvan used to elucidate the inconceivable nature of God and his relationship to his energies. In the context of Acintya-bhedābheda, they used three analogies in particular: gold nuggets in relation to a gold mine; a drop of water compared to an entire ocean; and sunshine in relation to the sun. Contemporary Gauḍīya Vaishnava writer Kuṇḍalī Dāsa nicely sums up all three:

> Lord Caitanya's teaching of simultaneous oneness and difference between God and the individual souls is called in Sanskrit *acintya-bhedābheda-tattva*. He and His followers have given examples to illustrate this truth. One example is that of the gold nugget and the gold mine. Under chemical analysis, gold nuggets are seen to be qualitatively one with a whole mine of gold, but the quantitative difference is unquestionable. If one were given the choice to own one or the other between the two, it's inconceivable that one would choose the nugget . . . . Another example is that of a spark and a fire. Though both have the quality of giving off heat and light, the quantities of the energies they emit are vastly different . . . . Probably the most graphic example of simultaneous oneness and difference is that of sunlight and the sun. Like the Lord, the sun is the energetic source of unlimited energy. Its rays are comparable to the unlimited souls emanating from the Lord. The rays are simultaneously one with the sun and yet different from it. We may welcome a few sunrays into our room through the window, but we would never extend the same invitation to the sun itself.[7]

The key concept here is quality in relation to quantity. The sun, for example, might be seen as the sum total of all fire, and while qualitatively it shares its "fire quality" with sunshine, the latter issues forth in lesser quantity. Thus, in terms of God and his energies, we see that in one sense they are identical in nature—that is to say, we, and everything that emanates from God, are qualitatively one with him—and yet, in another sense, they are fundamentally different. God is great, and his energies are small, which is a quantitative consideration. This is the mystery of any given agent and the *śakti* that emanates from it. Dr. Kapoor explains this in terms of fire and its capacity to burn:

> We cannot think of fire without the power of burning; similarly, we cannot think of the power of burning without fire. Both are identical. Fire is nothing except that which burns; the power of burning is nothing except fire in action. At the same time, fire and its power of burning are not absolutely the same. If they were absolutely the same, there would be no sense in saying "fire burns." It would be enough to say "fire." "Fire burns" would involve needless repetition, for "fire" would mean the same thing as "burns." Besides, if there were no difference between fire and its power, it would not be possible to neutralize the power of burning in fire by means of medicines or mantra, without making fire disappear altogether.[8]

Extrapolating freely, Ravi Gupta confirms that the principle of Acintya-bhedābheda can be extended beyond its central focus, which is the relationship between God and his energies. Gupta traces this extended theory to Jīva Goswāmī himself, who indeed shows that the teaching is not merely a theological principle, related to God, but a far more inclusive one, applicable to all aspects of matter and spirit.[9]

We thus learn that reconciliation of oneness and difference is essential for a full experience of reality. Such reconciliation creates a higher synthesis in which man is truly able to perceive his place in the universe, harmonizing the disparate elements of existence. This sense of balance had already been expressed in the *Bhagavad-gītā*, hinting at Mahāprabhu's doctrine of Acintya-Bhedābheda long before it was officially formulated.

For example, in the *Gītā's* 18th chapter, there is a section where Krishna describes various kinds of knowledge. He separates them into goodness, passion, and ignorance. Naturally, when knowledge comes by way of passion or ignorance, it is stilted, hyperbolizing one side or the other, without balance. But when it is derived through the virtue of goodness, it embodies harmony. "That knowledge by which one undivided spiritual nature is seen in all beings, though simultaneously divided into innumerable forms," Krishna says, "should be understood as being in the mode of goodness."[10] This non-differential evenness of perception, so representative of the mode of goodness, is illuminating and accommodates both sides of reality. It therefore sits well with the doctrine of Acintya-bhedābheda. It asks us to see the "divided" and the "undivided" simultaneously, promoting a sort of middle path, which takes into consideration both sides of every equation. In this way, the truth of Acintya-bhedābheda embraces all of reality.

Bengali scholar Shukdeb Bhowmick articulates this all-encompassing aspect of Śrī Chaitanya's teaching as follows:

> Gaudiya-Vaishnavism advocates the middle path of monism in pluralism, identity in difference, unity in diversity . . . . The absolute and the relative, the one and the many, the order and the disorder, the cosmos and the chaos, have their relative roles to play. At the end all are bound together in the all-abiding, all-comprehensive perfect Being who runs as a thread through infinite parts, diverse personalities and interacting relations that constitute the universe as a whole . . . . It is the real philosophy of harmony and order since it does not brush aside disorder and disharmony, differences of parts and relations, as mere illusory appearances . . . . It is a philosophy of affirmation and not of negation . . . . This philosophy builds a solid bridge between man and divinity, between the relative and the Absolute, between the part and the whole.[11]

The *Gītā* initially articulates this idea in cryptic terms and then enunciates it more clearly. In 9.4, for example, Krishna says (in Prabhupāda's translation):

"By Me, in My unmanifested form, this entire universe is pervaded. All beings are in Me, but I am not in them." Here, Krishna is basically saying that he is simultaneously one with and different from his creation. He then underlines this truth in the subsequent verse (9.5): "And yet everything that is created does not rest in Me. Behold My mystic opulence! Although I am the maintainer of all living entities and although I am everywhere, I am not a part of this cosmic manifestation, for My Self is the very source of creation." Thus, even in the *Gītā*, Śrī Chaitanya's doctrine of inconceivable unity in diversity can be found in seedlike form.

GRASPING THE UNGRASPABLE

Still, Acintya-bhedābheda is beyond comprehension, as indicated by the prefix, *acintya* ("inconceivable"). It is important that the word be properly understood. It basically refers to that which lies beyond argument, logic, and philosophical speculation. In other words, *acintya* can correctly be applied to anything that is truly spiritual. Nonetheless, scholars have argued that a more appropriate translation might be "paradoxical," or even "mind-boggling," since under the right conditions the "inconceivable" can, according to religious doctrine, become conceivable, at least to a certain extent.[12]

For example, in the *Bhagavad-gītā*, Krishna describes the soul as *acintya* (2.25), but the entire *Gītā*—and, in Vaishnava circles, the entire spiritual pursuit—involves discovering and eventually directly perceiving the nature of the soul. Later in the *Gītā* (8.9), Krishna tells Arjuna of his (Krishna's) "inconceivable form" (*acintya-rūpam*), but Arjuna actually sees this form as the text unfolds. How, then, is it inconceivable? Clearly, Gauḍīya Vaishnavism offers a method by which one might grasp the ungraspable. Indeed, the concept of *acintya* indicates a truth that cannot be reached by normal methods, but which *can,* say Gauḍīyas, be known by revelation, or even by knowledge that is passed down from master to disciple in disciplic succession (*paramparā*).

Baladeva Vidyābhūṣaṇa, the great Gauḍīya commentator of the 18th century, wrote that the inconceivable can be apprehended through scriptural revelation.[13] When he writes about the interrelationship between God (*īśvara*) and the soul (*ātmā*), he tends to address the concept of inconceivability as a matter of course. But to reconcile this, he inevitably suggests recourse to scripture. It is through this, says Baladeva, that we can access that which is beyond experimental knowledge.[14] That is, if something is inconceivable, then it can only be understood by consulting knowledge that is beyond human jurisdiction. For Baladeva, this means taking shelter of India's revealed wisdom texts, which are said to have supernatural origin.

The renowned Vaishnava *sannyāsin*, B. R. Śrīdhara Mahārāja makes clear the Gauḍīya doctrine of how to conceive the inconceivable. He tells us that it is simply illogical to assume that an all-powerful God would be unable to reveal himself to others: "There are channels by which the infinite descends," Śrīdhara Mahārāja intimates to us. "The infinite cannot be contained in a limited sphere, as I've just said, but if He is really infinite, then He has the power of making Himself known in all His fullness to the finite mind. When out of His own prerogative, he takes the initiative and reveals Himself to the devotee, there is actual perception of Godhead, self-realization, transcendental revelation."[15]

Krishna affirms in the *Gītā* (18.55), too, that he can be known *as he is,* that is, "in truth" (*tattvataḥ*), by the confidential process of devotional service (*bhakti*). In this way, say the Gauḍīya Vaishnava *ācāryas*, the inconceivable (*acintya*) can be accommodated by a finite mind and become accessible to the sincere practitioner. Indeed, if we deny God's ability to effect such revelation, as Śrīdhara Mahārāja insists, we are, by implication, attempting to limit the Unlimited.

ACINTYA-BHEDĀBHEDA: HISTORY AND COMMENTARY

Although there were numerous forms of Bhedābheda ("oneness and difference") philosophy prior to the time of Śrī Chaitanya, it was the Master himself who first conceived of it in terms of its inconceivability and as a way of harmonizing all traditional systems of thought.[16]

Soon after Mahāprabhu's time, Jīva Goswāṃī, one of the Six Goswāṃīs of Vrindāvan, gave it its formal title, "Acintya-bhedābheda." This has been documented in his masterwork, *Sarva Saṃvādinī*, specifically where he comments on his own *Paramātmā Sandarbha* (Anuccheda 77, 78). The context is revealing: While exploring the various traditions of "difference" (*bheda*) in the history of Sanskrit literature, he distinguishes the philosophical system he inherited through Śrī Chaitanya, writing, *sva-mate tu acintya-bhedābhedaḥ* ("but my view is Acintya-bhedābheda"). Though the general idea had appeared in the writing of his predecessors, including both Sanātana and Rūpa Goswāmīs, he was the first to actually coin the term.[17] But in these early years of the lineage, it was rarely used as an official name for Śrī Chaitanya's form of Vedānta.

Almost two hundred years later, in the 18th century, Jīva Goswāmī's successor, Baladeva Vidyābhuṣaṇa, elaborated on the doctrine in his famous *Govinda-bhāṣya* (commentary on the *Vedānta-sūtra*). Systematically drawing on sacred texts, the teachings of previous masters, and logic to prove the legitimacy of Acintya-Bhedābheda, he finally established it as the official school of the Gauḍīya Sampradāya.[18]

Nearly a century after that, Bhaktivinoda Ṭhākura developed Baladeva's ideas further. In 1892, he published a book called *Vaishnava-siddhānta-mālā*. Its fifth chapter fully explains Acintya-bhedābheda Vedānta in the context of Indian philosophy. He begins by showing how it is distinct from Advaita Vedānta, asserting that difference (*bheda*) is real and not imaginary or illusory, a claim that is often associated with Śaṅkara and his followers. God and all living beings are eternally distinct, Bhaktivinoda says, even if they engender a certain oneness as spiritual entities eternally connected in loving relationship (*bhakti*).[19]

He goes on to explain that those who accept the philosophy of *bhedābheda*—in any of its various permutations—are reaching for a more complete view of reality, whereas those who only propound either *bheda* or *abheda*, separately, will necessarily be confronted by a one-dimensional truth. He says that various Vaishnava *sampradāyas* express this reality in their own ways, according to the specifics of their lineage, and that there is no actual disagreement between them. This is because they are all ultimately *saviśeṣa-vādīs* (those who believe in eternal distinction). In this sense, none of them adhere to Śaṅkara's doctrine of *kevalābheda* (only oneness), which, according to Bhaktivinoda, is clearly fallacious.[20]

Bhaktivinoda expanded on these ideas in *Mahāprabhura Śikṣā*,[21] published the same year as *Vaishnava-siddhānta-mālā*. Here he explains that Acintya-bhedābheda is the culmination of all Vedic thought. He does this by showing that it is the most inclusive of all philosophical systems and the most accommodating in terms of Vedic injunction. His argument runs as follows: The *Vedas* express the truth in various ways. Sometimes they promote monism, saying that God is ultimately formless, and, in other verses, they support theistic Vedānta, pointing to a personal God. That being the case, says Bhaktivinoda, it is odd that none of India's established philosophical traditions, which seek to legitimate Vedic understanding, succeed in fully accommodating both sides of the spectrum.

In other words, Indian philosophy reveals two extreme positions: Advaita (oneness, formlessness) and Dvaita (duality, God with form). Both extremes can be seen as supporting one or the other of the various Vedic perspectives, but not both. Now, there are Vaishnava schools, Bhaktivinoda reminds us, that *do* recognize both Advaita and Dvaita—but not equally. So, what we have, essentially, are either extreme positions that accept certain Vedic statements but in doing so automatically decry the others, and we have traditions that seek to accommodate both sides but nonetheless tend to emphasize one or the other. Acintya-bhedābheda resolves the problem: Only in this all-inclusive philosophy, Bhaktivinoda says, do we find equitable treatment of both sides of the Vedic argument, and for this reason it is to be considered the perfect Vedic philosophy.

In Bhaktivinoda's words: "Exclusive duality, exclusive monism, pure monism or qualified monism [the standard Vaishnava schools]—these philosophies all agree with *some* of the statements of the Vedic scriptures, but contradict other such statements. But the philosophy of Acintya-bhedābheda is a philosophy that agrees with and accommodates all the statements of scripture."[22]

CONCLUDING REFLECTIONS

Gauḍīya Vaishnava scholar Graham Schweig argues that the etymology of the word *bhakti* reveals clear indication of Acintya-bhedābheda. Its verbal root *bhaj*, he observes, primarily means both "to share" and "to divide," as we have explained in our previous chapter on *bhakti*. Nonetheless, this paradoxical nature of the word itself takes on new meaning in light of the present subject. Schweig elaborates:

> In *bhakti*, a "dividing" or difference (*bheda*) is always maintained between the soul and God . . . . Simultaneously, there is always a "sharing" or oneness (*abheda*) between the soul and God . . . . In Vaishnava *bhakti*, there must always be this difference or "division" between the soul and God which allows for a devotional union consisting of reciprocal "sharing" between both. Thus, on the one hand, there is never an absolute duality between the soul and God, as there is in the deistic relationship to the numinous, and, on the other hand, there is never an absolute dissolution of the individuality of the soul or God (as there is in the union of monistic conceptions) . . . . This etymological definition of *bhakti* as oneness and difference reflects Chaitanya's philosophy of "inconceivable oneness and difference" (*acintya-bhedābheda*).[23]

We can sum up with one of Śrīla Prabhupāda's many clear if also seemingly enigmatic assertions, much loved by his disciples: "There is nothing in existence not related with Śrī Kṛṣṇa. In a sense, there is nothing but Śrī Kṛṣṇa, and yet nothing is Śrī Kṛṣṇa save and except His primeval personality."[24] Or as the *Vishnu Purāṇa* (1.16.78) tells us: "There is nothing different from it, yet it is different from everything."[25] This is Acintya-bhedābheda in a nutshell.

NOTES

1. Many philosophical thinkers throughout history, from the West as well as the East, have approximated Acintya-bhedābheda in their pursuance of ultimate reality. Glimmers of the doctrine can be found in the teachings of Heraclitus (c. 535–c. 475 BCE), in the West, and in that of his contemporary, Lao Tzu, author of the *Tao Te*

Ching, in the East: These teachers famously gave us "the fundamental law of the universe," that is, the unity of opposites. This was eventually articulated as *Coincidentia Oppositorum*, a Latin phrase that in fact means, "coincidence of opposites." This, in essence, points to Acintya-bhedābheda. In the writings of Śrī Chaitanya's followers, however, we see this idea fully developed as a distinct and sophisticated philosophical system of knowledge.

2. For more on Hegel in this context: (https://plato.stanford.edu/entries/hegel-dialectics/). For more on Hegel in relation to Vaishnavism: (http://mexpostfact.blogspot.com/2015/12/hegels-holiday.html).

3. Ibid.

4. The aphorism "*śakti śaktimator abhedaḥ*" is found in many ancient texts and is widely accepted as a general Vedāntic principle, as quoted by Śrīla Prabhupāda: See *Caitanya-caritāmṛta* (Madhya 6.163), purport. The Vrindāvan Goswāmī's used the phrase (or slightly altered versions of it) in their work as well. Two examples are Rūpa Goswāmī's *Laghu bhāgavatāmṛta* (5.246) and Jīva Goswāmī's *Bhagavata Sandarbha* (Anuccheda 8, *Sarva Saṁvādinī*), both quoted from the much earlier *Bhargava Tantra*.

5. *Vibhinnāṁśa* is a word that is pregnant with meaning. The *Mahā-varāha Purāṇa* defines the soul as similar to a portion of the Supreme: "The Supreme Lord is known in two ways: in terms of his plenary expansions (God) and his separated expansions (living beings). The plenary expansions are hardly distinguishable from their source, both in terms of their capabilities and their forms. These are the many types of *avatāras*. But the *separated* expansions, the living entities (*vibhinnāṁśa*), are different, possessing only minute potency and endowed with the Lord's powers only to a small extent." (*svāṁśaś cātha vibhinnāṁśa, iti dvidhā śa iṣyate, aṁśino yat tu sāmarthyaṁ, yat-svarūpaṁ yathā sthitiḥ, tad eva nāṇu-mātro 'pi, bhedaṁ svāṁśāṁśinoḥ kvacit, vibhinnāṁśo 'lpa-śaktiḥ syāt, kiñcit sāmarthya-mātrayuk*). Quoted by Prabhupāda in his commentary to *Śrīmad Bhāgavatam* 10.87.20.

6. O. B. L. Kapoor, *The Philosophy and Religion of Śrī Caitanya* (New Delhi: Munshiram Manoharlal, 1977), 151–152.

7. See Kuṇḍalī Dāsa, "The Counterfeit of Spiritual Life" in *Back to Godhead*, Vol. 23, No. 9, 1988 (http://btg.iskcondesiretree.com/Back_To_Godhead_-_html_format/1988/246_-_BTG_Year-1988_Volume-23_Number-09.html#3).

8. O. B. L. Kapoor, op. cit., 153.

9. Ravi M. Gupta, *The Caitanya Vaiṣṇava Vedānta of Jīva Gosvāmī* (New York: Routledge, 2007), 50–52.

10. See *Bhagavad-gītā* 18.20 (*sarva-bhūteṣu yenaikaṁbhāvam avyayam īkṣateavibhaktaṁ vibhakteṣutaj jñānaṁ viddhi sāttvikam*).

11. Shukdeb Bhowmick, *The Theory of Acintya-bhedābheda* (Kolkata: Sanskrit Pustak Bhander, 2004), 14–15.

12. See Alessandro Graheli, "Narration and Comprehension of Paradox in Gauḍīya Literature," in *Rivista di Studi Sudasiatici* 2 (2007), 183–184. For more on the Gauḍīya Vaishnava conception of God in relation to inconceivability, see Steven J. Rosen, "Krishna: Lord of Paradox" in *The Agni and the Ecstasy: Collected Essays of Steven J. Rosen* (UK: Arktos Media Ltd., 2012), 56–58.

13. Bhakti Chatterjee, *The Literary Contribution of Baladeva Vidyābhūṣaṇa* (New Delhi: Sastra Publishers, 1996), 22–23.

14. Ibid.

15. See Śrīla B. R. Śrīdhara Mahārāja, "The Descent of the Holy Name: A Gauḍīya Vaiṣṇava Perspective" (http://bvml.org/SBRSM/tdothn.html).

16. It should be underlined that although various schools of Bhedābheda existed prior to Gauḍīya Vaishnavism, Jīva Goswāmī's particular formulation is unique, mainly because of its emphasis on *acintya* or "inconceivability." Here's how this is so: First of all, despite their well-known use of the term "Bhedābheda," Bhāskara (c. 9th century) and Vijñānabhikṣu (c. 16th century), for example, tend to emphasize *abheda* ("oneness") as opposed to the simultaneous unification of both *bheda* and *abheda*, a principle to which a thoroughgoing Bhedābheda system must adhere. Nimbarka (c. 13th century) and Jīva Goswāmī, on the other hand, optimize the Bhedābheda relation by acknowledging an equal emphasis on both sides of the equation. However, Nimbārka does not address just how the Lord and pure souls themselves are inherently constituted. Is there within each of them an internal hierarchical structure of sameness and difference with which one must reckon? If so, does Bhedābheda apply to only part of such a structure or to all of it? This is explained in Jīva's thesis by use of the term *acintya* (which is known as *viśeṣa* in Mādhva's school and in later Gauḍīya texts as well). Each spiritual entity, Jīva teaches, is fundamentally identical to all of its own forms and qualities, even if these forms and qualities appear different from each other and are not always externally manifested. By developing this line of thought, Jīva shows how only the term *Acintya*-bhedābheda comprehensively addresses the entire truth of the Lord and his energies, making his system of knowledge, according to Gauḍīya Vaishnavas, both the most natural and complete explanation of Vedānta. For more on these points, see Andrew Nicholson, *Unifying Hinduism: Philosophy and Identity in Indian Intellectual History* (New York, N.Y.: Columbia University Press, 2010), 45–46, 49, particularly for all pre-Gauḍīya Bhedābheda conceptions. Jīva Goswāmī's *Bhagavat-sandarbha*, trans., Satyanarayana Dasa (Vrindavan: Jiva Institute of Vaishnava Studies, 2014), Anuccheda 25, 244, alludes to the essence of the *acintya/viśeṣa* principle, that is, how the Lord and all atomic souls are inconceivably identical to their own respective attributes, but a more complete discussion of this occurs in B. N. K. Sharma, *History of the Dvaita School of Vedānta and its Literature* (Delhi: Motilal Banarsidass, reprint, 2000), 588–590.

17. See Satyanārāyaṇa Dāsa in his commentary to *Bhagavata Sandarbha* 16.3, where he writes: "It was Śrīla Jīva Gosvāmī, in fact, who coined the term Acintya-bhedābheda-vāda (inconceivable simultaneous distinction within oneness) to name the philosophy propounded by Śrī Caitanya Mahāprabhu and His followers." See Satyanārāyaṇa Dāsa, trans., *Śrī Bhagavata Sandarbha* (Vrindavan, UP: Jiva Institute of Vaishnava Studies, 2014), 149.

18. See Kiyokazu Okita, *Hindu Theology in Early Modern South Asia: The Rise of Devotionalism and the Politics of Geneology* (Oxford University Press, 2014), 249–251. Okita explains that while Baladeva thoroughly addresses Acintya-bhedābeda in terms of its theological underpinnings, he does not use the phrase per se, suggesting it was not yet in common usage. Instead, because he wanted to show the Gauḍīya connection to its predecessors, Baladeva uses the Madhva concept of *viśeṣa*

("differentiating capacity") and Rāmānuja's notion of *apṛthak-siddhi* ("inseparability") to prove the logical and scriptural basis of Acintya-bhedābheda.

19. *Vaishnava Siddhānta Mālā*, Chapter Five (http://www.krishnapath.org/Library/Goswami-books/Bhaktivinoda-Thakura/Bhaktivinoda_Thakura_Vaisnava_Siddhanta_Mala.pdf). Bhaktivinoda also devotes an entire section of *Jaiva Dharma* (Chapter 18, Prameya: Bhedābheda-Tattva) to the subject, significantly using the word *tattva* ("conclusive truth") for Mahāprabhu's philosophy while using *vāda* ("theory," "proposition," "thesis") for other Vedāntic teachings. See Bhaktivinoda Ṭhākura, *Jaiva-Dharma, the Essential Function of the Soul*, trans., Śrīla Nārāyaṇa Mahārāja (Mathura: Gaudiya Vedanta Publications, 2002). He does the same in *Śrī Chaitanya Śikṣāmṛta* 1.3.5, which again is a lengthy elaboration on the subject, and he further includes Acintya-bhedābheda as the eighth principle in his "Daśa Mūla Tattva," or the ten most important teachings of the *Vedas*. See *Daśa Mūla Tattva: The Ten Foundational Truths of Śrī Chaitanya Mahāprabhu's Philosophy* (Vrindavan, India: Rasabihari Lal & Sons, 2000).

20. Ibid.

21. See Bhaktivinoda Ṭhākura, *Mahāprabhura Śikṣā*, Chapter 9 (http://gosai.com/chaitanya/saranagati/html/siksa/siksa-9.html).

22. Ibid.

23. See Graham M. Schweig, "Axiological Analysis in Phenomenological Method: A Study of the Hermeneutic Task in Comparative Religion," unpublished Th.M. thesis, Harvard Divinity School, April 1984, 41f.

24. See *Caitanya-caritāmṛta*, Ādi 1.51, purport.

25. Quoted in Andrew J. Nicholson, *Unifying Hinduism,* op. cit., 53–54.

Chapter 8

Śrī Chaitanya and Other Traditions

For Gauḍīya Vaishnavas, there are no "other" traditions. This is not to say that they arrogantly see themselves as the only tradition worth acknowledging. Rather, they see all theistic traditions as but various expressions of Sanātana-dharma, "the eternal duty," revealed in various ways according to time, place, and circumstance. "Everyone is a Vaishnava," say the Gauḍīya masters. "It is simply a question of degree."

This is succinctly expressed in the *Caitanya-caritāmṛta*, Madhya 20.108–109: "The living being is constitutionally an eternal servant of Krishna (*haya-krishnera 'nitya-dāsa'*). This is because we are all intimately connected to the Lord as his marginal energy, simultaneously one with and different from him, like a spark of sunshine coming from a huge fire."[1] In other words, regardless of what particular religion we embrace, we are intimately connected to God as his devotee—call him what you will, Krishna, Allah, Adonai, etc.—and religion, to one degree or another, basically refers to our recognition of that fact.

This is elaborated upon by Vaishnava theologian Bhaktivinoda Ṭhākura, and his words are worth repeating at length:

> The word "Vaishnavism" indicates the normal, eternal and natural condition, functions and devotional characteristics of all individual souls in relation to Vishnu, the Supreme, the All-pervading Soul. But an unnatural, unpleasant and regrettable sense has been attributed to the word making one understand by the word *Vaishnava* (literally a pure and selfless worshipper of Vishnu) a human form with twelve peculiar signs (Tilak) and dress on, worshipping many gods under the garb of a particular God and hating any other human form who marks himself with different signs, puts on a different dress and worships a different God in a different way and designated by the words "Shaiva," "Shakta," "Ganapatya," "Jaina," "Buddhist," "Mohammedan," "Christian," etc.

> Vishnu, the Supreme, All-pervading Soul, gives life and meaning to all that is . . . . As the service of the master is the fundamental function of the servant, so the service of Vishnu is natural and inherent in the *jiva* [soul] and it is called "Vaishnavata" or "Vaishnavism" and every *jiva* is a Vaishnava. As a person possessing immense riches is called a miser if he does not display and make proper use of them, so *jivas* when they do not display Vaishnavata are called Non-Vaishnavas or Avaishnavas though in reality they are [in fact Vaishnavas]."[2]

In other words, Bhaktivinoda, as an articulate representative of Mahāprabhu's universal religion of love, highlights its nonsectarian and all-embracing nature, proposing that all living beings are Vaishnavas, whether they self-identify that way or not. He sees Vaishnavism not as yet another dogmatic, insular religious tradition, but rather as a developed science of spirituality, with methods and insights as useful to practitioners of any and all other religions as they are to those who see themselves as Vaishnavas. Further, he indicates that the bodily markings (*tilāka*) and other external signs of Vaishnavism are just that—external—and that the essence of the tradition is based on the soul's connection to Vishnu, or Krishna—God—in a bond of eternal love.

Bhaktivinoda talks about how religious differences arise in his 1886 Bengali book, *Caitanya-śikṣāmṛta*:

> In different regions, things such as the locations of bodies of water, air currents, mountains and forests, and the availability of foodstuffs and clothing all vary. Consequently, differences naturally occur in people's appearance, social status, occupation, and style of dressing and eating. Each nationality has a peculiar disposition of mind, and thus various conceptions of the Supreme Lord, although the same in essence, appear superficially dissimilar. As people in different places rise above their aboriginal condition and gradually develop culture, science, law, and devotion to God, their means of worship also diverge in terms of language, costume, kinds of offerings, and mental attitudes. Considering all these secondary differences impartially, however, we find no discrepancy. As long as the object of worship is the same, there is no harm. Therefore Lord Chaitanya has specifically ordered that we should execute our own service to the Supreme Lord in the mode of pure goodness and at the same time refrain from ridiculing the religious codes of others.[3]

One may wonder, therefore, if Vaishnavas ever become judgmental, assessing members of other religions—or even those of their own—as good or bad. Of course they do. In fact, this is true in all religions—there are broad-minded, discerning practitioners able to accommodate the naturally occurring variegatedness of religious expression, and those who believe that if spirituality is not executed in a very specific way, it is virtually useless.

Availing himself of an already existing Vaishnava schema, articulated, for example, by the *Śrīmad Bhāgavatam* (11.2.45, 46, 47), Bhaktivinoda attributes this diversity to three levels of consciousness, embodied by devotees who are at various stages in their spiritual development: (1) *Kaniṣṭha-adhikārī* is the beginning level, and here one knows that they should adhere to a particular religious path, but their feeling, understanding, and learning are underdeveloped. They can be easily swayed from their resolve because their faith is not strong. Bhaktivinoda also refers to them as *komala-śraddhās*, or "those of tender faith." (2) Next comes the stage of *madhyama-adhikārī*, a devotee who has deeply imbibed the teachings and has a natural proclivity to share it with others. Such a person is determined on the path and makes rapid advancement. (3) Finally, the most advanced devotees are *uttama-adhikārī*, or those who see the essence of spiritual truth. Such a person is vastly learned, completely dedicated, and an inspiration to others.[4]

In the current context, *kaniṣṭha-adhikārīs* commonly find fault with others and have difficulty seeing any harmony between apparently diverse traditions; the *madhyama-adhikārī* is more open to resonance, and can understand the essential, unifying truth that undergirds various forms of religion; and the *uttama-adhikārī* has fully developed his or her universal vision, and is able to appreciate all forms of spirituality as just so many ways of approaching the same absolute truth.

These three levels of spiritual seekers can be found in any religious tradition, with *uttama-adhikārīs* appreciating all traditions as being one in essence.

Along these lines, Bhaktivinoda invokes an image that emphatically brings home the urgent need to transcend the stultifying effects of sectarianism: "The eleventh obstacle for the Vaishnava is sectarianism, which takes the shape of a forest fire. Due to sectarianism, a person will not accept anyone outside of his own group as a Vaishnava, and as a result he faces many obstacles . . . . Therefore, one must extinguish this forest fire by abandoning this unfortunate mentality."[5]

According to Bhaktivinoda, one who can rise above sectarianism and thus taste the higher levels of Krishna Consciousness—regardless of one's chosen path—is someone who has found the essence of religion. He uses two significant terms in this regard: *sāragrāhin* ("essence seekers") and *bhāravāhin* ("burden bearers"). The former, as the name implies, reaches for essential truth; such a person never mistakes peripheral aspects of a given religion for its central doctrine. The latter does just the opposite: the *bhāravāhin* tends to focus on nonessentials, unconsciously elevating them to a higher status than they deserve.

While the *sāragrāhin* embraces his religion thoughtfully and insightfully, the *bhāravāhin* is generally a fundamentalist, clinging to literal interpretations even when unwarranted and imbibing a superficial view of his tradition's teachings.[6] Bhaktivinoda views Sāragrāhī Vaishnavism as the true teaching of Śrī Chaitanya, and of all religion, and he sees lesser forms of Vaishnavism as various samplings of what goes awry when religious traditions miss the point.

Interestingly, in this mood of seeing all religion as representing a continuum to ultimate spiritual revelation, Bhaktivinoda offers a unique interpretation of Pañcopāsanā.[7] While Pañcopāsanā is generally seen as the worship of India's five major deities—Durgā, Sūrya, Gaṇeśa, Shiva, and Vishnu—Bhaktivinoda explains it in a different way. He sees it as *a hierarchy of religious categories*, not as a literal statement on specific divinities per se. In other words, for Bhaktivinoda, the gradual progression of religious consciousness, as seen around the world, was anticipated in India by the worship of her five prominent deities.

For example, he begins with Durgā, the Goddess. This is known as Śākti-dharma in India, but throughout the world there are various kinds of Goddess worship, from the recognition of a female force in the universe to the worship of nature and the world we see around us, whether in the form of pantheism or panentheism or what have you. As Gauḍīya Vaishnava scholar Abhishek Ghosh writes: "In Bhaktivinoda's system, Śāktism is a paradigmatic faith in which the individual or collective 'ultimate concern' is to find absolute truth within manifest nature (*prakṛti*) in the phenomenal world . . . . This is . . . most common among the primal forms of human civilization and represents the first step in the spiritual quest of mankind."[8] In this category, Bhaktivinoda includes elements of deism, animism, shamanism, Earth religion, Neopaganism, Shintoism, and so forth.

The next level is associated with the sun, known as Sūrya-dharma. Bhaktivinoda says that as one matures beyond the earth, one develops an appreciation for the heavens, recognizing the sun, especially, as the giver of life, providing heat and the ability to grow crops. "Coming to this understanding," writes Ghosh, "the Sauryas (the second level) make it the object of their worship."[9] The Aztecs of Mexico and certain tribes of Africa, among others, are known for sun worship.

Bhaktivinoda then refers to a higher form of worship wherein one realizes that animated living entities supersede energetic abstractions or even life-giving stars and constellations. It is at that point that Gaṇeśa comes into focus. As Ghosh tells us, "In the hierarchical model, when individuals realize that the basic level of consciousness present in animals is higher than matter, and that consciousness is the ultimate force that animates matter, they come to the next level of spiritual evolution. This third level is called the Gānapatya level."[10]

After this, Bhaktivinoda next turns his spotlight on the dawning of human consciousness, albeit still compromised by material concerns and as yet failing to capture the essence of theism proper. "The fourth level of spiritual progress, the Śaiva," Ghosh asserts, "comes when individuals realize the more complex nature of the human level of consciousness relative to the animalistic. Bhaktivinod suggests that religions like Jainism and Buddhism, which strive to perfect human consciousness, are on this level."[11]

Vaishnava-dharma represents the culmination of this evolution, and arises when individuals realize that they are tiny beings (*jīva*) who are meant to serve and worship a supreme being (*upāsanā*). Ghosh concludes, ". . . the fifth and final level is the Vaishnava . . . . According to Bhaktivinod, the core of Christianity and Islam is also Vaishnavism (and the reverse: Christianity and Islam are the core of Vaishnavism) . . . . Bhaktivinod concludes his discussion by saying that all the various religious traditions of the world have an otherworldly (*pāramārthaka*) aim that can be classified into the five levels of spiritual progress."[12]

This sense of religious hierarchy, along with the universalism and nonsectarianism that it suggests, can be found in the earliest moments of the Gauḍīya Vaishnava tradition. For example, in the person of Haridāsa Ṭhākura, who was an intimate associate of Śrī Chaitanya, we see a twofold instance of the tradition's egalitarian and nonsectarian nature.

First, Mahāprabhu chose Haridāsa as the "Nāmācārya" of the tradition, that is, "the exemplary teacher of the holy name." This is significant because Haridāsa was born in a Muslim family. In the India of Mahāprabhu's time, Brahmins tended to engage sectarian bias, especially against foreigners, and were deeply concerned about ritual purity. Even a moment's casual association with a "non-Hindu" could be grounds for expulsion from respectable Hindu society. However, Mahāprabhu couldn't be less concerned with social stratification (even if he honored the customs of the day in terms of practical everyday affairs). He looked at a person's spiritual quality and nothing more. Haridāsa showed by his dedication to the name (and his insightful teaching about it) that he was highly qualified as a Vaishnava. Thus, he is honored in the *Caitanya-caritāmṛta* (Antya 11.99), for instance, as "he who has revealed the importance of the holy name"[13] and was lauded by all of Mahāprabhu's followers as being the Nāmācārya. Bhaktivinoda states this in his book, *Harināma-cintāmaṇi* (Chapter 14, Verse 3).[14]

Secondly, Gauḍīya Vaishnavism's nonsectarianism is also clear from Haridāsa's teaching. In the *Caitanya-bhāgavata* (Ādi 16), for example, we find an episode in which Haridāsa was taken to task for purportedly having disgraced his Islamic heritage by the sin of apostasy. Indeed, it was the Muslim king himself who accused Haridāsa of this capital offense. Thus, for openly associating with the "idolatrous" Hindus, and for persistently honoring their "false" God by reciting the spurious "holy names," Haridāsa was tried and adjudged an offender.

To this, "Haridāsa simply laughed, marveling at how illusion engulfs people. (75) In a sweet and humble manner, he said to the king, 'I beg you to hear me, O respected one. The Supreme Lord is one without a second. Hindus and Muslims have different names for God, according to their respective languages, but, from the spiritual point of view, the Lord is one. This is confirmed in both the Purāṇas and the Koran." (76–77)[15] He then elaborated on the importance of nonsectarianism and the oneness of God.

This philosophy comes from Mahāprabhu himself. In his *Śikṣāṣṭakam*, for example, he glorifies the name of God, who, he says, "has hundreds of millions of names."[16] For the tradition, this means that his potency pervades any legitimate name of God, not only those of Indian origin. The exact word used in this connection is *bahudhā* ("various kinds," "diverse," "many"), which is also found in the Ṛg-vedic verse, "The learned tell us of one reality that is expressed in various ways." (1.164.46, *ekaṁ sad viprā bahudhā vadanti*) Even in that earlier Vedic context, it is often used to show the catholic nature of the entire Hindu tradition: Truth is one, but it is known by various names. Chaitanya Vaishnavism fully adheres to this all-embracing and broad-minded spirit.

ŚRĪ CHAITANYA AND THE JUDEO-CHRISTIAN TRADITION

There is no record of Mahāprabhu interacting with representatives of the Judeo-Christian faith, even if their presence in India had long been established by the time of his appearance. The earliest Jews, for example, arrived well before the Common Era. Eventually, Jewish merchants came en masse for purposes of trade, since their religion in general has little interest in conversion. Historical documents give us more information about their presence in India from the 11th century onwards, with the first Jewish communities arising along the western coast and in the south as well. Jewish migrations in the 16th and 17th centuries, slightly after Mahāprabhu's time, created important settlements in northern India and Kashmir, and, today, three distinct denominations are known in the subcontinent: the Bene Israel, the Cochin Jews, and the White Jews from Europe.[17]

Although any overt connection is unlikely, the mystical Jewish tradition enjoys certain similarities with Mahāprabhu's Vaishnavism, particularly in regard to the holy name. A few brief biblical examples will underscore this parallel: "The name of the Lord is like a strong tower: the righteous runneth into it and are safe." (*Proverbs*, 18.10) In *Psalms*, King David proclaims, "I will praise the name of God with a song." (*Psalms*, 69.30) And, "O give thanks unto the Lord: Call upon His name: Make known His deeds among the people. Sing unto Him, sing psalms unto Him: talk ye of all His wondrous works. Glory ye in His holy name." (*Psalms*, 105.1–4) "From the rising of the sun to the place where it sets—from east to west—the name of the Lord is to be praised" (*Psalms*, 113.3). "Praise Him with the timbrel and dance: Praise Him with stringed instruments and organs. Praise Him upon the loud cymbals." (*Psalms*, 150.4–5) With such verses in mind, no doubt, Israel Baal Shem Tov (1699–1761), the great Jewish mystic, founded Hasidism, a popular Chaitanyaite-like movement within Judaism, in which members sing and dance in glorification of God's name.[18]

As far as Christianity goes, we find its earliest representatives in India in as early as 52 CE, when the Apostle Thomas appeared on the Malabar Coast. In the centuries that followed, others, such as Pantaenus, a Greek philosopher from Alexandria, set sail for the land of the Ganges, usually for missionary purposes. But their mission was initially small. That would change with time. In 1542, for example, Jesuit missionary Francis Xavier and his followers baptized tens of thousands in a single month, and many more as years went by. Still, Bengal and its neighboring states were spared mass conversion. While it is true that Portuguese missionaries and various traders appeared there in the 16th century, the British East India Company did not allow missionary work until 1813.[19] Whatever the case, there is virtually nothing in Mahāprabhu's biographies suggesting interaction, pro or con, with the Christian community.

Nonetheless, many Christian writers have noted correlations between Gauḍīya Vaishnavism and Christian philosophy, and some have even compared Mahāprabhu to Jesus or the saints. For example, the reverend John Morrison of Calcutta, lecturing at the University of Glasgow in 1906, calls attention to "the new power of Christ's personality" and credits Jesus for the resurgence of Chaitanya's movement in India: "A Christ-like man, indeed, in many ways, Chaitanya was, and the increased acquaintance of educated Bengal with Jesus Christ naturally brought Chaitanya to the front."[20]

A year later, Shushir Kumar Ghose writes, "If it is a fact that a Messiah was born in Judea 1900 years ago, it seems not unreasonable to suppose that, in other places, other Messiahs might appear at periods of the history of the world, and in different localities. Thus the advent of Jesus Christ establishes the possibility of the divine character of Sree Gauranga; and, in the same way, the advent of Sree Gauranga establishes the possibility of the advent of Jesus Christ."[21]

In 1925, historian Melville Kennedy published one of the first Western academic studies of Mahāprabhu's life and mission, devoting an entire section to Śrī Chaitanya in light of Christianity.[22] There have been numerous such studies since Melville's work, but few have articulated Mahāprabhu's "Christ-like" nature as sensitively as Christian theologian John Moffitt:

> If I were asked to choose one man in Indian religious history who best represents the pure spirit of devotional self-giving, I would choose the Vaishnavite saint

> Chaitanya, whose full name in religion was Krishna-Chaitanya, or "Krishna consciousness." Of all the saints in recorded history, East or West, he seems to me the supreme example of a soul carried away on a tide of ecstatic love of God. This extraordinary man, who belongs to the rich period beginning with the end of the fourteenth century, represents the culmination of the devotional schools that grew up around Krishna . . . . Chaitanya delighted intensely in nature. It is said that, like St. Francis of Assisi, he had a miraculous power over wild beasts. His life in the holy town of Puri is the story of a man in a state of almost continuous spiritual intoxication. Illuminating discourses, deep contemplation, moods of loving communion with God, were daily occurrences.[23]

In modern times, Śrīla A. C. Bhaktivedānta Swami Prabhupāda has embraced Jesus as one of his own, citing Christ's personal life as paradigmatic of ideal Vaishnava character and proof of his divinity. Ravi Gupta summarizes: "In his commentary, and when he discusses it in lectures, Prabhupāda offers Jesus as the ideal example . . . . He repeatedly points out Jesus' tolerance (*titikṣu*) in the face of great suffering, his compassion (*kāruṇika*) toward those who crucified him, and his desire to do good for everyone (*suhṛd*). Prabhupāda even offers Jesus as an example of someone who had no enemies, for although the world is a 'treacherous' place, a *sādhu* himself does not bear enmity toward anyone . . . . Prabhupāda explains that Jesus should also be regarded as a *śaktyāveśa avatāra* because he 'preached' about the glorification of the Supreme Lord' and 'sacrificed everything for preaching the glories of the Lord.'"[24]

Śrīla Prabhupāda even refers to Jesus as "my guru."[25] Indeed, if a contemporary Gauḍīya Vaishnava leader of Prabhupāda's stature sees Jesus as his own spiritual master, and even as an *avatāra*, Chaitanyaite nonsectarianism and universalism become ipso facto established as irrevocable and unassailable.

ŚRĪ CHAITANYA AND INTERRELIGIOUS DIALOGUE

In Mahāprabhu's Bengal, there were very few "other" religions, that is, those outside the Vedic/Hindu cultural milieu. His interaction with the Muslim tradition was briefly addressed in a prior chapter and earlier in this one.[26] I will look at yet another of his exchanges with Islam in this section, albeit in relation to Sufism, the Islamic mystical tradition. It is said that the Master also met Guru Nanak,[27] who would become the founder of Sikhism, and a certain group of Buddhist monks, too.[28] Both incidents will be briefly addressed below. In addition to this, he interacted with numerous adherents of the Advaita Vedānta school, which is an alternate tradition, and members of the other Vaishnava Sampradāyas as well. He met Śāktas, Jains, tribals, and others as he traveled throughout India, sharing his loving devotion with anyone who would hear him.[29] Some of these exchanges will now be addressed.

I would like to begin, however, with one brief caveat, a Gauḍīya Vaishnava apologetic on behalf of the tradition. In Mahāprabhu's exchange with "others," he seems to convert as much as share. This speaks to the hierarchical conception mentioned above. Mahāprabhu acknowledged all theistic paths as part of a continuum, but he did see truth in terms of higher and lower, or complete versus partial. Accordingly, with peerless circumspection, he often tried to help others understand his notion of the Supreme, though never forcefully, and always through scriptural quotation and logic. Moreover, when he saw that a beneficial purpose would be served by preserving a given individual's devotional perspective, he did so, encouraging them on the path even if it were different from his own.

For example, when visiting South India, he came upon Veṅkaṭa Bhaṭṭa and his family, who were members of the Rāmānuja Sampradāya, worshippers of Lakṣmī-Nārāyaṇa. While Mahāprabhu clearly expressed to Veṅkaṭa the superiority of Krishna over Vishnu (albeit in conjunction with affirming the ontological equality of the divinities), he did leave Veṅkaṭa to worship as he saw fit, without attempting to dissuade him from his path. Indeed, it is even said that he was "happy" to see Veṅkaṭa's devotion.[30]

A similar instance occurs with Mahāprabhu's devotee Murāri Gupta, who worshiped Rāma instead of Krishna. Although Mahāprabhu initially tried to sway him to the worship of Krishna, he concluded that it was proper and appropriate for Murāri to worship according to his inner *bhāva*.[31]

These examples might seem negligible, since they are only slight variations on Mahāprabhu's tradition. But they make a point. While Mahāprabhu knew the efficacy and surpassing virtues of the path he espoused, and though as an outpouring of his fervent devotion he so ardently wished to share it with others, he always respected individual needs and encouraged stepwise evolution to the highest goal. But, by the same token, when he sensed that people could go higher, he enthusiastically tried to assist them in approaching that end. That being said, when it was clear that they were worshipping to their capacity and that the best possible situation for them was the path that they were already on, he encouraged them to continue unabated.

We will now turn to an episode in which Mahāprabhu encounters a group of Sufi soldiers who worshiped an impersonal Absolute.[32]

After briefly visiting Vrindāvan, Śrī Chaitanya and his four traveling companions—Balabhadra Bhaṭṭācārya and his assistant, Rājaputa Krishnadāsa and an unnamed Sanoḍiyā Brahmin—began a homeward journey toward Purī. Just before leaving Krishna's holy land, Mahāprabhu heard a cowherd boy playing on his flute, which reminded him of Krishna. This caused him to swoon, foam at the mouth in a fit of ecstasy, and fall unconscious. Soon after, a group of ten Muslim soldiers of the Pāṭhāna military order arrived. When they saw Mahāprabhu's four fellow travelers standing over the Master's body, they assumed that they were dacoits who had attacked the young *sannyāsī*, trying to poison him and steal his valuables. Fortunately, Śrī Chaitanya quickly regained consciousness.

Realizing that outward appearances placed his traveling companions in grave jeopardy, with them possibly being mistakenly punished as criminals, he related to the soldiers what had happened in his own way. Rather than explaining the nature of his uncommon ecstatic transformations, he attributed his fainting to epilepsy (*mṛgī-vyādhite*),[33] adding that his four traveling companions are merciful friends who take care of him when he has such episodes. (*Caitanya-caritāmṛta*, Madhya 18.184) As he spoke, he noticed that one of the soldiers was wearing the black robes of a Sufi mystic and that the others were addressing him as a saintly person. (185) So Mahāprabhu started to talk to him of love of God and the nature of the Absolute. And when the saintly soldier started to glorify God's impersonal feature on the basis of the Koran, Śrī Chaitanya refuted him. (187)

The Muslim philosopher basically adhered to Advaita-brahma-vāda, the impersonal Brahman conception, with which Mahāprabhu was quite familiar.[34] Deeply considering Mahāprabhu's counterarguments, the Pāṭhāna was stunned, unable to speak. (188) Śrī Chaitanya added that although, in his opinion, the Koran is primarily based on impersonalistic philosophy, at least when viewed from a certain perspective, it concludes by establishing the existence of a personal Absolute. (189) After the Pāṭhāna accepted that premise, Mahāprabhu developed his arguments from there and concluded by saying: "The Koran accepts the fact that ultimately there is only one God. He is full of opulence, and his bodily complexion is blackish (*śyāma-kalevara*)." (190) To this, the saintly Muslim leader replied, "All that you have said is true. While it is so written in the Koran, our own authorities can neither understand it nor accept it." (199) As this conversation came to a close, the group of Pāṭhānas all became Śrī Chaitanya's followers, and the Master gave the one in black robes the name Rāmadāsa, thus initiating him into Gauḍīya Vaishnavism.[35]

A similar incident occurred with a group of Buddhist monks.[36] *Caitanya-caritāmṛta*, Madhya 9, relates the story as follows: As Mahāprabhu traveled south, he met with representatives of various traditions. One of them was a Buddhist who happened to be revered as a learned scholar. With a group of his followers, he approached Mahāprabhu and began to explain the basic principles of Buddhism, hoping to impress the Master with his knowledge (text 48). However, Śrī Chaitanya countered him, point for point, and dismantled his conception with strong logic. (51) Unfortunately, those listening to this conversation began to laugh, causing the Buddhist leader and his followers to feel both shame and fear. (52) Because of this, they plotted against

Mahāprabhu, even though such scheming was beneath them. This was their plan: they would graciously bring him a plate of food, not telling him that it was unoffered according to Vaishnava practice. Then, upon consuming it, he would be humiliated, for a devotee of his stature would never eat unoffered food.

Bringing him the plate according to plan—and telling him it was *mahā-prasāda*, or the highest caliber of sacred edibles—their ruse would soon backfire. (53) Just as he was about to consume it, a large bird appeared out of nowhere, picking up the plate in its beak and flying away. (54) As the bird was in mid-flight, the untouchable food fell on the gathered Buddhists, with the plate itself hitting the chief Buddhist in the head. (55) Because the plate was made of metal, it cut him, causing him to fall to the ground, unconscious. (56) Seeing their leader in this condition, his disciples cried aloud, begging Śrī Chaitanya to forgive them and to help. (57) Mahāprabhu then advised them, "You should all chant the names of Krishna very loudly, and also chant it in the ear of your spiritual master." (59) When they did as Mahāprabhu said, the Buddhist teacher regained consciousness and immediately began chanting the name himself. (61) Thus, they all became Mahāprabhu's disciples.[37] Here again we see the power of Mahāprabhu's presence—his cogency in debate, personal charisma, purity of chanting, and overwhelming spirituality often made those in his presence want to follow him and live according to his teachings.

Next, a more congenial episode exists that chronicles the interreligious encounter between Śrī Chaitanya and the great saint Guru Nanak. Although clearly from two different traditions, Mahāprabhu responded favorably to Guru Nanak's love for the holy name, and made no attempt to convert him.

We learn this from an Odiya manuscript known as the *Caitanya-bhāgavata*. According to that text, there was a mysterious meeting between the two luminaries of Indian tradition, a meeting that is not detailed in any of the other authorized biographies.[38] It may be that since Īśvara Dāsa, the author, was himself from Odisha, he was privy to information that was not available to the other biographers.

The scene is the great Ratha-yātrā festival at Purī, where hundreds of thousands gather together to glorify Krishna in the form of Lord Jagannāth. In the section of the Odiya manuscript where this is described, two verses are particularly significant: "Śrī Chaitanya, the Supreme Lord, joined in *kīrtana* with Guru Nanak, who was accompanied by his disciple Sarang. Also in attendance were Rūpa and Sanātana, the two brothers, and Jagāi and Mādhāi. They all chanted and danced together, feeling indescribable bliss." (*Caitanya-bhāgavata*, Chapter 61, text 4) The second verse runs as follows: "In the congregational chanting led by Śrī Chaitanya and Guru Nanak, Purushottama Dās [Svarūpa Dāmodara] was also there. Two others, Jaṅgalī and Nandinī [disciples of Sītādevī], joined them. With them were also Gopāla Guru and Nityānanda. They all performed ecstatic *kīrtana* in Jagannāth Purī, relishing each other's association." (*Caitanya-bhāgavata* Chapter 64, text 13)[39]

These verses are crucial in the present context because they mention Śrī Chaitanya and Guru Nanak in the company of prominent disciples, allowing readers to be certain that this is the same Chaitanya and Nanak with which their traditions are familiar. Thus, we see a perfect interreligious encounter, in which both parties, in mutual respect, sing and dance in glorification of God. There is no attempt to change each other's path. Followers of both Śrī Chaitanya and Guru Nanak might learn from the example of the Masters and live together in harmony, despite external differences.

MĀYĀVĀDA: A PHILOSOPHICAL IMPROPRIETY

But as we have seen, Mahāprabhu clearly assessed religion according to certain standards, and there were particular philosophical faux pas that he would never tolerate. One such indiscretion was impersonalism, as we have seen, particularly as embodied in Advaita Vedānta, so typical in the India of his day. Thus, Mahāprabhu made the succinct proclamation that Māyāvādīs, or those who de-personalize God, were in fact Lord Krishna's most blatant offenders (*māyāvādī kṛṣṇe aparādhī*).[40]

In the *Caitanya-caritāmṛta*, Mahāprabhu corrects the misconceptions of two deeply learned Māyāvādīs: Sārvabhauma Bhaṭṭācārya, who we have mentioned previously, and Prakāśānanda Sarasvatī, the famous philosopher of Benares. When Mahāprabhu met Sārvabhauma, the latter expressed a desire to lecture on the *Vedānta-sūtra* for him. These are terse philosophical texts that sum up all of Vedic knowledge. Sārvabhauma was, after all, widely known as "king of the logicians," and he wanted to share both his wealth of learning and his expertise in debate with the young *sannyāsī* sitting before him. Although Sārvabhauma had some sympathy for devotional explanations, he was a leader among Advaita Vedāntists and espoused Māyāvādī philosophy according to the tradition of Śaṅkarācārya. Nonetheless, he began his lengthy instruction, Kavirāja Goswāmi tells us, in the presence of the Master.

In utter silence, for seven consecutive days, Mahāprabhu listened patiently as Sārvabhauma elaborated his pedantic disquisition. But at the end of those seven days, the refulgent Chaitanya broke his silence with a shower of eloquence, which resoundingly countered each and every Māyāvādī conclusion Sārvabhauma had offered, showing with unparalleled cogency the superiority of personalistic thought. Impressed by Śrī Chaitanya's profound commentary, Sārvabhauma submitted to him as a disciple and immediately composed 100 verses celebrating Mahāprabhu's character.[41]

As for Prakāśānanda Sarasvatī, the *Caitanya-caritāmṛta* tells us that he, too, was a follower of Śaṅkara's Advaita Vedānta. And while Sārvabhauma was well known throughout the subcontinent, Prakāśānanda enjoyed even greater fame, with over 60,000 disciples. Mahāprabhu met him in Benares on his way to Vrindāvan. The leading *sannyāsīs* there didn't understand Mahāprabhu. Because he was always chanting and dancing rather than studying, meditating, and debating, as *sannyāsīs* should, the Benares renunciants wrote him off as an illiterate sentimentalist. Free of pride and undisturbed by their erroneous estimation of his position, Mahāprabhu, in silence, humbly accepted their criticism.

But after they expressed their doubts, he offered them an in-depth explanation of the holy name. Moved by his sermon, which, according to the biographer, was not only scripturally and logically accurate but also full of *bhāva*, or deep spiritual emotion, they could understand that this was no ordinary personality in their midst, and they asked him to comment on the proper import of Vedānta.

According to their desire, he then delivered a thorough explication of Vedāntic thought, establishing the personal Absolute on the basis of the *sūtras* themselves and showing the limitations of Śaṅkara's understanding. After an extensive elaboration, in which he revealed how the cryptic Vedānta texts are actually in support of Krishna *bhakti*, Śrī Chaitanya persuasively answered all their philosophical challenges, resulting in a shift in their consciousness. Thus, Prakāśānanda and all his followers came to see shortcomings in the impersonal explanation of divinity. Like Sārvabhauma, they surrendered to Mahāprabhu's mission, such that Prakāśānanda and all of his followers engaged in ecstatic *saṅkīrtana* with Mahāprabhu and his intimate associates.[42]

Mahāprabhu's silencing of the Māyāvādīs was considered a major step forward for the *bhakti* movement in Medieval India. However, the Eastern hemisphere is still inclined to impersonalistic and voidist thought, as are certain philosophers in the Western world. Indeed, we find Śaṅkara-like intimations in the writings of Plotinus, Spinoza, George Berkeley, and Georg Wilhelm Friedrich Hegel, among others. That being said, theistic thinkers, largely associated with the Judeo-Christian tradition, present a strong voice in favor of God's personhood as well, if carefully avoiding anthropomorphism. In the end, philosophers East and West will continue to either directly or indirectly represent Śaṅkara's perspective. And devotees of a personal deity will continue to counter them.

THE FOUR SAMPRADĀYAS

According to Kavirāja Goswāmī, Mahāprabhu met with followers of all four major Vaishnava Sampradāyas—the Nimbārka (Kumāra), the

Rāmānuja (Śrī), the Mādhva (Brahmā), and the Rudra (Vallabha). While he accepted them as legitimate Vaishnavas, he adopted the position of teacher while in their midst, presumably to "take them further," as per his accepted mission.

The first recorded encounter with a bona fide representative of a major Vaishnava lineage occurred when Chaitanya met with the renowned scholar/poet Keśava Bhaṭṭa, also known as Keśava Kāśmīrī. Though the *Caitanya-caritāmṛta* makes no mention of Bhaṭṭa's association with the Nimbārka Sampradāya, focusing instead on the encounter itself and its momentous outcome, later texts make the connection clear. For example, according to Bhaktivinoda Ṭhākura, Keśava Kāśmīrī was in fact a reincarnation of Nimbārka himself.[43] Gérard Colas, a modern scholar of the tradition, writes that Keśava Kāśmīrī "is the first whose historical association with the Braj area is certain. His direction is marked by the revival of the Nimbārka tradition and the propagation of its teachings all over India."[44] Colas further notes that Keśava Kāśmīrī is the 29th *ācārya* in the Nimbārka lineage,[45] establishing him as an historical Nimbārka personality in the time of Śrī Chaitanya.

The meeting between the two of them occurred early in Mahāprabhu's career. At that time, the Master, still known as Nimāi Paṇḍita, defeated him in philosophical argument, mainly by using the technicalities of Sanskrit grammar and poetics. To establish his intellectual and scholarly superiority over Śrī Chaitanya, whom he regarded as a mere child of small learning, Kāśmīrī flaunted his own prodigious literary skill by rapidly and spontaneously composing 100 brilliant lines of Sanskrit verse in praise of the Ganges.

But it was Kāśmīrī who, in the next instant, suffered crushing defeat, "hoist in his own petard," when the youthful Master astounded him (and all others in attendance) by replying with a stinging literary critique of Kāśmīrī's verse. Focusing on one verse of the hundred, Mahāprabhu left everyone speechless, first by reciting the verse verbatim, after having heard it only once in the whirlwind of its creation, and then by identifying its numerous literary flaws and elaborately analyzing each, one by one, thereby greatly diminishing the glamour of Kāśmīrī's vaunted erudition and literary skill. Soon after, Kāśmīrī accepted Śrī Chaitanya's preeminent position as a divinity.[46]

The next meeting with a bona fide Vaishnava of another tradition occurred much later, this time with a member of the Rāmānuja lineage. After Mahāprabhu took *sannyāsa*, he met Vyeṅkaṭa Bhaṭṭa, a senior priest at the Śrīraṅgam temple in South India. Vyeṅkaṭa was at that time a prominent member of the Śrī Sampradāya, systematized by Rāmānuja in the 12th century. This lineage emphasizes the awe and reverence side of worship, focusing, as it does, on Lakṣmī and Vishnu as opposed to Rādhā and Krishna. Kavirāja Goswāmī gives a detailed account of Vyeṅkaṭa's meeting with Mahāprabhu, especially regarding their discussion of their respective deities.

Through numerous light-hearted arguments, delivered in a friendly, loving way, Mahāprabhu shows Vyeṅkaṭa the importance of intimacy over power, amorousness over awe and reverence. While Mahāprabhu clearly has respect for Vyeṅkaṭa's dedication to Lakṣmī-Vishnu, and says as much, he wants to leave him with the understanding that Krishna supersedes Vishnu. Mahāprabhu thus makes evident, using scripture and logic, that Vishnu's magisterial bearing (*aiśvarya*) is subservient to Krishna's sweet and intimate nature (*mādhurya*). Vyeṅkaṭa understands Mahāprabhu well and praises his insight. Having thus accomplished his mission, the Master sees no need to convert Vyeṅkaṭa. He expanded the compass of the Śrī Sampradāya's spiritual discourse to include more intimate phases of transcendental love, and that was enough. And so, after this, he traveled further south.[47]

His meeting with representatives of the Mādhva tradition is less benign, but that clearly has more to do with the particular devotees involved than with the tradition itself. In fact, Kavirāja Goswāmī tells us (Madhya 9.252) that Mahāprabhu deemed these Madhvites unduly proud of their Vaishnavism (*'vaiṣṇavatā' sabāra antare garva jāni'*), and that it was important to curb their pride. And this makes sense. After all, Mahāprabhu's lineage would later align with the Mādhva Sampradāya, so it was not Madhva philosophy as such that he objected to.

Referred to here as Tattvavāda ("the philosophy of truth"), to distinguish it from Māyāvāda, the Madhvites who interacted with Mahāprabhu met him in Uḍupī, a stronghold of Madhvite devotion. Their leader, who was learned in the scriptures and the philosophical conclusions of Vaishnavism, began to speak to him, and they had a cordial exchange. It began very much like the conversation with Rāmānanda Rāya, with the Madhvite leader promoting Varṇāśrama and social duty as the pinnacle of spiritual truth. Mahāprabhu of course countered him by presenting more fundamental spiritual realities, particularly those centered on chanting the holy name. The leader of the Tattvavādīs could see his purity of purpose and the logic of his presentation, and therefore he accepted his conclusions. Still, he remained faithful to his Madhvite tradition. Mahāprabhu left him with important words about an aspect of their Sampradāya that is indeed praiseworthy: "You see the form of the Lord as ultimate truth."[48]

Finally, Mahāprabhu had meaningful exchange with Vallabha Bhaṭṭa (also known as Vallabhācārya) while they were both in Purī. Kavirāja Goswāmī detailed this in Antya 7, entitling the chapter, "The Meeting of Śrī Chaitanya Mahāprabhu and Vallabha Bhaṭṭa." In summary, Vallabha and Mahāprabhu enjoyed friendly exchange and conversation, talking about everything from the wonderful devotees in Purī to the exalted *rasas* of intimate relationship with Krishna. The Master dined at his home, with many of his associates, and engaged in *kīrtana* with him.

Key philosophical contributions from each of the four Sampradāyas, as accepted by Śrī Chaitanya

Source	*Contribution to Gauḍīya practice (sādhana-bhakti)*		*Contribution to Gauḍīya ontology (sambandha-jñāna)*	
Madhva	*kevala-advaita-nirāsana*	The complete refutation of Śaṅkara's Advaita philosophy	*sac-cid-ānanda-nitya-vigraha*	The Lord as His body of eternity, knowledge, and bliss
	kṛṣṇa-mūrti-sevana	The worship of the physical image of Śrī Kṛṣṇa in the temple		
Rāmānuja	*ananya-bhakti*	The concept of unalloyed devotion free from *karma* and *jñāna*	*śakti-siddhānta*	The Lord's energies
	bhakta-jana-sevā	Service to the devotees		
Viṣṇusvāmī	*tadīya-sarvasva-bhāva*	The sentiment of total dependence on Śrī Kṛṣṇa	*śuddha-advaita-siddhānta*	Pure non-dualism, that is, non-dualism that is devoid of the imperfections associated with Śaṅkara's Advaita philosophy
	rāga-mārga	The path of spontaneous devotional service		
Nimbārka	*ekānta-rādhikāśraya*	The need of taking exclusive shelter of Śrī Rādhā	*nitya-dvaita-advaita-siddhānta*	Eternal dualism and non-dualism
	gopī-bhāva	The exalted mood of the *gopīs'* love for Śrī Kṛṣṇa		

But then, one day, Vallabha came before Mahāprabhu with a *Śrīmad Bhāgavatam* commentary he had written, asking him to appraise it. He recited some of it for him, but Śrī Chaitanya expressed little interest, feeling Vallabha too proud to accurately convey the teachings of such a sacred text. Vallabha then took shelter of Gadādhara Paṇḍita, who showed him some necessary attention and mercy.

All would have been well and good except for the following. On one particular day, Vallabha again presented his commentary on the *Bhāgavatam* before Mahāprabhu, but this time he altogether transgressed the sanctity of Vaishnava etiquette: he impugned Śrīdhara Swami, the revered 15th-century commentator, by boasting that his own *Bhāgavatam* commentary surpassed that of Śrīdhara.[49] Responding to the audacity of the assertion and to the remarkable insensitivity Vallabha modeled by his boasting, Mahāprabhu offered harsh words, for he considered the very notion of surpassing Śrīdhara Swami to be blasphemy.

After some time, Vallabha considered deeply, Kavirāja Goswāmī tells us, and was able to see what was at the heart of Mahāprabhu's criticism: "He is reacting to my pride, because I foolishly present myself as a learned scholar. Therefore, his harsh language is meant to rectify me, destroying my inappropriate hubris."[50] With this in mind, Vallabha apologized and humbly submitted himself before Mahāprabhu, who then accepted him: "Śrī Chaitanya said, 'You are both a greatly learned scholar and a great devotee.'"[51] Further, says Kavirāja Goswāmī, "Mahāprabhu was very pleased with him."[52]

Śrī Chaitanya accepted certain philosophical contributions from each of these four Sampradāyas that he considered particularly valuable. In certain of Bhaktivinoda Ṭhākura's books, he briefly mentions exactly what those contributions are. On the opposite page, we include a chart[53] that illustrates Bhaktivinoda's thesis.

NOTES

1. *Caitanya-caritāmṛta*, Madhya 20.108–109 (*jīvera 'svarūpa' haya-kṛṣṇera 'nitya-dāsa,' kṛṣṇera 'taṭasthā-śakti' 'bhedābheda-prakāśa,' sūryāṁśa-kiraṇa, yaiche agni-jvālā-caya, svābhāvika kṛṣṇera tina-prakāra 'śakti' haya*).

2. Bhaktivinoda Ṭhākura and Bhaktisiddhānta Sarasvatī, *Vaishnavism and Nam-Bhajan* (Madras: Sri Gaudiya Math, 1968, reprint), 2–3. Incidentally, Bhaktvinoda's use of the word "Mohammedan" is simply a matter of adhering to the conventions of his time. It was not considered pejorative in his Bengal, as it often is today. The current term in favor is "Muslim."

3. Bhaktivinoda Ṭhākura, "The Nectarean Teachings of Śrī Caitanya, Part 1," trans., Gopīparāṇadhana Dāsa Brahmacārī, in *Back to Godhead*, Volume 11, No. 2,

1976 (http://www.backtogodhead.in/the-nectarean-teachings-of-sri-caitanya-part-1-by-srila-bhaktivinoda-thakura/).

4. These three levels are found throughout Gauḍīya Vaishnava literature. For a particularly meaningful discussion of the levels in general and also in relation to Christian theology, see Abhishek Ghosh, "Vaiṣṇavism and the West: A Study of Kedanath Datta Bhaktivinod's Encounter and Response, 1869–1909," Ph.D. thesis, The University of Chicago, 2014, 181–185.

5. See Bhaktivinoda Ṭhākura, *Śrī Krishna-saṁhitā* (Calcutta: Isvarchandra Basu, 1879), 8.22 (*sampradāya-virodho 'yam dāvānalo vicintyate*).

6. Abhishek Ghosh, "Vaiṣṇavism and the West: A Study of Kedanath Datta Bhaktivinod's Encounter and Response, 1869–1909," op. cit., 179–182.

7. Literally, "five" (*pañca*), "worship, meditation" (*upāsanā*). It refers to Hinduism as commonly understood, especially in the modern world: There are innumerable gods of which five are most prominent—they are all to be worshiped equally.

8. Abhishek Ghosh, "Vaiṣṇavism and the West: A Study of Kedanath Datta Bhaktivinod's Encounter and Response, 1869–1909," op. cit., 216–217.

9. Ibid.

10. Ibid.

11. Ibid.

12. Ibid.

13. "Everyone began to chant, 'All glories to Haridāsa Ṭhākura, who revealed the importance of chanting the holy name of the Lord!'" (*sabe gāya,—"jaya jaya jaya haridāsa nāmera mahimā yeṅha karilā prakāśa*). This is likely the origin of Haridāsa's identity as the Nāmācārya. See also Antya 5.86: "The glories of the holy name were manifested through Haridāsa Ṭhākura . . . ." (*haridāsa-dvārā nāma-māhātmya-prakāśa* . . . .).

14. Bhaktivinoda writes: "It is due to your teaching that the people of this age attain auspiciousness. You are the potent *ācārya* (teacher) of the holy name." It should also be noted that Rūpa and Sanātana Goswāmīs, although of Brahmin birth, had long been employed by the Muslim occupational government of Bengal. According to the Hindu social standards of the time, this made them no better than "foreigners," who were generally frowned upon. Nonetheless, Mahāprabhu accepted them with open arms as leaders of his movement, for they exhibited the learning and character of higher echelon devotees.

15. Bhaktisiddhānta Sarasvatī's commentary on these verses illuminate the Gauḍīya position: "The Supreme Person is one, eternal, and non-dual being—the same Supreme Personality found in all religious traditions. He is the Lord of Hindus, Muslims, young, old, male, female, and all souls. Hindus and non-Hindus who are ignorant of spiritual truth foolishly oppose each other by imagining two different Gods with diverse names, but when they abandon such discrimination and difference of opinion and impartially consider their respective religious scriptures, the Purāṇas and the Koran, they will rise beyond such differences and see the Absolute Truth as one harmonious reality."

16. This is a loose translation of *bahudhā* (various kinds, many) found in contemporary versions of *Śikṣāṣṭakam*. See, for example, Swami Prabhupāda's translation (http://www.harekrsna.de/Siksastaka/Siksastakam-E.htm).

17. For more, see Nathan Katz, *Who Are the Jews of India?* (Berkeley: University of California Press, 2000). Also see information on the Jews of India online (http://www.jewishvirtuallibrary.org/india-virtual-jewish-history-tour).

18. "Baal Shem" actually means "Master of the Name." (Tov means "good," thus making the founder of Hasidism, "master of the good name.") He was known especially for his philosophy of *devekus nigunim*—"songs that transcend syllables and sound." This is comparable to Śrī Chaitanya's *kīrtana*. There is a beautiful story about the Baal Shem Tov that highlights how similar his philosophy is to Vaishnavism. I will paraphrase the story here: Rabbi Israel Baal Shem Tov was once asked, "Why do your followers burst into song and dance at the slightest provocation? Is this the behavior of healthy, sane individuals?" The Baal Shem Tov responded with a story: "Once, a musician came to town. He stood on a street corner and began to play. People who stopped to listen became enthralled, unable to leave, and soon a large crowd developed around the young musician. Before long, everyone present naturally moved to the rhythm of the music, and started to look like a party of intoxicated dancers. Just then, a deaf man walked by and, witnessing the scene, wondered: 'Has the world gone mad? Why are these people jumping up and down, waving their arms and moving in these odd ways in middle of the street?'" Concluding his story, the Baal Shem Tov said, "The Hasidim are moved by the spiritual melody that issues forth from G-d's creation. If this makes them appear mad to those who cannot hear, should they therefore terminate their dancing?" See Eliezer Steinman, "The Dancing Jews" (http://www.chabad.org/library/article_cdo/aid/421876/jewish/The-Dancing-Jews.htm/sc/em_share).

19. See Robert Eric Frykenberg, *Christianity in India: From Beginnings to the Present* (Oxford University Press, 2010); also see D. Dennis Hudson, *Protestant Origins in India: Tamil Evangelical Christians, 1706–1835* (Grand Rapids, M.I.: Wm. B. Eerdmans Publishing, 2000). Other online information (http://www.smithsonianmag.com/travel/how-christianity-came-to-india-kerala-180958117/).

20. John Morrison. *New Ideas in India During the Nineteenth Century: A Study of Social,Political, and Religious Developments* (Edinburgh: George A. Morton, 1906), 199. Quoted in Ravi M. Gupta, "God or Guru?: Jesus in the Thought of Swami Prabhupāda" *Journal of Vaishnava Studies*, Volume 21, No. 1 (Fall 2012), 219–225.

21. Shishir Kumar Ghose, *Lord Gaurāṅga, or Salvation for All*, Vol. 2, Second Edition (Calcutta: P. K. Ghose,1907), 10.

22. Melville Kennedy, *The Chaitanya Movement: A Study of the Vaishnavism of Bengal* (London: Oxford University Press, 1925).

23. John Moffitt, *Journey to Gorakhpur: An Encounter with Christ Beyond Christianity* (New York, N.Y.: Holt, Rinehart, and Winston, 1972), 129, 135–136.

24. Quoted in Ravi M. Gupta, "'He is our master': Jesus in the Thought of Swami Prabhupāda" in *Journal of Hindu-Christian Studies*, Volume 23, Article 7 (2010), 2–3 (http://dx.doi.org/10.7825/2164–6279.1459).

25. His Divine Grace A. C. Bhaktivedānta Swami Prabhupāda, *The Science of Self-Realization* (Los Angeles, C.A.: Bhaktivedanta Book Trust, 1994, reprint), 135–136.

26. "Bakhtiar Khilji, a Turk, swept across eastern India at the turn of the 12th century, causing Lakshman Sen to flee his kingdom in 1202," Jan Brzezinski writes. "He conquered large parts of Bengal and established Muslim dominance that would last

until 1757. There is little evidence that there were forced conversions of non-Muslims in Bengal. However, Muslim rulers did give patronage to Sufi preachers, who thus enjoyed a certain psychological and economic advantage. Some features of Islam that shared a common ethos with aspects of Bengali native religious tendencies were anti-casteism and simplification of ritual. Sufi practices that undoubtedly had an influence on Vaishnavism were communal singing (*sama*) and meditation using beads (*dhikr*). The Sufis also appeared to share a sympathy for ecstatic or experiential religion, such as is found in many of the Bengali religious groups, in particular Vaishnavism. The Persian legend of Layla and Majnun (the madman), which is often interpreted allegorically by Sufi mystics, also has parallels with the erotic themes of Krishna mythology." See Jan Brzezinski, "An overview of Bengali religious history prior to Śrī Chaitanya" for more on the interaction of Islam (Sufism) and Chaitanya Vaishnavism (http://jagadanandadas.blogspot.com/2007/01/overview-of-bengali-religious-history.html).

27. I am grateful to Guy L. Beck for bringing the meeting of Guru Nanak and Śrī Chaitanya to my attention. See Guy L. Beck, "Historic Meeting at Puri," in *The Sikh Review* 24 (November, 1976), 53–59. Although this meeting is not mentioned in the standard biographies of Śrī Chaitanya, it is found, exclusively, in an early Odiya manuscript known as *Caitanya-bhāgavata* (not to be confused with Vrindāvandāsa's work of the same name). In Raghubir Singh Tak's paper, "Guru Nanak in Oriya Sources," he mentions an Odiya palm-leaf manuscript preserved in the Jagannāth Temple Museum. This manuscript, he writes, tells us the story of Śrī Chaitanya and Guru Nanak visiting Purī at the same time, and thus coming into contact with each other. The Odiya manuscript was donated by the Prachi Samiti in Cuttack, to Utkal University, Bhubaneshwar, where it was edited by Rai Bahadur Arthabaltaba Mohanty and published by the University in 1953. The author does not provide any date for the *Caitanya-bhāgavata*, but Prabhat Kumar Mukhopadhaya assesses it as a product of the 16th century. Bimanbehari Majumdar, however, suggests that it is quite possibly from a later period, perhaps the 18th century. (http://www.harekrsna.com/sun/features/11–09/features1565.htm) For a general overview of Sikhism in relation to the Gauḍīya tradition, see Sunil Kumar Das, *Śrī Caitanya and Guru Nanak: A Comparative Study of Vaiṣṇavism and Sikhism* (Calcutta: Rabindra Bharati University, 1985).

28. See *Caitanya-caritāmṛta*, Madhya 9.47–62.

29. For more on Mahāprabhu's interaction with other traditions, see Kenneth R. Valpey, "Circling in on the Subject: Discourses of Ultimacy in Caitanya Vaiṣṇavism," in Ravi M. Gupta, ed., *Caitanya Vaiṣṇava Philosophy* (Burlington, V.T.: Ashgate Publishing Company, 2014), 1–26.

30. See *Caitanya-caritāmṛta*, Madhya 9. Especially see 9.109: "Being a Vaishnava in the Rāmānuja-sampradāya, Veṅkaṭa Bhaṭṭa worshiped the deities of Lakṣmī and Nārāyaṇa (Vishnu). Seeing his pure devotion, Śrī Caitanya Mahāprabhu was very much satisfied. (*bhakti dekhi' prabhura tuṣṭa haila mana*).

31. See *Caitanya-caritāmṛta*, Madhya 15.137–156. The following verses are especially pertinent: "Śrī Chaitanya said, 'I repeatedly encouraged Murāri to find attraction in Krishna, saying to him, "My dear Gupta, Śrī Krishna, Vrajendra-kumāra, is the epitome of sweetness." (138) Just to test your conviction, I repeatedly asked you

to change your worship from Lord Rāma to Lord Krishna. (155) But in the end, I congratulated Murāri, saying, 'Indeed, you are the incarnation of Hanumān. Because of this, you are the eternal servant of Lord Rāma. Why should you give up his worship and the nectar of his lotus feet?'" (156).

32. See *Caitanya-caritāmṛta*, Madhya 18. See especially Madhya 18, Texts 162–211.

33. June McDaniel clarifies the distinction between ecstatic states and epilepsy, particularly in regard to Śrī Rādhā and Śrī Chaitanya. See June McDaniel, *The Madness of the Saints: Ecstatic Religion in Bengal* (Chicago: The University of Chicago Press, 1989), 82–84. Interestingly, many modern psychologists relegate mystical experience to deviant mental states, some even going so far as to call it a form of epilepsy. Most psychologists will admit, however, that even if there is some material, cerebral explanation for religious experience, it is merely an *external* explanation, the mechanism through which it occurs, and does not necessarily nullify or negate the experience itself or the subtle, otherworldly underpinning it might suggest. Along these lines, the psychologist William James wrote in *The Varieties of Religious Experience* (14–15): "Even more perhaps than other kinds of genius, religious leaders have been subject to abnormal psychical visitations. Invariably they have been creatures of exalted emotional sensitivity liable to obsessions and fixed ideas; and frequently they have fallen into trances, heard voices, seen visions, and presented all sorts of peculiarities which are ordinarily classed as pathological . . . . To plead the organic causation of a religious state of mind in refutation of its claim to possess superior spiritual value is quite illogical and arbitrary. [Because if that were the case], none of our thoughts and feelings, not even our scientific doctrines, not even our dis-beliefs, could retain any value as revelations of the truth, for every one of them without exception flows from the state of the possessor's body at the time. Saint Paul certainly once had an epileptoid, if not an epileptic, seizure, but there is not a single one of our states of mind, high or low, healthy or morbid, that has not some organic processes as its condition." (Quoted in "Transcendent Experience and Temporal Lobe Epilepsy" by Clifford Pickover: http://www.meta-religion.com/Psychiatry/The_Paranormal/trascendent_experiences.htm#ixzz4X0U1Qnaf).

34. It should be pointed out here that, like most religious scriptures, the Koran can be interpreted in both personal and impersonal ways. Overall, in the Koran, God is very much a "person," but great pains are taken not to anthropomorphize him. See David Norcliffe, *Islam: Faith and Practice* (Portland, Oregon: Sussex Academic Press, 1999), 56–60.

35. The conversation with the Pāṭhānas is interesting on a number of levels. First of all, it goes beyond the usual debate between personalism and impersonalism. As the Gauḍīya scholar Rādhāgovinda Nātha asserts, there are basically three categories of reality expressed here, which tallies with observable reality. That is to say, the Abrahamic faiths as traditionally understood do not exactly endorse the same sort of impersonalism that is expressed in the Indic traditions. Rather, they acknowledge that God is a person, as Vaishnavas do, but they tend to deny that this person has any distinct form, or that he could ever be perceived or articulated in any way. Dimock and Stewart, drawing on Rādhāgovinda Nātha, elaborate on this point when commenting

on the Pāṭhāna episode. Basically, they say that Mahāprabhu first argues that God has qualities, as opposed to being a God without qualities—and he does so, the text says, on the basis of Muslim scripture. Then, once the Sufi soldier agrees that a personal God is a higher conception, Mahāprabhu elaborates the full Vaishnava implications of personalism (i.e., God has a specific blackish form, and so on). In other words, Mahāprabhu cleverly helped the Sufi soldier advance from impersonalism to partial personalism, as per the Abrahamic faiths, and then to Vaishnava particularity, which covers new ground in personal-impersonal discourse. See Edward C. Dimock, Jr. and Tony K. Stewart, *The 'Caitanya Caritāmṛta' of Kṛṣṇadāsa Kavirāja*, op. cit., 608–609.

36. See endnote 28.

37. Despite the obvious Vaishnava-centric dimension of this story, the Buddha himself is seen as a *śaktyāveśa avatāra* and is highly lauded in the Vaishnava tradition. There are diverse notions about the Buddha's true identity, and even Buddhist tradition itself teaches that there are many Buddhas. However, it is generally agreed that when we speak of the Buddha of history, we are referring to Siddhartha Gautama. It is a complex subject, and so I will refer readers to three books from the Vaishnava perspective: Śrīla Bhakti Prajñāna Keśava Goswāmī Mahārāja, *Vaiṣṇava Vijaya: The Life History of Māyāvādism* (Atlanta, Georgia: Gaudiya Vaishnava Press, 1996, reprint); Śrī Śrīmad Bhaktivedānta Nārāyaṇa Mahārāja, *Beyond Nirvāṇa* (Mathura: Gaudiya Vedanta Publications, 2003); and Steven J. Rosen, *From Nothingness to Personhood: A Collection of Essays on Buddhism from a Vaishnava-Hindu Perspective* (New York: FOLK Books, 2003). Also regarding Buddha's identity: According to Jīva Goswāmī, Buddha appears when two thousand years of the Kali age have passed: *tataḥ iti ayaṁ kaler abda-sahasra-dvitīye gate vyaktaḥ*. See Jīva Goswāmī, *Krishna-sandarbha*, Volume I, Anuccheda 24. Rūpa Goswāmī says this, too, in his *Laghu-bhāgavatāmṛta* (1.3.91–92). That would put the date at approximately 3,000 years ago. For Vaishnavas, however, the critical point is not when he appeared on earth, but that he was an *avatāra* of Vishnu. This is stated in the *Śrīmad Bhāgavatam* (1.3.24), in the *Gīta-govinda's daśāvatāra-stotram*, and elsewhere.

38. See endnote 27.

39. See Trilochan Singh, *Guru Nanak: The Founder of Sikhism, A Biography* (Delhi: Gurdwara Parbandhak Committee,1969), 60–62. Also informative are a number of Sikh websites (http://www.searchsikhism.com/sri-guru-nanak-dev-ji/meeting-between-guru-nanak-and-chaitanya).

40. This is *Caitanya-caritāmṛta*, Madhya 17.129. Mahāprabhu's unequivocal stance on this has carried to the present day. See for example, *Caitanya-caritāmṛta*, Adi 7.99, purport. Prabhupāda writes: "The Māyāvādīs say that the ultimate source of everything is impersonal, and in this way they deny the existence of God. Saying that there is no God is direct denial of God, and saying that God exists but has no head, legs or hands and cannot speak, hear or eat is a negative way of denying His existence. A person who cannot see is called blind, one who cannot walk is called lame, one who has no hands is called helpless, one who cannot speak is called dumb, and one who cannot hear is called deaf. The Māyāvādīs' proposition that God has no legs, no eyes, no ears and no hands is an indirect way of insulting Him by defining Him as blind,

deaf, dumb, lame, helpless, etc. Therefore although they present themselves as great Vedāntists, they are factually *māyayāpahṛta-jñāna*; in other words, they seem to be very learned scholars, but the essence of their knowledge has been taken away."

41. See *Caitanya-caritāmṛta*, Madhya 6.110–232.

42. See *Caitanya-caritāmṛta,* Ādi 7.38–145, and Madhya 25.4–116. See also Vasudeva das, "Śrī Caitanya as a teacher of Vedānta: the Philosophy of the *Vedānta-sūtra* as Presented in the *Caitanya-Caritāmṛta*," *Journal of Vaishnava Studies*, Volume 25, No. 1 (Fall 2016), 205–209.

43. See *Navadvipa-dhāma-mahatmya*, Parikramā-khaṇḍa, Chapter 16 (http://nitaaiveda.com/Compiled_and_Imp_Scriptures/Navadvipa_Dhama_Mahatmya/Parikrama_Khanda/Bilvapaksa_and_Bharadvaja-tila.htm).

44. Gérard Colas, "History of Vaiṣṇava Traditions: An Esquisse" in Gavin Flood, ed., *The Blackwell Companion to Hinduism* (Oxford: Blackwell Publishing, 2003), p. 253.

45. Ibid.

46. See *Caitanya-caritāmṛta*, Ādi 16. 25–109.

47. See *Caitanya-caritāmṛta*, Madhya 9.102–146.

48. See *Caitanya-caritāmṛta,* Madhya 9.228–250.

49. See *Caitanya-caritāmṛta*, Antya 7.113 (*bhāgavate svāmīra vyākhyāna kairāchi khaṇḍana, la-ite nā pāri tāṅra vyākhyāna-vacana*).

50. See *Caitanya-caritāmṛta*, Antya 7.123–124 (*āpanā jānāite āmi kari abhimānase garva khaṇḍāite mora karena apamāna*).

51. See *Caitanya-caritāmṛta*, Antya 7.131 (*prabhu kahe—"tumi 'paṇḍita' 'mahā-bhāgavata' dui-guṇa yāhāṅ, tāhāṅ nāhi garva-parvata*).

52. See *Caitanya-caritāmṛta*, Antya 7.141 (*mahāprabhu tāre tabe prasanna ha-ilā*).

53. This chart is based on Bhaktivinoda Ṭhākura's presentation in *Navadvīpa-dhāma-māhātmya* 16.52–56 (for *sādhana-bhakti* contributions) and *Mahāprabhurā Śikṣā,* pariccheda 9 (for *sambandha-jñāna* contributions). See Bhaktivinoda Ṭhākura, *Navadvīpa-dhāma-māhātmya* 16.52–56, trans., Bhakti Kamal Tyagi Maharaja (Nabadwip: Sri Caitanya Saraswat Math, 2015), 350–351; and Bhaktivinoda Ṭhākura, *Śrī Caitanya Mahāprabhu ki Śikṣā* (Hindi translation of *Mahāprabhurā Śikṣā*) 9th pariccheda, trans., Bhaktivedānta Nārāyaṇa Mahārāja (Mathura: Gaudiya Vedanta Samiti, 2005), 105. Special thanks to Gerald Surya for the chart.

Chapter 9

Rāmānanda Rāya

The Viceroy of Devotion

The Sanskrit tradition of the *Vedas* often uses conversational format (*saṃvāda*) to convey spiritual truth. One of the earliest examples of this appears in the *Ṛg-veda*, where Mitra and Varuṇa teach through extended dialogue. Prajāpati and Indra, Yājñavalkya and Maitreyī, and many others do the same. Most Upanishads, in fact, center on the edifying exchanges that occur between spiritual teachers and their students. This dialogical technique is prominent in later texts as well. In the *Mahābhārata*, for example, we see Draupadī and Satyabhāmā, Yakṣa and Yudhiṣṭhira, and Krishna and Arjuna (as in the *Bhagavad-gītā*) having meaningful back and forth.

But of all such verbal interchange, the 17th-century *Caitanya-caritāmṛta* (Madhya 8) gives us what is arguably the most profound. It involves a conversation between Chaitanya Mahāprabhu and Rāmānanda Rāya, a well-stationed viceroy in South India who is considered among the Master's most intimate followers. For Gauḍīya Vaishnavas, these informal talks embody the highest and most confidential aspects of *bhakti* philosophy.

Apropos of this, perhaps, the very act of dialogue between these two turns all social and religious conventions on their head. For example, Chaitanya is a Brahmin and a *sannyāsī*, whereas Rāmānanda is a Śūdra and a householder.[1] Consequently, under normal circumstances, they would never be seen in prolonged conversation. But there is yet another, more startling transgression of societal norms, central to this interaction: this exchange does not find Mahāprabhu instructing his follower but rather it is the other way around—Rāmānanda Rāya is put into the position of teacher, and the Master becomes his willing pupil.[2]

This is because Rāmānanda is a special devotee: It is sometimes said that Mahāprabhu took *dīkṣā*, regular initiation, from Īśvara Purī; he then took *sannyāsa*, the renounced order, from Keśava Bhāratī; and for entrance into the transcendental pastimes of Krishna in Vrindāvan, he took *rāga-mārga* initiation from Rāmānanda Rāya.[3] Of course, Īśvara Purī, Keśava Bhāratī, and Rāmānanda Rāya never thought of themselves as Śrī Chaitanya's *guru*. They were simply complying with the Master's wishes, which was to show by example how *bhakti* is properly pursued.

The *Caitanya-caritāmṛta*, Madhya 8.204–205, asserts that the help of a *sakhī*, or a *gopī*, is required if one wants to make progress in developing love for Śrī-Śrī Rādhā-Krishna (*sakhī vinā ei līlāya anyera nāhi gatisakhī-bhāve ye tāṅre kare anugati*), especially in the realm of *mādhurya-rasa*. Only through following in the footsteps of such souls might one reach the perfectional stage of life.[4] "In *mādhurya-rasa*," B. R. Śrīdhara Mahārāja tells us, "the guru is seen in the form and spirit of a *sakhī*, a maidservant of Rādhārāṇī (*guru rūpa sakhī*). Rāmānanda Rāya was Viśākhā-sakhī,[5] the right-hand personal attendant of Śrīmatī Rādhārāṇī."[6] Therefore, Mahāprabhu set an example by taking pertinent instruction from his dear devotee who was absorbed in *gopī-bhāva*, or the mood of a *gopī*. In our recreation of these teachings, we will primarily follow the *Caitanya-caritāmṛta*, Madhya 8.

THE CONSEQUENTIAL MEETING

When Mahāprabhu left Purī for his tour of South India, Sārvabhauma Bhaṭṭāchārya suggested that he search out Rāmānanda Rāya,[7] referring to him in superlatives: "exalted" "learned," and so on. "No other devotee is his equal in terms of '*rasa tattva*,'" he said.[8] Mahāprabhu decided to take Sārvabhauma seriously.

Thus, on his journey south, after quickly visiting the famous temple of Jiyaḍa-nṛsiṁha, Mahāprabhu made his way to the Godāvarī River, hoping to meet Rāmānanda there. This is in Vidyanagar Rajahmundry, present-day Kobura (Kovvur) in the East Godavari district of Andhra Pradesh. Rāmānanda was governor of the entire area, serving under King Pratāparudra, and normally took his bath at a small part of the Godāvarī known as Goṣpada-ghaṭ. Mahāprabhu thus searched out that exact spot, with the clear intention of meeting this great devotee. And as fate would have it, Kavirāja Goswāmī tells us, Rāmānanda happened to approach just as Mahāprabhu was about to bathe. Rāmānanda was accompanied by both his royal retinue and many Brahmins, who were chanting Vedic *mantras*.

Attracted by Mahāprabhu's effulgence and demeanor, Rāmānanda had his assistants lower his palanquin and, alighting in his kingly manner, proceeded to offer obeisance. They greeted each other and embraced, as if reuniting after many births. Both felt the onset of divine emotions, the *Caitanya-caritāmṛta* tells us, experiencing the highest forms of transcendental love in each other's company.

Without wasting a moment, Mahāprabhu expressed a desire to hear about Krishna, specifically asking Rāmānanda to talk about the ultimate goal of life (*sādhyera*).[9] And so the conversations began. In these talks, the tradition tells us, the reader is presented with complete knowledge of *krishna-tattva, rādhā-tattva, prema-tattva*, and *rasa-tattva*, that is, the fundamental truths regarding Śrī Krishna; his eternal consort Śrī Rādhā; the love they share between themselves and with others; and the varieties of relationships God enjoys with his intimate associates, respectively.

Initially, Rāmānanda replied that the ultimate goal of life is to perform Vishnu-bhakti, devotional service to Lord Vishnu, by executing one's prescribed duties according to his or her social position. As evidence, he quoted a verse from the *Vishnu Purāṇa* (3.8.8). While social interaction and one's station in life are no doubt important, even for one pursuing spiritual perfection, this is hardly the ultimate goal of life.

Thus, Mahāprabhu responded, "What you have just said is only external. Please augment this truth, telling me something more (*eho bāhya āge kaha āra*)." This will become a familiar refrain for the first part of the conversation. By making Rāmānanda repeatedly reconsider his answers, Mahāprabhu extracts higher and higher knowledge from him. And with every suggestion about the possible goal of life, Rāmānanda gives colorful proof-texts, enhancing their intensely philosophical back and forth.

After his initial answer about using one's social position in service to the Lord—and Mahāprabhu's rejection of it—Rāmānanda suggested the following: "The essence of all perfection is to completely offer Krishna the results of one's activities." To buttress his case, he supported this notion with the *Bhagavad-gītā*'s final teaching (18.66): "Abandon your regular duty and replace it with surrender to Krishna." But Mahāprabhu still wanted more. "This is also external," he said.

So at this point, Rāya proposed *jñāna-miśrā-bhakti*, or devotion mixed with empiric knowledge. This, he said, is the essence of perfection. Nonetheless, Mahāprabhu again protested: *eho bāhya āge kaha āra*—"this, too, is merely external. Please go further."[10] Rāmānanda Rāya again conceded, amending his position: "Pure devotional service *devoid* of speculative knowledge (*jñāna-śūnyā bhakti*) is in fact the ultimate goal of life."

Though this certainly indicated a higher level of purity, Mahāprabhu still expressed dissatisfaction. Clearly, in the Master's estimation, the ultimate goal should not be contaminated or compromised by anything material, no matter how subtle. *Karma-miśrā-bhakti*, or devotion that is hampered by materialistic activity, is rejected along with *jñāna-miśrā-bhakti*, or devotion mixed with knowledge, as stated above. These lesser forms of spirituality have been termed *biddha-bhakti*, or "devotion with blemishes." Ultimate truth must go further, beyond the realm of even unmixed devotion (*jñāna-śūnyā bhakti*). Mahāprabhu was prompting Rāmānanda to articulate this more clearly.

PURE LOVE OF GOD

The ultimate goal of life, from Mahāprabhu's perspective, is a form of *bhakti* that is unhampered by action (*karma*) or knowledge (*jñāna*), whether ordinary or even extraordinary. In other words, real purity, paramount devotion, goes beyond all common conceptions of pious activity, or spirituality, existing in a higher realm of unmotivated and ceaseless love. And so, Rāmānanda at this point utters four verses, beginning in Madhya 8.67, in which he quotes the *Bhāgavatam*.[11] Here he says that pure love of God—*prema-bhakti*—is the essence of all perfection. (*prema-bhakti-sarva-sādhya-sāra*)

Mahāprabhu acknowledges this to be true, affirming that Rāmānanda's current position is fully acceptable (*eho haya*). This, in fact, is a major turning point in the conversation. No more is Mahāprabhu characterizing Rāmānanda's explanation as external (*eho bāhya*).

Encouraged by his Master, Rāmānanda then talks about engaging in activities that foster this love with both "faith" (*śraddhā*) and transcendental "greed" (*laulyam*), a concept to which we will return in the following chapter. Again Mahāprabhu concedes that all this is true, even if he still wants his interlocutor to go further, to define exactly what he means by *prema-bhakti*. It is then that Rāmānanda enunciates the five *rasas*, or the deep, loving relationships one can have with Krishna.

Kavirāja Goswāmī clearly bases much of this upcoming section on Rūpa Goswāmī's *Bhakti-rasāmṛta-sindhu*, Western Quadrant, Waves 1–5, where the five primary *rasas*—neutral (*śānta*), service (*dāsya*), friendly (*sakhya*), parental (*vātsalya*), and romantic (*mādhurya*)—are elaborately explained. *Mādhurya-rasa*, arguably the most important of these five, is further outlined in Śrī Rūpa's follow-up treatise, *Ujjvala-nīlamaṇi*.

And so this section of the Rāmānanda Samvāda similarly focuses on *rasa* theology, highlighting its hierarchical development. It illuminates each stage sequentially up to the ultimate, most coveted phase, the realm of conjugal *rasa*. The criterion for establishing this hierarchy is intensity of emotion, which progressively develops as one goes from the initial *rasas* to the final one, and the fact that each higher *rasa* contains certain elements of those that come before it. (It should be noted, however, that all *rasas* are also, from another perspective, considered equal, or absolute, because all beings, including God, thrive in a diversity of relationships and, in fact, Krishna relishes them all.)

Briefly, those given to neutral or peaceful (*śānta*) relationships are tranquil in their service. These souls experience complete satisfaction simply by pleasing Krishna through their prayerful presence, with little or no interaction. Śrī Rūpa describes their emotional experience (*bhāva*) as being similar to that of *yogīs*, but whereas the *yogīs* want to realize the self (*ātman*), those in *śānta-rasa* want exchange with the Lord.

Higher than this is the mood of a loving servant (*prita-bhakti-rasa, dāsya-rasa*), which, Śrī Rūpa tells us, is based on a sense of profound respect. In this relationship, Krishna manifests in the mood of a superior or perhaps even a protective elder, and the devotees who relate to him in this way lovingly function as doting servants or younger relatives.

Greater intimacy crystalizes into transcendental friendship or companionship (*preyo-bhakti-rasa, sakhya-rasa*), and, at least in the initial stages, still has the seeds of awe and veneration (*gaurava-sakhya*). This can mature into a more equal relationship (*viśrambha*) and sometimes Krishna can even be seen as one's inferior, wherein one, with great confidence, acts as though they supersede him (*viśvāsa-maya*). But this sense of superiority is a transcendental phenomenon, merely enacted for the relishing of relationship.

Still further along the continuum, Śrī Rūpa describes parental affection (*vātsala-bhakti-rasa*), which is nurturing and protective. This is a form of love that completely absorbs the devotee in Krishna, but not with the same intensity as the conjugal mood. An important distinction must be made here: unlike the teaching commonly received in the Judeo-Christian tradition, where God is revered as the ultimate father, *vātsalya-bhāva* is the reverse—God is nurtured by a loving devotee who takes a position as his guardian.

The supreme devotional *rasa,* leading to the highest type of religious experience, is romantic love (*mādhurya-bhakti-rasa*), based on the mood of amorous affection. *Mādhurya* means "honey-sweet" and "intoxicating." *Śṛṅgāra,* another word for the same *rasa,* means "passionate" and even "sexual." *Ujjvala* is yet another term for this category of love, meaning "fully blossomed and brilliant."[12] These terms give a sense of what this *rasa* is trying to convey.

All living entities have a particular relationship with Krishna, say the Gauḍīya texts, fitting into one of the above five. But they have moved away from this relationship over uncountable lifetimes of forgetfulness. The goal of spiritual practice, we learn, is to become reinstated in this relationship and thus return to Krishna.

While the above is a summary of Śrī Rūpa's analysis, we now return to Rāmānanda Samvāda and specifically how *rasa* theology is presented in that particular section of the *Caitanya-caritāmṛta.*

Rāmānanda responds to Mahāprabhu's latest question, about defining *premā*, by outlining the four higher categories of relationship (*rasa*), beginning with the first two: the mood of a servant (*dāsya-rasa*) and the mood of a friend (*sakhya-rasa*).[13] Contemporary Gauḍīya Vaishnava master Nārāyaṇa Mahārāja offers an insight here, preparing readers for the higher order of love that is yet to come:

> Up until this point, Śrīman Mahāprabhu has said, "*Eho haya*—this is good," but now to this He replies, "*Eho uttama*—this is the topmost." Prior to *sakhya-rasa* being mentioned, whatever scriptural evidence that had been presented had mainly referred to the practitioner who comes in the category of an ordinary living entity; but here the discussion embarks upon the subject of the *nitya-siddha-parikaras*, or the eternally perfected associates of the Lord. The devotees of *śānta* and *dāsya-rasa* are controlled by Bhagavān, but from the stage of *sakhya-rasa* onward, Bhagavān is controlled by His devotee.[14]

In other words, from the *rasa* of friendship (*sakhya*) forward, the love is so intense that God himself becomes subservient to it, that is, he allows himself to be governed by such a devotee's love.

Thus, after discussing *sakhya-rasa* and *dāsya-rasa*, Rāmānanda glorified the nurturing mood of a parent (*vātsalya-rasa*), and, finally, *kāntā-prema*, or *mādhurya-rasa*, the highest form of love, passionate and romantic—a love that belongs only to Krishna's female girlfriends, the *gopīs*. Using scriptural evidence and logic, Rāmānanda demonstrated how *kāntā-prema* is the ultimate in spiritual loving affairs, and that to follow in the *gopīs*' footsteps is how one attains this purest love for God. Starting with Madhya 8.79, then, Rāmānanda elaborates the subtleties of the *gopīs*' love, and Mahāprabhu is delighted.

Although the love of the *gopīs* seemed like it would be the final answer, it was not. Surprisingly, Mahāprabhu entreated him to go further still, and Rāmānanda Rāya was more than happy to comply.

ŚRĪMATĪ RĀDHIKĀ: A LOVE SUPREME

Thus, Rāmānanda began to describe the intimate and exclusive mood of Śrīmatī Rādhārāṇī as the pinnacle of transcendental love of Godhead. Mahāprabhu relished this part of the conversation immensely, asking Rāma Rāya to more fully describe the relationship of the divine couple, with special emphasis on *rasa-tattva* and *prema-tattva*.

Rādhā-prema, especially, is evoked in Madhya 8.98 as higher than the highest—the ultimate jewel of perfection (*sādhya-śiromaṇi*). If the love of the *gopīs* is the highest thing there is, the confidential and singular love of

Rādhā surpasses even that! Then, in Madhya 8.100, Rāmānanda quotes the *Bhāgavatam* verse (10.28.30) about the mysterious *gopī* who runs off with Krishna, and over the course of many verses to follow, reveals that it was Śrī Rādhikā herself.

Hearing this, Mahāprabhu could not contain his joy: "Please continue! The unmitigated nectar that flows from your mouth brings me incalculable joy"[15] In fact, after hearing about Rādhārāṇī's sweet relationship with Krishna, Mahāprabhu confirmed that he had achieved his goal: "That for which I have come has now been satisfied. Through you I have come to understand the blissful goal of life and the process of attaining it."[16] But there was still something more, Mahāprabhu said, and he begged Śrī Rāmānanda to reveal it to him.

At this point, Rāmānanda admitted that he could go no higher, that it was beyond his capacity and realization. But, he said, he was not speaking his own words anyway: it was the Master who was speaking *through* him, and these highest subjects could be conveyed only by him, in any case.[17]

Rāmānanda Rāya then began to evoke these higher subjects by telling Mahāprabhu more about Krishna-tattva, Rādhā-tattva, and the love that these two divine personalities feel for each other, just to prepare him for the ultimate knowledge he was about to express.[18] Then—as if to signal the highest point in this transcendental conversation—Rāmānanda began to intone a self-composed song revealing the truth of *prema-vilāsa-vivarta*.[19] This Sanskrit phrase refers to an esoteric level of spiritual trance in which feelings of love in separation become impossible to contain—it is the highest dimension of *mahābhāva*, and, from the Gauḍīya perspective, engenders the purest love imaginable. *Prema-vilāsa-vivarta* is a form of divine madness (*divyonmāda*), causing one to see everything in relation to Krishna and mistaking even material objects as part of his *līlā* (*vivarta* means "opposite" or "bewilderment"). The typical example is Rādhikā seeing a black *tamāla* tree and embracing it with intense love, thinking it is Krishna.

Upon Rāmānanda's singing, Mahāprabhu gently prevented his devotee from speaking further, indicating that the emotional intensity and the nature of the truths being revealed had become too confidential: "Śrī Chaitanya, in the ecstasy of divine *premā*, immediately covered Rāmānanda's mouth with his own hand."[20] The later tradition would take this as highly suggestive symbolism, that is, confidential subjects should not be uttered in the presence of those who are less qualified. Mahāprabhu himself only spoke about such things in the presence of Svarūpa Dāmodara, Rāmānanda Rāya, and a few others, setting an example for generations to come.

In this way, after some ten days and nights of continuous immersion, hearing and discussing confidential topics about Rādhā and Krishna, Rāmānanda and Śrī Chaitanya would go their separate ways.[21] But only for a short time, for they planned to reunite in Purī, and that would happen soon enough.

Before leaving each other on the banks of the Godāvarī, however, Rāmānanda confessed something significant to Mahāprabhu, leading to the ultimate revelation of the Master's supreme form, that is, his true identity as Krishna enhanced by the mood and complexion of Rādhā. This is revealed in a series of verses beginning with Madhya 8.268: "At first, I saw you in the form of a *sannyāsī*," Rāmānanda says, "but now I see you as Śyāmasundara, the beautiful darkish cowherd. (268) You also appear like a brilliant sculpture of some sort,[22] your entire form covered by a golden luster. (269) You are holding a flute to your mouth, and your eyes dart in all directions due to your uncontrollable ecstasy." (270) Mahāprabhu then assures him that this vision is a natural byproduct of his heightened spiritual perception. (272) Rāmānanda responds by asking him to nonetheless reveal his truest form. (278) At that point, Rāmānanda realizes just who is standing before him: "My dear Lord, I can now see that you have assumed the ecstatic love and bodily complexion of Śrīmatī Rādhārāṇī." (279) And indeed, Mahāprabhu shows him that rare and confidential form in which he is both Rādhā and Krishna. (282)

But it is too much to bear, and Rāmānanda Rāya falls unconscious.

With the soothing touch of his transcendental hands, Kavirāja Goswāmī says, Mahāprabhu restores Rāmānanda to external consciousness, and then he lovingly embraces him. At that time, he asks him to not reveal this form or identity to anyone. He wants to keep his divinity secret, so he could go on with his mission of spreading the holy name in the guise of a devotee, and continue experiencing the mood of Rādhā among his associates.

CONCLUDING REFLECTIONS

Toward the end of Madhya 8, Kavirāja Goswāmī offers a list of thirteen questions and answers, a mere sampling of the kind of back and forth that Mahāprabhu and Śrī Rāmānanda so relished. Modern Gauḍīya Vaishnava leader Satsvarūpa Dāsa Goswāmī compares it to a sort of Vaishnava "catechism," which for Christians is a summary of essential theological principles issued in question and answer format.[23] Here are a few of those found in the *Caitanya-caritāmṛta*:

Mahāprabhu: "What is the best education?"
Rāmānanda: "Devotion to Krishna."
Mahāprabhu: "What is the greatest activity for all living beings?"
Rāmānanda: "To be Krishna's servant."
Mahāprabhu: "What makes one truly wealthy?"
Rāmānanda: "Love of Rādhā-Krishna."

Mahāprabhu: "What is the greatest misfortune?"
Rāmānanda: "To not have the association of Krishna's devotees."[24]

In this way, Mahāprabhu would ask questions and Rāmāmanda Rāya would answer, sometimes in terse, one-sentence responses and, other times, elaborating in a detailed way, as in the earlier part of Madhya 8. Over the centuries, the Vaishnava *ācāryas* have extrapolated and commented on Rāmānanda's teachings, to make explicit that which is mostly implicit in the *Caitanya-caritāmṛta*. Their books constitute a storehouse of literature on love of God.

There is much to be gleaned from Rāmānanda Samvāda, beginning, on the most basic level, with emphasis on the all-important *guru*-disciple relationship. And Śrīla Prabhupāda underscores how crucial this point is in his book, *In Search of the Ultimate Goal of Life*:

> The method of approach and the manner of humility exhibited by Lord Caitanya to Rāmānanda is the ideal for approaching a bona fide *tattva-darśī* or a master of transcendental knowledge . . . . In the *Bhagavad-gītā*, it is recommended that one approach the spiritual master for supramundane knowledge under the protection of service and surrender accompanied by relevant inquiries. Lord Caitanya, as the ideal teacher and practical demonstrator of the teachings of the *Bhagavad-gītā*, teaches us by His approach to Rāmānanda Rāya. He shows that a person desirous of knowing the transcendental science must not be proud of his material acquisitions of education and wealth, which are very insignificant to the transcendentally situated spiritual master from whom we should be very keen to understand the science of devotion.
>
> If somebody approaches the bona fide spiritual master with the vanity of mundane pride in respect to his heredity, wealth, education, or personal beauty and without the necessary qualifications of surrender, service, and relevant inquiry, surely such a person will be honored outwardly by the spiritual master, but the spiritual master will decline to bestow transcendental knowledge upon the student who by his attitude of mundane vanity is rendered unqualified. Such a proud student is actually a *śūdra* and he has no access to spiritual knowledge for want of the necessary qualifications mentioned above. Thus the *śūdra* student, instead of availing himself to the mercy of the spiritual master, goes to hell as a result of his mundane vanity.
>
> Rāmānanda Rāya was born in the family of a *śūdra* and was also a *gṛhastha* in terms of the system of *varnāśrama-dharma*. Lord Caitanya appeared in the family of a highly cultured *brāhmaṇa* of Navadvīpa and was in the topmost rank of the *sannyāsa āśrama*. Therefore, in terms of the *varnāśrama* system, Rāmānanda Rāya was in the lowest status while Lord Caitanya was in the highest status; yet, because Rāmānanda was a master in the art of transcendental knowledge, Lord Caitanya approached him as one should approach a guru. He did so for the benefit of us all.[25]

NOTES

1. Rāmānanda's status as a Śūdra is worthy of further research. Generally, he was considered a Kāyastha, a sub-caste often associated with Kṣatriya-dharma and also identified, particularly in Bengal, with landowners. They are often scribes as well. Still, Kāyastha origins are inevitably linked with Śūdra status. See S. N. Sadasivan, *A Social History of India* (New Delhi: A.P.H. Publishing, 2000), 257. Prabhupāda offers the following explanation in his commentary to *Caitanya-caritāmṛta*, Madhya 7.63, purport: "Śrī Rāmānanda Rāya belonged to the *karaṇa* class, which is the equivalent of the *kāyastha* class in Bengal. This class is regarded all over India as *śūdra*. It is said that the Bengali *kāyasthas* were originally engaged as servants of *brāhmaṇas* who came from North India to Bengal. Later, the clerical class became the *kāyasthas* in Bengal. Now there are many mixed classes known as *kāyastha*. Sometimes it is said in Bengal that those who cannot claim any particular class belong to the *kāyastha* class. Although these *kāyasthas* or *karaṇas* are considered *śūdras*, they are very intelligent and highly educated. Most of them are professionals such as lawyers or politicians. Thus in Bengal the *kāyasthas* are sometimes considered *kṣatriyas*. In Orissa, however, the *kāyastha* class, which includes the *karaṇas*, is considered in the *śūdra* category. Śrīla Rāmānanda Rāya belonged to this *karaṇa* class; therefore he was considered a *śūdra*. He was also the governor of South India under the regime of Mahārāja Pratāparudra of Orissa."

2. This reversal of roles was addressed by Krishnadāsa Kavirāja Goswāmī in his *Caitanya-caritāmṛta, Madhya* 8.1. In Prabhupāda's translation: "Gaurāṅga [Chaitanya] is like the ocean of spiritual truths; he filled the cloud named Rāmānanda with the nectar of devotion to himself. Rāmānanda then rained down that same nectar on the very ocean from which it had come, producing the jewels of transcendental knowledge." In the *Bhagavad-gītā*, Arjuna hears from Lord Krishna, but here—Krishna (in the form of Śrī Chaitanya) hears from his devotee (Rāmānanda), who, according to tradition, is an incarnation of Arjuna (Rāmānanda Rāya). See endnote 4.

3. B. R. Śrīdhara Deva Goswāmī, *The Search for Sri Krishna: Reality the Beautiful* (San Jose, CA: Guardian of Devotion Press, 1986), 133–134.

4. Ibid.

5. As stated in Chapter Three (endnote 55): There are diverse opinions about Rāmānanda Rāya's spiritual identity. According to the *Gaura-gaṇoddeśa-dīpikā* (124), ". . . Rāmānanda Rāya is the incarnation of Lalitā-gopī, Arjuniya-gopī, and Paṇḍava Arjuna." But according to Dhyānachandra Goswāmī's *Śrī Gaura-Govindārcana-Smaraṇa-Paddhati*, Text 214, Rāmānanda Rāya is Viśākhā. Thus, the tradition offers a certain latitude when it comes to Rāmānanda's previous incarnation. That being said, the mass of Gauḍīya stalwarts tends to accept Dhyānachandra's version. In the late 17th century, for example, Viśvanātha Chakravartī writes in his *Gaura-gaṇa-svarūpa-tattva-candrikā* (text 79): "The illustrious *gopī* named Arjunika (or Arjuniya), a plenary portion of Viśākhā, has now become Rāmānanda Rāya , the dear friend of Chaitanya." Bhaktivinoda Ṭhākura clearly expresses this preference, too, in his commentary on *Caitanya-caritāmṛta* (Madhya 8.23), and Prabhupāda, while elsewhere giving credence to the Lalitā option, also comments on Madhya 8.23

in the same way, writing, "Śrīla Rāmānanda Rāya was an incarnation of the *gopī* Viśākhā. Since Śrī Caitanya Mahāprabhu was Lord Kṛṣṇa Himself, there was naturally an awakening of love between Viśākhā and Kṛṣṇa." In the *Caitanya-caritāmṛta*, Madhya 10.53, Śrī Chaitanya himself tells Bhāvānanda Rāya, Rāmānanda's father, who he is in the eternal play of Krishna: "You are Paṇḍu, and your wife is Kuntī. Your five sons are the five Paṇḍavas." This is perhaps the origin of seeing Rāmānanda Rāya as Arjuna, who was one of the five Paṇḍavas.

6. B. R. Śrīdhara Deva Goswami, *The Search for Sri Krishna: Reality the Beautiful,* op. cit., 134.

7. Some biographical information: Born in Orissa as a member of the *karaṇam* caste (similar to the Kāyasthas of North India), Bhāvānanda Rāya—Rāmānanda's father—had five sons, Vāṇīnātha, Gopīnātha, Kalānidhi, Sudhānidhi, and Rāmānanda, who was the eldest. According to the *Bhajana-nirṇaya*, Rāmānanda was the disciple of Rāghavendra Purī and grand-disciple of Madhavendra Purī. (http://www.bvml.org/SBBTM/p_srr.html).

8. *Caitanya-caritāmṛta*, Madhya 7.64–66.

9. Ibid., Madhya 8.57.

10. Ibid., Madhya 8.64. (*prabhu kahe,—"eho bāhya, āge kaha āra"rāya kahe,—"jñāna-miśrā bhakti--sādhya-sāra*). The rejection of *jñāna-miśrā-bhakti* as the ultimate goal is significant. Traditionally, Vedic scholars cherish knowledge as a most valuable spiritual commodity. But for Mahāprabhu it is little more than a distraction.

11. Responding to Mahāprabhu's rejection of his initial answers, that is, that of adhering to social position and the importance of devotional work and the cultivation of knowledge, Rāmānanda offers this *Bhāgavatam* verse (10.14.3) as a sort of culminating response: "If one can do away with speculative knowledge and at the same time use one's body, mind, and words to glorify Krishna's personality and activities, as pure devotees do, dedicating their lives to such endeavors—even while remaining properly situated in one's established social position—one can fully conquer the Supreme Lord, although he is generally unconquerable by anyone within the three worlds. (*jñāne prayāsam udapāsya namanta eva, jīvanti san-mukharitāṁ bhavadīya-vārtām, sthāne sthitāḥ śruti-gatāṁ tanu-vāṅ-manobhir, ye prāyaśo 'jita jito 'py asi tais tri-lokyām*)

12. See Vraja Kishor, "Flavors of Love" (https://vicd108.wordpress.com/2014/02/10/flavors-of-love/).

13. One might question why *śānta-rasa* (the "neutral" or "peaceful" relationship) seems to be given short shrift in this context. Usually, the primary *rasas* are enumerated as five, beginning with *śānta*, but Gauḍīyas tend to emphasize the higher four (see *Caitanya-caritāmṛta*, Ādi 3.19). This is because *śānta* is sometimes associated with Brahman, or worship of the impersonal absolute. Also, in *śānta-rasa*, there is no real feeling of passionate attachment to Krishna. Rather, knowledge (*jñāna*) seems to outweigh devotion (*bhakti*) in this particular *rasa* (See *Caitanya-caritāmṛta,* Madhya 19.218 and *Bhakti-rasāmṛta-sindhu* 2.5.18), making it more akin to *yoga* than it is to Vaishnavism. Additionally, *Bhakti-rasāmṛta-sindhu* 3.1.7 says that the object of *śānta-rasa* (or its *viṣaya-ālambana*) is four-armed Vishnu as opposed to two-armed Krishna, which could also explain why it is de-emphasized among Gauḍīyas. That

being said, it is understood that trees, lakes, and other "inanimate" paraphernalia of the spiritual realm, sometimes even cows, partake of the *śānta* mood. And, clearly, there are distinctions and gradations within the *rasa* itself, as witnessed by the fact that the nine *yogīs* named Kavi, Havi, Antarikṣa, Prabuddha, Pippalāyana, Avirhotra, Drumila, Camasa and Karabhājana; the four Kumāras (Sanaka, Sanandana, Sanatkumāra and Sanātana); and even Prahlāda are sometimes cited examples of *śānta-rasa*. As a side-note, the Rāmānanda Rāya conversation does include mention of *śānta* some verses later. See, for example, Prabhupāda's translation of Madhya 8.86: "As the qualities increase, so the taste also increases in each and every mellow. Therefore the qualities found in *śānta-rasa, dāsya-rasa, sakhya-rasa* and *vātsalya-rasa* are all manifest in conjugal love [*mādhurya-rasa*]." Finally, in Rūpa Goswāmī's *Bhakti-rasāmṛta-sindhu* (Western Quadrant, First Wave), fifty-one verses are dedicated to describing *śānta-rasa*, which clearly make it a legitimate part of Gauḍīya philosophy.

14. Śrī Śrīmad Bhaktivedānta Nārāyaṇa Gosvāmī Mahārāja, *Śrī Rāya Rāmānanda Sam5āda* (Vrindavan: Gaudiya Vedanta Publications, 2009), 83.

15. *Caitanya-caritāmṛta*, Madhya 8.101.

16. Ibid., Madhya 8.117–118.

17. Ibid., Madhya 8.121–122.

18. It should be clear that the *premā* discussed here is not in any sense mundane or material, that is, it is not the kind to which we are accustomed in the material world (*jaḍa-prema*), although it may externally appear to share some of the same characteristics. Rather, Vaishnava texts identify the mundane counterpart as a form of lust (*kāma*), even when it appears wholesome and pure, as in a mother's love for her child. Upon careful scrutiny, they say, one finds that love in this world tends to bear certain selfish characteristics, however subtle that may sometimes be; it is only a shadow of spiritual love, the highest form of which occurs between Rādhā and Krishna. Gauḍīya texts describe the difference between mundane love and spiritual love as being comparable to the difference between iron and gold—although both are metals, one has tremendous value, while the other does not. See *Caitanya-caritāmṛta*, Ādi 4.164 and 165.

19. The words *prema-vilāsa* refer to "playful activity that arises from the purest kind of love"; *vivarta* means "mistaking one thing for something else." Counter-intuitively (since it involves a type of illusion), this rare stage of divine love is considered the zenith of spiritual realization.

20. *Caitanya-caritāmṛta*, Madhya 8.193 (*preme prabhu sva-haste tāṅra mukha ācchādila*).

21. According to Madhya 8.291–294, they spent ten nights together discussing these esoteric subjects.

22. I am aware that the word used in this verse, *kāñcana-pañcālikā*, more accurately translates as "a doll made of gold." But I don't think that the English word "doll," in a modern context, accurately conveys what Rāmānanda was trying to say. *Pañcālikā* can also be rendered as "puppet," or a small doll that can be seen as a type of marionette or figurine. In essence, he was saying that Mahāprabhu looked like a small, animated, golden statue of some sort.

23. See Satsvarūpa Dāsa Gosvāmī, *From Copper to Touchstone: Favorite Selections from the Caitanya-Caritāmṛta* (Port Royal Pennsylvania: GN Press, Inc., 1996), 234.

24. See *Caitanya-caritāmṛta* 2.8.245–257.

25. His Divine Grace A. C. Bhaktivedanta Swami Prabhupada, *In Search of the Ultimate Goal of Life: Śrī Rāmānanda Samvāda* (Vermont: Gosai Publishers, 1993), 47–48.

Chapter 10

Rāgānuga-bhakti

Śrī Chaitanya's Special Gift

Chaitanya Mahāprabhu's unique contribution to the *bhakti* tradition and through it to spiritual aspirants the world over cannot be overstated. True, previous to Mahāprabhu, the secrets of *bhakti*'s most recondite phase, *mādhurya-rasa*, had been conveyed in the writing of Vidyāpati, Caṇḍīdāsa, and Jayadeva, among others, and important elements of that knowledge had begun to percolate through the tradition's evolving conversation. But, in fact, it was not until Śrī Chaitanya's appearance that the world received, not just a fleeting glimpse but an unabbreviated and unabated portrait of Śrī Rādhā's superlative love, enriched by teachings that elaborately developed an understanding of its character, its mood, and its behavior. Moreover, Śrī Chaitanya illumined a path, Rāgānuga-bhakti, whereby aspirants could enter fully into the highest phases of love of God, teaching chiefly by his life narrative.[1]

The *bhakti* journey begins with *sādhana*, or "*bhakti* in practice." Rūpa Goswāmī devotes the entire second chapter of his *Bhakti-rasāmṛta-sindhu* to analyzing this initial phase, explaining that there are two types of practice: Vaidhī (in texts 1.2.6–269) and Rāgānugā (in 270–309). Vaidhī emphasizes the rules and regulations of scripture and is primarily motivated by fear of sinful reactions. Rāgānugā, on the other hand, is motivated by a deep, inner yearning that impels one to follow in the footsteps of those with passionate devotion.

While both forms of *bhakti* are ultimately performed to achieve *premā*, or pure love of God, the practice of Vaidhī leads to Vishnu in Vaikuṇṭha (or sometimes Krishna in Dvārakā, who is similarly majestic) whereas Rāgānuga leads to Krishna in Vraja, the highest portion of Vaikuṇṭha. That latter destination is the stated goal of the Gauḍīya Vaishnavas.

Rūpa Goswāmī further distinguishes these two kinds of love in 1.4.5–8, where he refers to the Vaidhī-bhakti kind of love as *mahimāyukta* ("mixed with a sense of awe") and the Rāgānugā variety as *kevala* ("pure"). In this way, on whichever path one chooses to tread, *sādhana* leads first to Bhāva-bhakti, or the dawn of love of God, and then to Premā-bhakti, or the highest aspect of devotional love: "Now, Sādhana-bhakti will be defined," Rūpa Goswāmī writes. "Actions of the senses, which produce the stage of *bhāva*, are called Sādhana-bhakti. This advanced stage of Bhāva-bhakti is based on one's eternal *sthayi-bhāva*, or permanent emotion, which is not created, but simply manifests within the soul by the spiritual energy of the Lord."[2]

But before any of this can be understood, it should be clear where Śrī Chaitanya fits in, for none of this information was available until he and his Six Goswāmīs appeared in India and revealed it, both by extensive writings that expressed its nuances in clear language, and by their living example.[3]

It begins, say the Goswāmīs, with Krishna, who had three "unfulfilled desires," and wished to descend in the form of Śrī Chaitanya in order to fulfill those desires. As expressed in the *Caitanya-caritāmṛta*: "This *avatāra* specifically manifests to spread the chanting of the holy name and love of God. While this is true, it is only the external reason for his incarnation. One should know the internal reason (*antaraṅga*)—the confidential reason—for his appearance as well."[4]

Kavirāja Goswāmī then reveals the inner reason: "There is, in fact, a more central or underlying motivation (*mukhya-bīja*) for Lord Krishna to appear in this way, stemming from his own ontological position as the foremost enjoyer of loving exchanges (*rasika-śekhara*)."[5] This esoteric reason for his appearance is divided into three.

"The first of these three reasons," Kavirāja Goswāmī tells us, "was to relish the ontological character of Śrīmatī Rādhārāṇī, the prime reciprocator of love of Krishna. She loves him more than life itself, and so Krishna wanted to experience that same love from her unique perspective. Thus, the first reason for Mahāprabhu's appearance was to experience or understand the glory of Rādhikā's love (*śrī-rādhāyāḥ praṇaya-mahimā kīdṛśo vā*), which is her very essence. The second esoteric reason for his appearance was to deeply understand the sweetness of his own nature. Lord Krishna is sweetness personified, and by accepting the form of Chaitanya Mahāprabhu, the perfect devotee, he could experience the truth of that sweetness firsthand, as only Rādhārāṇī can (*anayā eva āsvādyo yena adbhuta-madhurimā kīdṛśo vā madīyaḥ*). The third reason for which Lord Chaitanya appeared was to enjoy the bliss tasted by Rādhā as a result of loving him (*saukhyaṁ cāsyā mad-anubhavataḥ kīdṛśaṁ veti*). 'Surely,' Krishna thought to himself, 'there is no greater pleasure than loving me, and Rādhārāṇī does this better than anyone.'"[6]

But, lest we misunderstand Śrī Chaitanya's overflowing magnanimity, Gauḍīya teachers are quick to point out that his intense eagerness to experience Śrī Rādhā's unique brand of love in no way diminished his intense eagerness to share that most refined height of loving devotion with all living beings. Accordingly, the *Caitanya-caritāmṛta* (Ādi 4.15–16) informs us that, "Krishna's desire to appear in this world can be traced to two primary reasons: He wanted to taste the sweet essence of love of God (*prema-rasa*), and he wanted to propagate that devotion to the world at large through the path of spontaneous attraction (*rāga-mārga bhakti loke karite pracāraṇa*). Thus he is known as the super-excellent taster of all spiritual relationships and as the most merciful of all."

In Śrīla Prabhupāda's commentary to the above verse, he writes, "Lord Krishna wants to make known *to all the conditioned souls* that He is more attracted by Rāga-bhakti than Vaidhī-bhakti, or devotional service according to rules and regulations."[7] (emphasis added) Here, Prabhupāda, as an important contemporary voice in the Gauḍīya tradition, tells us that Rāga-bhakti should be made accessible to all conditioned souls—not only to those who are advanced on the path—at least as an option. Why? So that they may, when ready, be prepared to pursue it. More, they should learn about it because it is, according to the tradition, Lord Krishna's preference.

Krishna says it himself in the *Caitanya-caritāmṛta,* "Everywhere in the world people worship me, God, according to scriptural injunctions [Vaidhī-bhakti]," he proclaims. "But simply by following such principles one does not attain the loving mood of the Vraja devotees." (Ādi 3.15) "Knowing that I am God Almighty, common religious practitioners revere me with awe, but such majestic devotion is compromised and does not attract me." (Ādi 3.16) "When one performs such dutiful religious activity with esteem and reverence, it takes them to Vaikuṇṭha where they achieve the four kinds of liberation." (Ādi 3.17) "But one who cherishes pure devotion to me, embracing me as his servant, friend, child, or beloved—considering me his equal or inferior—I allow myself to become subordinate to such a person, out of love." (Ādi 4.21–22) "Hearing about the pure love of the residents of Vraja, these devotees will worship me on the path of spontaneous love (*rāga-marga*), abandoning all rituals of religiosity and fruitive actions." (Ādi 4.33)

This preference, clearly articulated in the *Caitanya-caritāmṛta* and mentioned above by Śrīla Prabhupāda, is not meant to minimize Vaidhī-bhakti. In fact, the tradition expects that, in most cases, it is through Vaidhī that people will generally secure a foothold, at least initially. Conditioned souls naturally begin with discipline, rules, regulations, and worship of the Lord in awe and reverence. As such, Vaidhī is required. Although the path of Rāgānugā is not dependent on any hard and fast prerequisite, as we shall soon see, a true Rāgānuga-bhakta will never neglect Vaidhī, as exemplified by the Six Goswāmīs of Vrindāvan. But the ultimate goal should be clear as well.

Rūpa Goswāmī points out in *Bhakti-rasāmṛta-sindhu* 1.2.295 that those aspiring for Rāgānuga-bhakti must, as a matter of course, follow in the footsteps of those who reside in Vraja, engaging both their practitioner body (*sādhaka-rūpeṇa*) and their spiritual body (*siddha-rūpeṇa*). This is what *rāgānugā* literally means (*rāga* = "passion," and *anuga* = "to follow on the path."): The paradigmatic inhabitants of the spiritual world are called Rāgātmikā-bhaktas. It is they who have spontaneous, passionate love for God. Those who wish to follow in their wake are called Rāgānugā-bhaktas, that is, "those who follow those with passion."

Now, how does one follow such exalted souls? Does one simply *imitate* them or *follow them* in a more measured way?[8] Who are the inhabitants of Vraja? These are some of the questions we will now address.

Without doubt, Nanda, Yaśodā, Rādhikā, and so on, are inhabitants of Vraja, for they eternally exist in Krishna's celestial kingdom. But "inhabitants of Vraja" would also include the great souls who reside on the earthly plane, in terrestrial Vraja, that is, Śrī Rūpa Goswāmī, Sanātana Goswāmī, and others. In light of this notion, and to address Śrī Rūpa's statement about following the inhabitants of Vraja *in both practitioner and perfected bodies*, Jīva Goswāmī and Viśvanātha Chakravartī offer the following explanation—and this is critical for the practice of Rāgānuga-sādhana:

> Mental performance with the *siddha-rupa* [perfected body] is to be done in a manner that follows Śrī Rādhā, Lalitā, Visākhā, Śrī Rūpa Mañjarī, and other *gopīs*. But physical performance, with the *sādhaka-rupa* [practitioner body], is to be done in a manner that follows Śrī Rūpa, Sanātana, and the other Vrindāvan Goswāmīs.[9]

Kavirāja Goswāmī elaborates: "There are both external and internal methods for pursuing the path of Rāgānuga-bhakti. Even when one is self-realized, with one's external body (*sādhaka-dehe*) one follows all scriptural injunctions, especially hearing and chanting. But within one's mind, using one's eternal body (*siddha-deha*), one serves Krishna in Vrindāvan, all day and all night."[10] This is *rāgānugā* in a nutshell.

In other words, on the path of Rāgānuga-bhakti, there are two forms with which the practitioner engages in spiritual service. As the tradition developed after the time of Śrī Chaitanya, it became clear that it was the death knell of devotional life to confuse the two.[11] Rāgānugā chiefly involves inner mediation and developing a spiritual identity from within, but the practitioner must also cultivate *bhakti* from without, embracing the externals as strictly as the Six Goswāmīs of Vrindāvan.

Modern-day Gauḍīya practitioner and scholar Dhanurdhara Swami elaborates:

> The connection between Vaidhī-bhakti and Rāgānuga-bhakti in Gauḍīya Vaishnavism is analyzed clearly in the last section of *Śrī Bhakti-sandarbha*.

> [Anuccheda 312] If one lacks *ruci*, a natural taste for devotion, Śrī Jīva explains, one must be vigilant to consciously regard scriptural injunctions. If such a person tries to spontaneously execute devotional service out of attachment, he will fall prey to the whims of the mind and lose fixity in his practice. Still, however, [Śrī Jīva] insists, such a person should execute *rāgānuga-bhakti*. To resolve the apparent contradiction, he then offers an example of how such a devotee, one on the level of *vaidhī-bhakti*, can chant the *gopāla-mantra* while mixing both obligatory (*vaidhī*) and spontaneous (*rāga*) moods. Remaining consciously fixed in one's spiritual practices out of duty (*vaidhī-bhakti*), one should consciously cultivate a taste for Vraja (*rāgānuga-bhakti*) by thinking of the meaning of the mantra while visualizing "Śrī Krishna along with His associates, who all are attracted by the sound of his flute at the time of the milking of the cows."[12]

The path of Rāgānuga-bhakti is often seen as an extension of Vaidhī-bhakti, something that naturally evolves sequentially—and, indeed, it can certainly arise in this way. But, more accurately, it is an entirely different realm of practice, with different orientation, concepts of divinity, procedures, goals, and destinations. In this practice one seeks to become a divine participant in Krishna-līlā. To reiterate, Rāgānuga-bhakti is defined as the processes of devotion that allow one to follow the inhabitants of Vraja. In other words, the eternal associates of Krishna are seen as exemplary models of devotion, and *rāgānugā* means to practice following in their footsteps, to pursue their mood of spiritual passion.

GETTING TO THE HEART OF THE MATTER

David L Haberman summarizes the essence of Rāgānuga-sādhana: "The goal of Rāgānuga Bhakti Sādhana is to shift identity . . . [to] the 'perfected form' (*siddha-rūpa*), which is one's true and ultimate identity. Salvation, to the Gauḍīya Vaishnavas, is unending participation in the cosmic drama, and the skills of the actor are employed in pursuit of the true identity which allows such participation."[13]

Michele Voss Roberts elaborates:

> In the process of initiation to the *rāgānugā* path, devotees discover their true relationship to Kṛṣṇa as a servant, friend, guardian, or lover. This identity is a person's *siddha-rūpa*, or perfected body, which resides in the eternal realm of Kṛṣṇa. Through a process of mentally remembering Kṛṣṇa's pastimes, devotees progressively shift their identities onto that body. David Haberman likens the resultant "total identification with and absorption in" one's devotional identity to contemporary acting techniques developed by Constantin Stanislavski. "At first, practitioners merely copy the character they are striving to become. But the

successful practitioner's goal is to become so totally identified with a character in the Vraja-līlā that he or she *really is* that character."[14]

Roberts's words should be carefully understood. She is not suggesting that we become the Rāgātmikā personality we follow—and certainly not the person we worship. Otherwise, she would be describing the grave offense of *ahaṅgrahopāsana*, that is, thinking oneself to be the transcendental devotee one is following. This is forbidden. One should never think, "I am Rādhā, I am Lalitā, I am Viśākhā," and so on. As Prabhupāda writes: "The process of transcendental realization is to follow in the footsteps of the associates of the Supreme Lord; therefore if one thinks himself to be a direct associate of the Supreme Lord, he is condemned. According to authorized Vaiṣṇava principles, one should follow a particular devotee, and not think of himself as Kṛṣṇa's [direct] associate."[15] Accordingly, Roberts is saying that we meditate on ourselves as serving a particular personality in the *līlā*, and then we take on the identity of that servant in due course—the servant, not the person we are serving.

In the above quote, Roberts mentions the various types of relationships (*rasa*) one can pursue in Rāgānuga-bhakti, and this is important. Rāgānuga-bhakti, being modeled on Rāgātmikā, is generally divided into two categories: the followers of those with "romantic desire" (*kāmānuga*), who are solely in the mood of Mādhurya-rasa (conjugal love), and the followers of those who relish "other relationships in *bhakti*"(*sambandhānugā*), who may be engaged as a servant, a friend, or in a parental mood. Rūpa Goswāmī mentions this in *Bhakti-rasāmṛta-sindhu* (1.2.288–290). The highest level, he says, is the path of *kāmānuga*, the path of the *gopīs*, and this topmost path is the special contribution of Śrī Chaitanya.

Whether one chooses *kāmānuga* or *sambandhānugā*, however, the process involves deep meditation and the development of one's internal spiritual body. These are intensive practices that require devotional attainment and rigorous discipline. Thus, the process can only begin, say the Gauḍīya *ācāryas*, when one has the appropriate qualifications.

That being said, the initial qualification seems simple enough. Rāgānuga-bhakti begins with *lobha*, or *laulyam*—the "greed" or single-minded determination to attain the mood of a Rāgātmikā-bhakta. In common parlance, of course, "greed" is not something to aspire to, especially in spiritual circles. The meaning in this context is different, however. It refers to a complete dedication to one's subject, or the unwavering and undistracted determination to achieve one's goal. And it is this very hyper-focused determination that is required if one is to take up the practice of Rāgānuga-bhakti.[16]

Śrī Rūpa's *Bhakti-rasāmṛta-sindhu* (1.2.309) tells us that the "only way this type of transcendental greed arises is through the mercy of Krishna or his pure devotee." In other words, Krishna might arbitrarily bless someone or such a person might be continuing in his or her spiritual journey from a previous life. More than likely, a sincere soul will hear a devotee chanting, or reciting Krishna's pastimes, or witness something else related to Krishna, and this causes something to stir deep within.

Whatever the case, it can arise anywhere along the devotional path. Viśvanātha Chakravartī Ṭhākura indicates that it can arise even as one is still clearing away unwanted habits (*anartha-nivṛtti*), that is, still in the conditioned stage of life: "Now it will be described how the Rāgānugā-bhakta gradually advances through the stages of *anartha-nivṛtti*, *niṣṭhā* (steadiness), *ruci* (sustained taste for spiritual life), and *āsakti* (loving attachment)—all the way to the stage of *premā* (pure love) and the direct attainment of one's cherished deity.[17]

With *lobha*, one initially experiences a general attraction toward Rāga-bhakti, which becomes refined and enhanced through continued hearing and chanting—and internal meditation.[18] All of this being the case, it is generally understood that if one has not attained *niṣṭhā*, or a high level of steadiness in one's devotional practice, or, more, *ruci*, a genuine taste for spiritual life, one will not be able to legitimately perform *līlā-smaraṇam*, meditation or remembrance of Krishna, which is the main practice of Rāgānuga-sādhana. Jīva Goswāmī explains this in his *Bhakti-sandarbha* (Anuccheda 312) as follows:

> The path of Rāgānuga-bhakti is embraced simply by feeling special regard for specific Rāgātmikā associates of Lord Krishna. Still, if a person has not developed *ruci* as defined above, if a genuine taste has not yet sprouted (*ajāta-ruci*), one should still perform Rāgānuga-bhakti in conjunction with the practices of Vaidhī-bhakti . . . . Those who have acquired this taste (*jāta-ruci*) and are respected within a larger community should also perform *rāgānugā* mixed with *vaidhī* in order to set an accommodating example for others. As one engages both practices, *vaidhī* should be performed in such a way that it becomes one in nature with *rāgānugā*.

Dhanurdhara Swami elaborates,

> In other words, those not on the level of taste (*ruci*), although acting out of duty, should still cultivate an attraction to the mood of the eternal residents of Vrindāvan . . . by applying to their spiritual practices their aspirations and thoughts concerning Vraja-bhakti according to their realization.[19]

As one advances in the practice, one will eventually require familiarity with one's own spiritual form. It is only then, in fact, that one can perform Rāgānuga-bhakti proper. The practitioner can be introduced to this form by way of personal realization or through the grace of one's guru. This is called "Siddha Praṇālī." As we learn from Bhaktivinoda Ṭhākura's work, in particular, Siddha Praṇālī is generally a confidential interaction between guru and disciple, where the guru might say, "This is my eternal identity in Vraja-lilā. I will now reveal to you who you are, too, so you can effectively assist me in our service."[20]

In the final chapter of Bhaktivinoda Ṭhākura's *Hari-nāma-cintāmaṇi*—and elsewhere in his writings as well—he describes the details of *siddha-praṇālī-dīkśā,* beginning with *ekādaśa-bhāva*: "In order to fulfill one's desire to attain *ujjvala-rasa* [*mādhurya-rasa*] there are eleven items that form one's spiritual identity: relationship (*sambandha*), age (*vayasa*), name (*nāma*), form (*rūpa*), group (*yūtha*), dress (*veśa*), assignment (*ājñā*), residence (*vāsa*), service (*sevā*), highest ambition (*parākāṣṭhā*), and feeling one's self protected and maintained (*pālyadāsī*)." These eleven items are traditionally conferred on the disciple during initiation, or sometime thereafter, according to one's readiness. The conferral serves to define an internal spiritual identity that the *sādhaka* gradually learns to use to participate in Krishna *līlā.*[21]

Just how such a spiritual identity is implemented is described as follows: "The *sādhana* relating to these eleven items is executed in five progressive stages: *śravaṇa-daśā* (the stage of hearing), *varaṇa-daśā* (the stage of accepting), *smaraṇa-daśā* (the stage of remembering), *āpana-daśā* (the stage of maturing), and *sampatti-daśā* (the stage of attainment)."[22]

If either guru or disciple is not highly qualified, the process simply doesn't work. As Bhaktisiddhānta Sarasvatī Ṭhākura has said,

> By attaining *anartha-nivṛtti*, one's *svarūpa* is automatically awakened, and the eternal mode of thinking that is innate to it manifests . . . . The spiritual identity has eleven aspects (*ekā-daśa-bhāva*) . . . . There are many cases of unscrupulous gurus who artificially force-feed these designations on unqualified practitioners, but we cannot call this the mark of spiritual perfection. Those who have achieved the perfection of being fixed in their spiritual identity (*svarūpa-siddhi*) have attained such a realization through internal revelation and the spiritual master's only involvement in these matters is to help the further advancement of a disciple. As a practitioner progresses toward spiritual perfection, all these things are revealed naturally within the heart that sincerely seeks service.[23]

It should be clear that Bhaktisiddhānta Sarasvatī and others in his line were not opposed to *ekādaśa-bhāva* and its related practices, but were cautious about its inappropriate and premature implementation, which he found to be rampant in the modern age.

PERFECTED SPIRITUAL BODY

If one finds a legitimate guru, and if one is personally qualified to perform such advanced *sādhana*, Bhaktivinoda Ṭhākura tells us, three progressive "bodies" are used for attaining the Supreme: the Siddha-deha, the Svarūpa-siddhi, and the Vastu-siddhi.[24]

The first body, the Siddha-deha, is used for the practice of Rāgānuga-bhakti-sādhana. This is a mentally conceived body that perfectly suits the desired meditation. According to Viśvanātha and others, as stated above, this can begin early in one's devotional life, whenever genuine *laulyam*, or greed, arises. At this time, one graduates from haphazard reflection on Krishna-līlā to methodical cerebration, focusing on the Aṣṭa-kālīya-līlā (the eight periods of Krishna's day) with heart and soul, a detailed meditation that serves to bring practitioners into Krishna's world via intense contemplation.[25]

The Siddha-deha allows meditation while one is still in bodily form. This is necessary because one cannot interact with Krishna through one's material identity. Therefore, the Siddha-deha serves the function of a go-between, of sorts, allowing interaction with transcendence. It is the seed of one's "new" identity and the medium through which one develops relationship with Krishna.

By worshipping the Lord in this way, Bhaktivinoda says, the devotee inevitably meets Krishna face to face. At that point, the soul's pure spiritual form is manifested without any coverings and one can purely serve the Divine Couple in the spiritual world. This sense of identity perfection, which grows out of the Siddha-deha, is known as Svarūpa-siddhi, and it is the form with which one perfectly engages in *rasa* with Krishna. This is achieved while one is still embodied, though it is in the higher echelon of spiritual advancement, where one experiences *bhāva*, or the dawn of true love.

Meditation in the realm of Svarūpa-siddhi leads to concrete perfection: Vastu-siddhi. This is the body one acquires by taking birth in the womb of a *gopī*, first in a universe where Krishna engages in his manifested pastimes in the material world, and then this same body transforms into the totally spiritual body that engages with Krishna in the spiritual realm, far beyond the material universe.[26] Bhaktivinoda sums up:

> At the stage of *bhāvāpana* (Svarūpa-siddhi), the faculty of transcendental vision appears, and at that time, the *sādhaka* can have *darśana* of his *sakhī* [*gopī*], and also yūtheśvarī Śrīmatī Rādhikā. Even after having *darśana* of Golokanātha Śrī Krishna, the *sādhaka*'s realization is not steady at all times until he achieves the stage of *sampatti-daśā* (Vastu-siddhi), in which his gross and subtle bodies are destroyed. In *bhāvāpana-daśā*, the pure *jīva* [soul] has full command over the inert gross and subtle bodies. However, the secondary result of *sampatti-daśā*, the stage in which Krishna's mercy is fully manifested, is that the connection of the *jīva* with this mundane world is completely cut off. *Bhāvāpana-daśā* is called Svarūpa-siddhi, and in *sampatti-daśā* one attains Vastu-siddhi.[27]

TWO STREAMS OF THOUGHT

Though several Vaishnava communities express the above in various ways, with nuances of difference, there are two that deserve our attention. Along with the vision of Rūpa Goswāmī, Raghunāth Dāsa Goswāmī, and Krishnadāsa Kavirāja Goswāmī, the names of Gopāla Guru Goswāmī,[28] Dhyānacandra Goswāmī,[29] and Siddha Krishnadāsa Bābā[30] should be mentioned. These latter three have each composed manuals for engaging in Rāgānuga-bhakti-sādhana, collectively known as the *paddhati-traya*. Interestingly, Gopāla Guru Goswāmī and Dhyānacandra Goswāmī are lauded by Bhaktivinoda throughout his writings, particularly in *Jaiva Dharma*, and are thus considered important personalities in both communities under discussion.

The two streams of thought in the Gauḍīya Sampradāya have been called the internal and the external methods of Rāgānuga-bhakti.[31] According to this theory, Mahāprabhu gave Svarūpa Dāmodara Goswāmī, his confidential servant, access to both, and this was then bequeathed to his assistant Raghunāth Dāsa Goswāmī and to Gopāla Guru Goswāmī. The internal method, specifically, was directly passed to Dāsa Goswāmī, and these same techniques and teachings are found in the works of Rūpa Goswāmī. Their method—which might be called the "Rūpa-Raghunāth method"—was passed on to Kavirāja Goswāmī, who offers obeisance to Rūpa-Raghunāth throughout his *Caitanya-caritāmṛta* and *Govinda-līlāmṛta*. Narottama Dāsa Ṭhākura, too, embraces the Rūpa-Raghunāth mood in his writings and, apropos of this, offers deep respects to them overtly.

In this system, emphasis is on the chanting of the holy name and on receiving the seed of *ekādaśa-bhāva* in that holy name, imperceptibly. Then, through pure chanting, one's internal identity blossoms and, at a very advanced stage, can be augmented by *līlā-smaraṇam*, generally aided by an instructing guru or by one's own initiating guru, who offers specifics of one's *siddha-deha*. If one's guru is not still in physical frame, the information can come to a sincere disciple in meditation.

The above is called the internal method because there is no external conferral of *ekādaśa-bhāva*, or a literal, articulated *praṇālī* (succession of *rāgānuga* teachers), nor is there the "giving" of one's spiritual identity, at least not overtly, at the time of *dīkṣā* or soon thereafter—these are the key differences found in the external tradition, which will be outlined below. Before doing so, however, let it be said that this internal tradition was embraced by Bhaktisiddhānta Sarasvatī and the Gauḍīya Maṭha, and thus by Śrīla Prabhupāda and his International Society for Krishna Consciousness (ISKCON).

The external tradition also comes by way of Svarūpa Dāmodara Goswāmī. It was passed on to Vakreśvara Paṇḍita, who gave it to Gopāla Guru

Goswāmī, who in turn gave it to Dhyānachandra Goswāmī. This was largely a tradition that originated and subsisted in Jagannāth Purī, at least initially (as opposed to the internal method, which, through Dāsa Goswāmī, came to Vraja early on). Eventually, the external method came to Vraja, too, as we see today in the traditions of the Rādhā-kuṇḍa *bābājīs* and others. In this method, one is "externally" given one's *ekādaśa-bhāva*—which is why it is called the external method—and is taught how to meditate on his or her spiritual form via the Aṣṭa-kālīya-līlā schema. Interestingly, the external method is also endorsed in Bhaktivinoda Ṭhākura's *Jaiva Dharma*, who, it should not go unmentioned, was living in Purī for the greater part of his devotional career.

Bhaktivinoda, in his wisdom, decided to give the external method to his son Lalitā Prasāda and the internal method to his other son, Bhaktisiddhānta Sarasvatī. Why? Because Lalitā Prasada was inclined to pure internal *bhajan*, without any inclination to leave the precincts of Mahāprabhu's holy land, while Sarasvatī Ṭhākura, also inclined to pure internal *bhajan*, was an effective preacher as well, whom Bhaktivinoda was in fact grooming for taking the philosophy and practice of Gauḍīya Vaishnavism to all parts of the world.

The internal method, with its focus on chanting the holy name and the principles of Vaidhī-bhakti, would be the appropriate means for those who were disinclined to deep *bhajan*, or who were trying to pursue Krishna Consciousness in the world. The ultimate goal of this method, of course, is the same as that of the external method, if attempting to attain it more gradually, according to one's *adhikāra*: The goal is to evolve to a point where one can truly focus on Krishna. This occurs by perfecting the chanting to a point where such accomplishment leads to proper *smaraṇam*. Both the internal and the external methods of *rāgānuga bhajan* are seen as legitimate and embraced by various factions of the Gauḍīya Sampradāya. It is given to disciples according to their inclination and according to the mission and temperament of the respective *guru*.

A few concluding notes on the importance of chanting in relation to the practice of *smaraṇam*: One requires a pure heart for such remembrance, lest it be performed with distraction and incompetence. Therefore, Jīva Goswāmī recommends *kīrtana* over *smaraṇam*, as a means to the same end. This is so that when the heart becomes pure through ecstatic chant, deep meditation will arise as a matter of course.[32] Along these lines, Sanātana Goswāmī explains in *Bṛhad-bhāgavatāmṛta* that there is a very special, synergistic relationship between *kīrtana* and *smaraṇam*: "By congregational chanting the joy of meditation grows, and by meditation the sweet joy of congregational chanting grows. In our own experience, the two methods fortify one another and are therefore actually one."[33]

Bhaktivinoda Ṭhākura wrote a Bengali song, "*Śaraṇāgati*," to express such ideas. One line in particular is pertinent in the present context, so although I have quoted it in a previous chapter, it bears repeating here: "When the holy name fully blossoms it takes me to Vrindāvan and reveals its love. It gives me my own spiritual body, keeps me at Krishna's side, and gradually disintegrates the mortal frame."[34] Thus, in the very last line of Bhaktisiddhānta Sarasvatī's song, "Vaishnava Ke" (text 19), he leaves us with this: "The power of congregational chanting can automatically awaken remembrance of the Lord . . . ." (*kīrtana-prabhave, smaraṇa svabhave*).

MAÑJARĪ BHĀVA: MORE THAN AN ADDENDUM

An analysis of Rāgānuga-bhakti would be incomplete without some discussion of Mañjarī bhāva, which is a central focus for Rāgānuga-bhaktas in both streams of the Gauḍīya Sampradāya.[35] Basically, a *mañjarī* is a very young and qualified girl who tends to the needs of Śrī Rādhikā and her *gopī* friends. Thus, given the Sampradāya's emphasis on Śrī Rādhā, Mañjarī-bhāva, or the mood and acceptance of a *mañjarī* form in the spiritual world, is of extreme importance.

This is amplified by Mahāprabhu's teaching (found in *Padyāvali* 74), *gopī-bhartur pada-kamalayor dāsa-dāsa-dāsānudāsaḥ*, that is, the devotee aspires not for direct service to Śrī-Śrī Rādhā-Krishna but to be "the servant of the servant of the servant of the lotus feet of the master of the *gopīs*, Śrī Krishna." Mañjarī-bhāva goes one step further: It does not aspire to the service of the devotees of Krishna's devotees but to those of Śrī Rādhā, specifically.

Technically, it might be understood as follows: There are two kinds of *mādhurya-bhāva*: *sambhogecchātmikā* (the mood of Krishna's direct lovers) and *tad bhāvecchātmikā* (the mood of an indirect amorous accomplice). In *Bhakti-rasāmṛta-sindhu* (1.2.299), Rūpa Goswāmī elaborates: "The devotional mood of wanting to *assist* Śrī Rādhā and other prominent *gopī* leaders in their secret meetings with Śrī Krishna—as opposed to enjoying him themselves—is called *tad-bhāvecchātmikā* . . . ." (*tad-bhāvecchātmikā tāsāṁ bhāva mādhurya kāmitā*). While Rūpa offers both options for Rāgānuga-sādhana—meditating on oneself as a *gopī*, or as an assistant to the *gopīs*, that is, direct and indirect service—it becomes clear that the indirect mood is the proper aspiration for Gauḍīya Vaishnavas.[36]

In terms of their emphasis on Rādhā, *mañjarīs* are unique. Unlike other *gopīs*, who love Krishna (Krishna-snehādhikā) or who love Rādhā and Krishna equally (Sama-snehādhikā), these *gopīs* are completely devoted to Rādhikā (Rādhā-snehādhikā). This is called Bhavollas-rati, as mentioned in *Bhakti-rasāmṛta-sindhu* (2.5.128, *bhavollasa itiryate*). Such *gopīs* live to assist Rādhikā, and want nothing in return. They are innocent, partially because they are younger than the other *gopīs*,[37] and because of this innocence, their purity knows no equal. Theirs is a totally selfless and naïve love, and is, in its own way, comparable to Rādhikā's.

As Rādhikā's most intimate devotees, they long to see her happiness—even more than she longs for it. In this respect, it is said that they feel the truest form of spiritual empathy (*anukampa*)—her pleasure is their pleasure, and they experience simple, unfettered enjoyment in working together to please her. Thus, they are called "*mañjarīs*" or "tender buds" in relation to Rādhā, who is the ultimate flower. These buds, the *ācāryas* tell us, tremble with the greatest pleasure when the bee known as Krishna visits that flower, who is their life and soul. As Nārāyaṇa Mahārāja says, ". . . the *mañjarī* tastes something special, which even the flower does not taste, in the sense that the flower does not tremble as the *mañjarī* does. Similarly, the maidservants of Śrīmatī Rādhikā experience a pleasure in being Her maidservant, which She Herself does not experience . . . ."[38]

As an extension of the flower analogy, it should be noted that the word *mañjarī* actually means "a cluster of flower-buds," as opposed to a single flower, and so, as indicated above, they tend to work together as friends, rather than as a solitary heroine. The only true heroine in their eyes is Rādhā, who perpetually belongs to Krishna.

The *mañjarīs* are also known as *pālyadāsī*, or "protected, beloved servants," and the sense of protection they feel in service to Rādhā further enhances their supreme happiness. The *mañjarīs* are, by definition, *kiṅkari*, literally, "whatsoever-doers." In the material world, such a person is considered lowest, a slave, but in the spiritual realm, which is the exact opposite of the material realm, it is considered the highest: the lowly maidservant of Śrī Rādhikā is thus the most sought-after position among Gauḍīya Vaishnava *sādhakās*.

Thus, in Mañjarī-bhāva, the dignity of the highest paradigmatic individuals in the spiritual realm is preserved, for no one can aspire to their position. One can only be their servants, or their *mañjarīs*. As Michelle Voss Roberts writes,

> The greatest intimacy with God is withheld. No one may aspire to the role of Rādhā, Kṛṣṇa's favorite and eternal divine counterpart. Although Rūpa's texts appear to hold open the possibility of identification with one of the other *gopīs*, he himself chooses the role of a *mañjarī*, one of Rādhā's friends or attendants; and many of Rūpa's followers imagine themselves as a servant of such an attendant. The paradigm of loving the lover of Krishna, and of enjoying their erotic play as a bystander, spectator, or minor participant, becomes the standard for later Gauḍīya Vaiṣṇavas. For them, the *rasa* of devotional love is best savored from afar.[39]

Among all *mañjarīs*, Śrī Rūpa is the leader, and, at least according to the line of Bhaktivinoda Ṭhākura, one must follow him/her in both his identities as

Rūpa Goswāmī and as *mañjarī* par excellence. But before one can attempt the latter, one would do well to excel in the former. Therefore, Jīva Goswāmī writes in *Bhakti-sandarbha*, Anuccheda 275.3: "If one's heart has become pure by surrender, and never abandons hearing and singing the names, forms, attributes and pastimes of the Lord, one can perform *smaraṇam*, or divine remembrance." To follow Rūpa Goswāmī in both his forms is called Rūpānuga Vaishnavism, and, for Bhaktivinoda and his followers, this is the highest achievement in spiritual life.

It was Raghunāth Dāsa Goswāmī who originally coined the term "Rūpānuga" in his seminal work, *Manaḥ-śikṣā* (text 12). In this way, both historically and conceptually, it goes back to the very beginnings of the Gauḍīya Sampradāya. Bhaktivinoda augmented our knowledge of Rūpānuga Vaishnavism in his book, *Gītāmālā*, in a chapter specifically titled, "Rūpānuga Bhajana Darpaṇa." In that chapter he mentions the word in several of his songs, making clear that Gauḍīya Vaishnavas should follow in Śrī Rūpa's footsteps.

In conclusion, the practice of Rāgānuga-sādhana in general, and Mañjarī-bhāva, in particular—along with its natural extension of Rūpānuga Vaishnavism—ultimately leads one to deep meditation on one's *siddha-rūpa* (eternal spiritual form), and is thus an advanced process, necessitating determination and qualification. By chanting the holy name under the guidance of self-realized souls, the tradition tells us, one can gradually attain this higher dimension of spiritual accomplishment, reaching the goal of Śrī Chaitanya's method.

The entire path of Chaitanya Vaishnavism can be understood by analyzing the various dimensions of the word "*bhava*," which, through its several grammatical permutations, indicates movement from a rudimentary awareness of material existence to a fully awakened spiritual understanding of life. In its most basic form, the word *bhava* refers to mere "being," "the material world," or even "the act of becoming." This is where we all start, with a modicum of awareness of our existence as distinct entities, attempting to find our way in the world of three dimensions. However, when one seriously engages in the spiritual pursuit, awareness expands and at the same time becomes more subtle. Consequently, emotions intensify and the word *bhava* also undergoes a transformation to become "*bhāva*." Here, the long "a" changes the word into one that indicates "feeling" or "developed emotion." The macron indicates an enhancement of being, where our true existence begins to unfold and life embraces deeper meaning. In its highest sense, the word now indicates that we have achieved the initial intimations of true spiritual love. But Chaitanya Vaishnavism goes still further, revealing the most developed form of *bhāva* as a state of ecstasy called "*mahābhāva*." This is a realm of love that is shared only between divinities; specifically, it refers to the love that Śrī Rādhā feels for Lord Krishna. That overflowing, uncontainable love bursts forth like a geyser or hot spring, spraying the diaphanous mist of its transformative essence on the most sincere of devotees.[40] It is this love, *mahābhāva*, that Śrī Chaitanya felt in his heart of hearts, that he exhibited, and which we witness in his life and teachings.

NOTES

1. Many great books and articles—written by both devotees and scholars—have appeared in recent years to explain the esoteric teachings of Rāgānuga-bhakti. To name just a few: David L. Haberman, *Acting as a Way of Salvation: A Study of Rāgānugā-Bhakti-Sādhana* (New York, N.Y.: Oxford University Press, 1988); Barbara A. Holdrege, *Bhakti and Embodiment: Fashioning Divine Bodies and Devotional Bodies in Kṛṣṇa Bhakti* (New York, N.Y.: Routledge, 2015); Uttamasloka dasa (Ron Marinelli), *The Realization and Manifestation of Your Eternal Identity: Identity Transformation Through Rāgānugā-Bhakti* (Vedic Institute for Advanced Studies, 2012); Swami B. V. Tripurāri, *Śrī Guru-Paramparā* (Mill Valley, California: Harmonist Publishers, 1998); Dhanurdhara Swami, "Śrīla Bhaktisiddhānta and Rāgānuga-Sādhana-Bhakti" in *Journal of Vaishnava Studies*, Volume 18, No. 1 (Fall 2009), 125–149; and a special issue on "Rāgānuga-Bhakti and Visualization" in the *Journal of Vaishnava Studies*, Volume 1, No. 3 (Spring 1993).

2. *Bhakti-rasāmṛta-sindhu*, 1.2.2.

3. Tradition attributes the first revelation of *mādhurya-bhāva* and its consequential Rāgānuga-bhakti to Madhavendra Purī, the spiritual master of Mahāprabhu's spiritual master. But no one would deny that this flame of love was enhanced by Mahāprabhu and his followers. For more on tracing the source to Madhavendra Purī, see the work of Śrīla B. R. Śrīdhara Mahārāja: "Śrī Madhavendra Purī is the sprout of the great tree of devotional love represented in the world by Śrī Chaitanya Deva. Śrī Madhavendra Purī comes from the line of Śrī Madhva, the *ācārya* of the pure Dvaita (dualistic) philosophy. . . . Although the services to Krishna as the *gopīs* rendered them in Vrindāvan were not unknown in Mādhva Maṭhas [temples], the object of their service was Bāla Gopāla, and thus their mood of service could naturally only be in *vātsalya-rasa*, or parental affection. . . . The first effective start of *mādhurya-rasa-upasana*, or consort-service to the youthful Krishna, was really given by Śrī Madhavendra Purī." See Śrīdhara Mahārāja, "The Pontifical Position of Madhavendra Puri" (http://gosai.com/writings/the-pontifical-position-of-madhavendra-puri).

4. *Caitanya-caritāmṛta*, Ādi 4.5, 6.

5. *Caitanya-caritāmṛta*, Ādi 4.103.

6. *Caitanya-caritāmṛta*, Ādi 4.230. (*śrī-rādhāyāḥ praṇaya-mahimā kīdṛśo vānayaivā-svādyo yenādbhuta-madhurimā kīdṛśo vā madīyaḥsaukhyaṁ cāsyā mad-anubhavataḥ kīdṛśaṁ veti lobhāttad-bhāvāḍhyaḥ samajani śacī-garbha-sindhau harīnduḥ*)

7. This is especially significant because certain contemporary devotees seem to have an aversion to Rāgānuga-bhakti, perhaps considering the practice beyond their scope, both intellectually and in terms of spiritual capacity. But here Prabhupāda

makes clear that it is a legitimate part of the tradition, and that all souls should familiarize themselves with its truths, preparing for a time in which they might find themselves ready to pursue it. Krishna himself says he prefers Rāgānugā to Vaidhī-bhakti: (http://prabhupadabooks.com/cc/adi). Prabhupāda often expressed caution about prematurely attempting Rāgānuga-sādhana, but with that caveat, he also often highlighted how important it really is: "Vaidhī-bhakti, that is apprenticeship. Real *bhakti, parā-bhakti*, that is *rāgānuga-bhakti*. This *rāgānuga-bhakti*, we have to come after surpassing the *vaidhī-bhakti*. In the material world, if we do not try to make further and further progress in devotional service, if we are simply sticking to the shastric regulation process and do not try to go beyond that. . . . That is not real honey. You have to open the bottle of the honey and lick up the real honey, then you'll get taste. That is advancement of spiritual knowledge." See Prabhupada, Lecture on *Śrīmad Bhāgavatam* 1.2.33, Vrindāvan, November 12, 1972 (http://vaniquotes.org/wiki/Vaidhi-bhakti,_that_is_apprenticeship._Real_bhakti,_para-bhakti,_that_is_raganuga-bhakti).

8. The tradition has made much of the distinction between merely "imitating" (*anusāra*) and "following in the footsteps" (*anuga*). Imitation is often associated with Prākṛta-sahajiyās, a disparate group of practitioners who tend to emphasize left-hand tantric practices. The orthodox tradition has labeled them "Imitationists." For a detailed analysis, see Suhotra Swami, "Deviant Vaiṣṇava Sects" (http://www.kkswami.com/texts/vows/reference/deviant-vaisnava-sects.php).

9. Quoted in David L. Haberman, *Acting as a Way of Salvation*, op. cit., 106. The specific verses may be found in Viśvanātha Chakravartī Ṭhākura, *Rāga Vartma Chandrikā: A Moonbeam to Illuminate the Path of Spontaneous Devotion,* trans., Bhaktivedānta Nārāyaṇa Mahārāja (Mathura: Gaudiya Vedanta Publications, 2001), 42–51. Also, Viśvanātha Chakravartī Ṭhākura, *Śrī Bhakti-rasāmṛta-sindhu-bindu: A Drop of the Nectarine Ocean of Bhakti-rasa*, trans., with commentary by Bhaktivedānta Nārāyaṇa Mahārāja (Mathura: Gaudiya Vedanta Publications, 1996), 121–122.

10. See *Caitanya-caritāmṛta*, Madhya 22.156–157 (*bāhya, antara—ihāra dui ta' sādhana'bāhye' sādhaka-dehe kare śravaṇa-kīrtana'mane' nija-siddha-deha kariyā bhāvanarātri-dine kare vraje kṛṣṇera sevana*).

11. The prime example is Rūpa Kavirāja (not to be confused with Rūpa Goswāmī), whose plight is elaborately described in David L. Haberman, *Acting as a Way of Salvation, op. cit.*, 98–108. Michele Voss Roberts summarizes: "Theoretical justification for practices such as cross-dressing may have been provided by Rūpa Kavirāja, who opined that the physical body, the *sādhaka-rupa*, undergoes an ontological transformation imperceptible to the uninitiated. One's meditation on Kṛṣṇa's *līlā* becomes so complete that the behavior of this transformed body will 'in all ways' be the same as the *siddha-rūpa*. The practitioner's body becomes free from ordinary social rules and the injunctions of the preliminary stages of devotional practice (*vaidhī-bhakti*). This radical interpenetration of the two bodies of the devotee has not been common, however, and Rūpa Kavirāja was excommunicated by a Vaiṣṇava synod at Jaipur in 1727." See Michelle Voss Roberts, *Tastes of the Divine: Hindu and Christian Theologies of Emotion* (New York: Fordham University Press, 2014), 78. Today, there are

still Rādhā-kuṇḍa *bābājīs* and others who attempt this practice, following the thought process of Rūpa Kavirāja.

12. See Dhanurdhara Swami, "Śrīla Bhaktisiddhānta and Rāgānuga-Sādhana-Bhakti," in *Journal of Vaishnava Studies*, op. cit., 142.

13. David L. Haberman, *Acting as a Way of Salvation*, op. cit., 4.

14. Michele Voss Roberts, *Tastes of the Divine: Hindu and Christian Theologies of Emotion*, op. cit., 76–77.

15. See A. C. Bhaktivedanta Swami Prabhupada, *Teachings of Lord Caitanya* (New York, N.Y.: ISKCON Books, 1968), Chapter 31, 321. For more on *ahaṅgrahopāsana*, see Śrīla Nārāyaṇa Mahārāja, "The Five Principles of Rāgānuga-Bhakti" (http://www.purebhakti.com/teachers/bhakti-discourses-mainmenu-61/57-discourses-2010/1150-the-five-principles-of-raganuga-bhakti.html).

16. On the importance of "greed" on the path of *rāgānugā*, see Bhakti-*rasāmṛta-sindhu* 1.2.292: *tat tad bhāvādi mādhurye śrute dhīr yad apekṣate, nātra śāstraṁ na yuktiṁ ca tal lobhotpatti lakṣaṇam*. See also Viśvanātha Chakravartī's *Rāga-vartma-chandrikā* 1.3: *vaidhi-bhaktir bhavet śāstraṁ bhaktau cet syāt pravartakam, rāgānugā syac ced bhaktau lobha eva pravartakaḥ*.

17. *Rāga-vartma-chandrikā* 2.7 (*atha rāgānugā-bhakti majjanasyānartha-nivṛtti-niṣṭhā-rucy-āsakty-antaraṁ prema-bhūmikārūḍhasya sākṣāt svābhīṣṭa-prāpti-prakāraḥ pradarśyate*). It is here that we learn that *lobha* can arise from early on in the life of a practitioner. See also verse 8: *sa ca lobho rāga vartma vartināṁ bhaktānāṁ guru-padāśraya lakṣaṇam ārabhya svābhīṣṭa vastu sākṣāt prāpti samayam abhivyāpya*. Whenever *laulyam* or *lobha* arises, one should heed its call, albeit with certain reservations. Bhaktivinoda Ṭhākura, for example, warns that the prospective practitioner should be attentive to his own qualifications (*adhikāra*) or lack thereof: "If one tries to contemplate one's *siddha-deha* without sufficient qualification, one's contemplation is rendered useless due to lack of strength; such a person's entire *bhajan* is thereby ruined. This is called Sahajiyā-bhāva, and it is completely opposed to pure *bhajan*. (*adhikāra nā labhiyā siddha-deha bhāveviparyaya buddhi janme śaktira abhāve*). *See Bhaktivinoda Thakura, Bhajana-rahasya* 1.10.

18. See *Rāga-vartma-chandrikā* 1.8.

19. Dhanurdhara Swami, "Śrīla Bhaktisiddhānta and Rāgānuga-Sādhana-Bhakti" in *Journal of Vaishnava Studies*, op. cit., 142.

20. "The idea that your guru 'gives' you your *ekādaśa-bhāvas* is also a point of contention. Bhaktivinoda Ṭhākura sometimes implies that the *guru* gives these details, but it's not always clear whether he means the *guru* gives the knowledge of these details and how the process works, versus giving the specifics to the disciple. In *Harināma-cintāmaṇi* he indicates clearly that the development of one's *ekādaśa-bhāvas* is a collaborative endeavor between the disciple and *guru*. . . . The *guru* teaches the disciple the theory and guides him according to his manifest inclinations, and makes sure the disciple's conceptions are all within acceptable parameters. And this is not necessarily done at the time of *dīkṣā* either. It should only be done when the disciple has clearly manifested a strong desire for a particular *rasa*. The qualification of *lobha* for a particular *rasa* must be there or it would be premature and inappropriate." (personal correspondence with Uttamaśloka Dāsa, 1.20.16)

21. Quoted in Shukavak Dāsa, "ISKCON's Link to Sādhana-Bhakti Within the Caitanya Vaishnava Tradition," in Steven J. Rosen, ed., *Gaudiya Vaishnavism and ISKCON: An Anthology of Scholarly Perspectives* (Vrindavan: Rasbihari Lal & Sons, n.d.), 534 (*sādhite ujjvala rasa, āche bhāva ekādaśa, sambandha, vayasa, nāma, rūpa/ yūtha, veśa, ājñā, vāsa, sevā, parākāṣṭhāśvāsa, pālya-dāsī ei aparūpa//*). See also Dhyānachandra's *Paddhati*, verse 93.

22. Ibid.

23. This is taken from the correspondence of Śrīla Bhaktisiddhānta Sarasvatī, November 17, 1930, *Patravali* 2.89–90 (http://www.harekrsna.com/sun/editorials/03–06/editorials277.htm). His disciple, Śrīla Prabhupāda, is equally skeptical of easy access to Siddha-praṇālī and Rāgānuga-sādhana. The following is from a garden conversation on June 23, 1976, New Vrindavan, West Virginia. When a devotee asks Prabhupāda about attaining one's *svarūpa*, or natural form, the guru responds as follows: "First of all, *anartha-nivṛtti*. You are accustomed to so many bad habits. First of all try to rectify it, then talk of *svarūpa*. Where is your *svarūpa*? Simply wasting time. A man is diseased, he's thinking, 'When I shall be cured I shall eat, go to this hotel, I shall eat like this.' First of all cure, then talk of eating this and that. *Svarūpa* . . . . When you are cured, that is *svarūpa*. So long you are not cured, what is the use of talking *svarūpa*? First business is cure yourself. *Anartha-nivṛtti*. That is *anartha-nivṛtti*. Then *svarūpa* will come. That is the *bābājīs*. In Vrindāvan, you have seen? Siddha-praṇālī." And then later in the same conversation: "Up to *anartha-nivṛtti*, you have to struggle very hard with determination, and then automatically everything will come." (https://old.prabhupadavani.org/main/Bhagavad-gita/GT186.html).

24. See Uttamaśloka Dāsa (Ron Marinelli), *The Realization and Manifestation of Your Eternal Identity: Identity Transformation Through Rāgānugā-Bhakti*, op. cit., 164, 165, 185, 202, 207.

25. This meditation can be found in early Gaudīya manuals for meditation; in a short poem written by Rūpa Goswāmī; in Kavirāja Goswāmī's *Govinda-līlāmṛta* (http://www.harekrsna.de/Asta-kaliya-nitya-lila.htm), which is the most famous version; in Viśvanātha Chakravartī's *Krishna-bhāvanāmṛta*; and also in a work by the *mahant* Siddha Krishnadasa Bābāji of Govardhana (*Gaura-Govinda-līlāmṛta-guṭika*). Interestingly, the tradition also developed a meditation for Mahāprabhu's eight times of the day, "Mahāprabhor-aṣṭa-kālīya-līlā," originated by Gopāla Guru Goswāmi/ Dhyānachandra Goswāmī. It was developed by Viśvanātha Chakravartī and could later also be found in the writing of Siddha Krishnadasa Bābājī.

26. This analysis is clear throughout the writings of Bhaktivinoda Ṭhākura and other Gauḍīya *ācāryas*. It has been crystalized for a modern audience in Uttamaśloka Dāsa (Ron Marinelli), *The Realization and Manifestation of Your Eternal Identity: Identity Transformation Through Rāgānugā-Bhakti, op. cit.*, especially in his chart on 153.

27. See Śrīla Bhaktivinoda Ṭhākura, *Jaiva Dharma, Our Eternal Nature*, trans., Śrī Śrīmad Bhaktivedānta Nārāyaṇa Mahārāja (Mathura: Gaudiya Vedanta Publications, 2002), Chapter 40, 863–864.

28. Gopāla Guru Goswāmī (mid-15th century) was a disciple of Vakreśvara Paṇḍita, a contemporary of Śrī Chaitanya. In fact, Gopāla Guru himself is known to

have had the Master's association on many occasions. He is famous for his meditation text, the *Gaura-govinda-arcana-smaraṇa-paddhati* ("A guidebook to Gaura-Govinda's Deity worship and remembrance"). He was a prominent Odiya Vaishnava in Mahāprabhu's time.

29. Dhyānacandra Goswāmī was Gopāla Guru Goswāmī's disciple, well known for his *smaraṇa-paddhati*, which bears the same name as his guru's text. In fact, in terms of content, his work is almost identical to that of his teacher, though he has added sections about Gaura-līlā-*smaraṇa*, including meditations for one's spiritual body in Gaura-līlā.

30. Siddha Krishnadāsa Bābā (circa, 19th century) was a *sādhu* from Govardhan, near Vrindāvan. He elaborated in his writings on both Krishna and Mahāprabhu's Aṣṭa-kālīya-līlā, as stated above. See his *Śrī Śrī Bhavana-sāra-saṅgraha, Naimittika-līlās*, and *Yogapitha Sevā*. His most esteemed work is his *Gaura-Govinda-līlāmṛta-guṭika*.

31. For more on the distinctions between these two methods, see Prabhupāda Dāsa, *"Follow Rūpa-Raghunātha": The Science of Self Realization & Entering Into Krishna's Līlā* (Self-published, 2012). He bases his analysis on Bhaktivinoda Ṭhākura's *Jaiva Dharma* (Chapter 39): "Śrī Chaitanya instructed Svarūpa Dāmodara to disseminate *rasa-upāsanā*, the process of *bhajan* consumed by *rasa*. Accordingly, he composed his diaries on *rasa-upāsanā* comprising two sections: *antaḥ-panthā*, the esoteric, internal means of attainment, and *bahiḥ-panthā*, the exoteric means of attainment. The esoteric process was entrusted to Raghunāth Dāsa Goswāmī, as amply exhibited in his books, while the exoteric was given to Vakreśvara Paṇḍita . . . ."

32. See *Bhakti-sandarbha*, Anuccheda 256, where Śrī Jīva gives the sequence of proper *sādhana*, saying that hearing and chanting necessarily come first, focusing, progressively, on the name, form, qualities and pastimes, in that order. After this, one properly pursues *smaraṇam*. Also see Anuccheda 276: "A pure heart is required . . . for remembrance (*smaraṇam*). Therefore, it is not as effective as *kīrtana*." Viśvanātha Chakravartī also supports the notion that *smaraṇam* is dependent on *kīrtana*: *atra rāgānugāyāṁ yan mukhyasya tasyāpi smaraṇasya kīrtanādhīnatvam avaśyaṁ vaktavyam eva | kīrtanasyaiva etad yugādhikāratvāt sarva-bhakti-mārgeṣu sarva-śāstrais tasyaiva sarvotkarṣa-pratipādanāc ca*. See *Rāga-vartma-chandrikā* 1.14.

33. See Sanātana Goswāmī's *Bṛhad-bhāgavatāmṛta* 2.3.148 and 153.

34. Bhaktivinoda Ṭhākura, *Śaraṇāgati: Śrī Nāma-māhātmya*, Verse 7.

35. The seminal text on this subject is *Mañjarī-svarūpa-nirūpaṇam* by Kuñja Bihārī Dās Bābājī (1896–1976). See translation by Jan Brzezinski (https://flowingnectarstream.files.wordpress.com/2015/02/manjari-svarupa-nirupana-2.pdf).

36. Both Jīva Goswāmī and Viśvanātha Chakravartī, in their commentaries on Śrī Rūpa's *Bhakti-rasāmṛta-sindhu* (1.2.306), emphasize the importance of this indirect method of assisting Śrī-Śrī Rādhā-Krishna's assistants.

37. The primary *gopīs*, like Viśākhā and Lalitā, are roughly fourteen years old, whereas *mañjarīs* are envisioned as a year or two younger, and they are often described as prepubescent.

38. See Śrī Śrīmad Bhaktivedānta Nārāyana Gosvāmī Mahārāja, "On Rāgānuga-bhakti," 1991 (http://www.purebhakti.com/teachers/bhakti-discourses-mainmenu-61/57-discourses-2010/1146-on-raganuga-bhakti.html).

39. See Michelle Voss Roberts, *Tastes of the Divine: Hindu and Christian Theologies of Emotion, op. cit.*, 96. Although Voss uses phrases in this paragraph like "imagine themselves," which might make practitioners balk, her overall analysis holds true.

40. This analysis of the various forms of *bhāva* and particularly the metaphor of a geyser can be traced to the work of Graham Schweig, who develops these ideas in his co-authored volume with Tamal Krishna Goswami: *A Living Theology of Krishna Bhakti: Essential Teachings of A. C. Bhaktivedanta Swami Prabhupāda* (New York, N.Y.: Oxford University Press, 2012), 203–205. It should be understood that *mahābhāva* is a highly technical term indicating the pinnacle of divine love. While any aspect of *mahābhāva* is considered "advanced" (*rūḍha*), it reaches its zenith in its more "highly advanced" (*adhirūḍha*) form. The preliminary stage of this topmost exalted love is known as *mohana-adhirūḍha-mahābhāva*, to which the Vraja *gopikās* and others have access. This penultimate level is in itself incomparable and inexhaustible, and rarely achieved. Still, there is a more fully mature phase found only in the heart of Śrī Rādhā (and thus in the heart of Mahāprabhu as well): *mādana-adhirūḍha-mahābhāva*. Therefore, she is often referred to as the very form of *mahābhāva* (Mahābhāva-svarūpiṇī). Additionally, *mohana* and *mādana* in relation to *mahābhāva* refer, respectively, to being separated from and meeting with Krishna.

Afterword

Mahāprabhu Comes West

pṛthivīte āche jata nagarādi grama
sarvatra pracāra haibe mora nāma
"My name will spread to every town and village of the world."

—Śrī Chaitanya (*Śrī Caitanya-bhāgavata*, 4.126)

The above verse is well known to all members of the Gauḍīya community, particularly its prophetic dimension: Some 500 years ago, Mahāprabhu indicated that his name (or the name of Krishna) would resound and be appreciated around the world. For most devotees, this would be the origin of the movement's mandate to go West, and to spread Śrī Chaitanya's universal teaching to all corners of the globe.

But what was meant by "the world" (*pṛthivīte* or *pṛthivī*) in 16th-century India? Did it encompass the vast kingdoms and countries beyond the subcontinent? Was it *the* world, as we know it today, including the "New World," which was, at the time, being "discovered" by historically notable agents of European imperialism, controversial adventurers like Vasco da Gama and Christopher Columbus? Or was it a more humble understanding of what the world might include?[1] Abhishek Ghosh, in fact, argues that it may not have embraced the wide-ranging definition we now attribute to it:

> Today one can only speculate in what sense Caitanya or Vṛndāvandāsa may have used the word "*pṛthivī*" in its sixteenth- or seventeenth-century contexts and whether he actually intended to take his *saṁkīrtana* beyond South Asia. The "world" could have included the various tribes and kingdoms mentioned in the *Bhāgavata Purāṇa* or the *Mahābhārata*, such as Khāsa, Hundra, Pulinda, and so on, or the kingdoms of Kāśi, Gāndhara, and others, though the geographical areas these people or kingdoms inhabited is subject to debate. If we were to

stretch the semantic limits of the word *pṛthivī*, we could perhaps even include Eurasia and the Middle East among sixteenth- and seventeenth-century Bengali xenology, as the ruling Turks and later the Moghuls were aware of the extent of these regions because of trade links.[2]

Whatever the truth of the matter, the Gauḍīya tradition has come to see it as a prediction of the highest order. Bhaktivinoda Ṭhākura recognizes it as an intimation of Mahāprabhu's universalism, envisaging the creation of a "world church" as Chaitanya's mission, a veritable Godsend for all people, irrespective of caste, creed, gender, race, age-group, and so on:

> The *dharma* preached by Chaitanya Mahaprabhu is universal and not exclusive . . . . The principle of *kīrtana* as the future church of the world invites all classes of people, without distinction of caste or clan, to the highest cultivation of the spirit. This church, it appears, will spread worldwide and replace all sectarian churches, which exclude outsiders from the precincts of the mosque, church, or temple.[3]

Or further:

> Lord Chaitanya did not advent Himself to liberate only a few men of India. Rather, His main objective was to emancipate all living entities of all countries throughout the entire universe and preach the Eternal Religion. Lord Chaitanya says in the *Chaitanya Bhagavata* (Antya 4.126): "In every town, country and village, My name will be sung." . . . Very soon the unparalleled path of *hari-nama-sankirtana* will be propagated all over the world. Already we are seeing the symptoms. Already many Christians have tasted the nectar of divine love of the holy name and are dancing with *karatalas* [hand cymbals] and *mridangas* [drums]. Educated Christians are ordering these instruments and shipping them to England . . . . Oh, for that day when the fortunate English, French, Russian, German and American people will take up banners, *mridangas* and *karatalas* and raise *kirtan* through their streets and towns. When will that day come? Oh, for the day when the fair-skinned men from their side will raise up the chanting of Jaya Sacinandana, Jaya Sacinandana ki jaya [All Glories to Lord Chaitanya! All Glories to Lord Chaitanya!] and join with the Bengali devotees. When will that day be? On such a day they will say, "Our dear Brothers, we have taken shelter of the ocean of Lord Chaitanya's Love; kindly embrace us. When will that day come? That day will witness the holy transcendental ecstasy of the Vaishnava-*dharma* [the eternal religion of devotional service to the Lord] to be the only *dharma*, and all the sects and religions will flow like rivers into the ocean of Vaishnava-*dharma*. When will that day come?"[4]

Bhaktivinoda worked diligently to make his vision a reality. He wrote, edited, and published over 100 books on Vaishnavism as well as a monthly journal in

Bengali, the *Sajjana-toṣaṇī*. Although he never traveled West himself, he was duly represented by his literature, which he sent by post to numerous far-off destinations. His work reached the desks of assorted scholars in the British Empire, including the Royal Asiatic Society of London, in whose journal it received a favorable review. It also arrived and was accepted by several prestigious academic libraries, such as that of McGill University in Montreal, Canada, and the University of Sydney in Australia. The famous American Transcendentalist, Ralph Waldo Emerson, another recipient of Vaishnava literature sent by the Ṭhākura, wrote back to acknowledge his receipt and appreciation.[5]

Of special significance was the little booklet that Bhaktivinoda sent to McGill. The bulk of it would have been curious to the scholars there, with its exotic-looking text, written in Sanskrit. Its title: "Śrī Śrīmad Gaurāṅga-līlā-smaraṇa-maṅgala-stotram," 104 verses summarizing the life and teachings of Śrī Chaitanya Mahāprabhu.[6] More important, in a sense, since the bulk of its receivers would have been unfamiliar with Sanskrit, was the 47-page prefatory essay—in English. This was called *Shri Chaitanya Mahaprabhu: His Life and Precepts*, a small treatise that would be the West's initial introduction to the golden *avatāra* of love.

INITIAL EXPANSION

Interestingly, in the generation immediately following Mahāprabhu and the Six Goswāmīs, there was an important journey that helped fulfill Śrī Chaitanya's prophetic proclamation—but this expedition traveled eastward, not west. And it occurred not outside the subcontinent but within her borders. This journey would serve to solidify Śrī Chaitanya's movement and thus constitute a first step in bringing his message to foreign shores. The movement needed organization and consistency, a formalization that would later lead to solidarity and the systematic dissemination of its teachings.

This began with that journey east: Stalwart disciples of Jīva Goswāmī—Śrīnivāsa, Narottama, and Śyāmānanda—were deputed to bring the literature of the Goswāmīs out of Vrindāvan and throughout India, particularly to the eastern provinces of Bengal, Manipur, and so on. The intrigue and tremendous effort involved in this journey have been well documented.[7]

But the main point is this: As of the 1570s, the writings of the Goswāmīs, which had served well in systematizing Śrī Chaitanya's teachings, were largely confined to Vrindāvan, leaving the devotees in Bengal and other parts of India without access. As a consequence, the movement was temporarily fragmented, and various deviant theories began to arise, even among the orthodox. Thus, Śrī Jīva's transcendental triumvirate was sent east with the authorized literature, hoping to resolve the deficiencies of an otherwise loosely knit spiritual movement. Their mission was largely successful.

More, it led to an important council, of sorts. The meeting at Kheturi, in the Rajshahi district of East Bengal, was more than the poignant birthday celebration it facilitated (in honor of Śrī Chaitanya). Some fifty years after the Master's departure, this well attended meeting of Vaishnavas from all over the subcontinent served to further organize the movement, sifting out much peripheral and nonessential dogma from the minds of Śrī Chaitanya's then considerable following. This council was convened somewhere between 1580 and 1585.[8]

The chief organizers—Narottama Dāsa, Śrīnivāsa Āchārya, and Jāhnavā Devī, the wife of Nityānanda—had had direct association with the Goswāmīs of Vrindāvan, thus allowing them personal insight into their teachings. Jāhnavā Devī, especially, took a leading role in the festival and its ecclesiastic function, as noted in *Bhakti-ratnākara, Prema-vilāsa*, and *Narottama-vilāsa*, and was able to synthesize Śrī Chaitanya's philosophy into one coherent doctrine.[9] The large number of Vaishnavas from all parts of India who attended the festival—reportedly in the thousands—eventually went back to their respective regions with a consistent and uniform view of Mahāprabhu's thought and mission. The movement was now in fact a movement.

The rich history of that movement's subsequent peaks, valleys, and plateaus need not concern us here, but a signal highpoint was to occur more than a century later. This came with the rise of Viśvanātha Chakravartī and Baladeva Vidyābhūṣaṇa.[10] As for Viśvanātha, known as "the crest jewel of the Vaishnavas" because of his pure devotion, scholarship, and mystical insights into the Gauḍīya scriptures, he almost singlehandedly reclaimed the movement from newly arising compromised sects and misunderstandings or parochial interpretations of scripture.[11]

Baladeva Vidyābhūṣaṇa, Viśvanātha's equally scholarly disciple, served to formally clarify and re-articulate Gauḍīya doctrine on his *guru*'s order, enabling the tradition to win wide acceptance under Jai Singh II's rule (in the early- to mid-1700s) and respectability among the more orthodox Vaishnava traditions of the time.[12]

GROWING PAINS

After Baladeva Vidyābhuṣaṇa, the Vaishnava community in Bengal contended with a brief period of adjustment to the technologies and social structures of encroaching European modernity. At this time, there was a burgeoning of Vaishnava Bābājī movements and the growth of Vaishnavism among the masses through landholder patronage. The printing press was still new, but even prior to this devotees were producing handwritten copies of texts like *Caitanya-caritāmṛta*, *Caitanya-bhāgavata*, and so on. Despite the transition of power between Mughal and British empires, there were huge Vaishnava fairs and festivals in many parts of Bengal, and regions like Khardaha and Ambika-kalna were institutions unto themselves.

As time passed, however, Gauḍīya Vaishnavism developed a questionable reputation among the Intelligentsia, mainly because of the proliferation of *sahajiyā* sects,[13] facilitated by the mass production of their sectarian literature. It was Batatalā Press, in particular, founded in the Hooghly district of West Bengal, that catered to this growing *sahajiyā* audience.[14] Throughout the 18th century, in fact, Calcutta became one of the subcontinent's fastest growing supporters of the printed word. It was here that the East India Company introduced printing to facilitate trade, which, in turn, served to consolidate the British Empire. The Baptist Mission Press at Serampur, to cite but one example, was among India's most popular printing enterprises, establishing itself just north of Batatalā toward the end of the 18th century. Its initial publications were, of course, Bengali translations of the Gospels and assorted Christian tracts meant for the conversion of Hindus, even if the Press eventually published translations of the Indian epics and other Hindu texts as well.

With the advent of Ram Mohan Roy (1772–1833), a major intellectual influence in the late 18th and early 19th centuries, all of this was exacerbated. He conceived a Hindu reform movement known as the Brahmo Samaj, and while his intentions were noble, they were somewhat ill-conceived. He sought to dispel sentimentalism and irrational thought among his peers. Largely a reaction to Christian missionaries, whose critique of Hindu traditions included disparaging perspectives on image worship, class division, and so on, his Brahmo Samaj was also a reaction to rampant *sahajiyāism*. He responded by reconstituting Hinduism in a way that would be acceptable to the rising Bhadralok (literally, "civilized people," as opposed to the Chọtalok, or "smaller people"), Bengal's then emerging class of "gentlefolk," who were influenced by British science, culture, religion, and philosophy.

In essence, Ram Mohan attempted to "sanitize" the Krishna tradition, censoring it and presenting it with "more acceptable" terminology. Bankim Chandra Chatterjee (1838–1894) and others followed his approach, if in their own way. Dayananda Saraswati (1824–1883), founder of the Arya Samaj, yet another Hindu reform movement, advocated a return to Vedic customs and practices. But the net result of these many endeavors was that pure Gauḍīya teaching was becoming more and more obscure.

Certainly there were Vaishnava luminaries during this period as well, devotees who endeavored to preserve the tradition as it is: Baladeva's disciple Nanda Miśra, for example, wrote commentaries on his teacher's works that were studied by those who were serious about the tradition. His famous grand-disciple, a generation removed, Madhusūdana Bābājī of Sūrya-kuṇḍa, and Krishna Dāsa Bābājī of Govardhan (circa late 18th and early 19th century) would inspire a wide variety of Vaishnavas by the intensity of their private practice. Not least was Jagannāth Dāsa Bābājī (1776–1894), who became known as the "commander in chief" of the Gauḍīya Vaishnavas.

Bijoy Krishna Goswami (1841–1899), a prominent social reformer and religious personality in Bengal during the British period, was born into the lineage of Advaita Ācārya.[15] Still, he adopted the practice of Chaitanya Vaishnavism later in life, after leaving the Brahmo Samaj, the Hindu reform movement mentioned above. In due course, Bijoy Krishna became an influential spokesperson for Mahāprabhu's mission. His disciple, Bipin Chandra Pal (1858–1932), was an Indian nationalist who briefly visited America and Europe in 1899. His stay was short, however, and in less than a year he returned to India.

Toward the end of the nineteenth century, Shishir Kumar Ghosh (1840–1911) established the Gauranga Samaj along with a publishing house and English newspaper, both called the "Amrita Bazar Patrika." Sometime before this, he had published the widely read *Amiya Nimāi Carita*, a six-volume Bengali work on Śrī Chaitanya (which was eventually translated into English and abridged as *Lord Gaurāṅga or Salvation for All*). With the help of Bhaktivinoda and Rādhikānātha Goswāmī, he initiated the well-known periodical, *Vishnupriyā Pātrikā*, though Bhaktivinoda opted out of the project early on, feeling it too nationalistic and political in orientation. Several other small organizations, such as Priyanath Nandi's Krishna Chaitanya Tattwa Pracharini Sabha and Atul Krishna Goswami's Gaudiya Vaishnava Sanmilani, also amassed a following at this time.

During this same general period, Śrī Haridāsa Goswami (1867–1946) produced a life of Mahāprabhu in two large Bengali volumes, originally published in 1906. Because of its formidable size, resembling the mammoth *Mahābhārata*, it was called the *Śrī Chaitanya-bhārata*.[16] This work and others like it served to remind Bengalis of their Chaitanyaite roots. As a result, important Gauḍīya communities began to emerge, such as the one in Bāghnāpārā, from which hailed the prolific Bipina Bihārī Goswāmī (1850–1919). His most significant writings include the *Harināmāmṛta-sindhu* and the *Daśa-mūla-rasa*, a masterwork that summarizes the gamut of Vaishnava thought. It was Bipina Bihārī who formally initiated Bhaktivinoda into the Gauḍīya Sampradāya.

With Bhaktivinoda, as we have seen throughout this book, new life was thrust into Gauḍīya articulation and dissemination. There was prodigious use of the printing press and the ancient teachings were, for the first time on a large scale, made easily available to the masses in the English language. And, as noted above, there was a concerted attempt to bring the ancient Vaishnava culture to the West, retaining intact the authentic thesis and praxis of its noteworthy forebears.

We have elaborated on Bhaktivinoda's work elsewhere, but here we should mention that it was his scholarly and determined son, Bhaktisiddhānta Sarasvatī, who would achieve the impossible, sending missionaries to the Western world and implanting Gauḍīya-siddhānta into the hearts of many. But before taking a closer look at this consequential course of events, we turn to other Gauḍīya Vaishnava missionaries who also expanded westward.

PREMĀNANDA BHĀRATĪ AND MAHĀNĀMBRATA BRAHMACHARI

Although not connected to Bhaktivinoda and the line he represented, another branch of the Gauḍīya Sampradāya migrated to America with a similar mission in mind. Bābā Premānanda Bhāratī (1857–1914) may well have been the first Gauḍīya missionary in the modern era to cross the ocean, Bipin Chandra Pal's brief visit, mentioned above, notwithstanding. A follower of the controversial figure Prabhu Jagatbandhu Sundar (1871–1921), Bhāratī spent time in Paris and London before arriving in New York City, where, in 1902, he established the "Krishna Samaj," a society dedicated to the worship of Śrī Krishna. A few years later, in 1907, he relocated to Los Angeles, where he inaugurated what may have been the first Krishna temple in the West.[17]

While in the States, he produced several books—*Shree Krishna: The Lord of Love*; *Shree Krishna's Messages and Revelations*; *American Lectures*; *Indian Lectures, First Series*; and *Jim*, which was essentially a response to Rudyard Kipling's *Kim*—and a periodical, *Light of India*, which gained for him numerous followers, by some accounts nearly 5,000. He is even said to have had a fruitful correspondence with Count Leo Tolstoy.[18] In recent years Gerald Carney is known for having conducted extensive research on Bhāratī and his work, producing a number of articles and renewed interest in an otherwise little known *sādhu* from India.[19]

Mahānāmbrata Brahmachari (1904–1999) was yet another Vaishnava *sādhu* who came West early on, albeit several decades after Premānanda Bhāratī. Although Brahmachari lived most of his life in his native Bengal, he spent a fruitful period in Chicago between 1933 and 1939. By the time he arrived, he already had his master's degree in Sanskrit and Western philosophy from the University of Calcutta. While in the States, he was admitted to the University of Chicago, where he completed his postgraduate work in the philosophy of Jīva Goswāmī in 1937.

His monastery had sent him West to attend a conference called the World Fellowship of Faiths in Chicago. The first World Parliament of Religions conference of 1893, held in that same city, had been a huge success, with reverberations that reached him in his homeland. However, it was Swami Vivekānanda who represented "Hindu" teaching at that inaugural conference, meaning that the intellectuals of the West would come to identify Hinduism with Vivekānanda's particular brand of Neo-Vedānta and not Vaishnavism. Brahmachari reasoned that if he could go and give a similar series of lectures, specifically about Vaishnavism, he could balance the view Westerners had developed about the Hindu religion. Thus, at the World Fellowship of Faiths held during Chicago's Second World's Fair in 1933, Brahmachari made his mark.[20] Still, Swami Vivekānanda's rendition largely prevailed.

Other major events occurred during Mahānāmbrata's Western stay. For example, he had meaningful exchange with Thomas Merton (1915–1968), the famous Trappist monk, writer and mystic. A chance meeting in New York's Grand Central Station in 1938, when Merton was still a college student at Columbia University, led to a subsequent meeting and a friendship that would last a lifetime.[21] Merton, the story goes, had developed an interest in Eastern thought, but Mahānāmbrata insisted that he first look into the mystical literature of his own tradition, such as the works of St. Augustine and Thomas à Kempis's *The Imitation of Christ*. Taking Brahmachari's advice seriously, Merton soon found the rich literary resources of Christianity. The rest, as they say, is history.

Mahānāmbrata's literary output increased during this period as well. In addition to contributing his Ph.D. thesis on Jīva Goswāmī, he published numerous books, including *Vaiṣṇava Vedānta*, *Fundamental Thoughts*, and *Mahaprabhu Sri Krishna-Chaitanya: His Unparalleled Personality and Philosophy*. By the time of his departure, he was so highly esteemed that his death was covered by *The New York Times*.[22]

Śrī Krishna Prem (1898–1965) is another important Vaishnava of the early 20th century, though a bit afield in terms of our present study—rather than an Indian coming westward, this is a Western seeker going East. Born Ronald Henry Nixon, he became a British fighter pilot in the World War I and ended up with a teaching position at the University of Lucknow. While there, he met Monika Chakravarti, the wife of the university's vice-chancellor, and eventually accepted her as his spiritual teacher. She was affiliated with the Rādhā-ramaṇa Temple in Vrindāvan and soon became a well-known spiritual leader named Yashoda Ma.

Together, in 1930, they founded an ashram at Mirtola, near Almora, where they taught and practiced a strict form of Gauḍīya Vaishnavism. By the mid-1940s, Yashoda Ma had passed away and Śrī Krishna Prem, which is the name she had given him, succeeded her as head of the *ashram*.[23] He produced several books during his period as a monk, including *The Yoga of the Bhagavat Gita*; *Initiation Into Yoga: An Introduction to the Spiritual Life*; and *The Search for Truth*.

Ferdinando Sardella opines that Śrī Krishna Prem may well have been "the first European to embrace Vaishnavism in India."[24] David Haberman augments this by saying that he "was perhaps the first Westerner to tread the path of Krishna-bhakti, and was certainly the first to have any official affiliation with the Gauḍīya Vaishnavism of Braj."[25] Of interest are the last words Śrī Krishna Prem uttered on his deathbed, moments before his demise in November of 1965: "My ship is sailing."[26] We will return to this utterance at the end of the chapter.

BHAKTISIDDHĀNTA SARASVATĪ'S DISCIPLES

Contemporaneous with Mahānāmbrata Brahmachari's work in Chicago, Bhaktivinoda's son, Bhaktisiddhānta Sarasvatī, succeeded in fulfilling his father's dream of sending Mahāprabhu's teachings West. First, in 1918, he founded an institution known as the Gauḍīya Maṭha, specifically for disseminating Vaishnava teachings through the publication and distribution of books, large Hari-nāma festivals, and by training his followers to lead exemplary Vaishnava lives.

A benchmark of Sarasvatī Ṭhākura's uncommon prowess as a spiritual leader was his remarkable aptitude for attracting, inspiring, and effectively engaging an extraordinarily gifted set of leaders, responsible, under his direction, for creating and maintaining a massive institution. Among the most prominent and influential of his disciples and followers are three sets of brothers who worked diligently to help him make the Gauḍīya Maṭha a success: Ananta Vasudeva, later called Bhakti Prasād Purī Mahārāja, was one of Śrīla Bhaktisiddhānta's right-hand men. He was the younger brother of Bhakti Pradīpa Tīrtha Mahārāja, a disciple of Bhaktivinoda Ṭhākura who was sent as a missionary to the West (we will return to this in a few paragraphs). Śrī Kuñjabihārī Vidyābhūṣaṇa (known as Kuñja Da, "elder brother"), another of Bhaktisiddhānta's right-hand men, would become known Bhakti Vilāsa Tīrtha Mahārāja—he was the brother of Sambidānanda Dāsa, one of the other devotees who would eventually be sent abroad. And, finally, Bhakti Kevala Audulomi Mahārāja, *ācārya* of the Gauḍīya Mission after Bhakti Prasād Purī Mahārāja, was the brother of Śrī Bhakti Prajñāna Keśava Mahārāja, who was founder of the Śrī Gauḍīya Vedānta Samiti and spiritual master of Śrīla Nārāyaṇa Mahārāja, a noted contemporary Vaishnava of international fame. These men, along with several others, such as Sundarānanda Vidyāvinoda, B. P. Purī Mahārāja, B. D. Mādhava Mahārāja, B. H. Bon Mahārāja, and B.

R. Śrīdhara Mahārāja, assisted Śrīla Bhaktisiddhānta as spiritual architects of the Gauḍīya Maṭha.

These highly qualified disciples, working diligently with the preternaturally gifted Sarasvatī Ṭhākura, spread Gauḍīya Vaishnavism in an unprecedented way. The tradition was alive and well and in the capable hands of a master. Bhaktisiddhānta Sarasvatī was successful beyond anyone's dreams, perhaps even Bhaktivinoda's, and the mission engulfed the subcontinent.

In addition to the opening of temples and various publishing interests, Sarasvatī Ṭhākura began a number of important periodicals, catering to educated audiences in Bengali, Assamese, Odia, Hindi, and, yes, English. He produced a daily Bengali newspaper, *The Nadiya Prakash*; a weekly magazine, *The Gaudiya*; and a monthly journal in English and Sanskrit, *The Harmonist* (which was a continuation of his father's magazine, *Sajjana-toṣaṇī*).

Focusing on urban areas, the Gauḍīya Maṭha attracted a coterie of wealthy supporters who gave considerable financial contributions toward the building of new religious structures and progressive, outdoor "diorama" exhibitions, which were essentially theistic museums that used creative displays and three-dimensional forms to illustrate Gauḍīya Vaishnava philosophy. In his lifetime, Bhaktisiddhānta Sarasvatī had seen 64 Gauḍīya Maṭha branches emerge with multitudes embracing the strict practices of Vaishnava behavior. By his herculean efforts, the chanting of Hare Krishna resounded throughout cities and villages alike, just as it had in Mahāprabhu's time.

Again, especially significant for this study is the fact that, because of the Gauḍīya Maṭha's success, which included financial assets, Bhaktisiddhānta Sarasvatī was able to send devotees to the West. Thus, in 1933, Bhakti Pradīpa Tīrtha Mahārāja, Bhakti Hridaya Bon (Vāna) Mahārāja,[27] Bhakti Saraṅga Goswāmī, and Sambidānanda Dās set sail for Western shores and, that very summer, introduced Śrī Chaitanya's teachings to the King and Queen of England, among other prominent dignitaries. Soon afterwards, the first Western *ashram* appeared in London, compliments of Daisy Cecilia Bowtell (1887–1981), a British woman who donated her home to the mission. She would eventually be initiated as Vinode Vani Dasi, making her the first Western woman to embrace Gauḍīya Vaishnavism.

A Gauḍīya Maṭha center also soon appeared in Berlin, bringing forth ready and waiting seekers, such as Ernst-Georg Schulze, soon to become Sadānanda Swami (1908–1977), and Walther Eidlitz (1892–1976), who would author several noted books on Gauḍīya Vaishnavism.[28] A center opened in Burma as well, showing potential for further expansion. But soon the mission began to wane. With the premature departure of Sarasvatī Ṭhākura (1937), the Gauḍīya Maṭha's preaching lost unified energy and momentum. As is witnessed often, upon the disappearance of a charismatic polymath and organizational genius like Bhaktisiddhānta Sarasvatī, many of the bereaved disciples slackened in their commitment, settling into conventional lives, a number even leaving the mission to pursue other interests.

THE "KRISHNA CONSCIOUSNESS" MOVEMENT

And then the unexpected happened. There was one lone, sincere, and pure-hearted devotee, not a *sannyāsī* at the time, but a married man engulfed in business and everyday life. His name was Abhay Charan De. He had met Bhaktisiddhānta Sarasvatī in 1922, and took initiation from him some eleven years later. From their very first meeting, he dreamed of fulfilling his master's desire to spread the teachings of Śrī Chaitanya in the English language, which was the specific instruction Bhaktisiddhānta had given him, and to travel to America, so that he might offer these teachings to the modern world.

Self-consciously intent on carrying out his guru's order, and assisted by numerous, apparently adventitious circumstances, over the next period of years Abhay prepared himself for the extraordinary mission his guru requested he fulfill. Eventually, in the year 1959, he took *sannyāsa* and sequestered himself at the famous Rādhā-Dāmodara temple in Vrindāvan, studying and chanting and beseeching the Lord for mercy. He knew that to accomplish his master's mission would require purity, learning, and determination. So he cultivated these qualities, and emerged as Śrīla A. C. Bhaktivedānta Swami, who, several years after arriving in the West, would become known as "Prabhupāda," or "the master at whose feet other masters sit."[29]

History shows that Prabhupāda took the mission seriously. He was practically penniless when he arrived in New York by freighter in 1965, a stranger in a strange land. But his remarkable determination produced an amazing outcome: after almost a year of great difficulty, reversals, and life-threatening challenges, at the advanced age of 70, this gentle soul from Calcutta established his International Society for Krishna Consciousness (ISKCON) in the summer of 1966. Under his careful guidance, the Society grew—within a mere decade—into a worldwide coalition of almost one hundred *ashrams*, schools, temples, institutes, restaurants, and farm communities. Mahāprabhu had come West.

As an addendum, we may remember that in November of 1965, on his deathbed, Śrī Krishna Prem had been documented as saying, "My ship is sailing." What he didn't know, of course, was that the sublime "ship of Śrī Krishna Prem" had, indeed, already set sail, just a few months earlier, headed for Western shores.[30] On board was the remarkable A. C. Bhaktivedānta Swami Prabhupāda, and in the Swami's heart he carefully bore with him across the great expanse of sea, as a gift of divine love, the transcendental teachings of Śrī Chaitanya Mahāprabhu.

NOTES

1. As Ghosh argues, it is unlikely that "the world" indicated Western Europe, the Americas, or Australia in precolonial times. He refers readers to *An Atlas and Survey of South Asian History* (Armonk, New York, N.Y.: M. E. Sharpe, 1995), 100–104. For more on the exploitative and imperialistic agenda of both Columbus and Vasco da Gama, among others, see Eric Toussaint, "Globalization from Christopher Columbus and Vasco da Gama until today" (http://www.cadtm.org/spip.php?page=imprimer&id_article=3205).

2. See Abhishek Ghosh, "Vaiṣṇavism and the West: A Study of Kedanath Datta Bhaktivinod's Encounter and Response, 1869–1909," Ph.D. thesis, The University of Chicago, 2014, 3–4.

3. Bhakti Vinoda Thakur, *Sri Caitanya Mahaprabhu: His Life and Precepts* (Calcutta: K. Dutt, 1896), 60.

4. See Bhaktivinoda Ṭhākura, "Nityadharma Suryodoy," in *Sajjana-toṣaṇī* 4.3, 1885, 8–10. Although Bhaktivinoda had long since passed from this world, his prophetic words—anticipating a time when "English, French, Russian, German and American people will take up banners, *mṛdangas* and *karatālas* and raise *kīrtana* through their streets and towns"—indeed came to pass. When Śrīla A. C. Bhaktivedānta Swami Prabhupāda brought Mahāprabhu's mission to Western shores in 1965, such international *kīrtana* became a reality that would have no doubt pleased both Bhaktivinoda and Mahāprabhu himself.

5. See Shukavak N. Dasa, *Hindu Encounter with Modernity: Kedarnath Datta Bhaktivinoda, Vaishnava Theologian* (Los Angeles: Sanskrit Religions Institute, 1999), 89–92.

6. Accompanying the verses we find a Sanskrit commentary known as the *Vikāśinī-ṭīkā* by "the renowned *paṇḍita* of Navadvīp," Mahā-mahopādhyāya Śitikaṇṭha Vācaspati, of whom we know nothing, there being no known historical record of his life and accomplishments.

7. See Narahari Chakravarti, *Śrī Bhakti-ratnākara*, in Bengali (Calcutta: Bagbazar Gaudiya Mission, 1987, reprint); Narahari Chakravarti, *Narottama-vilāsa*, in Bengali (Murshidabad: Radharaman Press, 1921, reprint); and Nityananda Das, *Prema-vilāsa*, in Bengali (Calcutta: Mahesh Library, 1999, reprint). In English, see Tony K. Stewart, *The Final Word: The Caitanya Caritāmṛta and the Grammar of Religious Tradition, op. cit,* especially Chapter One, "Facing the Peril of Disintegration, 3–43. Also see Steven J. Rosen, *The Lives of the Vaishnava Saints: Shinivas Acharya, Narottam Das Thakur, and Shyamananda Pandit* (New York, N.Y.: FOLK Books, 1991).

8. See Jagadananda Das (Jan Brzezinski), "Keeping Faith with Kheturi, Part II (http://jagadanandadas.blogspot.com/2015/08/keeping-faith-with-kheturi-part-ii.html).

9. For details see Hitesranjan Sanyal, "Transformation of the Regional Bhakti Movement" in Joseph T. O'Connell, ed., *Bengal Vaiṣṇavism, Orientalism, Society and the Arts* (East Lansing, Michigan: Asian Studies Center, Michigan State University, 1985). See also Eben Graves, "Padāvali-Kīrtan: Music, Religious Aesthetics, and Nationalism in West Bengal's Cultural Economy," Ph.D. Dissertation, The University of Texas at Austin, 2014, Chapter One.

10. It is difficult to date Viśvanātha and Baladeva. Scholars present diverse views, usually with good reasons, but the most likely dates would be something along these lines: Viśvanātha Chakravartī (c. 1643–1730) and Baladeva Vidyābhūṣaṇa (c. 1695–1793).

11. See Daśaratha Suta Dāsa, *The Story of Śrīla Viśvanātha Cakravartī Ṭhākura* (Union City, Georgia: Nectar Books, 1991). Also see online material (http://gaudiya-history.iskcondesiretree.com/sri-visvanatha-cakravarti-thakura/).

12. See Kiyokazu Okita, *Hindu Theology in Early Modern South Asia: The Rise of Devotionalism and the Politics of Genealogy* (Oxford, UK: Oxford University Press, 2014); A. P. Burton, "Temples, Texts, and Taxes: The *Bhagavad-gītā* and the Politico-Religious Identity of the Caitanya Sect," Ph.D. thesis, The Australian National University, 2000; and Michael and Nancy Wright, "Baladeva Vidyābhūṣaṇa: The Gauḍīya Vedāntist," *Journal of Vaishnava Studies*, Volume 1, No. 2 (Winter 1993), 159–84.

13. The Vaishnava-Sahajiyā movement in Bengal can be traced to both Hinduism and Buddhism, originating in as early as the 8th or 9th centuries of the Common Era. Initially, the word *sahaja* ("easy" or "natural") merely indicated those who have innate devotion. However, it soon became identified with what the orthodox tradition views as a "cheap," "imitative" practice in which human coupling and sexuality have been confused with Vaishnava *sādhana*, so that ordinary living entities try to emulate the love of Rādhā and Krishna. It is frowned upon by the Vaishnava community as defined by the Six Goswāmīs of Vrindāvan.

14. See Ramakanta Chakravarti, *Vaiṣṇavism in Bengal 1486–1900* (Calcutta: Sanskrit Pustak Bhandar, 1985), 392–393.

15. There are Vaishnavas who descend from family dynasties linked to Mahāprabhu's direct associates, either through blood lineage or relation to disciples. For example, Bijoy Krishna Goswami, as stated, belonged to the Advaita-vaṁśa, which originated with Advaita Ācārya's son Krishna Miśra. Similarly, there exists a Nityānanda-vaṁśa, by way of Jāhnavā and her son Vīrabhadra Goswāmī, and also through Rāmachandra Goswāmī, Nityānanda's adopted son. The Gadādhara-parivāra, to cite yet another example, descends through any of Gadādhara Paṇḍita's many disciples. We find this Gadādhara tradition most famously represented in the modern era through Śrī Haridāsa Shastri Mahārāja (1918–2013), a teacher and scholar of considerable renown. His disciple, Dr. Satyanārāyaṇa Dāsa Bābājī, founded The Jīva Institute of Vaishnava Studies, an important contemporary Vaishnava organization. Similarly, there are lineages stemming from Gopāla Bhaṭṭa Goswāmī, Śrīnivāsa Ācārya, Lokanātha Goswāmī, Narottama Dāsa Ṭhākura, and others.

16. I am grateful to Neal Delmonico for directing my attention to this important Gauḍīya Vaishnava tome. For more, see *On Associating with Great Ones—Śrī Kanupriya Goswami (Based on lectures collected and edited in Bengali by Śrī Gauraraydas Goswami, Introduced, translated, and annotated by Neal Delmonico* (Kirksville, Missouri: Blazing Sapphire Press, 2014), xiv.

17. *Śrī Krishna: Lord of love* was recently republished in a handsome hardbound edition, with additional materials, under the general editorship of Neal Delmonico. It includes a lengthy introductory essay by Gerald Carney summarizing the life and

work of Bābā Premānanda Bhāratī. See Premānanda Bhāratī, *Śrī Krishna: The Lord of Love* (Kirksville, Missouri: Blazing Sapphire Press, 2007).

18. Ibid. The Leo Tolstoy correspondence is reproduced on lxxvii-lxxxiv.

19. See, for example, Gerald Carney, "Bābā Premānanda Bhāratī (1857–1914), an Early Twentieth-Century Encounter of Vaishnava Devotion with American Culture: A Comparative Study," in *Journal of Vaishnava Studies,* Volume 6, No. 2 (Spring, 1998), 161–88. See also "Bābā Premānanda Bhāratī's 'Privileged View' of Christianity," in *Journal of Vaishnava Studies*, Volume 13, No. 1 (Fall, 2004), 77–102.

20. See Francis X. Clooney, "In Memoriam: Mahanambrata Brahmachari (December 25,1904–October 18, 1999)." *Merton Annual* 13 (2000), 123–26 (http://merton.org/ITMS/Annual/13/Clooney123–126.pdf).

21. Merton and Brahmachari had a great amount of respect and admiration for each other. This is a matter of public record, affectionately mentioned in Merton's autobiography. See Thomas Merton, *The Seven Storey Mountain* (New York, N.Y.: Harcourt Brace & Co., 1948), 194–198.

22. See Gustav Niebuhr, "Mahanambrata Brahmachari Is Dead at 95," *The New York Times*, November 1, 1999 (http://www.nytimes.com/1999/11/01/world/mahanambrata-brahmachari-is-dead-at-95.html).

23. "Krishna Prem, Śrī (1898–1965) Western-born Vaishnavite Guru" in Constance Jones, Constance and James D. Ryan, *Encyclopedia of Hinduism* (New York, N.Y.: Infobase Publishing, 2006), 246.

24. Ferdinando Sardella, *Modern Hindu Personalism: The History, Life, and Thought of Bhaktisiddhānta Sarasvatī* (New York, N.Y.: Oxford University Press, 2013), 143.

25. David L. Haberman, "A Cross-Cultural Adventure: The Transformation of Ronald Nixon," in *Religion*, Volume 23, No. 3 (July 1, 1993). 223.

26. Ibid., 221.

27. Bhakti Hridaya Bon Mahārāja's initial three years in Europe, including England, Germany, and Czechoslovakia, were augmented by additional trips to America, Japan, and Burma in 1939–1941, and then again to Germany, Austria, Belgium and Scandinavia in 1960. He undertook yet another journey to the U.S.A. and Canada in 1974–1975.

28. Most significantly, *Kṛṣṇa-Caitanya: Sein Leben und Seine Lehre* (Stockholm: Almqvist & Wiksell, 1968) and the autobiographical tale, *Unknown India: A Pilgrimage into a Forgotten World* (London: Rider, 1952). Eidlitz had received the name Vamandas from a guru prior to meeting Gauḍīya Vaishnavas. Once Bon Mahārāja initiated him, his name became Bimala Krishna Vidyavinode Dasa, though many continued to call him Vamandas.

29. For more on Prabhupāda's life and the early days of ISKCON, see Satsvarūpa Dāsa Goswāmī, *Śrīla Prabhupāda Līlāmṛta*, Vol 1–2 (Los Angeles, C.A.: Bhaktivedanta Book Trust, 1980–82, 2002, reprint); Hayagriva Dasa, *The Hare Krishna Explosion: The Birth of Krishna Consciousness in America* (New Vrindaban: Palace Press, 1985); Ranchor Prime, *When the Sun Shines: The Dawn of Hare Krishna in Britain* (Sweden: Bhaktivedanta Book Trust, 2009); Mukunda Goswami, *Miracle on Second Avenue: Hare Krishna Arrives in New York, San Francisco, and London 1966–1969*

(Badger, C.A., Torchlight Publishing, 2011); Dinatarini Devi, *Yamuna Devi: A Life of Unalloyed Devotion* (Alachua, Florida: Unalloyed, Inc., 2014); Shyamasundar Das, *Chasing the Rhinos with the Swami* (Self-published, 2016); and Joshua M. Greene, *Swami in a Strange Land: How Krishna Came to the West* (San Rafael, C.A.: Mandala Publishing, 2016).

30. "Śrī Krishna Prem" literally means, "love for Krishna," and it is this that Prabhupāda was taking to the Western world. While Śrī Krishna Prem was using the expression, "My ship is sailing," in its most common sense, that is, "I am now leaving my present body," the more profound reading, given that Prabhupāda started his journey only several months earlier—by ship—was that Mahāprabhu's teaching of divine love was already en route to the Western world. The divine coincidence of Śrī Krishna Prem's utterance thus begs to be expressed.

Bibliography

PRIMARY SOURCES

Baṃsal, Nareśa Chandra, *Caitanya sampradāya: siddhānta aura sāhitya* (Agra: Vinoda Pustaka Mandira, 1980).

Chakravartī, Narahari, *Narottama-vilāsa* (Murshidabad: Radharaman Press, 1921, reprint).

———, *Śrī Bhakti-ratnākara* (Calcutta: Bagbazar Gaudiya Mission, 1987, reprint).

Dāsa, Haridāsa, *Gauḍīya Vaiṣṇava Abhidhāna*, 4 parts in 2 vols. (Navadvīpa: Haribola Kuṭīra, 471 GA. [1957]).

Dāsa, Kuñjavihāri, *Mañjarī-svarūpa-nirūpana*, 2nd edition (Rādhākuṇḍa, UP: Kṛṣṇacaitanya Śāstra Mandira at Vrajānandagherā, 489–90 GA. [1975–1976]).

Dāsa, Locana, *Chaitanya-maṅgala,* ed. Bhakti Kevala Audulomi (Calcutta: Gaudiya Mission, 1979).

Dāsa, Nityānanda, *Prema-vilāsa*, in Bengali (Calcutta: Mahesh Library, 1999, reprint).

Dāsa, Vṛndāvana, *Caitanya-bhāgavata,* ed. *Nitāikaruṇākallolinī ṭīkā* by Rādhāgovinda Nātha, in Bengali, 6 vols. (Kalikātā: Sādhanā Prakāśanī, 1964).

Gosvāmin, Jīva, *Bhāgavata-sandarbha*, ed. Śyāmalāla Gosvāmī (Calcutta: Śyāmalāla Gosvāmī, 1915).

———, *Bhāgavata-sandarbha,* 2 vols, Puridasa edition (Vrindavan: Haridasa Sharma, 1951).

———, *Bhakti-sandarbha*, ed. Bengali translation by Rādhāraman Gosvāmī and Kṛṣṇagopāla Gosvāmī (Calcutta: University of Calcutta, 1962).

———, *Paramātmā-sandarbha,* with the Gopālatoṣaṇī of Śyāmdās (Vrindavan: Vrajagaurav Prakāśan, 1999).

Gosvāmin, Rūpa, *Bhakti-rasāmṛta-sindhu*, with the commentaries of Jīva Gosvāmin, Mukundadāsa Gosvāmin, and Viśvanātha Chakravartin, ed. Bengali translation by Haridāsa Dāsa (Navadvīpa: Haribol Kuṭhīr, 1945).

———, *Padyāvali of Rūpa Gosvāmin: An Anthology of Vaishnava Verses in Sanskrit,* ed. Sushil Kumar De (Dacca: University of Dacca, 1934).
———, *Ujjvalanīlamaṇi,* ed. Bengali translation by Haridasa Dāsa, with the *Svātmapramodinī ṭīkā* of Viṣṇudāsa (Navadvīpa: by the editor at Haribola Kuṭīra, 1955).
Guha, Manindranath, *Śrī-Śrī Caitanya-śikṣāṣṭakam* (Calcutta, self-published, 1964).
———, *Śrīman-nāmāmṛta-sindhu-bindu,* 2nd edition (Sri Vrindavan, India: Savitri Guha, n.d.).
Jānā, Nareśacandra, in Bengali, *Vṛndāvanera chaya gosvāmī* (Calcutta: Calcutta University Press, 1970).
Karṇapūra, Kavi, *Gaura-gaṇoddeśa-dīpikā,* Bengali trans. by Ram Narayan Vidyaratna, ed., Ramdev Miśra, 4th edition (Berhampore: Radharaman Press, 1922).
———, *Chaitanya-candrodaya-nātaka* (Benares: Chowkhambha, 1966).
Kavirāja, Kṛṣṇadāsa, *Govinda-līlāmṛta,* ed. Haridāsa Dāsa, in Bengali (Navadvīpa Śrī-śrī-gauḍiya-gaurava-grantha-guccha, 1949).
———, *Śrī Caitanya Caritāmṛta of Kṛṣṇadāsa Kavirāja,* Nātha, Rādhāgovinda, ed. in Bengali, 4th edition, 6 vols. (Calcutta: Sādhanā Prakāśanī, 1962).
———, *Śrī-Śrī Chaitanya Caritāmṛta with commentaries by Bhaktivinoda Ṭhākur and Bhaktisiddhānta Sarasvatī* (Kalikata: Sri Chaitanya Gaudiya Matha, second edition, 1992).
Mahārāja, Śrī Śrīmad Bhakti Prajñāna Keśava, "Acintya-bhedābheda." in *Śrī Gauḍīya Pātrikā* (Bengali): vol. 9, issues 3–10 (May–December, 1957) and 12 (February, 1958); vol. 10, issues 2–4 (April-June 1958) and 7–10 (September–December, 1958).
Majumdar, Bimanbehari, in Bengali, *Śrī Caitanya Cariter Upādān* (Calcutta: University of Calcutta, 1959).
Mukhopadhyay, Harekrishna, ed., in Bengali, *Vaiṣṇava Padāvalī,* 1st edition (Kolkata: Sahitya Samshad, 1961).
———, *Bāṅgālāra Kīrtana O Kīrtanīyā* (Kolkata: Sahitya Samsad, 1971).
Nātha, Rādhāgovinda, *Gauḍīya-vaiṣṇava-darśana,* 5 vols. (Kalikātā: Prācyavāṇī Mandira, 1965).
Sanyal, Hiteshranjan, in Bengali, *Bāṁlā Kīrtaner Itihās* (Kolkata: K.P. Bagchi & Company, 1989).
Sarasvatī, Bhaktisiddhānta, ed., in Bengali, *Śrī Caitanya-bhāgavata of Vṛndāvana Dāsa Ṭhākura,* 3rd edition (Calcutta: Bāgbāzār Gauḍīya Maṭha, 1961).
———, ed., in Bengali, *Śrī Śrī Śikṣāṣṭakam, Anuvṛtti-sahitam* (Calcutta: Kunjabihari Vidyabhusana, Sri Gaudiya Math, n.d.).
Svāmin Śrīdhara, *Bhāvārtha-Dipikā: Commentary on the Bhāgavata Purāṇa in Sanskrit,* ed. Jagadisa Lala Sastri (Delhi: Motilal Banarsidass, 1983).
———, *Śrīdhara Swami's Commentary on the Śrīmadbhāgavat Mahāpurāṇam,* ed. Pandit Rāmteja Pāndeya (Delhi: Chaukhambā Sanskrit Pratiṣthān Pub, 2011).
Ṭhākura, Bhaktivinoda, *Śrī Krishna-saṁhitā* (Calcutta: Isvarchandra Basu, 1879).
———, "Śikṣāṣṭaka Baṅga-bhāṣā," in *Sajjana-toṣaṇī,* Bengali, vol. 3, issue 9, 1886, 101–112.

———, *Sanmodana-bhāṣya and Vivṛti,* in Bengali (Dhaka: Bhakti Pradipa Tirtha Maharaja, Gaudiya Mission, 1921).

———, *Jaiva-dharma,* ed. Bhakti Dayita Mādhava Gosvāmī, with an introduction by Bhaktisiddhānta Sarasvati (Kalikātā: Śrī Caitanya Gauḍiya Maṭha, 1989).

Thakur, Lochan Das, *Śrī Caitanya-maṅgala* (Calcutta: Bagh Bazaar Gaudiya Mission, 1991).

Vamana Maharaja, Bhakti Vedanta, ed. *Śrī Caitanya-Śikṣāṣṭaka,* in Bengali (Mathura: Gaudiya Vedanta Samiti in 1984).

Vidyābhūṣaṇa, Baladeva, *Govinda-bhāṣya,* commentary on the *Brahma-sūtras,* ed. Kṛṣṇadāsa Bābā (Rādhā-kuṇḍa: Kṛṣṇadāsa Bābā, 1954).

———, *Prameya-ratnāvalī,* edited and translated by Haridāsa-Śāstrī with the Kantī-mālā commentary of Kṛṣṇadeva Sārvabhauma Bhaṭṭācārya (Vṛndāvana: Gadādhara-gaura-hari Press, 1981).

Vidyavinoda, Sundarananda, in Bengali, *Acintya-bhedābheda-vāda* (Calcutta: Gaudiya Mission, 1951).

Yadunandanadāsa, *Karṇānanda,* in Bengali, ed. Rāmanārāyaṇa Vidyāratna (Murshidabad: Haribhaktipradāyinī Sabhā, 1891).

SECONDARY SOURCES

Babaji, Ananta Dasa, translation, *Sri-Sri Siksastakam: The Eight Instructions of Sri Caitanya Mahaprabhu, with the commentary of Radhakunda Mahanta Pandita* (Radha-kunda, Mathura District, U.P.: Sri Krishna Caitanya Sastra Mandira, n.d.).

Bake, Arnold A., "Kirtan in Bengal." in *Indian Art and Letters,* n.s. XXI (1947), 34–40.

Basham, A. L. "Interview with A. L. Basham." in *Hare Krishna, Hare Krishna: Five Distinguished Scholars on the Krishna Movement in the West,* ed. Steven J. Gelberg (New York: Grove, 1983), 162–195.

Beck, Guy L., *Sonic Theology: Hinduism and Sacred Sound* (Columbia, South Carolina: University of South Carolina Press, 1993).

———, "An Introduction to the Poetry of Narottam Dās." in *Journal of Vaishnava Studies,* vol. 4, issue 4 (Fall 1996), 17–52.

———, "The Devotional Music of Śrīla Prabhupāda." in *Journal of Vaishnava Studies,* vol. 6, issue 2 (Spring 1998), 125–140.

———, *Alternative Krishnas: Regional and Vernacular Variations on a Hindu Deity* (Albany, NY: State University of New York Press, 2005).

———, "Kīrtan and Bhajan," in *Brill's Encyclopedia of Hinduism,* vol. II, 585–598, ed. Knut A. Jacobsen (Leiden: Brill Academic Publishers, 2010), 585–598.

———, *Sonic Liturgy: Ritual and Music in Hindu Traditions* (Columbia, South Carolina: University of South Carolina Press, 2012).

Berendt, Joachim-Ernst, *The World is Sound Nada Brahma: Music and the Landscape of Consciousness* (Rochester, Vermont: Destiny Books, 1983).

Bhakti Tirtha, Swami, *Reflections on Sacred Teachings, Volume One: Sri Siksastaka* (Washington, D.C.: Hari-Nama Press, 2002).

Bhattacharya, Deben, *Love Songs of Chandidas: The Rebel Poet-Priest of Bengal* (New York: Grove Press, 1969).

———, *Love Songs of Vidyapati*, ed. W. G. Archer (New York: Grove Press, 1970).

———, *The Mirror of the Sky: Songs of the Bauls of Bengal* (Prescott, Arizona: Hohm Press, 1999).

Bhatia, Varuni, "Devotional Traditions and National Culture: Recovering Gauḍīya Vaishnavism in Colonial Bengal" (PhD thesis, Columbia University, 2009).

Bhowmick, Shukdeb, *The Theory of Acintya-Bhedābheda* (Kolkata: Sanskrit Pustak Bhandar, 2004).

Bon, Bhakti Hridaya, *My First Year in England: Report of My Activities in the West from May 1933 to May 1934* (London: Gaudiya Mission, 1934).

———, *Second Year of the Gaudiya Mission in Europe* (London: Gaudiya Mission, 1935).

Bose, Manindra Mohan, *The Post Caitanya Sahajiyā Cult* (Delhi: Gian Publishing House, 1986, reprint).

Brahmachari, Mahanamabrata, *Vaiṣṇava Vedānta*: *The Philosophy of Śrī Jīva Gosvāmī* (Calcutta: Das Gupta and Co., 1974).

Broo, M., *As Good as God: The Guru in Gauḍīya Vaiṣṇavism* (Åbo: Åbo Akademi University Press, 2003).

———, "The Vrindavan Goswāmins on *Kīrtana*." in *Journal of Vaishnava Studies*, vol. 17, issue 2 (Spring, 2009), 57–71.

Brooks, Charles R. "Hare Krishna, Radhe Shyam: The Cross-Cultural Dynamics of Mystical Emotions in Brindaban." in *Divine Passions: The Social Construction of Emotion in India*, ed. Owen M. Lynch (Berkeley: University of California Press, 1990).

———, "The Blind Man Meets the Lame Man: ISKCON's Place in the Bengal Vaishnava Tradition of Caitanya Mahāprabhu." in *Journal of Vaishnava Studies,* vol. 6, issue 2 (March–April 1998), 5–30.

———, *The Hare Krishnas in India* (Princeton, NJ: Princeton University Press, 1989).

Bryant, Edwin, and Ekstrand, Maria, eds., *The Hare Krishna Movement: The Post-charismatic Fate of a Religious Transplant* (New York: Columbia University Press, 2004).

Bryant, Edwin F., "The Date and Provenance of the *Bhāgavata Purāṇa*." in *Journal of Vaishnava Studies,* vol. 11, issue 1 (Fall, 2002), 51–80.

———, *Krishna: The Beautiful Legend of God—Śrīmad Bhāgavata Purāṇa Book X* (New York: Penguin Books, 2003).

———, ed., *Krishna: A Source Book* (New York: Oxford University Press 2007).

———, *Bhakti Yoga: Tales and Teachings from the Bhāgavata Purāṇa* (New York: North Point Press, 2017).

Brzezinski, Jan K., "Jīva Gosvāmin's *Gopāla-campū*," PhD thesis, School of Oriental and African Studies, University of London, 1992.

———, "Women Saints in Gauḍīya Vaiṣṇavism." in *Vaiṣṇavī: Women and the Worship of Kṛṣṇa,* ed. Steven J. Rosen (Delhi: Motilal Banarsidass, 1996).

———, "The Parampara Institution in Gaudiya Vaishnavism." in *Journal of Vaishnava Studies,* vol. 5, issue 1 (Winter 1996–1997), 151–182.

———, "Does Kṛṣṇa Marry the Gopīs in the End? The *Svakīya-vāda* of Jīva Gosvāmin." in *Journal of Vaishnava Studies,* vol. 5, issue 4 (Fall, 1997), 49–110.

———, "Śrī Chaitanya's *Śikṣāṣṭakam.*" in *Journal of Vaishnava Studies*, vol. 12, issue 1 (Fall 2003), 87–111.

———, "Jīva Goswāmin: Biography and Bibliography." in *Journal of Vaishnava Studies,* vol. 15, issue 2 (Spring, 2007), 51–80.

Capwell, Charles, *The Music of the Bauls of Bengal* (Kent, Ohio: Kent State University Press, 1986).

Cakravartī, Viśvanātha, *Gaura-gaṇa-svarūpa-tattva-candrikā*, translation, Demian Martins (Vrindavan, U.P.: Jiva Institute, 2015).

Carney, Gerald T., "The Erotic Mysticism of Caitanya." in *Journal of Dharma,* vol. 4, issue 2 (1979), 169–177.

———, "The Theology of Kavikarṇapūra's *Caitanyacandrodaya*, Act II," Ph.D. Thesis (Fordham University, 1979).

Chakravarti, Ramakanta, *Vaiṣṇavism in Bengal: 1486–1900* (Calcutta: Sanskrit Pustak Bhandar, 1985).

Chakravarti, Sudhindra Chandra, *Philosophical Foundations of Bengal Vaiṣṇavism* (Calcutta: Academic Publishers, 1969).

———, "Bengal Vaiṣṇavism," in K. R. Sundararanjan and Bithika Mukerji, eds. *Hindu Spirituality: Postclassical and Modern* (New York: The Crossroad Publishing Company, 1997), 47–62.

Chandidasa, Baru, *Singing the Glory of Lord Krishna: The Sri Krishna Kirtana*, translated and annotated by M. H. Klaiman (Chico, CA: Scholars Press, 1984).

Chatterjee, A. N., *Srikrsna Caitanya: A Historical study on Gaudiya Vaisnavism* (New Delhi: Associated Publishing, 1984).

Chaudhuri, Dr. Roma, *Ten Schools of Vedanta*. Parts I, II, & III (Calcutta: Rabindra Bharati University, 1973, 1975, 1981).

Clooney, Frank X., and Stewart, Tony K., "Vaiṣṇava." in S. Mittal and G. Thursby, eds., *The Hindu World* (Abingdon: Routledge, 2004), 162–184.

Cole, Richard J., and Graham Dwyer, eds. *The Hare Krishna Movement: Forty Years of Chant and Change* (New York: I. B. Tauris, 2007).

Das, Gurcharan, *The Difficulty of Being Good: On the Subtle Art of Dharma* (New York: Oxford University Press, 2009).

Das, Paritosh, *Sahajiyā Cult of Bengal and Pancha Sakhā Cult of Orissa* (Calcutta: Firma KLM Pvt. Ltd., 1988).

Das, Radhamadhav, *Unity in Diversity: Shri Chaitanya's Achintya-Bhedabheda* (Florida Vedic College Press, 2012), http://ebooks.iskcondesiretree.com/pdf/His_Grace_Radhamadhav_Prabhu/Unity_in_Diversity.pdf

Das, Raghava Chaitanya, *The Divine Name* (Bombay, the author, 1954).

Das, Rahul Peter, *Essays on Vaiṣṇavism in Bengal* (Calcutta: Firma KLM: 1997).

———, "'Vedic' in the Terminology of Prabhupada and His Followers." in *Journal of Vaishnava Studies,* vol. 6, issue 2 (Spring 1998), 141–159.

Dasa, Gopīparāṇadhana, trans., *Śrī Bṛhad Bhāgavatāmṛta of Śrīla Sanātana Gosvāmī*, 3 vols. (Los Angeles: Bhaktivedanta Book Trust, 2002–2003).

———, *Śrī Tattva-sandarbha of Śrīla Jīva Gosvāmī* (Vrindavan: Girirāja Publishing, 2014).

Dāsa, Kuśakratha, translated, *Śrīla Vṛndāvana Dāsa Ṭhākura's Śrī Caitanya-bhāgavata*, Complete in One Volume (Alachua, Florida: The Kṛṣṇa Institute, 1994).

Dāsa, Ravīndra Svarūpa [William H. Deadwyler III], *Encounter With the Lord of the Universe: Collected Essays, 1978–1983* (Washington, DC: Gita-nagari Press, 1983).

———, "The Devotee and the Deity: Living a Personalistic Theology." in *Gods of Flesh Gods of Stone: The Embodiment of Divinity in India*, ed. Joanne Punzo Waghorne and Norman Cutler (New York: Columbia University Press, 1985), 69–87.

———, "The Scholarly Tradition in Caitanyaite Vaiṣṇavism." *ISKCON Review*, vol. 1, issue 1 (Spring, 1985), 15–23.

———, "The Contribution of Bhāgavata-Dharma Toward a 'Scientific Religion' and a 'Religious Science.'" in *Synthesis of Science and Religion—Critical Essays and Dialogues,* eds. T. D. Singh, R. Gomatam (San Francisco: Bhaktivedanta Institute, 1987), 366–380.

———, "Saṁpradāya of Śrī Caitanya." in *Vaiṣṇavism: Contemporary Scholars Discuss the Gauḍīya Tradition.* ed. Steven J. Rosen (New York: Folk Books, 1992), 127–140.

———, "Rādhā, Kṛṣṇa, Caitanya: The Inner Dialectic of the Divine Relativity." in *Journal of Vaiṣṇava Studies*, vol. 10, issue 1 (Spring, 2001), 5–26.

Dāsa, Rūpa Vilāsa, *A Ray of Vishnu: The Biography of a Śaktyāveṣa Avatāra Śrī Śrīmad Bhaktisiddhānta Sarasvatī Gosvāmī Mahārāja Prabhupāda* (Washington, MS: New Jaipur Press, 1988).

———, *The Seventh Goswami: A Biography of His Divine Grace Śrīla Saccidānanda Bhaktivinoda Ṭhākura* (Washington, MS: New Jaipur Press, 1989).

Dasa, Shukavak N., *Hindu Encounter with Modernity: Kedarnath Datta Bhaktivinoda, Vaishnava Theologian* (Los Angeles: Sanskrit Religions Institute, 1999).

———, "Bhaktivinoda and Scriptural Literalism," in *The Hare Krishna Movement: The Post-charismatic Fate of a Religious Transplant*, eds. Edwin F. Bryant and Maria L. Ekstrand (New York: Colombia University Press, 2004), 97–111.

Dasa, Dasaratha Suta, translated, "*Śrī Śikṣāṣṭakam*," in *The Songs of Bhaktivinoda Thakura, Saranagati and Gitavali* (Union City, Georgia: Nectar Books, 1994), 140–152.

Dasa, Sarvabhavana, translated, *Śrī Śikṣāṣṭakam: Eight Beautiful Instructions by Śrī Caitanya Mahāprabhu, with Sri Sanmodana Bhasyam of Srila Bhaktivinoda Thakura and Purports by Srila Bhaktisiddhanta Sarasvati Gosvami* (Bombay: Harmonist Publications, 1991).

Dasa, Satyanarayana, translated, *Śrī Bhagavata Sandarbha* (Vrindavan, UP: Jiva Institute of Vaishnava Studies, 2014).

Dāsa, Satyarāja, "Lord Chaitanya's Eight Teachings," A Five-Part Series on the *Śikṣāṣṭakam*, in *Back to Godhead*: "A Prophecy Fulfilled," (March–April 2002),

Volume 36, Number 2; "Teaching 1: Seven Effects of Chanting" (May–June 2002), Volume 36, Number 3; "Teachings 2 & 3: The All Powerful Names of God," (September–October 2002), Volume 36, Number 5; "Teachings 4 & 5: Resolute In Purpose," (November–December, 2002), Volume 36, Number 6; and "Teachings 6, 7 & 8: Symptoms of the Purest Love," (January–February, 2003), Volume 37, Number 1. [Reprinted in Steven J. Rosen, *Sonic Spirituality: A Collection of Essays on the Hare Krishna Maha-Mantra* (Vrindavan, U.P.: Rasbihari Lal & Sons, 2009)].

De, Sushil Kumar, ed. *The Padyāvalī: An Anthology of Vaiṣṇava Verses in Sanskrit Compiled by Rūpa Gosvāmin, a Disciple of Śrī-Kṛṣṇa-Caitanya of Bengal* (Dacca University Oriental Publications Series, No. 3. Dacca: The University of Dacca, 1934).

———, "Caitanya as an Author," *Indian Historical Quarterly* 10 (1934), 301–320.

Dehejia, Vidya, *Antal and Her Path of Love: Poems of a Woman Saint from South India* (Albany, New York: State University of New York Press, 1990).

Delmonico, Neal, "Sacred Rapture: A Study of the Religious Aesthetic of Rūpa Gosvāmin," Ph.D. Dissertation, The University of Chicago, 1990.

———, "Sacred Rapture: The Bhakti-Rasa Theory of Rūpa Goswāmin." in *Journal of Vaishnava Studies,* vol. 6, issue 1 (Winter 1998), 75–98

———, "Chaitanya Vaishnavism and the Holy Names." in *Krishna: A Sourcebook,* ed. Edwin F. Bryant (Oxford: Oxford University Press, 2007), 549–575.

Dimock Jr., Edward C., "The Place of Gauracandrikā in Bengali Vaiṣṇava Lyrics." in *Journal of the American Oriental Society,* vol. 78, issue 3 (1958), 153–169.

———, "Doctrine and Practice Among the Vaiṣṇavas of Bengal." in *History of Religions*, vol. 3, issue 1 (1963), 106–127. Reprinted in *Krishna: Myths, Rites and Attitudes*, ed. by Milton Singer (Hawaii: East-West Center Press, 1966), 41–63.

———, *The Place of the Hidden Moon: Erotic Mysticism in the Vaiṣṇava-Sahajiyā Cult of Bengal* (University of Chicago Press, 1966).

———, "The 'Nectar of the Acts' of Caitanya." in *The Biographical Process, Studies in the History and Psychology of Religion,* ed. Frank E. Reynolds and Donald Capps (The Hague: Mouton, 1976), 109–117.

Dimock, Edward C., Jr., and Levertov, Denise, translated, *In Praise of Krishna: Songs from the Bengali* (Chicago: The University of Chicago Press, 1981, reprint).

Dimock, Edward C., Jr., translated, and Stewart, Tony K. (ed.), *Caitanya Caritāmṛta of Kṛṣṇadāsa Kavirāja: A Translation and Commentary.* Harvard Oriental Series, vol. 56 (Cambridge, MA: The Department of Sanskrit and Indian Studies, Harvard University, 1999).

Eck, Diana L, "Krishna Consciousness in Historical Perspective." *Back to Godhead* vol. 14, issue 10 (1979), 26–29.

Edelmann, Jonathan B., "Argument and Persuasion: A Brief Study of *Kīrtana* in the *Bhāgavata Purāṇa.*" in *Journal of Vaishnava Studies*, vol. 17, issue 2 (Spring, 2009), 37–56.

Eidlitz, Walther, in German, *Kṛṣṇa-Caitanya: Sein Leben und Seine Lehre* (Stockholm Studies in Comparative Religion, no. 7. Stockholm: Almquist and Wiksell, 1968).

Elkman, Mark Stuart, *Jīva Gosvāmī's Tattvasandarbha: A Study on the Philosophical and Sectarian Development of the Gauḍīya Vaiṣṇava Movement* (Delhi: Motilal Banarsidass, 1986).

Entwistle, Alan W., *Braj: Centre of Krishna Pilgrimage* (Groningen: Egbert Forsten, 1987).

Eschmann, Anncharlott, Kulke, Hermann, and Tripathi, Gaya Charan, eds., *The Cult of Jagannāth and the Regional Tradition of Orissa* (South Asia Institute, Heidelberg University, South Asian Studies, no. 8. New Delhi: Manohar, 1978).

Flood, Gavin, "Hinduism, Vaisnavism, and ISKCON: Authentic Traditions or Scholarly Constructions?" in *ISKCON Communciations Journal* 3.2 (December 1995), 5–15.

Frazier, Jessica, *Reality, Religion, and Passion: Indian and Western Approaches in Hans-Georg Gadamer and Rūpa Gosvāmī* (Idaho Falls, ID: Lexington Books, 2008).

Fuller, Jason D, "Re-membering the Tradition: Bhaktivinoda Ṭhākura's 'Sajjanatoṣaṇī' and the Construction of a Middle-Class Vaiṣṇava Sampradāya in Nineteenth-Century Bengal." in *Hinduism in Public and Private: Reform, Hindutva, Gender, and Sampraday*, ed. A. Copley (New Delhi: Oxford University Press, 2003), 173–210.

———, "*Religion, Class, and Power: Bhaktivinode Thakur and the Transformation of Religious Authority Among the Gauḍīya Vaiṣṇavas in Nineteenth-Century Bengal*" PhD Thesis (University of Pennsylvania, 2005).

———, "Reading, Writing, and Reclaiming: Bhaktivinoda Thakura and the Modernization of Gaudiya Vaishnavism." in *Journal of Vaishnava Studies,* vol. 13, issue 2 (Spring, 2005), 75–94.

———, "A Path Fraught With Danger: Reflections on Aṣṭāṅga Yoga From Bhaktivinoda Ṭhākura's *Prema Pradīpa*." in *Journal of Vaishnava Studies,* vol. 14, issue 1 (Fall, 2005), 233–242.

Gelberg, Steven J., ed., *Hare Krishna, Hare Krishna: Five Distinguished Scholars on the Krishna Movement in the West* (New York: Grove Books, 1983).

Gerow, Edwin, "Jayadeva's Poetics and the Classical Style." *in Journal of the American Oriental Society*, vol. 109, issue 4 (1989).

Ghose, Shishir Kumar, *Lord Gauranga, or Salvation for All,* vol. 1, 2nd edition (Calcutta: P.K. Ghose, 1907).

Ghosh, Abhishek, "Vaishnavism in Bengal," in *Contemporary Hinduism,* ed. P. Pratap Kumar (London: Routledge, 2013), 178–189.

———, "Vaiṣṇavism and the West: A Study of Kedarnath Datta Bhaktivinod's Encounter and Response, 1869–1909," Ph.D. thesis, (University of Chicago, 2014).

Ghosh, Pika, *Temple to Love: Architecture and Devotion in Seventeenth-Century Bengal* (Bloomington: Indiana University Press, 2005).

González-Reimann, Luis A., *The Mahābhārata and the Yugas: India's Great Epic Poem and the Hindu System of World Ages* (New York: Peter Lang Inc., 2002).

Goswāmī, Jīva, *Bhagavata Sandarbha*, translated, Bhanu Swami (Chennai: Sri Vaikuntha Enterprises, 2013).

Goswami, Mukunda, *Miracle on Second Avenue* (Badger, California: Torchlight Publishing, 2011).

Gosvāmin, Rūpa, *Bhaktirasāmṛtasindhu*, translated with introduction and notes by David L. Haberman (New Delhi: Indira Gandhi National Centre for the Arts and Motilal Banarsidass Publishers, 2003).

Goswami, Shrivatsa, "Man and God Bound in Love: A *Vaiṣṇava* Approach." in *In Search of the Divine: Some Unexpected Consequences of Interfaith Dialogue*, ed. Larry D. Shinn (New York: Paragon House Publishers, 1987), 3–17.

———, "Acintya-bhedābheda." in *Vaiṣṇavism: Contemporary Scholars Discuss the Gauḍīya Tradition*, ed. Steven J. Rosen (New York: Folk Books, 1992. Reprinted, Delhi: Motilal Banarsidass, 1998), 249–259.

———, *Celebrating Krishna* (Vrindavan: Sri Caitanya Prema Samsthana, 2001).

Goswami, Tamal Krishna, with Schweig, Graham, *A Living Theology of Krishna Bhakti: Essential Teachings of A. C. Bhaktivedanta Swami Prabhupāda* (New York: Oxford University Press, 2012).

Graheli, Alessandro, "Narration and Comprehension of Paradox in Gauḍīya Literature." in *Rivista di Studi Sudasiatici*, vo. 12 (2007), 181–208.

Graves, Eben, "Chaitanya Vaishnava Perspective of the Bengali Khol." in *Journal of Vaishnava Studies*, vol. 17, issue 2 (Spring, 2009), 103–126.

———, "Padāvali-Kīrtan: Music, Religious Aesthetics, and Nationalism in West Bengal's Cultural Economy," Ph.D. Dissertation (The University of Texas at Austin, 2014).

Gupta, Ravi. M., "Walking a Theological Tightrope: Controversies of Sampradāya in Eighteenth-Century Caitanya Vaiṣṇavism." in *ISKCON Communications Journal* 11 (2005), 39–51.

———, *The Caitanya Vaiṣṇava Vedānta of Jīva Gosvāmī: When Knowledge Meets Devotion* (London: Routledge, 2007).

———, "On Conceiving the Inconceivable: Jīva Gosvāmī's Presentation of Acintyabhedābheda." in *Journal of Vaishnava Studies*, vol. 16, issue 2 (Spring, 2008), 103–117.

———, ed., *Caitanya Vaiṣṇava Philosophy: Tradition Reason and Devotion* (Farnham: Ashgate, 2014).

———, "Where One is Forever Two: God and the World in Jīva Gosvāmī's *Bhāgavata-sandarbha*," in *Caitanya Vaiṣṇava Philosophy: Tradition, Reason and Devotion*, ed. Ravi Gupta (England: Ashgate Publishing, 2014), 35–60.

Haberman, David L., *Acting as a Way of Salvation: A Study of Rāgānugā Bhakti Sādhana* (New York: Oxford University Press, 1988).

———, "Shrines of the Mind: A Meditative Shrine Worshiped in Mañjarī Sādhana." in *Journal of Vaishnava Studies*, vol. 1, issue 3 (Fall, 1993), 18–35.

———, "On Trial: The Love of Sixteen Thousand Gopees." in *History of Religions*, vol. 33, issue 1 (1993), 44–70.

———, *Journey through the Twelve Forests: An Encounter with Krishna* (New York and Oxford: Oxford University Press, 1994).

Hardy, Friedhelm, "Mādhavendra Purī: A Link between Bengal Vaiṣṇavism and South Indian *Bhakti*." in *Journal of the Royal Asiatic Society of Great Britain and Ireland*, vol. 106, issue 1 (1974), 23–41.

———, *Viraha-Bhakti: The Early History of Kṛṣṇa Devotion in South India* (Delhi: Oxford University Press, 1983).

Hawley, John S. "How Do the Gauḍīyas Belong? Kavikarṇapūra, Jaisingh II, and the Question of Sampradāya," in *Journal of Hindu Studies*, vol. 6, issue 2 (2013), 114–130.

———, *A Storm of Songs: India and the Idea of the Bhakti Movement* (Cambridge: Harvard University Press, 2015)

Hein, Norvin, "Caitanya's Ecstasies and the Theology of the Name," in *Hinduism: New Essays in the History of Religions* (Leiden: E.J. Brill, 1976).

Holdrege, Barbara A., "From Nāma-Avatāra to Nāma-Saṅkīrtana: Gauḍīya Perspectives on the Name." in *Journal of Vaishnava Studies*, vol. 17, issue 2 (Spring, 2009), 3–36.

———, "Meditation as Devotional Practice in Jīva Gosvāmin's Philosophy of Education," in *ISKCON Studies Journal,* vol. 2 (2014), 45–70.

———, *Bhakti and Embodiment: Fashioning Divine Bodies and Devotional Bodies in Kṛṣṇa Bhakti* (Abingdon: Routledge, 2015).

Hopkins, Thomas J., "The Social and Religious Background for Transmission of Gaudiya Vaisnavism to the West." in *Krishna Consciousness in the West*, eds. D. G. Bromley and L. D. Shinn (Lewisburg, PA: Bucknell University Press, 1989).

———, "Why Should ISKCON Study Its Own History?" *ISKCON Communications Journal*, vol 6, issue 2 (1998), 1–6.

Hudson, Dennis, *Krishna's Mandala: Bhagavata Religion and Beyond* (New York: Oxford University Press, 2010).

Kapoor, O. B. L., *The Philosophy and Religion of Śrī Caitanya* (New Delhi: Munshiram Manoharlal, 1977).

———, "Vṛndāvana: The Highest Paradise." in *Journal of Vaiṣṇava Studies,* vol. 1,issue 1 (Fall 1992), 42–49.

———, *The Saints of Vraja* (Caracas: Saravatī Jayaśrī Classics, 1992).

———, *The Gosvāmīs of Vṛndāvana* (Caracas: Sarasvatī Jayaśrī Classics, 1995).

———, *The Saints of Bengal* (Caracas: Sarasvatī Jayaśrī Classics, 1995).

Kennedy, M. T., *The Chaitanya Movement: A Study of Vaishnavism in Bengal* (Calcutta: Association Press, 1925).

Kinsley, David, "Without Kṛṣṇa, There is no Song." in *History of Religions,* vol. 12, issue 2 (November, 1972), 149–180.

Klostermaier, Klaus K., *Hindu and Christian in Vrindaban* (London: SCM Press, 1969).

———, "Hṛdayavidyā: A Sketch of a Hindu-Christian Theology of Love," in *Journal of Ecumenical Studies*, vol. 9, issue 4 (Fall 1972), 750–775.

———, "The *Bhaktirasāmṛtasindhubindu* of Viśvanātha Cakravartin." in *Journal of the American Oriental Society*, vol. 94, issue 1 (1974), 96–107.

———, "Will India's Past Be America's Future? Reflections on the Caitanya Movement and Its Potentials," in *Journal of Asian and African Studies*, vol. 15, issue 1–2 (January and April 1980), 94–103.

———, "The Education of Human Emotions: Śrīla Prabhupāda as a Spiritual Educator," in *ISKCON Communications Journal* vol. 4, issue 1 (June 1996), 25–32.

Lutjeharms, Rembert, "The Splendour of Speech: The Theology of Kavikarṇapūra's Poetics." Ph.D. thesis (University of Oxford, 2010).

Mahārāja, Śrī Śrīmad Gour Govinda Swami, *The Embankment of Separation* (Bhubaneswar, Orissa, Gopal Jiu Publications, 1996).

———, *Mathura Meets Vrindavan* (Bhubaneswar, Orissa, Gopal Jiu Publications, 2003).

Mahārāja, Śrī Śrīmad Bhaktivedānta Nārāyaṇa Gosvāmī, translation, and commentary, Viśvanātha Chakravartī Ṭhākura's *Śrī Bhakti-rasāmṛta-sindhu-bindu: A Drop of the Nectarine Ocean of Bhakti-rasa* (Mathura: Gaudiya Vedanta Publications, 1996).

———, *Viśvanātha Chakravartī Ṭhākura's Rāga Vartma Chandrikā: A Moonbeam to Illuminate the Path of Spontaneous Devotion* (Mathura: Gaudiya Vedanta Publications, 2001).

———, *Jaiva Dharma, Our Eternal Nature* (Vrindavan: Gaudiya Vedanta Publications, 2001).

———, *Śrī Rāya Rāmānanda Samvāda* (Vrindavan: Gaudiya Vedanta Publications, 2009).

———, *Śrī Śikṣāṣṭaka with Śrī Sanmodana Bhāṣyam and Vivṛti* (Mathura, U.P.: Gaudiya Vedanta Samiti, 1994; reprint, New Delhi, Gaudiya Vedanta Publications, 2011).

Majumdar, A. K., *Caitanya: His Life and Doctrine* (Bombay: Bharatiya Vidya Bhavan, 1969).

Majumdar, Biman Bihari, *Kṛṣṇa in History and Legend* (Calcutta: University of Calcutta, 1969).

Manring, Rebecca, *Reconstructing Tradition: Advaitācārya and Gauḍīya Vaiṣṇavism at the Cusp of the Twentieth Century* (New York: Columbia University Press, 2005).

———, "Does Kṛṣṇa Really need His Own Grammar? Jīva Gosvāmin's Answer." in *International Journal of Hindu Studies,* vol. 12, issue 3 (2008), 257–82.

———, *The Fading Light of Advaitācārya: Three Hagiographies* (New York: Oxford University Press, 2011).

Martins, Demian, "The concept of acintya-bheda-abheda," http://bkdemian.blogspot.com/2009/12/concept-of-acintya-bheda-abheda.html

Matchett, Freda, *Kṛṣṇa: Lord or Avatāra? The Relationship Between Kṛṣṇa and Viṣṇu* (London: Curzon, 2001).

McDaniel, June, *The Madness of Saints: Ecstatic Religion in Bengal* (Chicago: University of Chicago Press, 1989).

———, "The Tantric Rādhā: Some Controversies about the nature of Rādhā in Bengal Vaishnavism and the Rādhā Tantra," in *Journal of Vaishnava Studies,* vol. 8, issue 2 (Fall, 2000), 131–46.

Miller, Barbara Stoler, translation, *Love Song of the Dark Lord: Jayadeva's Gītagovinda* (New York: Columbia University Press, 1977).

Mitra, Kankana. "A Stylistic Pattern of Bengali Kirtan: Journey from Pada to Pala." in *Proceedings of the International Seminar on "Creating & Teaching Music Patterns"* (Kolkata: Rabindra Bharati University, 2013), 81–101.

Mukherjee, Prabhat, *History of the Jagannath temple in the 19th Century* (Columbia, Missouri: South Asia Books, 1977).

———, *History of the Chaitanya Faith in Orissa* (South Asian Institute, Heidelberg University, South Asian Studies, no. 10. New Delhi: Manohar, 1979).

———, *The History of Medieval Vaishnavism in Orissa* (Delhi: Asian Educational Services, 1981).

Nanda, Ajaykumar, *Śikṣāṣṭakam Commentary, "Kṛṣṇoddīpinī"* (Tirupati Rashtriya Sanskrit University, 2007).

Nath, Radha Govinda, "The Acintya-bhedābheda School." in *The Cultural Heritage of India: The Philosophies,* vol. 3, 2nd edition (Kolkata: Ramakrishna Mission Institute of Culture, 1953), 266–386.

Nicholson, Andrew J., *Unifying Hinduism: Philosophy and Identity in Indian Intellectual History* (New York: Columbia University Press, 2010).

O'Connell, J. T., "Social Implications of the Gauḍīya Vaiṣṇava Movement." Unpublished Ph.D. thesis, Harvard University, 1970.

———, "The Word 'Hindu' in Gauḍīya Vaiṣṇava Texts." in *Journal of the American Oriental Society,* vol. 93, issue 3 (July–September, 1973), 340–344.

———, "Caitanya's Followers and the *Bhagavad-gītā*: A Case Study in Bhakti and the Secular." in *Hinduism: New Essays in the History of Religion*, ed. Bardwell L. Smith (Leiden: E. J. Brill, 1976), 33–52.

———, "Were Caitanya's Vaiṣṇavas really Sahajiyās? The Case of Rāmānanda Rāya." in *Shaping Bengali Worlds, Public and Private*, ed. Tony K. Stewart (East Lansing: Asian Studies Center, Michigan State University, 1989), 11–22.

———, "Historicity in the Biographies of Caitanya." in *Journal of Vaishnava Studies*, vol. 1, issue 2 (Fall 1993), 102–132.

———, "Rāmānanda Rāya: A Sahajiyā or a Rāgānuga-bhakta?" in *Journal of Vaishnava Studies*, vol. 1, issue 3 (Spring, 1993), 36–58.

Okita, Kiyokazu, "A Caitanya Vaiṣṇava Response to the Nineteenth-century Bengal Renaissance Movement According to the Works of Bhaktivinoda Ṭhākura." in *Religions of South Asia*, vol. 2, issue 2 (2008), 195–214.

———, "Mādhva or Gauḍīya? The Philosophy of Baladeva Vidyābhūṣaṇa's *Prameyaratnāvalī*." in *Journal of Vaishnava Studies,* vol. 16, issue 2 (Fall 2008), 22–48.

———, "Caitanya Vaiṣṇavism on Trial: Continuity and Transformation in the Eighteenth Century." in *Caitanya Vaiṣṇava Philosophy: Tradition Reason and Devotion,* ed. Ravi Gupta (Farnham: Ashgate, 2014), 75–112.

———, *Hindu Theology in Early modern South Asia: The Rise of Devotionalism and the Politics of Genealogy* (Oxford: Oxford University Press, 2014).

Otto, Rudolf, *India's Religion of Grace and Christianity Compared and Contrasted* (New York: Macmillan, 1930).

Packert, Cynthia, "An Absent Presence In Vrindavana." in *Radha: From Gopi to Goddess*, ed. Harsha V. Dehejia (New Delhi: Niyogi Books, 2014), 50–57.

Paramadvaiti, B. A., *Our Family the Gaudiya Math: A Study of the Expansion of Gaudiya Vaishnavism and the Many Branches Developing around the Gaudiya Math* (Vrindavan: The Vrindavan Institute for Vaisnava Culture and Studies, 1999).

Potter, Karl H., *Encyclopedia of Indian Philosophies*, vol XIX: "Acintyabhedābheda Vaiṣṇava Philosophy" (Delhi: Motilal Banarsidass, 2015).

Prabhupāda, His Divine Grace A. C. Bhaktivedanta Swami, *Teaching of Lord Chaitanya* (Boston: ISKCON Press, 1968). Reprinted as *Teachings of Lord Caitanya, the Golden Avatar* (Los Angeles: Bhaktivedanta Book Trust, 1988).

———, translation, and commentary, *Śrīmad Bhāgavatam*, 12 vols (Los Angeles: Bhaktivednata Book Trust, 1972).

———, translation, and commentary, *Bhagavad-gītā As It Is* (Los Angeles, California, 1989, reprint).

———, translation, and commentary, *Śrī Īśopaniṣad* (Los Angeles, California, 1995, reprint).

———, translation, and commentary, Krishnadāsa Kavirāja Goswāmī's *Śrī Caitanya-caritāmṛta*, 9-volume set (Los Angeles, California, 1996, reprint).

Preciado-Solis, Benjamin, *The Kṛṣṇa Cycle n the Purāṇas: Themes and Motifs in a Heroic Saga* (Delhi: Motilal Banarsidass, 1984).

Prentiss, Karen Pechilis, *The Embodiment of Bhakti* (New York: Oxford University Press, 1999).

Prime, Ranchor, *The Birth of Kirtan: The Life & Teachings of Chaitanya* (San Rafael, California: Mandala Publishing, 2012).

Roberts, Michelle Voss, *Dualities: A Theology of Difference* (Louisville, Kentucky: Westminster John Knox Press, 2010).

———, *Tastes of the Divine: Hindu and Christian Theologies of Emotion* (New York: Fordham University Press, 2014)

Rosen, Steven J., *India's Spiritual Renaissance: The Life and Times of Lord Chaitanya* (New York: Folk Books, 1989).

———, *The Six Gosvamis of Vrindavan* (New York: Folk Books, 1991).

———, *The Lives of the Vaishnava Saints: Shrinivas Acharya, Narottam Das Thakur, Shyamananda Pandit* (New York: Folk Books, 1991).

———, *Śrī Pañca Tattva: The Five Features of God* (New York: Folk Books, 1994).

———, ed., *Vaiṣṇavism: Contemporary Scholars Discuss the Gauḍīya Tradition* (Delhi: Motilal Banarsidass, 1994).

———, *The Hidden Glory of India* (Sweden: Bhaktivedanta Book Trust, 2002).

———, "Who is Shri Chaitanya Mahaprabhu." in *The Hare Krishna Movement: The Postcharismatic Fate of a Religious Transplant*, eds. Edwin F. Bryant and Maria Ekstrand (New York: Columbia University Press, 2004), 63–72.

———, *Essential Hinduism* (Westport, Connecticut: Greenwood Publishing Group/ABC-CLIO, 2006; Lanham, MD.: Rowman & Littlefield, paperback edition, 2008).

———, *The Yoga of Kirtan: Conversations on the Sacred Art of Chanting* (New York: Folk Books, 2008).

Sailley, Robert, *Chaitanya et la dévotion a Krishna* (Paris: Dervy-Livres, 1986, French).

Sanyal, Hitesranjan, "Transformation of the Regional Bhakti Movement." in *Bengal Vaiṣṇavism, Orientalism, Society and the Arts,* ed. Joseph T. O'Connell (East Lansing, Michigan: Asian Studies Center, Michigan State University, 1985).

Sarbadhikary, Sukanya, *The Place of Devotion: Siting and Experiencing Divinity in Bengal-Vaishnavism* (Oakland, California: University of California Press, 2015).

Sardella, Ferdinando, "Bhaktisiddhānta Sarasvatī (1874–1937) Vaishnava Identity in Modern Dress." in *Journal of Vaishnava Studies*, vol. 15, issue 2 (Spring, 2007), 95–122.

———, *Modern Hindu Personalism: The History, Life, and Thought of Bhaktisiddhānta Sarasvatī* (New York: Oxford University Press, 2012).

Satyanand, Joseph, *Nimbarka: A Pre-Sankara Vedantin and His Philosophy* (New Delhi: Munshiram Manoharlal, 1997).

Schelling, Andrew, ed., *The Oxford Anthology of Bhakti Literature* (New Delhi: Oxford University Press, 2011).

Schweig, Graham M., "An Analysis of the Structure of Polarities in the Caitanya Vaishnava Tradition." Unpublished paper, Harvard Divinity School, December 1984.

———, "Synthesis and Divinity: Śrī Chaitanya's Philosophy of Acintya Bhedābheda Tattva," in *Synthesis of Science and Religion: Critical Essays and Dialogues*, ed. T. D. Singh, (Bombay: The Bhaktivedanta Institute, 1988), 420–429.

———, "Universal and Confidential Love of God: Two Essential Themes in Prabhupāda's Theology of *Bhakti*." in *Journal of Vaishnava Studies,* vol. 6, issue 2 (Spring 1998), 93–123.

———, *Dance of Divine Love: the Rāsa Līlā of Krishna from the Bhāgavata Purāṇa, India's Classic Sacred Love Story* (Princeton, NJ: Princeton University Press, 2005).

———, *Bhagavad Gita: The Beloved Lord's Secret Love Song* (San Francisco, California: Harper San Francisco, 2007).

———, "The *Upadeśāmṛtam* of Rūpa Gosvāmī: A Concise Teaching on Essential Practices of Kṛṣṇa *Bhakti*." in *Caitanya Vaiṣṇava Philosophy: Tradition, Reason and Devotion,* ed. Ravi M Gupta (Farnham: Ashgate, 2014).

Sen, Dinesh Chandra, *History of Bengali Language and Literature* (Calcutta: Calcutta University Press, 1911).

———, *The Vaiṣṇava Literature of Mediaeval Bengal* (Calcutta: Calcutta University Press, 1917).

———, *Chaitanya and His Companions* (Calcutta: Calcutta University Press, 1917).

———, *Chaitanya and His Age* (Calcutta: Calcutta University Press, 1922).

Sharma, B. N. K., *History of the Dvaita School of Vedānta and Its Literature: From the Earliest Beginnings to Our Own Times* (Delhi: Motilal Banarsidass, 2000, reprint).

Sharma, Krishna, *Bhakti and the Bhakti Movement: A New Perspective* (New Delhi: Munshiram Manoharlal, 1987).

Sherbow, Paul, "A. C. Bhaktivedanta's Preaching in the Context of Gaudiya Vaishnavism," in *The Hare Krishna Movement: The Post-charismatic Fate of a Religious Transplant* (New York: Colombia University Press, 2004), 129–146.

Sheridan, Daniel P., *Advaitic Theism of the Bhāgavata Purāna* (Delhi: Motilal Banarsidass, 1986).

———, *Loving God: Kṛṣṇa and Christ: A Christian Commentary on the Nārada Sūtras* (Leuven, Belgium: W.P. Eerdmans, 2007).

Siegel, Lee, *Sacred and Profane Dimensions of Love in Indian Traditions as Exemplified in the Gītagovinda of Jayadeva* (New York: Oxford University Press, 2nd edition, 1991).

———, *Gīta Govinda: Love Songs of Rādhā and Krishna* (New York University Press, Clay Sanskrit Library, 2009).

Sil, Narasingha, "Hiteś Rañjan Sanyāl's *History of Bāṅglā Kīrtan.*" in *Journal of Vaishnava Studies*, vol. 17, issue 2 (Spring, 2009), 73–93.

Slawek, Stephen. "Kīrtan: A Study of the Sonic Manifestations of the Divine in the Popular Hindu Culture of Banāras," Ph.D. Dissertation (University of Illinois at Urbana-Champaign, 1986).

Śrīdhara Dev Goswāmī's *Śikṣāṣṭakam* commentary: http://www.scsmathlondon.org/who-are-we/teachings/sri-siksastakam/

Śrīdhara, Swami B. R., *The Search for Sri Krishna: Reality the Beautiful* (San Jose, California: Guardian of Devotion Press, 1986).

———, *The Golden Volcano of Divine Love* (Nadiya, West Bengal: Sri Chaitanya Saraswat Math, 1996, reprint).

———, *Śrī Guru and His Grace* (Nabadvip: Sri Chaitanya Sāraswat Matha, 1999).

Srinivasachari, P. N., *The Philosophy of Bhedābheda* (Chennai, India: The Adyar Library, 1950).

Stewart, Tony K., "The Biographical Images of Kṛṣṇa-Caitanya: A Study in the Perception of Divinity," Ph.D. thesis (Department of South Asian Languages and Civilizations, The University of Chicago, 1985).

———, "On Changing the Perception of Caitanya's Divinity." in *Bengal Vaiṣṇavism, Orientalism, Society and the Arts*, ed. by Joseph T. O'Connell, South Asia Occasional Paper no. 35 (East Lansing, MI: Asian Studies Center, Michigan State University, 1985), 37–45.

———, "When Biographical Narratives Disagree: The Death of Kṛṣṇa Caitanya." in *Numen,* vol. 38, issue 2 (1991), 231–260.

———, "The Biographies of Śrī Caitanya and the Literature of the Gauḍīya Vaiṣṇavas." in *Vaiṣṇavism: Contemporary Scholars Discuss the Gauḍīya Tradition*, ed. Steven J. Rosen, foreword by Edward C. Dimock, Jr. (New York: Folk Books, 1992; reprint, Motilal Banarsidass, 1994), 101–125.

———, translation, "The Exemplary Devotion of the 'Servant of Hari.'" in *The Religions of South Asia in Practice,* ed. Donald S. Lopez, Jr. (Princeton: Princeton University Press, 1995), 564–577.

———, "When Rāhu Devours the Moon: The Myth of the Birth of Kṛṣṇa Caitanya." in *International Journal of Hindu Studies*, vol. 1, issue 2 (August 1997), 21–64.

———, "Reading for Kṛṣṇa's Pleasure: Gauḍīya Vaiṣṇava Meditation, Literary Interiority, and the Phenomenology of Repetition." in *Journal of Vaiṣṇava Studies,* vol. 14, issue 1 (Fall, 2005), 243–280.

———, *The Final Word: The Caitanya Caritāmṛta* and the Grammar of Religious Tradition (New York and London: Oxford University Press, 2010).

———, "Religion in the Subjunctive: Vaiṣṇava Narrative, Sufi Counter-Narrative in Early Modern Bengal." in *The Journal of Hindu Studies*, vol. 6 (2013).

———, "Caitanya," Oxford Bibliographies Online (New York: Oxford University Press, 2013): http://oxfordbibliographiesonline.com/

Swami, Bhakti Vikāsa, *Sri Bhaktisiddhānta Vaibhava*, vol. 3 (Surat: Bhakti Vikas Trust, 2009).

Swami, Subaladasa, "Lord Caitanya's Mission and Precepts—Parts One and Two." in *Back to Godhead*: *Śikṣāṣṭakam,* translation by His Divine Grace A.C.

Bhaktivedanta Swami Prabhupada, Commentary by Subaladasa Swami, vol 1, issue 49–50 (1972).

Taneja, Leena Aziza, "Tracing the Absence of Faith: Hermeneutics, Deconstruction, and the School of Gauḍīya Vaiṣṇavism," Ph.D. Thesis (The George Washington University, 2005).

Ṭhākura, Bhaktivinoda, *Shri Chaitanya Mahaprabhu, His Life and Precepts*, originally published in 1896 (Nabadwip: Shri Goudiya Vedanta Samiti, 1981, reprint).

———, *The Bhagavat, Its Philosophy, Ethics and Theology*, ed. Bhaktivilas Tirtha, 2nd edition (Madras: Madras Gaudiya Math, 1959).

———, *Shri Chaitanya Shikshamritam*, Bijoy Krishna Rarhi, translation (Madras: Sri Gaudiya Math, 1983, reprint).

———, *Śrīla Bhaktivinoda Ṭhākura's Gaurāṅga-līlā-smaraṇa-maṅgala-stotra—Auspicious Meditations on Lord Gaurāṅga,* Kuśakratha dāsa, translation (Los Angeles: Kṛṣṇa Institute, 1988).

———, *Śrīla Bhaktivinoda Ṭhākura's Śrī Navadvīpa-dhāma-māhātmya, Pramāṇa-khaṇḍa: The Glories of Śrī Navadvīpa, Evidence from Scripture,* Kuśakratha dāsa, translation (Los Angeles: Kṛṣṇa Institute, 1989).

———, *Śrī Hari-nāma-cintāmaṇi: The Beautiful Wish-Fulfilling Gem of the Holy Name*, Sri Sarvabhavana dasa Adhikari, translation (Bombay: Bhaktivedanta Books, 1990).

———, "Gītāvalī." in *The Songs of Bhaktivinoda Ṭhākura*, Daśaratha-suta dāsa, translation (Union City, GA: Nectar Books, 1994).

———, *Bhajana Rahasya* (Kalikata: Sri Chaitanya Gaudiya Matha, 2nd edition, reprint, 1996).

———, *Śrī Kṛṣṇa-samhitā,* Bhumipati Dāsa, translation (Vrindaban: Vrajraj Press, 1998).

———, *Daśa-mūla-tattva: The Ten Esoteric Truths of the Vedas,* Sarvabhāvana Dāsa, translation (Vrindaban: Rasa Bihārī Brothers, 2000).

———, *Jaiva Dharma, Our Eternal Nature*, Bhaktivedānta Nārāyaṇa Mahārāja, Araṇya Mahārāja, et al., translation (Mathura: Gauḍīya Vedānta Publications, 2002).

Thakura, Vrndavana dasa, *Sri Caitanya Bhagavata with commentary of Bhaktisiddhanta Sarasvati Gosvami Maharaja Prabhupada*, Bhumipati Dasa, translation, 7 vols (New Delhi: Vrajraj Press. 1998–2005).

Theodor, Ithamar, "The *Parinama* Aesthetics as Underlying *The Bhāgavata Purāṇa,*" in *Journal of Asian Philosophy* (Routledge, London and New York), Vol. 17, No. 2 (July 2007), 109–125.

———, "Ascending Notions of Personhood in the *Bhāgavata Purāṇa.*" *Religions of South Asia*, Equinox Publishers, London, vol. 2, issue 1 (2008), 45–63.

———, *Exploring the Bhagavad-gita: Philosophy, Structure and Meaning* (Surry: Ashgate Publishers, 2010).

———, *Exploring the Bhāgavata Purāṇa: The Language, Structure and Meaning of the 'Fifth Veda'* (New York: I. B.Tauris, 2015).

Tripurāri, Swami B. V., *Aesthetic Vedanta: The Sacred Path of Passionate Love* (San Rafael, California: Mandala Publishing, 1998).

———, *Śikṣāṣṭakam of Śrī Caitanya* (San Rafael, California: Mandala Publishing, 2005).

———, Jīva Goswāmī's *Tattva-Sandarbha* (Philo, California: Harmonist Publishers, 2011).

———, *Sacred Preface* (Palo Alto, California: Darshan Press, 2017).

Valpey, Kenneth R., *Attending Kṛṣṇa's Image: Caitanya Vaiṣṇava Mūrti-sevā as Devotional Truth* (Abingdon: Routledge, 2006).

———, "Gauḍīya Vaiṣṇavism," in *Brill's Encyclopedia of Hinduism*, vol. 3, ed. Knut A. Jacobsen (Leiden, The Netherlands: Brill, 2011), 312–328.

Various, *Sri Vrndavana Dhama Newsletter*, Aindra Dasa, "Siksastaka One"; Purushottama Dasa and Dr. Ajay Jani, "Siksastaka Two"; Prithu Dasa, "Siksastaka Three"; Kundali Dasa, "Siksastaka Four"; Kadamba Kanana Dasa, "Siksastaka Five"; Dhanurdhara Swami, "Siksastaka Six"; Bhurijana Dasa, "Siksastaka Seven"; Jadurani Devi Dasi, "Siksastaka Eight" (Raman Reti, Vrindavan: Krishna Balarama Mandir, vol. 2, no. 1, Gaura Purnima, 1994).

Wong, Lucian, "Negotiating History in Colonial Bengal: Bhaktivinod's *Kṛṣṇa-samhitā*." in *Journal of Hindu Studies*, vol. 7, issue 3 (2014), 341–370.

———, "Gauḍīya Vaiṣṇava Studies: Mapping the Field." *Religions of South Asia,* vol. 9, issue 3 (2015), 305–331. (http://www.academia.edu/29577275/Gauḍīya_Vaiṣṇava_Studies_Mapping_the_Field).

Wulff, Donna M., *Drama as a Mode of Religious Realization: the Vidagdhamādhava of Rūpa Gosvāmī*, American Academy of Religion, Academy Series (Chico, CA: Scholars Press, 1984).

———, "Radha: Consort and Conqueror of Krishna." in *Devi: Goddesses of India*, ed. John Hawley and Donna Wulff (Berkeley: University of California Press, 1998).

Index

Abhimanyu, *30, 37n50*
ācāryas, xxiv, 28, 80, 99, 128, 167, 178, 190n26
acintya, 124, 127–28
Acintya-Bhedābheda, xxii, 9, 81, 123–31
Advaitācārya, 4, 44, 45, 47, 50
Agni, 1
Ahimsa, 8
aiśvarya, 40, 41
Ajāmila, 90, 100n10
Ālvārs, 80
Analogy, 124–25
Arjuna, 19, 20
Aṣṭa-kālīya-nitya-līlā ("the eternal eightfold daily pastimes"), 25, 26, 35n34
avatāra, 2, 5, 8
avatārī, 8

Bhagavān, 10
Bhagavad-gītā, 19–20, 81, 126–28
Bhāgavata-māhātmya, 82–83, 85n28
Bhāgavatam, Śrīmad (*Bhāgavata Purāṇa*), 2, 3, *21, 27,89*
bhakti, xxi;
  as active service, 73–74;
  Bhakti Movement, 79–83;
  defined, 71–72, 84n10, 84n18;
  in practice, 75–78;
  nine stages, 120n28;
  saguṇa versus *nirguṇa*, 80–82.
  See also Vaidhī and Rāgānuga
Bhakti-rasāmṛta-sindhu, 75–76, 162, 178
Bhakti-sandarbha, 26, 92
Bhaktivinoda Ṭhākura, 9, 31, 42, 99, 115–16, 129–30, 133n19, 135–40, 180–81, 194–95, 198–99
bhāravāhin, 137
Bhārati, Bābā Premānanda, 199
Bharatī, Keśava, 53–54, 67n49, 159–60
Bhaṭṭa, Vyeṅkaṭa, 56, 148–49
bhāva, 75, 111, 186
Bhowmick, Shukdeb, 126
Bilvamaṅgala, 26
Brahman, 10
Brahmachari, Mahānāmbrata, 199–200
Brahma-saṁhitā, 19
Brahma-vaivarta Purāṇa, 29
Buddha, xxiii, 144–145, 156n37.
  See also Buddhist

Caitanya-bhāgavata, 39, 41, 42, 46, 50, 63n14, 193
Caitanya-caritāmṛta, 4, 6, 7, 40, 43, 64n23, 81, 89, 108, 114, 160, 174–75

Caitanya-candrodāya-nāṭakam, 39, 63n14, 113
Caitanya-maṅgala, 12n8, 39
Cakravartī, Nīlāmbara, 45
Caṇḍīdāsa, 26, 29, 80, 173
Chaitanya, Śrī:
assorted names, 46;
becomes a scholar, 47–48;
biographies, xxi, xix, 3, 5, 39, 40;
birth, 45;
childhood, 46–47;
conversion of Jagāi and Mādhāi, 50–52;
disappearance stories, 58–59, 68n62–63;
defeats Prakāśānanda Sarasvatī, 57;
explorations in English, 42–44;
first wife dies, 48;
goes to Puri, 55;
goes to South India, 55–56;
goes to Vrindāvan, 56–57;
identified, 39;
interacts with Chand Kazi, 52–53;
Jhārikhaṇḍa Forest, 59;
last twelve years in ecstasy, 57–58;
Mahāprabhu's miracles, 59–60;
meets Rāmānanda Rāya, 55, 159–65;
meets Rūpa and Sanātana, 56;
naming ceremony (*sannyāsa*), 53–54;
origin of *kīrtana* movement, 49–50, 65n40;
Rādhā and Krishna combined, as, xxi, 7, 8, 14–15n23, 40, 41, 42, 60–61, 72, 166;
reasons for descent, 174–75;
reveals himself in Krishna's various forms, 65n41, 166;
vital transformation (initiation), 48–49
Chaitanya Upanishad, 3, 12n11
Chaitanya Vaishnava tradition, xvii, xviii, xix, xx, xxi, xxiii, xxiv, 2, 8.
See also Gauḍīya Vaishnavism
Chakravartī, Viśvanātha, 26, 31, 35n34, 36n106, 102n33, 176, 179, 196, 205n10
Chandrāvalī, 112
Christianity, 141

De, S. K., 43
Dhātupāṭhaḥ ("recitation of word origins"), 74
Dhyānachandra Goswāmī, 26, 35n34, 67n55, 183, 190n25
Dimock, Edward C., xix, xxvi, 39, 43,
Dvārakā, xxi, 23

ekādaśa-bhāva, 180, 182–83, 189n20
Epilepsy, 144, 155n33

Gauḍīya (commentators), 4, 97
Gauḍīya Vaishnavism, 8, 9, 10, 11, 20, 194
Gaura-gaṇoddeśa-dīpikā, 6, 16n34, 66n44, 67n49, 67n55, 168n5
Ghosh, Abhishek, 138–39, 152, 193, 204n1, 204n2
Ghosh, Shishir Kumar, 42, 198
Gīta-govinda, 29
Gopāla Bhaṭṭa Goswāmī, 56
Gopāla Guru Goswāmi, 182, 190n25, 191n29
Gopāla *mantra*, 48
gopīs, xvii, xxvn3, 6, 27–28, 30–31, 36n42, 77–78, 136, 160, 164–65, 176, 178, 181, 184–85, 187, 191n37
Goswāmī, Satsvarūpa Dāsa, 74
Goswami, Shrivatsa, 82–83, 85n28
Govinda-bhāṣya, 128
Govinda-līlāmṛta, 26

Hari-bhakti-vilāsa, 97
Haridāsa, 50–52, 93, 139–40
Harivaṁśa, 23
Hawley, John Stratton, 80, 85n23
Heliodorus Column, 22

Hindu (Hinduism), xxv
Hopkins, Thomas J., 22
humility, 107–9

International Society for Krishna Consciousness (ISKCON), xix, xxvi, 182, 203, 206n29
Islam, 52–53, 66n44, 139–40, 144–45, 153–54n26, 155n34, 155n35

japa, xxi
Jayadeva, 29, 80, 173
Jesus, 33n18
Jewish, 140, 153n18
Jīva Goswāmī, xxii, xxv, 3, 5, 6, 26, 28, 30, 68n57, 77, 92, 128, 132n16
Judeo-Christian tradition, xxiii, 140, 147, 163

kairava, 118n5
Kali-santaraṇa Upanishad, 95, 102n35–36
Kali-yuga, 2
Kapoor, O. B. L., 124–25
Karṇapūra, Kavi, 6, 39, 40, 63n14, 113
Kāśmīrī, Keśava, 148
Kavirāja Goswāmī, Krishnadāsa, 4, 40, 41, 44, 114
Kazi, Chand, 52–53, 66n47
kīrtana, xxii, 52, 77, 87–103
Krishna, xvii, xviii, 3–5, 10, 19, 20, 25, 34–35n32, 34n31, 174;
  in history, 21–24, 34n30;
  Krishna's sweetness, xviii
Krishna Bhāvanāmṛta Mahāvākhya, 26
Krishna Prem, Śrī, 200–1, 207n30

Locana Dāsa Ṭhākura, 12n8
līlā, 63n28
līlā-smaraṇam, 179, 182, 209, 217

mādhurya, 10, 40, 41, 163
Mahā-mantra, xxii, 48, 93–98, 101n29, 115
Mahābhārata, xx
Mañjarī, 110, 185
Mañjarī-bhāva, 184–85
Mañjarī, Kaustūrī, 62n7
Mantra meditation, xxi
Māyāvādī, 47, 81, 146, 156n40
Megasthenes, 22
Miśra, Jagannāth, 45, 48
Moffitt, John, 141–42

nāma-apārādha, 97–98
Nāma-kīrtana, 87–89
Nanak, Guru, 142, 145–46, 154n27
Nārada Bhakti Sūtra, 74, 78
Nārāyaṇa, 20, 143
Nārāyaṇa Mahārāja, Śrīla, 35–36n39, 36n43, 164, 185
Narottama Dāsa, 88
Nimāi (Nimāi Paṇḍita), 45–50
Nityānanda, 4, 44, 51–52
Nonviolent Disobedience, 66n46
Nṛsiṁhadeva, 53

O'Connell, Joseph T., xix, xxv, 39

Padāvalī-kīrtana, 88
Padma Purāṇa, 9, 29, 92, 96
Padyāvali, 77, 114
Pañcha Tattva, *40, 44, 45*
Pañcopāsanā, 138–40
parakīya, 30
Paramātmā, 10
Paramātmā Sandarbha, 128
Pāṭhāna, 144, 155–56n35
Postage stamp, Mahāprabhu, xxvin8
Prabhupāda, A. C. Bhaktivedānta Swami, xxiv, 28, 30, 43, 74, 76, 130, 142, 203
Prakāśānanda Sarasvatī, xxiii, 146–47
Prahlāda Mahārāja, 5
Pratāparudra, King, 58
premā, 75, 106, 115–17, 162, 164–65, 170n17, 173, 175, 179
Purī, Īśvara, 48, 65n37, 159–60
Rādhā and Krishna (marriage), 29–30, 37n48, 37n50, 37n52

Rādhā (Rādhārāṇī), xxi, xxii, xxv, 6, 14n19, 27, 28, 29, 30, 31, 36n42, 36n44, 40, 94, 98, 107, 110, 112, 164, 174–75, 184
Rādhā-dāsyam, 31, 164
Rāgānuga-bhakti, xxiii, 75, 84n12, 173–78, 184, 186
Raghunātha Bhaṭṭa Goswāmī, xxv, 48
Raghunātha Dāsa Goswāmī, xxv, 191n31
Rāma, xxv, 94–95
Rāmānanda Rāya, xxiii, 26, 55, 67n55, 159–62, 167, 168n1, 168n5, 169n7
rasa, five varieties of (*śānta, dāsya, sakhya, vātsalya, mādhurya*), 78, 84n15, 162–64, 169n12
Rāsa-līlā, 27, 28, 95
Ṛg-veda, 1
Rūpa Goswāmī, xxiii, xxv, 3, 6–7, 25, 31, 57, 67–68n56, 75, 90–91, 93, 111, 114, 120n26, 152n14, 182, 184–86
Rūpānuga, 7, 186

Śacīdevī, 45, 46, 54
sādhana, 75
Śaivism, 8
Śāktism, 8
sampradāya, 9
Sanātana Dharma, xxiii, 9
Sanātana Goswāmī, xxiii, xxv, 67–68n56, 93
Śaṅkara, xxiii
saṅkīrtana, 5, 79, 87, 98
sannyāsa, 53
sāragrāhin, 137
Sarasvatī Ṭhākura, Bhaktisiddhānta, 7, 10, 43, 94, 98, 106, 114–16, 184, 199, 201–3
Sārvabhauma Bhaṭṭācārya, xxiii, 55, 146–47, 160
sāttvika-bhāvas, 111–12
Scholarship *vs.* devotion, xvii, xviii
Schweig, Graham M., 10, 27, 95, 130
Sen, D. C., 42
Shah, Hussein, 52
Shem, Baal, 153n18
Shiva, 115
Śikṣāṣṭakam, xxii, 105–21
Six Goswāmīs, xix, xxv, 31
smaraṇam, 9
Smartism, 8
Śrīdhara Mahārāja, B. R., 7, 10, 31, 128, 160
Śrī Rādhā. *See* Rādhā
Śrīvāsa, 50
Stavāmṛta Laharī, 31
Stewart, Tony K., 39, 40, 43
svakīya, 30
Svarūpa Dāmodara Goswāmī, 7, 41
Swami, B. T., 117
Swami, Śrīdhara (medieval commentator), 13–14n14, 151
Swami B. V. Tripurāri, 5, 117

Tattva Sandarbha, 5
Tattvavāda, 149
Tirtha Swami, B. P., 43

Ujjvala-nīlamaṇi, 28, 162

Vaidhī-bhakti, 75, 173–75
Vallabhācārya, 149, 151
Vallabha Sampradāya, 9
Varieties of Religious Experience, The, 155n33
Vedānta-sūtra, 54
Vedas, 1, 9, 106–8
Vidyābhūṣaṇa, Baladeva, 73, 127–28, 196, 205n10
Vidyāpati, 26, 80, 173
vipralambha (*viraha*), 27, 72–73
Vishnu, 1, 20, 40
Viśvarūpa (elder brother), 46, 47
Vrindāvandāsa Ṭhākura, 39, 50
Vyāsadeva, 27

World Ages, four (yuga), 1, 2, 4, 14n15

About the Author

Steven J. Rosen is a direct disciple of His Divine Grace A. C. Bhaktivedānta Swami Prabhupāda as well as a scholar in the fields of comparative philosophy and Vaishnava spirituality. He is the founding editor of the *Journal of Vaishnava Studies* and associate editor of *Back to Godhead* magazine. His 31 books include *The Hidden Glory of India* (Bhaktivedanta Book Trust, 2002); *Essential Hinduism* (Rowman & Littlefield, 2008); *Krishna's Other Song: A New Look at the Uddhava Gita* (Praeger/Greenwood, 2010); and *Christ and Krishna: Where the Jordan Meets the Ganges* (FOLK Books, 2011).